OMAN IN THE TWENTIETH CENTURY

Political Foundations of an Emerging State

J. E. PETERSON

CROOM HELM LONDON

BARNES & NOBLE BOOKS NEW YORK
(a division of Harper & Row Publishers, Inc.)

Croom Helm Ltd, 2–10 St John's Road, London SW11

British Library Cataloguing in Publication Data

Peterson, John E
Oman in the twentieth century.
1. Oman – History
I. Title
953'.5 DS247.065
ISBN 0–85664–629–6

Published in the U.S.A. 1978 by
HARPER & ROW PUBLISHERS, INC.
BARNES & NOBLE IMPORT DIVISION
Library of Congress Cataloging in Publication Data
Peterson, John E
Oman in the twentieth century.
Bibliography: p. 245
Includes index.
1. Oman—Politics and government. I. Title.
DS247.068P47 1978 320.9'53'5 78–761
ISBN 0–06–495522–2

Printed and bound in Great Britain by
Billing & Sons Limited, Guildford, London and Worcester

Contents

List of Abbreviations

ANM	Arab Nationalists' Movement
ARR	*Arab Report and Record*
BSOAS	*Bulletin of the School of Oriental and African Studies*
CAT	Civil Action Team
DLF	Dhufar Liberation Front
FA	Financial Adviser
FBIS	*Foreign Broadcast Information Service*—Middle East and North Africa
FO	Foreign Office; Foreign Office Records in the Public Records Office, London
GJ	*Geographical Journal*
HMG	Her/His (British) Majesty's Government
IA	Indian Army
IO	India Office; India Office Library and Records, London
IPC	Iraq Petroleum Company
JRAS	*Journal of the Royal Asiatic Society* (London)
JRCAS	*Journal of the Royal Central Asian Society* (later *Asian Affairs*)
JRUSI	*Journal of the Royal United Service Institution*
Lorimer's Gazetteer	J. G. Lorimer, comp., *Gazetteer of the Persian Gulf, 'Oman, and Central Arabia* (Calcutta: Superintendent, Government Printing, vol. 1, 1915; vol. 2, 1908. Reprinted Farnborough: Gregg International, 1970; Shannon: Irish Universities Press, 1970)
MEED	*Middle East Economic Digest*
MEJ	*Middle East Journal*
MLC	Muscat Levy Corps

MOFF	Muscat and Oman Field Force
MT$	Maria Theresa Dollar
NDFLOAG	National Democratic Front for the Liberation of Oman and the Arabian Gulf
NFR	Northern Frontier Regiment
PAM	Political Agent, Muscat
PDO	Petroleum Development (Oman) Ltd; Petroleum Development (Oman) Records at Mīnā' al-Faḥl, Oman
PDRY	People's Democratic Republic of Yemen (Aden)
PFLO	Popular Front for the Liberation of Oman
PFLOAG	Popular Front for the Liberation of the Occupied Arabian Gulf; Popular Front for the Liberation of Oman and the Arabian Gulf
PRPG	Political Residency/Resident in the Persian Gulf
R./Rs.	Rupee(s)
RAF	Royal Air Force
SAF	Sultan's Armed Forces
SAS	Special Air Service
TOS	Trucial Oman Scouts
UAA	United Arab Amirates

1. Central Oman – Geographical Provinces and Settlements

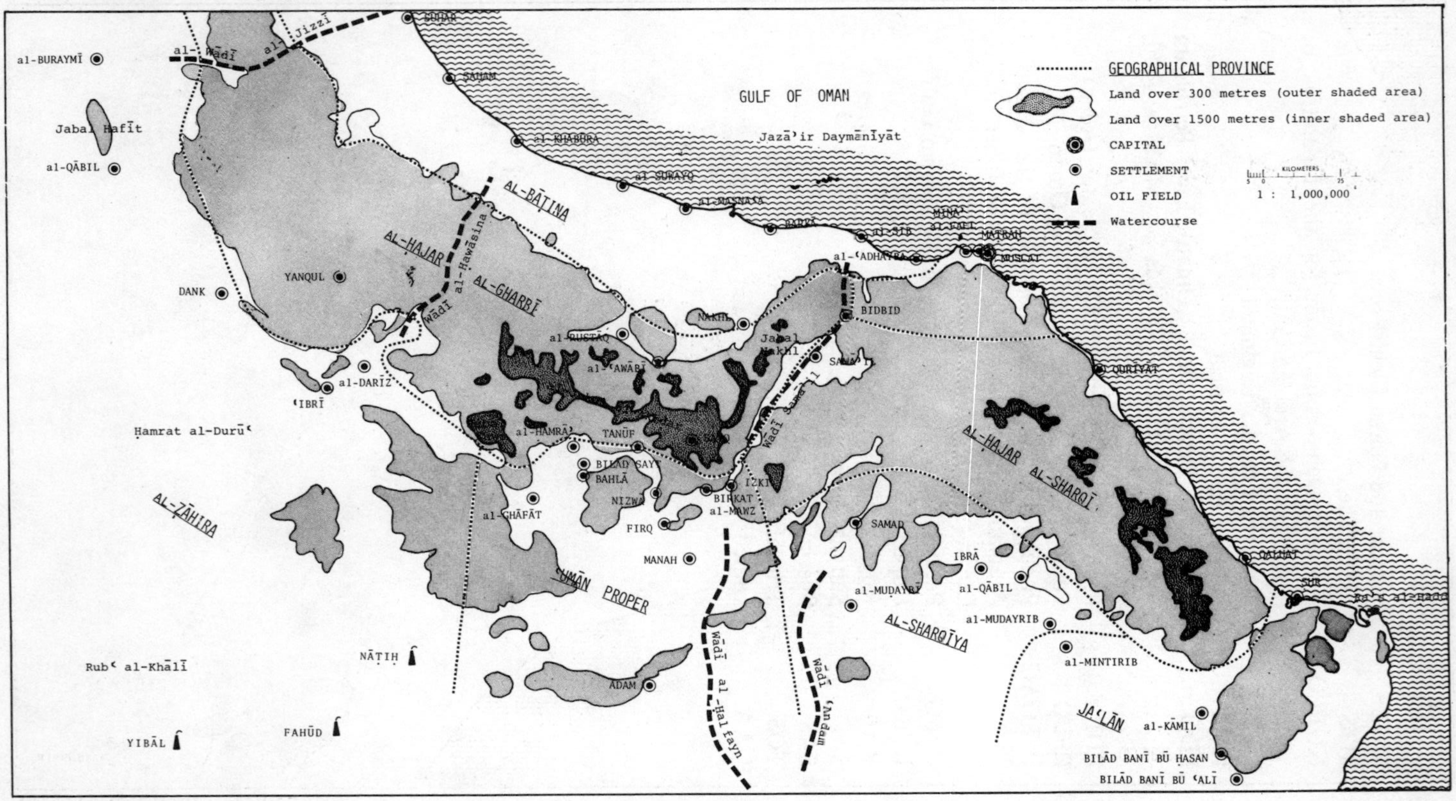

2. Central Oman — Tribes

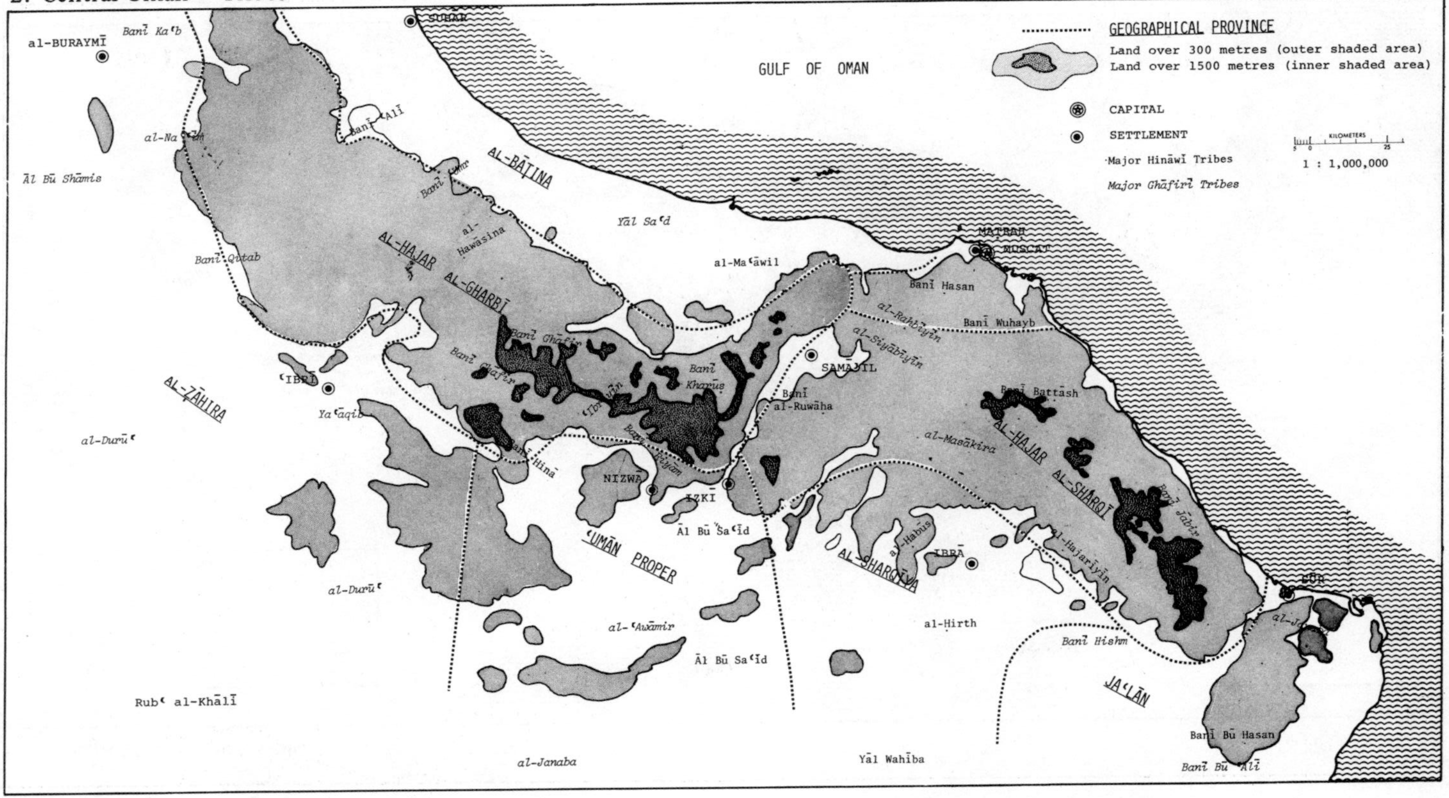

3. Governorate of the Capital

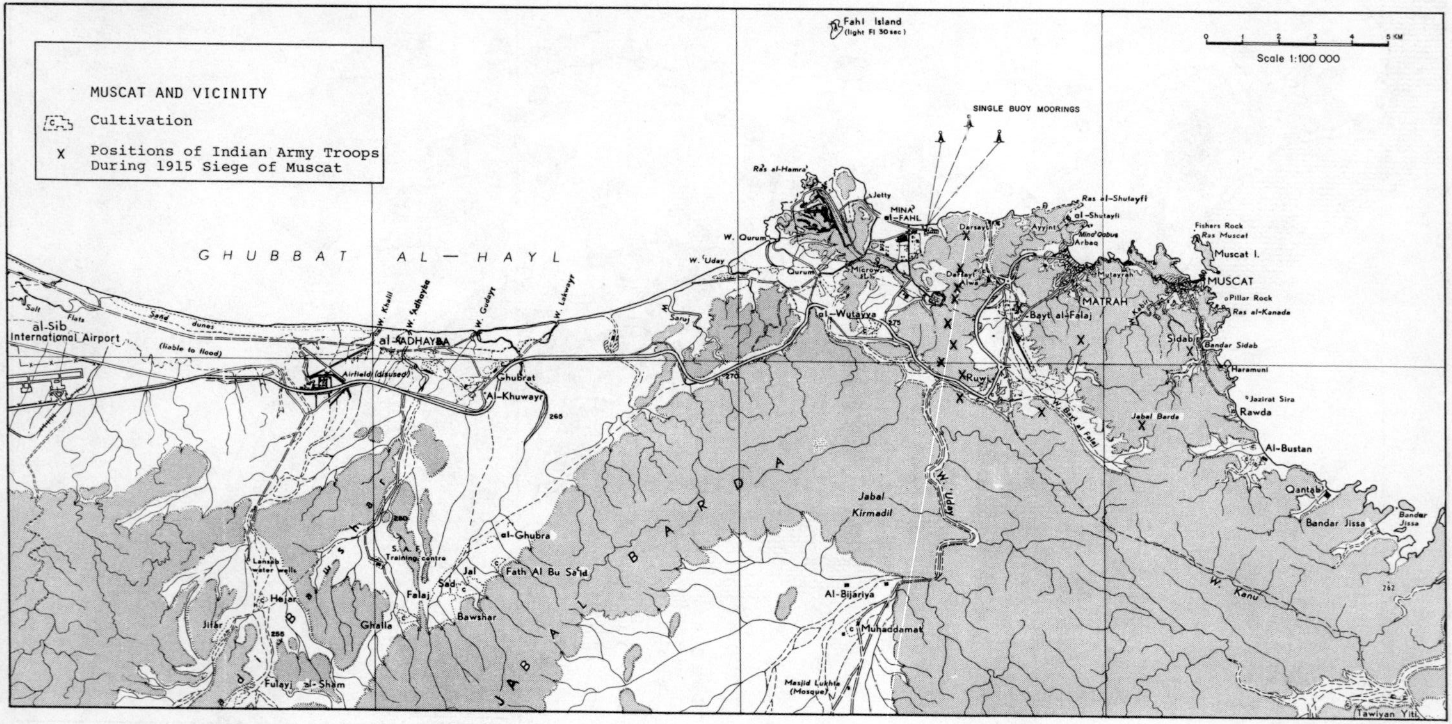

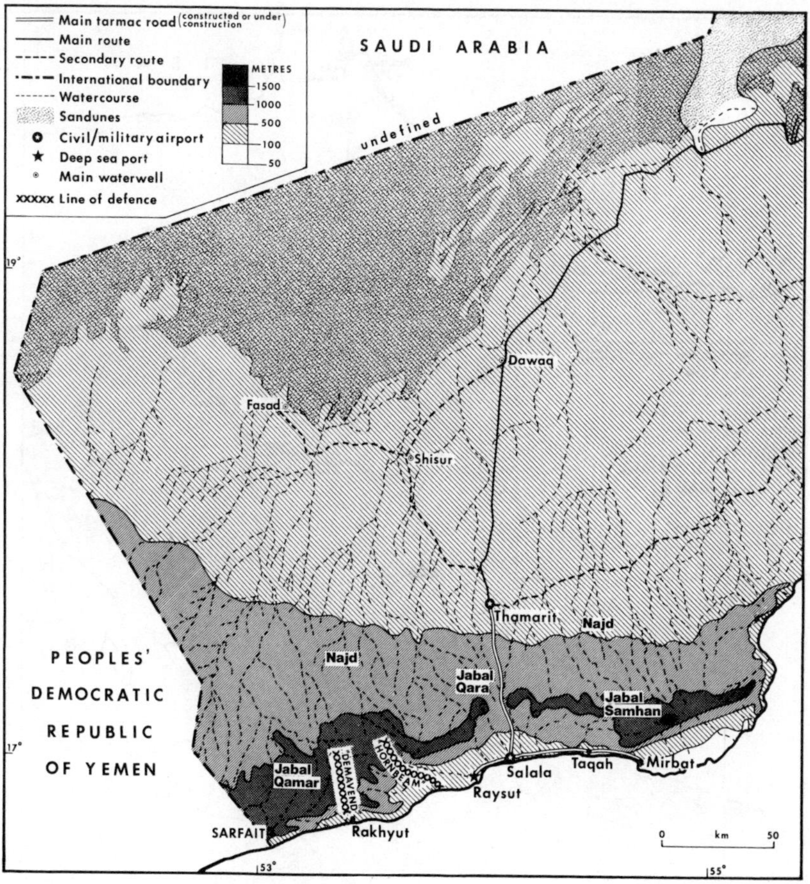

4. The War in Dhufar (reproduced from John Townsend, *Oman: The Making of the Modern State*, London, Croom Helm, 1977)

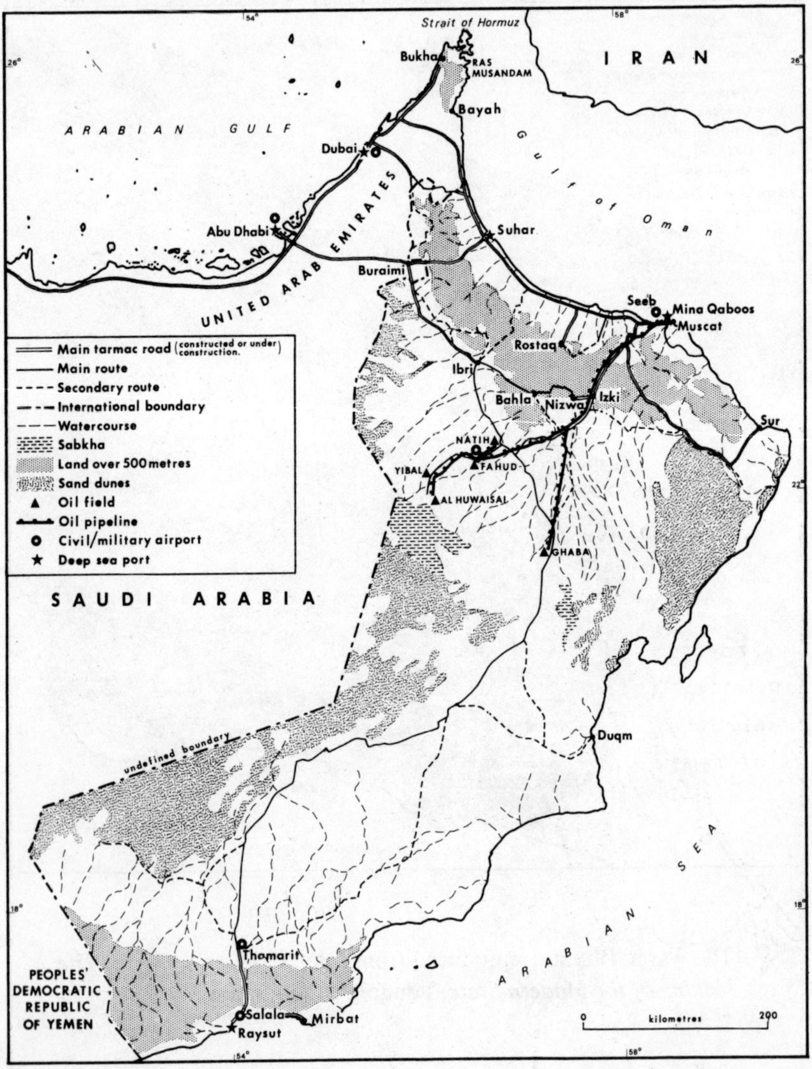

5. Oman (reproduced from Townsend, *Oman: The Making of the Modern State*)

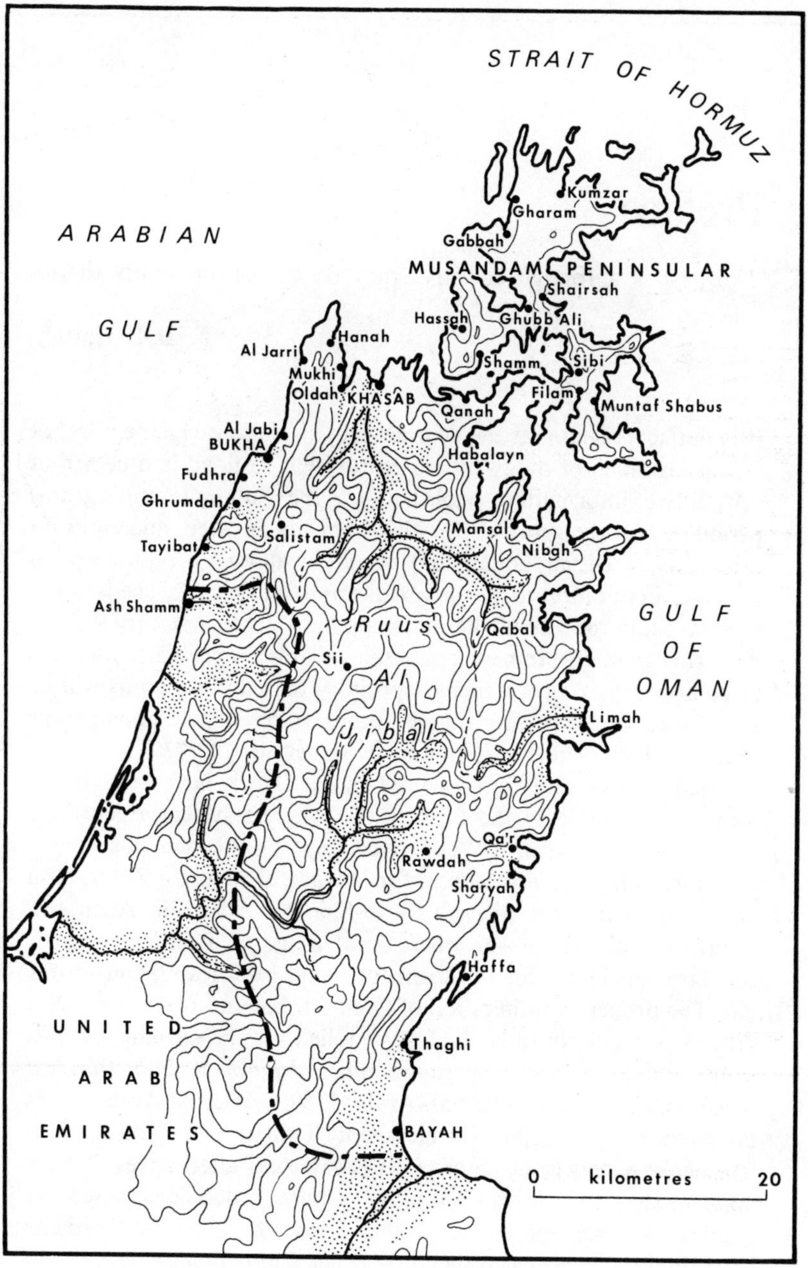

6. The Musandam Peninsula (reproduced from Townsend, *Oman: The Making of the Modern State*)

Preface

'The past is a foreign country: they do things differently there.'

L. P. Hartley

It is not surprising that the near absolute isolation which embraced Oman for much of the twentieth century has resulted in a dearth of substantive information published on the Sultanate during this period. Thus, the research for this book relied preponderantly on oral sources within Oman and on archival and oral sources in London, in addition to various books and articles published on the subject. State records of the Sultanate either have not survived the 1970 change in government or are unavailable for scholarly use. It is to be hoped that a permanent depository for official records will be established in Oman to enable future study of the momentous changes which were set in motion by the events of 1970.

Arabic words and phrases used in this work have been transliterated according to the Library of Congress system except in a few cases where either a Westernised form has become common—as in Oman for 'Umān, Muscat for Masqaṭ, Dhufar for Ẓufār, Abu Dhabi for Abū Ẓabī, Sharjah for al-Shāriqa, Aden for 'Adan and Yemen for al-Yaman—or where local usage of a variant form is standard—as in bin for ibn, banī for banū, bū for abū, and -īn for -ūn. The proper transliteration of Omani tribal and place names has proved particularly difficult. I have relied on the spelling used in Muḥammad bin 'Abd Allāh al-Sālimī, *Nahḍat al-A'yān bi-Ḥurrīyat 'Umān* (Cairo: Dār al-Kitāb al-'Arabī, 1380/1961); and Arabic maps prepared by Petroleum Development (Oman) Ltd. Vowelling is frequently a matter of choice between several alternatives; I have occasionally been forced to make arbitrary decisions based on queries made while in Oman. Arabic terms other than proper nouns have been italicised when they first occur and definitions have been added either in the text or in the Glossary (Appendix A). In addition,

I have found it convenient on occasion to refer to the entire period of the Āl Bū Sa'īd state as the 'Sultanate' and its rulers as 'Sulṭāns', although these terms were first applied in Oman by the British in the mid-nineteenth century and not generally adopted there until the beginning of the twentieth century or later. Likewise, the term 'Gulf' refers to the body of water variously known as the Arabian or Persian Gulf.

A brief explanation of the notes may be helpful. Citations of correspondence by British officials contained in the India Office Library and Records, London (IO), and the Foreign Office Records (FO) of the Public Records Office, London, have included or omitted names and/or titles as found in the original correspondence; titles have also been omitted occasionally when the official's position has been made clear by the preceding text. The place of origin of such correspondence has been included only in those cases where it differs from the official's normal duty station, as discussed in Chapter 5. English translations for the titles of journal articles and books in Arabic have been included in the bibliography. In addition, use of the phrases, *The Times* and the *Observer*, refer to the London newspapers.

It would be impossible to thank by name everyone who has helped me in the course of writing this book. I gratefully acknowledge the contributions of each of the many individuals in the US, England, the Gulf and Oman, who quite willingly discussed the subject with me. Special thanks must be made to at least some of those whose co-operation and generosity resulted in extended contact and discussion, frequently on more than one occasion. Among these individuals are Sayyid Ṭāriq bin Taymūr Āl Sa'īd, Sayyid Thuwaynī bin Shihāb Āl Sa'īd, Shaykh Sa'ūd bin 'Alī al-Khalīlī, 'Abd al-'Azīz bin Muḥammad al-Rawwās, John Townsend, Col. Malcolm Dennison, Brig. Colin Maxwell, William Peyton, Mohammed Lisanul Haq and Drs J. C. Wilkinson and T. M. Johnstone.

I also wish to thank the School of Advanced International Studies, the Shell Foundation, the India Office Library and Records, the Public Records Office, Petroleum Development (Oman) Ltd, and the Sultanate of Oman, together with their staffs and officials, for the generous co-operation and/or financial support extended to me. In particular, I must gratefully acknowledge my appreciation to Professor Majid Khadduri, for his many helpful comments and suggestions, and to Dr John Duke Anthony, who originally suggested the topic to me and was unstinting in his interest in and supervision of my work. I also wish to thank Ambassador Edward Henderson, who read the entire manuscript and gave many valuable comments and suggestions. I am indebted to David Cabitto for his help in the preparation of the maps.

Finally, I should like to say that the research for this book was made considerably easier and infinitely more enjoyable by the people of Oman, whose wide reputation for hospitality, generosity and openness is justly deserved.

CHAPTER 1

Introduction: Oman and its People

In 1970, Oman became the last Arab country to begin the attempt to break free from the fetters of traditional society and isolation and to adopt socio-economic development as a major policy goal.[1] If it could be said a few years previously that revolutionary Yemen was a medieval country 'rushing headlong into the fifteenth century', then the same expression could be applied to Oman even more aptly. Although Oman's attitude towards the 'modern world' was abruptly altered in 1970, the new face of the country's politics was firmly rooted in pre-1970 foundations: it remained a traditional monarchy, relying heavily on the support of the ruling family and with the advice of various expatriates, principally British.

Although the government's administrative structure was greatly expanded, the new ministries and departments were generally based on nuclei created in piecemeal fashion throughout the twentieth century. And, despite all the attention focused on the capital at Muscat and the character of the new administration centred there, Oman remained a tribal country. It was true that the events of 1970 and after had severely diminished the role of the tribes in Omani politics, nevertheless the tribal aspect, along with the country's geographic, nationalistic and religious characteristics, was at the heart of Oman's historical background and origins of development.

Oman has a very long history. It was brought into the fold of Islām during the time of the Prophet Muḥammad, traditionally through the efforts of 'Amr ibn al-'Āṣ, later to become the Muslim conqueror of Egypt.[2] It has remained an Islamic land ever since but has been cut off from the mainstream of Islamic society due to the isolationist nature of the Ibāḍī sect to which many of the inhabitants belong. The present state, the Sultanate of Oman, is descended from the classical Ibāḍī Imamates although far removed in political tone.[3] The present Sulṭān, Qābūs bin Sa'īd, is the fourteenth ruler of the Āl Bū Sa'īd dynasty, founded in 1744.

The Physical Setting

Wrapping itself around the eastern corner of Arabia, Oman's sea-coast extends from the entrance to the Arabian Gulf in the north to a point halfway along the Arabian Peninsula's southern coast which borders the Arabian Sea. Inland, Oman consists of successive zones of coastal plain, mountains and interior plateau, before merging into a sea of a different kind, the sands of the Rub' al-Khālī desert. In addition, the country is geographically capped by its southern and northern extremities: Dhufar and Musandam. The country bears a distinct resemblance to an island; consequently Omanis have turned their attention to overseas lands as much as to other parts of Arabia. In the course of modern history, Omani political authority has at one time or another held uncertain sway over the seven shaykhdoms now comprising the United Arab Amirates (UAA), al-Baḥrayn, part of the Iranian and Pakistani coasts, and Zanzibar and the East African littoral.

The geography of Oman has historically exercised a strong influence on the development of the country.[4] In a broad sense, the country falls into two largely self-contained divisions: the coast and the interior. The coast, relatively cosmopolitan and vulnerable, has always been open to invasion and to a melange of diverse foreign cultural influences while the interior traditionally served as the Arab and Ibāḍī fastness. Inaccessible to the outside, largely barren and xenophobic, the interior clung to tribal society and gave the outside world little consideration except as a threat to its security and purity. As the elected religious leadership of the interior was periodically transformed into a secular dynasty and sought to extend its control to the coastline, its religious and social ethic was superseded by a preoccupation with overseas expansionism.

Ultimately, this stage was followed by political collapse and retrenchment, with the interior once again withdrawing from the coast. The superior role of the interior heartland in Omani history *vis-à-vis* the marginal character of the coast was modified only after the rise of the Āl Bū Sa'īd dynasty of the last two centuries. This dynasty accomplished the transposition by their reliance on a second power base in East Africa. With the subsequent loss of Africa in the mid-nineteenth century, the Āl Bū Sa'īd of Oman, although based on the coast in contradiction to traditional historical practice, were maintained as the predominant political authority in Oman only by the arrival and then involvement of the British in Omani politics.

To a large extent, the social, economic and political organisation of Oman derives from the importance of oasis agriculture. The interior settlements are found in *wādīs* (water-courses) where date gardens can be irrigated by either natural waterflow or, more generally, by the ancient system of *aflāj* (singular, *falaj*). Introduced to the country by the pre-Islamic Persian inhabitants, the falaj is a man-made water channel, generally underground for part of its length and pierced at intervals by vertical shafts. When the Persian cultivators of Oman were displaced by the immigrating Arab tribes around the time of the introduction of Islām, the Arabs perpetuated the existing irrigation system and adapted their society and economy to fit the agricultural requirements.[5]

Although ill-suited to the new sedentary and irrigation-oriented agricultural practices, the traditional *badū* (nomadic) concept of tribal *dīra* (territory) was applied to the distribution of villages and agricultural lands acquired from the Persians.[6] The schismatic nature of tribal organisation was reinforced by the development of Ibāḍism, as described below, and resulted in a political system tending towards recurrent anarchy. Even the agricultural framework contributed to this tendency by its emphasis on the primary nature and self-sufficiency of the village unit.[7] The division of settlements along tribal and, to a certain extent, racial lines—i.e. north Arab and south Arab—contributed to the growth of two major tribal confederations encompassing most of the tribes of the country. This political dichotomy between the Ghāfirī and Hināwī alliances has been of fundamental importance in the exercise of Omani politics since its appearance in the early eighteenth century.[8]

The 'openness' of the coastal region stands in contrast to this disposition towards tribal autonomy. The exposure of coastal settlements to assault by both land and sea has resulted in a largely apolitical atmosphere allowing ethnocultural mixtures and frequent domination by secular and even non-Arab rulers. The consequent decline in the importance of the tribes there, combined with relatively bountiful resources in groundwater and fishing, contributed to the establishment of large, multi-tribal and multi-ethnic towns such as Muscat, Maṭraḥ and Ṣuḥār. As a result, while the interior has often been politically fragmented until recently, the coast has provided a solid territorial base for the Āl Bū Sa'īd dynasty.

Although the physical and psychological dichotomy between coast and interior up to the mid-twentieth century provided the most obvious division of Oman, the geography of the area admits to a large number of smaller units, frequently distinct politically as well as sometimes religiously and ethnically. Their political compartmentalisation in the past was dictated by the mountainous and desert terrain which separated them. This led to the development of balance-of-power systems among the tribes and tribal confederations, both on the provincial and local level. Despite their individuality, these geographical provinces have never been regarded as formal subdivisions of the larger political entity of Oman, whether the Sultanate or the Imamate. The lack of an intermediate unit between national and local governments is largely the result of the political influence of the tribes.[9]

The backbone of Oman, and one of the most important geographical provinces, is the Ḥajar mountain range, extending along a curve from the Musandam Peninsula in the north almost to Ra's al-Ḥadd, the easternmost point of the Arabian Peninsula, in the east, and crowned in the middle by the Jabal al-Akhḍar massif which reaches a height of over 10,000 feet. The mountains are generally regarded as comprising two regions—al-Ḥajar al-Gharbī (Western Ḥajar) and al-Ḥajar al-Sharqī (Eastern Ḥajar)—divided by the broad Wādī Samā'il, which also serves as the major artery between the coast and interior. The Western Ḥajar boasts the more important settlements, such as al-Rustāq, Nakhl and al-'Awābī, which hug the coastward side of the peaks. Of the major tribes, the Banī Kharūṣ, Ḥawāsina, Banī 'Umr and Banī 'Alī inhabit the coastal wādīs while the Banī Ghāfir, Banī Hinā, 'Ibrīyīn and Banī Riyām reside on the inland tracts. The Jabal al-Akhḍar is almost exclusively the territory of the Banī Riyām. The Eastern Ḥajar is less densely populated and its tribes play a lesser role in the country's politics. Samā'il, Bidbid and al-Ghubra, the major settlements, are found in the Wādī Samā'il, and the Banī Ruwāḥa, Siyābīyīn, Raḥbīyīn and Banī Jābir tribes are centred there. Other tribes, such as the Banī Baṭṭāsh, Masākira, Ḥajarīyīn and Banī Jābir, are found in the eastern part of the province.[10]

Nestled between the Ḥajar Range and the Gulf of Oman is the coastal plain of al-Bāṭina. Although it varies in width from between ten and fifty miles, little more than the first few miles inland from the coast are generally cultivated. This narrow strip is packed with date gardens throughout nearly the entire 175-mile length of the plain. Because of its agriculture and fishing potential, the Bāṭina is the most densely populated rural area in eastern Arabia. Its many coastal settlements, which include al-Sīb, Barkā, al-Maṣna'a, al-Suwayq, al-Khābūra, Ṣaḥam, Ṣuḥār and Shināṣ, are generally inhabited not only by several Arab tribes, but also by Baluchis, Indians and Africans of slave descent.[11] The principal Arab tribes are the Ma'āwil, Banī Ḥarrāṣ, Yāl Sa'd, Ḥawāsina, Banī 'Umr and Banī 'Alī.

Towards the east, the coastal plain gradually narrows and then terminates at the Qurum Hills. From then on, the coastline consists of a series of rugged escarpments and pocket bays until it gradually levels out again at Ra's al-Ḥadd. The area adjoining the Bāṭina at the Qurum Hills traditionally has not been regarded as a distinct province, but is sometimes simply considered to be a part of Muscat's hinterland. The first bay east of Qurum is Mīnā' al-Faḥl (formerly known as Sayḥ al-Māliḥ), used since the late 1960s as the loading point for Petroleum Development (Oman) Ltd (PDO), the country's major oil producer. Just beyond Mīnā' al-Faḥl lie the harbours of Maṭraḥ and Muscat, the Sultanate's major towns. Located in natural bowls formed by volcanic mountains, the capital of Muscat and the commercial centre of Maṭraḥ have long been the stronghold of the Āl Bū Sa'īd dynasty and are the settlements most transformed by the dramatic changes in Oman following the *coup d'état* of 1970. With a population upwards of 25,000, the twin towns have served as the principal meeting place between Oman and the outside world since the invading Portuguese built several story-book fortresses there in the sixteenth century, which still dominate the skyline of the towns. Farther down the coast stand the towns of Qurīyāt and Qalhāt, located on bays where large wādīs debouch into the sea.

Midway between the urban centre of Muscat/Maṭraḥ and Ra's al-Ḥadd lies another important port at Ṣūr. Long regarded for its shipbuilding and seafaring traditions and more recently as a centre of piracy and slave-running in the nineteenth century, Ṣūr serves as an entrepot centre for the hinterland of Ja'lān, traditionally the most isolated and xenophobic region of Oman. Ja'lān was long semi-independent of both Sultanate and Imamate and dominated by the rivalry between the Banī Bū 'Alī and Banī Bū Ḥasan tribes, although also inhabited by the Mashārifa, Banī Hishm, Janaba and Yāl Wahība. The few sizeable settlements include Bilād Banī Bū 'Alī, Bilād Banī Bū Ḥasan and al-Kāmil.

To the north of Ja'lān is the province of al-Sharqīya, which lies between the former and thc Eastern Ḥajar to its north. The Ḥirth tribe strongly dominated the province in the past, more so than any other tribe in any other province. Other tribes include the Ḥabūs, Masākina, Ḥajarīyīn, Āl Bū Sa'īd and Yāl Wahība. Plagued by persistent droughts in the twentieth century, many of the Sharqīya's inhabitants emigrated to Africa and subsequently returned. The settlements, including Ibrā, al-Qābil, al-Muḍayrib, al-Muḍaybī, Samad and those on the plain of Bidīya, are generally quite small.

Paralleling the inland curve of the Ḥajar mountains, al-Sharqīya shades into Oman province in the northwest. Also known as Oman proper or Jawf, this plateau region between the Jabal al-Akhḍar massif and the Rub' al-Khālī desert is the heart of Oman both geographically and culturally. It is shared by the most important of the Omani tribes, among them the Banī Hinā, Banī Riyām, Banī Ruwāḥa, Āl Bū Sa'īd and 'Ibrīyīn, and boasts the country's most ancient and revered towns, including the old Ibāḍī capital of Nizwā, as well as one-time capitals at Bahlā and Jabrīn, and the settlements of Tanūf (now destroyed), Birkat al-Mawz, al-Ghāfāt, al-Ḥamrā', Izkī, Manaḥ and Ādām.

To the northwest of this heartland lies the province of al-Ẓāhira (al-Dhāhira), important for being the traditional land route between Oman and the rest of Arabia; consequently as vulnerable to outside influences and invasions as the coast. Largely occupied by Sunnī (orthodox Muslim) tribes, it fell outside the scope of the Ibāḍī state and in recent times has occasionally come under the influence of Saudi Arabia. The province's major settlements include 'Ibrī, Yanqul, al-Darīz and Ḍank; notable tribes are the Ya'āqib, Banī Ghāfir, Na'īm, Banī 'Alī and Durū'. At al-Ẓāhira's western edge lies the oasis of al-Buraymī, a complex of nine villages strategically located at the crossroads of the Oman heartland, the regions of the Arabian Gulf and Saudi Arabia. Long coveted by Saudi Arabia, the oasis is presently divided between the Sultanate, with three villages, and the state of Abu Dhabi, now a member of the UAA, with six villages.[12] Besides serving as geographical parentheses to the country, both Dhufar and Musandam also exhibit historical, linguistic and ethnic differences from the rest of Oman: both are the home of ethnically distinct peoples who were never completely assimilated by the Arab migrations into the rest of Oman several millenia ago. In addition, the southern province of Dhufar was politically distinct from Oman until the last century when Oman's Āl Bū Sa'īd dynasty first established suzerainty over it. South Arabian (Ḥimyaritic) peoples such as the Mahrā and the Qarā predominate in the crescent-shaped mountains surrounding the coastal plain and the town of Ṣalāla.

There remains, finally, one major geographical area: the vast expanse of desert. Although it is the largest part of the country, it has played a marginal role in Omani history and culture, being populated by a half-dozen or so hardy nomadic tribes which continue the ageless traditions and life-styles of the Arabian badū. The Durū' form the largest of these tribes and their territory stretches along the Rub' al-Khālī from the borders of the UAA in the west almost to the Wādī Ḥalfayn in the east. To the east of this wādī, running north to south, lie the territories of two other major badū tribes, the Yāl Wahība and the Janaba. To their south, the smaller desert areas of the Barr al-Ḥikmān and the Jiddāt al-Ḥarāsīs are occupied by smaller tribal groups, such as the Ḥikmān, 'Ifār, Ḥarāsīs and the Baṭāhīra.

People and Religion

The foundations of the Omani state date back to the eastward migration of various Arabian tribal groups into the area several millenia ago. These peoples reached the Ja'lān region in about the second century AD and then moved north to challenge Persian supremacy in the area of al-Mazūn, roughly approximating what is now Oman province, where they were soon joined by other tribes moving southeast through the gateway of al-Buraymī.[13] The subsequent displacement of the Persians came as a result of the conversion of the Arab tribes to the new religion of Islām in the seventh century, and was followed by the development of a spirit of an Omani community (*umma* or *miṣr*) with the introduction of Ibāḍism, a variant form of Khārijism, to the country.[14] Traditionally, Ibāḍī leadership is vested in an Imām, who is nominated by the notables of the community and then elected by the public. The Imām must adhere to the tenets of the sect and provisions exist for his removal if necessary. Under adverse conditions, the Imām may remain in secrecy or the office exist in abeyance. The Imamate has no provision for a standing army. Generally speaking, Ibāḍism tends to be moderate in its requirements from its followers relative to other Islamic sects, yet Ibāḍī practice also displays a conservative nature that has influenced the recent history of Oman considerably.

Faced with persecution by the Umayyad governor of Iraq, many of the Ibāḍī Omanis resident in al-Baṣra returned to Oman and there established an Ibādī state in the mid-eighth century with al-Julandā bin Mas'ūd as Imām. Although the 'Abbasid caliphate, successor to the Umayyad state, and later the Saljūqs were able to subjugate Oman in the following centuries, they did so only briefly and the Oman heartland remained Ibāḍī and generally independent until recent times. The development of Ibāḍism as an integral part of the Omani national culture was complemented by the superimposition of the religious and political institution of the Imām on the tribal base of Omani society. The Imām's election, under a concept of double *bay'a* or *'aqd* (contract), reflected the method of choosing tribal shaykhs, as did the provision allowing the office of Imām to remain in abeyance when necessary.[15] The small Ibāḍī state, surrounded by an often hostile world of Sunnī Muslims and non-Muslims, assumed a defensive posture which combined with Oman's geography to influence the isolationist tendency of Omani politics and history. As a result, Oman has always looked inward to the ideals of the Ibāḍī state with its cultural and political centre at Nizwā.[16] The Omani state reached its classical zenith under the First Imamate of the ninth century, which was later to serve as the prime example of an ideal Ibāḍī state. But the achievements of this state subsequently lapsed into a series of historical cycles: elected Imāms were succeeded by secular dynasties which were overthrown by familial squabbling and groundswells of religious indignation. This pattern was the natural culmination of the centrifugal tendencies of the tribal system and the democratic ideals inherent in the Ibāḍī faith.[17]

The last complete cycle began with the creation of the Ya'rubī (plural, Ya'āriba) Imamate in the mid-seventeenth century.[18] Arising as a result of its eviction of the Portuguese garrisons from the coastal towns, this dynasty reached its apex through Omani expansion in the Arabian Gulf and along the East African littoral.[19] But the contrived election of a Ya'rubī minor as Imām in the early eighteenth century resulted in civil war which ended with the downfall of the dynasty and Persian occupation of Omani ports.[20] However, a Persian siege of Ṣuḥār was successfully resisted by the *wālī* (governor) who then became the focal point of resistance. After driving the Persians from their last Omani stronghold at Muscat, he was elected Imām in what looked to be the beginning of a new cycle. Although the first part of this cycle proceeded true to form, the resultant Āl Bū Sa'īd dynasty was preserved through the heretofore traditional period of decline by the emergence of Britain's interest in coastal Oman and her subsequent role as a protector of the Āl Bū Sa'īd.

Britain also sought influence in the country because of her role as the protector of Indian merchants who had taken up residence there. The existence of these and other non-Arab communities illustrates the point that, despite the predominant impact of Ibāḍism and the Arab tribal system on Oman's culture and history, the country is by no means culturally homogenous. Numerous ethnic and religious minorities inhabit Oman, some tracing their origins to before the Arab migrations while others are more recently arrived. There is diversity even among the Arab tribes, a significant number being Sunnī and not Ibāḍī, especially in Ṣūr, Ja'lān, al-Ẓāhira and Dhufar. Indeed, as the ethnic composition of Oman's minorities is frequently mixed and often difficult to ascertain, the distinguishing characteristic often lies in religion.[21] Nevertheless, the non-Ibāḍī role in the scope of national politics has been largely marginal, and non-Ibāḍīs have generally sought to safeguard their often precarious position by observing an apolitical neutrality.

Sunnīs form the largest non-Ibāḍī group in the country with adherents ranging from the tribes of the Ja'lān and al-Ẓāhira to the Baluchis of the Bāṭina coast. The latter were originally from the Makrān Coast of Iran and Pakistan and have emigrated to Oman in the last two centuries. There they became cultivators and fishermen and form the largest population group of both the Bāṭina and the Muscat/Maṭraḥ areas. Other Sunnīs are to be found among the ethnically distinctive tribes of Musandam and Dhufar. According to some authorities, the Shiḥūḥ tribe of the Musandam absorbed remnants of Oman's pre-Islamic population and a major section of the tribe employs an Arabic–Persian *patois* as its primary language.[22] The mountains of Dhufar contain three tribal groups: the Mahrā, Qarā and Śḥerā, which are distinct from the Arab tribes prevailing elsewhere in Dhufar.[23]

The third largest religious group is that of the Shī'īs.[24] The Shī'īs of Oman are concentrated along the Bāṭina coast and especially in the Muscat/Maṭraḥ region. Many are Khojas, members of a close-knit community originally from India but resident in Oman as merchants for several centuries. They inhabit a separate walled quarter in Maṭraḥ, known as Sūr al-Liwātīya, and also have communities in Ṣūr, Barkā, Ṣuḥār, al-Khābūra and al-Maṣna'a.[25] Another significant Shī'ī community is that of the Baḥārina, or

Baḥrānī in the singular. In Oman, the term is generally applied to Twelver Shī'īs of Iraqi or Persian background, who are also concentrated in the capital region and, like the Khojas, gravitate to trade as an occupation. Muscat is also the home of a small group of 'Ajam: Shī'īs of vague origin but believed locally to have come from Persia.[26]

The principal non-Muslim group is the Indian Hindu community, most of whom have resided in Muscat/Maṭraḥ and along the Bāṭina for several centuries, acting as one of the most important merchant communities of Oman. They are similar to the Khojas in their occupations and ties to India, but differ in religion and in the historical anomaly whereby the Hindus were granted British citizenship while the Khojas were left to become Omani citizens.[27] There are no indigenous Christian or Jewish communities in Oman although Christians were numerous in the pre-Islamic era and a small Jewish group is said to have existed in Ṣuḥār until the late nineteenth century.[28] The Arabian Mission of the Reformed Church of America was established in Muscat in 1893 and an Anglican mission functioned briefly in 1891.[29] A number of Christians, including Lebanese and Goans, have emigrated to the country since 1970 to find employment.

Adding to the ethnic heterogeneity are two classes of very small and largely unstudied groups which are scattered throughout Oman. One class consists of mostly unassimilated, probably pre-Arab individuals and families who have retained their distinctiveness by the specialised occupational functions they perform. These include the Bayādīr, who tend date gardens for pay in ḳind, the Bayāsira, who serve as semi-artisans, and the Zaṭūṭ, metalworkers, carpenters and performers of circumcision.[30] The other class concerns several minor tribal groups, particularly the Ḥarāsīs and the Baṭāḥira. These two tribes inhabit the southern part of the Sultanate between Dhufar and the Omani regions of the north. Ethnically, they seem to be mixed, having absorbed Arab as well as non-Arab elements, but the Ḥarsūsī and Baṭḥārī languages are said to be dialects of Mahrī.[31]

Although ethnic and/or religious minorities have generally sought to escape the attention of the Ibāḍī Arab majority, this has sometimes proved impossible. The Hindu merchants of the coast have on occasion been subjected to hostility on account of their religion. Resentment has been sparked by the British-protected status many Indians enjoyed in the past and also by envy over the relatively secure financial position which these merchants enjoyed in a poor and stagnant economy, which has not been fully eroded even since 1970.[32] Even Muslim groups, such as the Sunnī Banī Bū 'Alī of Ja'lān and the Qarā of the Dhufar mountains, have reacted by engaging in rebellion against the Muscat government in the nineteenth and twentieth centuries.[33]

On the other hand, minorities were able at times to profit by their removal from active political status. Automatically considered free from tribal bias, the Indian traders were able to continue their commercial role as middlemen between the coast and interior even during periods when the Muscat government's authority was limited to a handful of coastal towns. Likewise, the Arabian Mission of the Reformed Church of America was allowed to build a church in Muscat in the early twentieth century because it also provided almost the only medical care in the entire country until 1970.[34] In addition, the Āl Bū Sa'īd rulers, once the dynasty had grown away from its tribal and religious origins, gradually came to employ non-Ibāḍīs and non-Omanis as soldiers and guards. In the nineteenth century, Sunnī Muslims were brought in from the Ḥaḍramawt and central Arabia to garrison the forts in various towns and the country's present army, the Sultan's Armed Forces (SAF), was originally raised as a Baluchi mercenary force.

Although not generally regarded as an indigenous ethnic group, British residents in Oman have nevertheless exerted a certain influence on Omani society, ranging from an emulation of British manners and customs by members of the ruling family and other local intelligentsia in the capital to providing a target for moral and religious indignation by Ibāḍī religious leaders in the past.[35] Yet, in the final analysis, the British role in Oman is marginal like the other non-Arab and/or non-Ibāḍī minorities.

Life Patterns and Economy

The fundamental distinction in Omani life patterns has always been the dichotomy between *ḥaḍar* and badū, between the sedentary population of the towns and the nomads of the desert. It was as nomads that the first Arab tribes entered Oman—only later did they adopt the sedentary life-style of the earlier Persian inhabitants. This interplay between cultivation and nomadism reflects the differences in land productivity between the mountains and the wādīs on the one hand, and the sandy deserts on the other. Both the towndwellers and the badū exhibit mistrust of the other, whom they regard as inferior. In Oman, the tribal dīras of the nomadic tribes are restricted to the desert and the transitional zone between it and the settled plateaux behind the Ḥajar mountains, thus leaving the most productive area of the country to the settled population.[36] The role played by the badū in the economic and political life of the country has been of restricted importance. Their contact with the townspeople is largely limited to trade on a small scale: the badū sell camels, salt and charcoal in order to purchase such necessities as cloth, coffee, arms and ammunition. They may also own date palms in the towns of the desert fringe, such as 'Ibrī and Ādām, where they gather at harvest time. Politically, the major badū tribes have traditionally been allied with important settled tribes in a sort of client relationship but this alliance has diminished in importance with the decline of tribal society.[37]

The great majority of Oman's population, however, is settled and engaged in subsistence agriculture. There are two major cultivated regions in Oman. One consists of a narrow strip of land along the Bāṭina coast, two to five miles in depth and sandwiched between the beach and the parched coastal plain. The other is the largely barren and rocky interior where agricultural land is concentrated in irrigated oases lining the many wādīs. These oases usually consist of one or more settlements surrounded by date gardens and a few fields. Unlike the unbroken line of palms stretching along the Bāṭina, there is rarely any cultivation between oases. Most Omani cultivators own the land they work but the average holding is little more than six acres, due to the fragmentary effect of multiple inheritance under Islamic law.[38] Since all cultivation is dependent on irrigation, the choicest lands lie closest to the wells or aflāj and water is apportioned by complex methods under an elaborate system of rules administered by a 'hydrocracy' of ancient origin according to careful records kept from generation to generation.[39] The most common type of land use is a three-tiered system of crops. The most important of these is the date palm, which is grown on more than a third of all cultivated land. Frequently, limes, mangoes or bananas are grown in close proximity to the palms. In addition, there is often a groundcover of lucerne. Cereals, especially wheat, are sometimes grown at the end of a falaj after it has passed through the town and date gardens.[40] Traditionally, only the date and the lime have been consistently produced for market. Both were major exports in the past but haphazard commercial arrangements, political unrest and problems of supply during the two World Wars played an important part in the loss of established markets.[41]

Few variations from the traditional occupation of herder or farmer existed in the past.[42] Among the few were such status positions as wālī (governor of a town for the Sulṭān or Imām), *qāḍī* (religious judge) or teacher in a *kuttāb* (school for teaching the Qur'ān).[43] A career as an *'askarī* (armed retainer for a wālī), *wakīl* (supervisor of a falaj) or shopkeeper was also honourable, as was fishing in coastal areas. As pointed out above, the large merchants were usually Indian. Occupations such as metal-working and date tending were reserved for lower castes such as the Zaṭūṭ and Bayādīr. This traditional occupation pattern was disrupted in the mid-1950s when Petroleum Development (Oman) Ltd (PDO) undertook oil exploration in the interior. As a result, increasing numbers of tribesmen, especially among the badū tribes, were either occasionally or permanently employed by the oil company. After oil was discovered in the mid-1960s, PDO was instrumental in introducing a wage sector to the Omani economy by its requirements for truck-drivers and clerical help.

The country's meagre agricultural exports were supplemented in the twentieth century by fish products and some re-exports to the Gulf—while principal imports consisted of foodstuffs and cotton goods.[44] Oman faced an unfavourable balance of trade throughout most of the twentieth century, a contributing factor to the chronic insolvency of the government's treasury up to the 1930s.[45] The deterioration in Oman's trading position from its heyday of the early nineteenth century under the rule of Sa'īd bin Sulṭān resulted from several factors. These included the separation of Oman from its rich East African territories, Muscat's decline as an entrepot centre, a chronic state of unrest in the interior, and the depletion of its entrepreneurial community, especially many of the Indian merchant families.[46]

The impact of the world depression of the early twentieth century was even greater on the Oman interior than on the coast, due to a combination of an adverse shift in the terms of trade between the country's two regions and Oman's currency confusion. The only valid coin inland was the Maria Theresa dollar (MT$), a silver coin originally minted in Austria but later copied extensively for use in the Arabian Peninsula and elsewhere, although always with the same date of 1780. At the turn of the twentieth century, Sulṭān Fayṣal bin Turkī adopted the Indian rupee for use in the territories under his direct control, along with baizas of small value minted locally. The rise in world silver prices, combined with the loss of interior purchasing power due to less demand for dates and higher prices for rice and cotton imports, resulted in a dramatically shifting exchange rate: from a high of Rs. 255 per MT$ 100 in December 1917, the Maria Theresa dollar steadily appreciated until MT$ 100 equalled only Rs. 99 or less in 1938 and 1939.[47]

Most of Oman's trade, whether foreign or between the coast and interior, was heavily concentrated in Indian hands, both Hindu and Khoja.[48] These merchants generally sold imported goods through shops in Muscat, Maṭraḥ, Ṣūr and along the Bāṭina coast, and financed exports from the interior. Their near monopoly of trade rested on sound foundations: they were relatively well educated; they were able to raise necessary capital through extended family networks in the Indian subcontinent, to which they frequently shipped goods as well as from which they received imports; and, the Hindus being British subjects, they enjoyed the considerable protection of the Political Agent in Muscat (PAM), Britain's representative in the Sultanate, and consequently received compensation when their shops were disturbed during times of unrest. Nevertheless, the chaotic state of affairs of the late nineteenth and early twentieth centuries which resulted in trade disruption and frequent damage to merchandise, provoked an exodus by many in the Indian community. Those families that remained received their reward by being ideally situated to take advantage of the post-1970 economic boom in the Sultanate.[49]

Oman under the Āl Bū Sa'īd

The rise of the Āl Bū Sa'īd dynasty was unique in Oman's history. The dynasty relied more on chance and the fortunes of its founder for its creation than on the traditional route to power of a deeply religious candidate from an aristocratic family, as utilised by previous rulers.[50] The election of Aḥmad bin Sa'īd Āl Bū Sa'īd to the office of Imām was the result of his leadership in first successfully resisting a Persian siege while wālī of Ṣuḥār, followed by his expulsion of the Persian invaders from their last Omani foothold in Muscat in 1744. Aḥmad remained Imām and lived in the old Ya'rubī capital of al-Rustāq until his death in 1783.[51] His son Sa'īd thereupon was elected Imām but the new ruler was unable to control the internecine struggles of his family and was forced to yield power a year later to his son Ḥamad. Nevertheless, Sa'īd continued to reside at al-Rustāq for some three decades afterward, retaining the title of Imām while Ḥamad shifted the country's capital to Muscat.

The disdain the latter showed for the Imām's office emphasises the secular nature of the new regime. The removal of the ruler's residence to the coast signified more than just another episode in periodic forays into maritime expansionism by Oman's rulers: the abandonment of a capital with a central location for control of the tribally-balanced politics of the interior presaged a chronic schism between coast and interior that persisted for nearly two centuries. This fundamental shift was formally ratified by the 1792 Compact of Barkā, whereby Sulṭān bin Aḥmad, son of the dynasty's founder, was recognised as ruler of Muscat following the death of Ḥamad while his brother Sa'īd was allowed to keep al-Rustāq and the office of Imām and another brother, Qays, retained control of Ṣuḥār.

Neither Sulṭān bin Aḥmad (r. 1792–1804) nor his nephew, Badr bin Sayf (r. 1804–7), were able to establish a firm hold over the country and their reigns were marked by challenges from within the family as well as from the Muwaḥḥidūn (Wahhābīs) of central Arabia under the leadership of the Āl Sa'ūd. Badr was assassinated by his cousin, Sa'īd bin Sulṭān, who gradually extended his authority over Oman, defeated the Muwaḥḥidūn and raised expeditions against al-Baḥrayn and Ra's al-Khayma. But the consolidation of Āl Bū Sa'īd power in the eastern corner of Arabia gave way by 1829 to the attention paid by Sa'īd to East Africa.[52] Eventually his permanent residence was moved to Zanzibar where he received European emissaries and neglected Arabia, which had been left in the regency of his son Thuwaynī. Under Sa'īd's leadership, the Āl Bū Sa'īd dynasty became a major maritime force in the Indian Ocean on a par with the European powers in the area.[53]

The death of Sa'īd 'the Great' in 1856 was the first step in the rapid decline of Āl Bū Sa'īd fortunes. According to Sa'īd's wishes, Thuwaynī was to be the ruler of his Arabian dominions while another son, Mājid, was to have Zanzibar; but the two soon sought to supplant each other by intrigue and force. The subsequent British arbitration of the case began what was to develop into a heavy involvement in Omani affairs on the part of the Government of India. Indeed, 'British' policy in Oman and the Gulf until Indian independence in 1947 was generally much more a function of the Delhi government than Whitehall. The Government of India exercised political jurisdiction over the area, appointed the British officials in the Gulf, and acted almost independently of the India Office in London.[54]

In May 1860, the Coghlan Commission was set up to investigate the rival claims of Sa'īd's successors. On the commission's recommendation, the Government of India issued the Canning Award on 2 April 1861, whereby the African possessions of the Āl Bū Sa'īd became an independent state under Mājid who was also obligated to continue an annual payment of MT$ 40,000, begun in 1858 but dropped shortly afterwards, to the confirmed ruler of Muscat, Thuwaynī.[55] For the next twelve years, Oman suffered from the economic dislocation caused by the loss of Zanzibar, invasion by the Muwaḥḥidūn and from dynastic intrigues for control of Muscat. Thuwaynī was successful in thwarting the plans of his brother Turkī bin Sa'īd, but was assassinated by his son Sālim in 1866. Sālim received recognition by the British as ruler of Muscat but had to contend not only with Turkī but also with the emergence of a religious and tribal coalition of interior forces, led by 'Azzān bin Qays Āl Bū Sa'īd as elected Imām.[56] In 1868, 'Azzān's forces captured Maṭraḥ and then Muscat; Sālim unsuccessfully attempted to defend himself in one of the two Portuguese forts overlooking the harbour and then fled to Persia.

Initially, the new Imamate seemed militarily capable, as it successfully drove the Muwaḥḥidūn from al-Buraymī, but religiously intolerant, as it sought to lead the country back to the principles of the classical Ibāḍī state. The opinion of British officials that the Imamate's ruling triumvirate was composed of xenophobic bigots caused the Government of India to withhold recognition along with the Zanzibar Subsidy. Without the latter, the Imamate soon fell into financial difficulties. Previously loyal tribes were wooed to the cause of Turkī bin Sa'īd who was able to capture Muscat in early 1871 and restore the line of Aḥmad bin Sa'īd and Sa'īd bin Sulṭān to the Sultanate.[57]

Although Turkī received the blessing of the British, his reign was continually troubled by threats to his position. His first campaign was to wrest control of the Bāṭina from 'Azzān's younger brother Qays. Following the successful completion of that campaign, Turkī foiled an invasion by the ex-Sulṭān Sālim, who was later detained in Hyderabad by the British in 1873. A third Āl Bū Sa'īd challenge came from Turkī's brother, 'Abd al-'Azīz—but the latter agreed to recognise Turkī's authority in 1874 and remained in Muscat at

Turkī's side for a time.[58] The major threat, however, came from Ṣāliḥ bin 'Alī al-Ḥārithī, who occupied Maṭraḥ in 1874 and 1877 and laid siege to Muscat in 1883. Ṣāliḥ acted in league with 'Abd al-'Azīz on occasion and with Ibrāhīm bin Qays, the brother of 'Azzān bin Qays, at other times, unsuccessfully proposing both as candidates for Imām. The failure of these attempts was largely due to his inability to secure the co-operation of both the major tribal confederations. Consequently, the failure of the 1883 attack on Muscat and the rebels' subsequent withdrawal was followed by a nominal reassertion of the Sultanate's authority over the interior: Turkī even made a brief tour inland in 1886—the last Sulṭān to do so until Sa'īd bin Taymūr in 1955.

Turkī bin Sa'īd's natural death in 1888 was followed by the peaceful accession of his son Fayṣal—a transfer facilitated by the British who let it be known that the claims of 'Abd al-'Azīz and Turkī's eldest son Muḥammad would not be allowed. Fayṣal was faced with his father's problems of a restless interior and the schemes of Ibrāhīm bin Qays, who captured al-'Awābī soon after Fayṣal's accession, and 'Abd al-'Azīz, who failed in an abortive attack on Muscat in 1890 and was obliged to resettle in Bombay as a result. For the next few years, Ṣāliḥ bin 'Alī was occupied in quietly gathering support for his campaign and in 1895 the tribal leader managed to infiltrate his followers into Muscat, where they arose in the night and captured the town. This action was followed by a stalemate of nearly two months with Muscat as a 'no man's land' between the opposing forces of Ṣāliḥ bin 'Alī and the Sulṭān, who had retained possession of the harbour forts.

The presence of a British warship in Muscat harbour and the British warning that damage to the possessions of British subjects would not be tolerated were instrumental in producing successful negotiations between the combatants, the final result being Ṣāliḥ's withdrawal in return for a cash subsidy. The neutral position taken by the British during this siege owed a great deal to the strained relations between Delhi and the Sulṭān, and was compounded by the latter's dalliance with the French.

France, acting in league with Russia, had mounted a challenge during the 1890s to British supremacy in the Gulf. In Oman, this challenge took the form of re-establishing dormant diplomatic relations with Muscat, asserting the right of Omani vessels to fly the French flag, procuring the Sulṭān's permission for a coaling station near Muscat, and encouraging the flow of the Western Asia arms trade through Muscat.

The British response involved forcing Fayṣal to sign an agreement on 20 March 1891, whereby he undertook on behalf of his successors never to cede any portion of his territory except to the British. In addition, the Government of India publicly proclaimed that it would not tolerate another interior attack on the Muscat/Maṭraḥ region. Finally, Fayṣal was invited aboard a British cruiser at Muscat on 16 February 1899. There he was informed that if he did not revoke the promise of a coaling station to the French, he could watch the naval bombardment of his capital. He capitulated and British influence in the Sultanate was never questioned in the future.

The Sultanate's precarious hold on the interior continued to crumble throughout Fayṣal's reign. In March 1913, the two tribal confederations were sufficiently reconciled to allow the election of Sālim bin Rāshid al-Kharūṣī as Imām. Within months, the forces of the resurgent Imamate had captured the major settlements of the interior and gave the Government of India enough cause to fear for the safety of Muscat that Indian Army troops were despatched to defend the capital. In the midst of these defensive preparations, Fayṣal became ill and died on 5 October 1913.

Once again, succession to the throne was peaceful as Taymūr bin Fayṣal became Sulṭān with only minor objections from his older brother Muḥammad. The long-expected attack on the capital was launched in January 1915 and a nocturnal assault on the hills outside of Maṭraḥ was repulsed after heavy fighting. Contrary to the aftermath of previous unsuccessful assaults, the rebellion refused to subside. The Imamate remained a cohesive force and a *de facto* division of Oman into an autonomous interior and a coastal strip under the direct authority of the Sulṭān emerged. This situation was formalised by the Agreement of al-Sīb, signed in 1920 between the British PAM, R. E. L. Wingate, and various tribal leaders, which served as the major point of reference for the Sultanate's relationship with the interior for thirty-five years.

By the time of the negotiations at al-Sīb, the British had realised that their increasing involvement in Omani affairs, as demonstrated in the 1895 siege of Muscat, the 1899 ultimatum and the 1913–20 defence of the capital, could only become more entangling unless drastic steps were taken. The overhaul of Muscat's administrative machinery and a reworking of the state's financial affairs were necessary. Consequently, a Council of Ministers was organised in 1920, a British Financial Adviser introduced briefly in the same year, and a regular military force was imported from Baluchistan in 1921.

The customs was reorganised by a British expert and thereafter the department was headed by either Egyptian or Indian directors. Loans advanced by the Government of India freed the state from dependence on financing by the Indian merchants of Muscat; to secure the repayment of these loans another British Financial Adviser was seconded in 1925. During his tenure in this position, Bertram Thomas also assumed the position of *wazīr* (prime minister) and virtually ran the government during the Sulṭān's frequent absences. Taymūr had never been keen on being Sulṭān and had pleaded with the Viceroy of India for permission to abdicate soon after his accession. When his request, then and subsequently, was refused, Taymūr took to spending more and more time in Dhufar and India and returning to Muscat only infrequently and under great pressure.

The return of his son Sa'īd from education in India in 1929 eased the situation somewhat: Sa'īd assumed the role of President of the Council of Ministers and was generally regarded as regent. When Sa'īd reached the age of twenty-one, Taymūr was finally allowed to abdicate and his son assumed the title of Sulṭān in addition to the function early in 1932. In many ways, Sa'īd was considered by the British as the brightest hope for the Sultanate since Sa'īd bin Sulṭān. Yet it was to be with great relief that they eventually saw him deposed in 1970.

After a succession of three weak Sulṭāns, Sa'īd appeared to be the dynamic and intelligent leader that the country needed. By brutal economising, he soon managed to eradicate the Sultanate's long-term public debt. His campaign to reassert the personal authority of the Sulṭān over the Sultanate had shown results during his regency when the hitherto semi-independent wālī of Ṣuḥār was subjected to close control and the post of Financial Adviser was abolished in 1931. Sa'īd proved to be extremely skilful in manipulating subordinates, particularly when one considers the scarcity of trained individuals at his command. He healed the breach with the cadet line of Āl Bū Sa'īd by employing Aḥmad bin Ibrāhīm, a nephew of the late 'Azzān bin Qays, as his Minister of Internal Affairs and implemented a modest modernisation programme in his administration in the late 1930s and early 1940s. Although resentful of British domination of the Sultanate, he hid his feelings behind complete co-operation with Britain during World War II. Royal Air Force (RAF) installations dotted that part of the country under his control and, in return, Sa'īd received fairly substantial help in modernising his small armed forces.

In the mid-1940s, the Sulṭān was planning to use his military as a contingency group in his essentially peaceful plans to regain control of the interior. As early as 1937, he had used payments from a British oil company to pass on gifts to important tribal leaders and, by 1945, he had been in close agreement with nearly every figure of importance except the Imām. Imām Muḥammad bin 'Abd Allāh al-Khalīlī, the nephew of 'Azzān bin Qays's colleague, Sa'īd bin Khalfān, had been elected to his position in 1920 following the assassination of Sālim bin Rāshid. Over the years, Imām Muḥammad had gained considerable stature but by 1945 had fallen into poor health. Sa'īd's plan of moving quickly into the interior on Muḥammad's death was thwarted by the lingering presence of the Imām until 1954, by which time the position of the leadership in the interior had been altered considerably.

An important factor in the change in interior politics was the interest shown in the eastern part of the Peninsula by Saudi Arabia. In 1952, a Saudi military patrol occupied part of al-Buraymī oasis and was only removed in 1955. Soon after the restoration of Sultanate and Abu Dhabi control over the oasis, Sulṭān Sa'īd ordered his forces into the interior and easily crushed the new Imamate of Ghālib bin 'Alī al-Hinā'ī. The introduction of a PDO exploration team in the interior in 1954 had fuelled the controversy between the Sultanate and Great Britain on the one hand and the supporters of the Imamate, Saudi Arabia and the Arab nationalist camp on the other. A temporarily successful rebellion in 1957 by the leaders of the erstwhile Imamate was eventually put down permanently by a combined Sultanate–British assault on the Jabal al-Akhḍar retreat of the rebels in early 1959.

But even as one rebellion was winding down, the eccentricities of Sa'īd bin Taymūr were giving rise to another. Like his father, Sa'īd frequentiy preferred the relatively pleasant atmosphere of Ṣalāla to Muscat and after 1958 he remained in residence there until his removal as Sulṭān in 1970. But his petty restrictions on the lives of his Dhufari subjects led to the outbreak of isolated attacks on government vehicles which then escalated into first a Dhufar-nationalist rebellion and then became a vicious civil war pitting the government against Marxist–Leninist rebels supported by the leftist People's Democratic Republic of Yemen and the major Communist powers.

The rebellion was brought to an end only after Sa'īd had been usurped by his British-educated son Qābūs in a *coup d'état* in July 1970. With the change in leadership came a new commitment to economic and social development based on the discovery of oil in Oman in 1964 and its subsequent export in 1967. Although the post-1970 economic boom dramatically changed the face of Oman, the political nature of Qābūs's reign was thoroughly grounded in several fundamental themes which have dominated Omani politics throughout the twentieth century and even before. As changing circumstances brought increasingly stronger challenges to the viability of the Sultanate, these factors underwent modifications, the most recent of which was due to the effects of the 1970 *coup d'état*. Nevertheless, these themes continue to determine the broad course of the Sultanate's policies in the present, as much as in the past.

Notes

1. 'Oman' is a name susceptible to more than one definition. The Oman of this study is the territory encompassed by the Sultanate of Oman, formerly the Sultanate of Muscat and Oman, particularly from the turn of the twentieth century to the beginning of the 1970s. A more correct transliteration is 'Umān. For information on the origins of the word 'Umān, see J. C. Wilkinson, 'Arab–Persian Land Relationships in Late Sasānid Oman', *Proceedings of the Sixth Seminar for Arabian Studies* (1972), p. 46.

2. R. D. Bathurst, 'Maritime Trade and Imamate Government: Two Principal Themes in the History of Oman to 1728', in Derek Hopwood (ed.), *The Arabian Peninsula: Society and Politics* (London: George Allen and Unwin, 1972), p. 90.

3. The terms Sultanate and Imamate refer to the states ruled by a Sulṭān and an Imām. The use of the terms Sulṭān and Sultanate in Oman is a relatively recent phenomenon, whereas an Imām has been the religious and sometime political leader of the Ibāḍī sect for centuries.

4. The territory of the Sultanate differs from that of the traditional or geographical area of Oman by the inclusion of the southern province of Dhufar and the exclusion of the Arabian Gulf coast, formerly the Trucial Coast or Trucial Oman and now the UAA, in the north.

5. See Wilkinson, 'Arab–Persian Land Relationships', pp. 42–3, on the origins of the aflāj system.

6. J. C. Wilkinson, 'The Origins of the Omani State', in Derek Hopwood (ed.), *The Arabian Peninsula: Society and Politics* (London: George Allen and Unwin, 1972), pp. 73–4.

7. 'This preoccupation with distribution of water rights is reinforced by the fact that *aflāj* produce isolated, nucleated settlements. Each settlement therefore tends to form a self-sufficient hydrological society whose members must co-operate in water matters, whatever the tribal affiliation of the individual social units: indeed it is only really in irrigation matters that we can correctly speak of "villages" in Oman for . . . they are frequently made up of fortified quarters (*hārāt*) whose inhabitants are bitterly opposed to each other . . . ' J. C. Wilkinson, *The Organisation of the Falaj Irrigation System in Oman*, Research Paper No. 10, Oxford: School of Geography, July 1974.

8. The Ghāfirī–Hināwī dichotomy is discussed in greater detail in Chapter 4.

9. Some thought has been given recently to presenting the *wālīs* (local representatives of the Sulṭān) with additional responsibility as regional administrators.

10. It is difficult to assign the location of various tribes to one province or another, both because of the wide dispersion of many tribes and also due to the scarcity of information on Omani tribes. Consequently, this brief survey will list some tribes as inhabiting more than one province. An early tribal map of Oman was prepared by E. C. Ross and included in his article, 'Memorandum on the Tribal Divisions in the Principality of 'Oman', *Transactions of the Bombay Geographical Society*, vol. 19, pt. 3 (1873), pp. 187–98. Petroleum Development (Oman) Ltd has also prepared tribal maps of the Sultanate.

11. The various ethnic minorities of Oman are discussed below. The northwestern end of the Bāṭina is politically fragmented, with the UAA states of al-Fujayra and Sharjah (al-Shāriqa) exercising sovereignty among Omani enclaves.

12. The Abu Dhabi part of the oasis is sometimes referred to as al-'Ayn, after the name of the section's principal village. Al-Buraymī and its environs are also known as al-Jaw (Jau), after the plain in which it is situated.

13. An excellent discussion of the arrival of the Arabs in Oman is contained in Wilkinson, 'The Origins of the Omani State'.

14. The Khārijī sect, the first in Islām, was founded in al-Baṣra in opposition to the transfer of the Islamic state's leadership from the Prophet Muḥammad's son-in-law 'Alī to the Umayyad dynasty centred in Damascus. The sect soon divided into extremist and moderate parties. Among the latter was one founded in the last quarter of the seventh century by Abū Bilāl Mirdās bin Udayya al-Tamīmī and 'Abd Allāh bin Ibāḍ al-Murrī al-Tamīmī, from whence the name Ibāḍī. Whereas the hostility of the extremist party towards the Sunnī or orthodox body of Muslims assured its eventual eradication, the willingness of the moderates to coexist with non-Khārijis allowed the creation of Ibāḍī states in Oman, the Ḥaḍramawt and the Maghrib. Although the Ibāḍīs of the Ḥaḍramawt have since disappeared, communities still exist in the Mzab, Jabal Nafūsa and Jarba Island regions of North Africa, as well as in Oman. Discussions of the Ibādī tenets and states are found in J. C. Wilkinson, 'The Ibāḍī Imāma', *BSOAS*, vol. 39, pt. 3 (1976), pp. 535–51; Tadeusz Lewicki, 'al-Ibāḍīyya', *Encyclopedia of Islam*, 2nd edn, vol. 3, pp. 648–60; Roberto Rubinacci, 'The Ibāḍīs', in A. J. Arberry (general ed.), *Religion in the Middle East: Three Religions in Concord and Conflict* (Cambridge: Cambridge University Press, 1969), vol. 2, pp. 302–17; and Laura Veccia Vaglieri, 'L'Imamato Ibadita dell''Umān': La Ricostituzione dell'-Imamato Ibadita nell'interno dell''Umān', *Annali dell'Istituto Universitario Orientale di Napoli*, N.S. vol. 3 (1949), pp. 245–82. The spread of Ibāḍism to East Africa during the period of Omani control over that littoral was limited. 'There are practically no African Ibāḍīs. African Muslims asserted that the reason why 'Umani Arabs required their slaves to follow the Shā'fiyya of the coast was because of their attitude of racial superiority. You could only be born into Ibāḍism, the tribal religion of the waManga (Omani Arabs).' J. Spencer Trimingham, *Islam in East Africa* (Oxford: Clarendon Press, 1964), p. 81.

15. The first part of the bay'a requires the people to give complete allegiance to the Imām who is obligated to rule according to the precepts of the Qur'ān, the Sunna (the way of the Prophet) and the example provided by the first Imāms. If he fails in his duties, and does not formally repent, then the community is obligated to depose him. The second part concerns the election itself, whereby the notables of the community nominate a suitable candidate who is then presented to the public for their approval—without which a candidate can not legally be regarded as Imām. According to Ibāḍī tenets, the Imamate can be openly acknow-

ledged (*ẓuhūr*) or it may remain in a state of secrecy (*kitmān*), in which case it is not necessary to have an elected Imām. See Wilkinson, 'The Ibāḍī Imāma', and Lewicki, 'al-Ibāḍiyya'.

16. Due to its favourable and neutral location, its heritage as one of the first Arab settlements in eastern Arabia and as a centre of opposition to Persian control of pre-Islamic Oman, Nizwā has often served as the seat of the Ibāḍī Imamate. Consequently, it has become a symbol of Ibāḍī integrity and is sometimes referred to as 'al-Bayḍā", meaning white or pure.

17. 'It is easy to see that the Ibāḍī politico-religious ideology is an impractical basis for the permanent development of a state. It automatically develops a cycle which encompasses its own downfall. As the country is united so does its wealth and prosperity increase and the religious ideal weaken; the leadership becomes the prerogative of a single group and degenerates into temporal power (*saltanah*). There ensues a struggle for power in which tribal '*asabiyah* is brought into play and every potential weakness in the country exploited until full-scale civil war is the outcome. The situation is usually resolved by one or more of the parties calling in an outside power, normally with disastrous results for the Omanis in general.' Wilkinson, 'The Origins of the Omani State', pp. 78–9.

18. 'Clearly, during the Ya'rubi dynasty, control of succession to the imamate passed out of the hands of the '*ulama*'; for once full involvement in maritime trade had become possible, patronage dispensed by successive imams far exceeded anything experienced before. The rise of the dynasty coincided with a period of intense European competition for port facilities and trading agreements, with countries bordering the Arabian Sea and Persian Gulf, and the advantages offered by such agreements behooved the existence of a self-perpetuating form of government.' Bathurst, 'Maritime Trade and Imamate Government', p. 106.

19. A Portuguese fleet led by Affonso da Albuquerque had first appeared off Oman in 1507 and proceeded to sack many of the coastal towns. Permanent garrisons were established along the Oman coast in 1515. Later, increasing competition from the English, Dutch and Persians eroded the Portuguese position in the Indian Ocean and they were gradually forced to withdraw from many outposts along the Ocean's shores. A detailed account of Portuguese activities in Oman is contained in S. B. Miles, *The Countries and Tribes of the Persian Gulf*, 2nd edn (London: Frank Cass, 1966), pp. 137–200; and the subject is also covered by Bathurst, 'Maritime Trade and Imamate Government', pp. 94–9.

20. The Persian presence in Oman, originally at the invitation of one of the Ya'rubī contenders, is covered in Laurence Lockhart, 'Nādir Shāh's Campaign in 'Umān in 1737–1744', *BSOAS*, vol. 8, pt. 1 (1935–1937), pp. 157–71.

21. Another distinguishing mark is in language. One British Political Agent claimed that 'fourteen languages are spoken daily in the bazaars of Maskat and Matrah . . . ' William G. Grey, 'Trade and Races of Oman', *The Quarterly Journal of the Mythic Society*, vol. 2, no. 2 (Jan. 1911), pp. 60–1. These languages were Arabic, Persian, Baluchi, English, French, Swahili, Somali, Hindustani, Sindi, Gujerati, Portuguese/Goan, Pushtu, Armenian and Turkish.

22. More information about the Shiḥūḥ can be found in Bertram Thomas, 'The Musandam Peninsula and Its People the Shihuh', *JRCAS*, vol. 16, pt. 1 (1929), pp. 71–86; and N. L. Falcon, 'The Musandam (Northern Oman) Expedition, 1971/72', *GJ*, vol. 139, pt. 1 (Feb. 1973), pp. 1–19.

23. These peoples are discussed in greater detail at the beginning of Chapter 7.

24. Shī'ism, the largest sect in Islām to break away from orthodox Sunnism, holds that the Prophet Muḥammad's mantle of religious leadership was carried on through his grandsons rather than through the elected caliphs as accepted by the Sunnīs. The sect has been further subdivided according to the number of Imāms believed to have constituted the line of succession—the term Imām being

used in the sense of hereditary religious leader as distinct from the elected Imām of Ibāḍī tenets. Most Shī'īs today are Ithna'asharī or Twelver, *i.e.* they believe that there were twelve Imāms. The Islamic world's only predominantly Shī'ī country is Iran, although there are large Shī'ī communities in Iraq and al-Baḥrayn.

25. In Omani Arabic, Khojas are referred to as Liwātīya, singular, Lūtīya. Originally Ismā'īlī—or Sevener, another subsect of Shī'ism—followers of the Agha Khan, most Omani Khojas converted to Twelver Shī'ism several generations ago. Almost all of those who remained Sevener moved to Pakistan after its creation in 1948. Although mosques exist in Oman for the exclusive use of Shī'īs, the Khojas have their own mosques in Sūr al-Liwātīya. See A.Yusuf Ali, 'Khodja', *Encyclopedia of Islam*, 1st edn, vol. 2, pp. 960–2 and *Lorimer's Gazetteer*, vol. 1, pt. 2, pp. 2377–80. Additional information was gathered by interviews in Maṭraḥ in late 1974 and early 1975. An article of related interest is Noel Q. King and Seyyid Saeed Akhtar Risvi, 'The Khoja Shia Ithna-Asheriya Community in East Africa (1840–1967)', *Muslim World*, vol. 64, no. 3 (July 1974), pp. 194–204.

26. The word 'Ajam was used in classical Arabic to mean non-Arabs and was later applied to Persians in particular.

27. The option of British citizenship was extended to both communities in the nineteenth century but the subsequent registration of Indians at the Political Agency in Muscat was mostly limited to Hindus. See India Office Records (hereinafter cited as IO), R/15/3/337; Annual Muscat Administration Report for 1918. Later, the British and the Sulṭāns agreed to treat the Khojas as Omani citizens. After the phased British forfeiture of extraterritorial privileges in the 1950s and 1960s, many Hindus also adopted Omani citizenship.

28. S. B. Miles noted in the 1870s that Ṣuḥār's inhabitants included 'a dozen Jews, who have been gradually decreasing in numbers year by year'. 'On the Route Between Sohār and el-Bereymī in 'Omān, with a note on the Zatt, or Gypsies in Arabia', *Journal of the Asiatic Society of Bengal*, vol. 46, pt. 1, no. 1 (1877), p. 51. An American visitor to Muscat earlier in the nineteenth century noted that 'There are also a few Jews here, who, being unable to endure the tyranny and exaction of the Pacha of Persia, came to this settlement in 1828. They continue unmolested in the exercise of their customs and religion.' J. B. F. Osgood, *Notes of Travel or Recollections of Majunga, Zanzibar, Muscat, Aden, Mocha, and Other Eastern Ports* (Salem, Mass.: George Creamer, 1854), p. 94.

29. The first missionaries of the Arabian Mission arrived in Muscat in 1891 at the same time as Bishop French of the Anglican Church. The Americans went on to al-Baṣra but Bishop French died after a month in Muscat. See *Lorimer's Gazetteer*, vol. 1, pt. 2, pp. 2394–9. The Arabian Mission in Muscat was permanently established by Peter Zwemer in 1893; a brief attempt was made to establish another mission inland at Nakhl and a hospital was built at Maṭraḥ in 1908. Alfred DeWitt Mason and Frederick J. Barny, *History of the Arabian Mission* (New York: The Board of Foreign Missions, Reformed Church in America, 1926); and Samuel M. Zwemer, *Arabia: The Cradle of Islam* (New York: Fleming H. Revell, 1900).

30. The first two groups are discussed in J. C. Wilkinson, 'Bayāsirah and Bayādīr', *Arabian Studies*, vol. 1 (1974), pp. 75–85. S. B. Miles, 'Sohār and el-Bereymī', discusses the Zaṭūṭ, pp. 57–9. The second and third merit entries in *Lorimer's Gazetteer*, vol. 2. This volume consists of brief descriptions of place-names, tribes, ethnic groups, *et al.*, arranged alphabetically. Also see John Duke Anthony, with J. E. Peterson and Donald S. Abelson, *The Sultanate of Oman and the Amirates of Eastern Arabia: A Cultural and Historical Dictionary* (Metuchen, N. J.: Scarecrow Press, 1976). The singular forms for the three groups are Bīdār, Baysarī and Zuṭṭī, respectively.

31. Conversation with Prof. T. M. Johnstone, London, 27 September 1974. See Walter Dostal, 'Two South Arabian Tribes: al-Qara and al-Ḥarāsīs', *Arabian Studies*, vol. 2 (1975), pp. 33–41; T. M. Johnstone, *A Ḥarsusi Lexicon* (Oxford: Oxford University Press, 1976); C. D. Matthews, 'al-Baṭāḥira', *Encyclopedia of Islam*, 2nd edn, vol. 1, p. 1091; and ibid, 'al-Ḥarāsīs', *Encyclopedia of Islam*, 2nd edn, vol. 2, pp. 176–7.

32. The Ibāḍī fundamentalist revival of the Imamate, which held Muscat from 1868 to 1871, exhibited a virulent anti-Hindu streak which was a contributing factor to its fall when the Government of India refused to recognise it. Ravinder Kumar, 'British Attitudes Towards the Ibadiyya Revivalist Movement in East Arabia', *International Studies*, vol. 3, no. 4 (Apr. 1962), pp. 443–50.

33. A closer look at the Banī Bū 'Alī will be found in Chapter 4. The role of the Qarā in the Dhufar rebellion is discussed in Chapter 8.

34. Peter Zwemer, a member of the early Mission, was one of only two Westerners to visit the Jabal al-Akhḍar between 1837 and 1959. In addition, American Mission doctors travelled into the interior on various occasions in the first half of the twentieth century in order to treat interior notables at a time when even representatives of the Sultanate were unable to. Until 1970, there were only two hospitals in the entire country: the Mission's establishment in Maṭraḥ and the Muscat Hospital, originally part of the British Political Agency.

35. As shown later in Chapter 3, British individuals were responsible for reorganising the administration and military structure of the Sultanate beginning in the 1920s and British firms such as Grey-McKenzie and the British Bank of the Middle East have long played prominent roles in the country's economic life. The British cultural impact on Oman has been significant, accounting for such manifestations of Anglophilia as the overwhelming support shown in Muscat for the Allied cause in World War II, the education of the last three Sulṭāns in British-operated schools abroad, and the attraction that London has long shown for Omani travellers.

36. A minor exception to this generalisation is that of the *shāwīya*, singular, *shawāwī*: the nomadic sheepherders of the mountains. See Wilkinson, 'Arab-Persian Land Relationships', p. 45.

37. For more information on this subject, see Chapter 4.

38. According to the Whitehead Consulting Group's *Economic Survey of Oman 1972* (London: Harold Whitehead and Partners, 1972; unpaginated), land holdings average 6.2 acres on the Bāṭina and 7.1 acres in the interior.

39. J. C. Wilkinson provides an introduction to the subject in 'The Falaj Irrigation System'.

40. According to the Whitehead survey cited above, 37.5 per cent of the land is used for date palms, 15.5 per cent for lucerne, 10.3 per cent for onions, 9.9 per cent for limes, 3.3 per cent for wheat, 2.4 per cent for bananas, 1.1 per cent each for mangoes and tobacco, 0.7 per cent for garlic and 5.2 per cent for other crops. The same survey estimates the total number of palm trees in Oman to be 1,400,000.

41. Date exports suffered more in this respect than limes, partially due to unsatisfactory packing methods. According to a US Department of Agriculture report, the Sultanate exported 30,000 tons of dates at the turn of the century, some 1,000 tons of which went to the US. David G. Fairchild, 'Persian Gulf Dates and Their Introduction into America', US Department of Agriculture, Bureau of Plant Industry, *Bulletin* no. 54 (19 Dec. 1903), p. 12. Within a few decades, better packing methods and organisation of exports allowed Iraq to replace Oman as the primary supplier of Gulf dates to the US. For more information on the Gulf date trade, including the Sultanate, see *Lorimer's Gazetteer*, vol. 1, pt. 2, pp. 2294–307. A later assessment of the date trade in the area is to be

found in J. H. Stevens and E. Cresswell, 'The Future of Date Cultivation in the Arabian Peninsula', *Asian Affairs*, vol. 59 (N.S. 3), pt. 2 (June 1972), pp. 191–7.

42. Herding was one livelihood that both the ḥaḍar and badū populations have had in common. The nomad is heavily dependent on camels and goats while the sedentary population raises cattle and sheep in addition to goats. Estimates of livestock population in Oman, according to the Whitehead survey, include 45,000 head of cattle, 111,000 goats, 29,000 sheep and 5,100 camels. These figures exclude Dhufar where it is estimated that there are 23,000 head of cattle.

43. For a description of Oman's kuttābs, see Robert A. Mertz, *Education and Manpower in the Arabian Gulf* (Washington, D.C.: American Friends of the Middle East, 1972), pp. 62–5.

44. By way of example, principal exports in 1943–4 consisted of 34.5 per cent dry dates, 11.6 per cent wet dates, 9.9 per cent salted fish, 7.5 per cent tea, 3.9 per cent sardines, 2.8 per cent cotton piecegoods, 1.1 per cent sugar and 0.6 per cent coffee, according to their value in rupees. Primary destinations were: India, 56 per cent; Arabian Gulf, 29.2 per cent; Iraq, 6.2 per cent; and Ceylon and Persia, 2.9 per cent each. IO, R/15/3/339; Annual Muscat Administration Report for 1943. Major imports for 1942–3 were 28.6 per cent rice, 18.8 per cent cotton piecegoods, 19.1 per cent tea, 4.7 per cent wheat and wheat flour, 2.6 per cent twist, 1.6 per cent cement, 1.3 per cent coffee and 1.0 per cent sugar. Government of India, Political Agent, Muscat, *Muscat Trade Report 1942/43* (Simla: Government of India Press, 1943). In the early 1940s, India provided 68 per cent of the total imports, Africa 16.4 per cent, the Arabian Gulf 6.8 per cent, Aden 3.2 per cent, and Persia 3.0 per cent. IO, R/15/3/339; Annual Muscat Administration Report for 1941. Statistics on the Sultanate's foreign trade between 1874–1903 and 1894–1914 can be found in Robert G. Landen, *Oman Since 1856* (Princeton: Princeton University Press, 1967) and Briton Cooper Busch, *Britain and the Persian Gulf, 1894–1914* (Berkeley: University of California Press, 1967).

45. The Sultanate's trade deficit reached a maximum of over fifty *lakhs* of rupees in 1921–2 and in the 1930s it fluctuated between nine and fifteen lakhs. IO, R/15/3/337; Annual Muscat Administration Reports for 1911–1930; and R/15/3/338; Annual Muscat Administration Reports for 1934–1941. One lakh is equal to Rs. 1,00,000.

46. Robert G. Landen, in *Oman Since 1856*, has suggested that Oman's trade deterioration resulted from the introduction of European trading practices and steamship service to the Gulf region which disrupted Muscat's status as the premier entrepot centre in the area. This thesis has been rebutted by J. B. Kelly who contends that the reversal of Oman's fortunes began prior to the inauguration of steamship lines, started in the 1860s, and was particularly the result of the loss of Zanzibar with its larger population base, agricultural fertility and greater revenue potential, in addition to such factors as the decline of the slave trade and the political instability in Muscat. For a succinct presentation of thesis and counterthesis, see T. Cuyler Young (ed.), *Middle East Focus: The Persian Gulf*, Proceedings of the Twentieth Annual Near East Conference (Princeton: Princeton University Conference, 1969). Kelly has pointed out elsewhere that the initiation of the steamship services to the Gulf came about primarily for reasons not related to trade. For example, the British India Steam Navigation Company was established as a substitute for the Bombay Marine (Indian Navy) in carrying mail and providing reliable transport for the British political representatives in the area and their troops. J. B. Kelly, *Britain and the Persian Gulf, 1795–1880* (Oxford: Clarendon Press, 1968), pp. 564-5. Later services provided by the French, Germans and Russians in the 1890s were largely dictated by political ambitions in the area and proved unprofitable both politically and economically. Busch, *Britain and the Persian Gulf*.

47. Monthly average exchange rates between 1917 and 1927 are contained in the appropriate Annual Muscat Administration Reports. Bimonthly averages from 1927 to 1939 are given in the Muscat Intelligence Diaries of the Political Agent in Muscat (PAM). The use of various currencies in the Sultanate continued through Indian independence and the creation of the External (Gulf) Rupee in 1959, and was only resolved by the circulation of the Sa'īdī riyāl, later Omani riyāl, beginning on 7 May 1970. The Sultanate's currency problems in the nineteenth century are discussed in Landen, *Oman Since 1856*, pp. 127–31. Of related interest is the article by Michael E. Edo, 'Arabian Currency Arrangements Seen Evolving in Context of Rapid Change', *IMF Survey*, vol. 3, no. 23 (9 Dec. 1974), pp. 374–5; and the article on 'Bahrain Dinar, a Gulf Currency', in *Orient* (Hamburg), vol. 11, no. 1 (1970), pp. 3–5.

48. The role of Indians in Omani commerce is discussed in Landen, *Oman Since 1856*, pp. 131–44.

49. One prominent example is that of the W. J. Towell Company, originally an English business founded in the 1860s. In 1914, the firm's Khoja partner, Muḥammad Faḍl, assumed full ownership as well as succeeding his former English partner as US Vice-Consul. In the 1970s, his descendents, under the family name of Sulṭān, secured the Omani agencies for such products as Mazda, Unilever, Spinneys-1948, Pepsi Cola and Cheeseborough-Pond, and entered into partnership with the British firm, Taylor-Woodrow, on major construction projects. Another good example, albeit non-Indian, is that of Muscat merchant Yaḥyā Muḥammad Naṣīb. Both his maternal and paternal grandfathers were important members of the Muscat trading community at the turn of the century: the Baḥārnī Naṣīb Khān being the naval contractor for the British Political Agency and landing contractor for the Sulṭān while the Baluchi 'Alī bin Mūsā earned British enmity as a major arms merchant. In the 1970s, the grandson's Yaḥyā Enterprises held agencies for Peugeot, Sansui, General Electric, Pirelli and Marconi and have joined forces with another major British construction firm, Costain. Interviews with members of the Muscat/Maṭraḥ merchant community, 1974 and 1975.

50. The most complete history of modern Oman, covering the dynastic periods of the Nabāhina (1566–1624), the Ya'āriba (1624–1744) and the Āl Bū Sa'īd (from 1744 to the beginning of the twentieth century), is contained in *Lorimer's Gazetteer*, vol. 1, pt. 1, pp. 397–629. Lorimer later prepared a supplementary history on the Sultanate covering the period of 1908–1928. IO, B.400/P.4640/28; copy in R/15/1/4238. Another detailed work, contemporary to Lorimer, is S. B. Miles, *The Countries and Tribes of the Persian Gulf*. The broader scope of Omani history, from the entry of the Arab tribes to the mid-twentieth century, has been surveyed in articles by J. C. Wilkinson, R. D. Bathurst and J. B. Kelly in Derek Hopwood (ed.), *The Arabian Peninsula: Society and Politics* (London: George Allen and Unwin, 1972). The nineteenth century has been the period most completely covered by Western historians, particularly by Landen, *Oman Since 1856*; Kelly, *Britain and the Persian Gulf*; Busch, *Britain and the Persian Gulf*; as well as by Ravinder Kumar, *India and the Persian Gulf Region, 1858–1907; A Study in British Imperial Policy* (Bombay: Asia Publishing House, 1965). Published information on the twentieth century is relatively scarce. Other than the overviews given in Kelly's article for *The Arabian Peninsula* and the last chapter of Landen's book, substantive knowledge has generally been confined to memoirs or accounts of the three major rebellions, discussed below in Chapters 6 and 7. Classical Omani chronicles translated into English include G. P. Badger, *History of the Imâms and Seyyids of 'Umân, by Salîl-ibn-Razîk, from 661–1856* (London: Hakluyt Society, 1871), and Edward C. Ross, 'Annals of 'Oman, from early times to the year 1728 A.D.', *Journal of the Asiatic Society of Bengal*,

vol. 43 (1874). Further notes on Omani historical manuscripts are given in Wilkinson, 'The Origins of the Omani State', pp. 86–8. The *Tuḥfat al-A'yān bi-Sīrat Ahl 'Umān*, 5th edn (al-Kuwayt: Dār al-Ṭalī'a, 1974) of 'Abd Allāh bin Ḥumayd al-Sālimī serves as perhaps the standard history from the Omani point of view, and his narrative has been continued to the mid-twentieth century by his son, Muḥammad bin 'Abd Allāh al-Sālimī, in *Nahḍat al-A'yān bi-Ḥurrīyat* 'Umān (Cairo: Dār al-Kitāb al-'Arabi, 1380/1961). The following pages are intended to serve as a brief introductory survey of the development of the Āl Bū Sa'īd dynasty—detailed information and sources on the twentieth century will be found in the following chapters.

51. The date of Aḥmad's election is obscure. It is generally cited as 1744, although C. F. Beckingham concludes that it occurred in 1749. 'The Reign of Ahmad ibn-Sa'id, Imam of Oman', *JRAS*, vol. 28 (1941), pp. 257–60.

52. Oman's connection with the East African littoral predates Sa'īd bin Sulṭān's interest by approximately a thousand years, dating back to the period of the early Ibāḍī Imamates. Representative historical accounts of this long-standing relationship are to be found, *inter alia*, in Reginald Coupland, *East Africa and its Invaders, from the Earliest Times to the Death of Seyyid Said in 1856* (Oxford: Clarendon Press, 1931); W. H. Ingrams, *Zanzibar, Its History and Its People* (London: H. F. and G. Witherby, 1931); Richard Matheson Preece, 'Constitutional Development and Political Change in the Zanzibar Protectorate, 1890–1962' (unpublished Ph.D dissertation, Johns Hopkins University, 1975); and the articles by Gervase Mathew, G. S. P. Freeman-Grenville and Sir John Gray, in Roland Oliver and Gervase Mathew (eds.), *History of East Africa* (Oxford: Clarendon Press, 1963).

53. Britain sought Sa'īd's assistance in suppressing the slave trade and gained his signature on several agreements to further this end. Commercial treaties were concluded with the US in 1833, Britain in 1839 and France in 1844. After receiving an American ambassador in Zanzibar, Sa'īd sent the first Arab envoy to the US, who arrived in New York in April 1840. Hermann F. Eilts, 'Ahmad bin Na'aman's Mission to the United States in 1840: The Voyage of Al-Sultanah to New York City', *Essex Institute Historical Collections*, vol. 98, no. 4 (Oct. 1962), pp. 219–77. A biography of Sa'īd was later published by his grandson, Rudolph Said-Ruete, *Said bin Sultan (1791–1856), Ruler of Oman and Zanzibar: His Place in the History of Arabia and East Africa* (London: Alexander-Ouseley, 1929).

54. The relationship of Great Britain and the Government of India to Oman is discussed in detail in Chapter 5.

55. The payment was soon defaulted on by Mājid and then assumed by the British Government as the so-called 'Zanzibar Subsidy', and continued for the next century. The Canning Award was also notable for referring to the two rulers as 'Sulṭāns'. Having lost the title of Imām in 1784, the Āl Bū Sa'īd rulers had subsequently been known by their subjects as 'Sayyids' until the end of the nineteenth century when the term 'Sulṭān' finally became adopted in Muscat. For greater detail of the events leading up to the Canning Award, see Ravinder Kumar, 'The Dismemberment of Oman and British Policy Towards the Persian Gulf', *Islamic Culture*, vol. 36, no. 1 (Jan. 1962), pp. 8–19.

56. 'Azzān was the leader of a cadet line of Āl Bū Sa'īd based at al-Rustāq. Religious support for his investiture as Imām was marshalled by Sa'īd bin Khalfān al-Khalīlī, spokesman for the *muṭāwi'a*, singular *muṭawwi'*, the religious leaders known as '*ulamā*' by Sunnīs, while the chief tribal notable was Ṣāliḥ bin 'Alī al-Ḥārithī.

57. In the course of the fighting for Muscat, 'Azzān was killed, Sa'īd bin Khalfān was captured and put to death along with one of his sons and Ṣāliḥ bin

Alī had already left for his Sharqīya home, where he continued to direct attacks against Muscat for the next quarter century. ʻAzzān was the last Imām to rule in Muscat, as well as the last Āl Bū Saʻīd to hold the office of Imām.

58. During a period of severe depression experienced by Turkī in 1875, ʻAbd al-ʻAzīz acted as regent in Muscat while the Sulṭān withdrew to Gwadar on the Makrān Coast, and only reluctantly gave up the reins of power when Turkī returned a few months later.

PART ONE

Themes in Omani Politics

CHAPTER 2

The Sulṭāns and the Ruling Family

During the twentieth century up to 1970, the Sultanate knew only three Sulṭāns. Each of these individuals marked a distinct era in the history and development of the political structure of the state. Taymūr was as different from Fayṣal as Saʿīd was from Taymūr; nevertheless, all three exhibited a common thread of dynastic rule and typically traditional and Omani approaches to the events and factors facing the Sultanate. This thread was as much a product of the nature of the ruling family as it was of more obvious themes, such as the constitution of the country—both in the essentially Omani influences of the interior and the cosmopolitan tendencies of the coast—and the effect of the supervisory role of the British.

The direct and indirect influences of these Sulṭāns on the state cannot be understated; nor can the role played by the ruling family be minimised. In general, circumstances required the Sulṭāns to work administratively within the limitations of the ruling family. Without various members of the family, regardless of how incapable they may have been, the Sultanate could not have functioned, even in its customary, haphazard way.

Fayṣal Bin Turkī

If there was any predominant theme to the reign of Fayṣal bin Turkī, it was that the Sulṭān was more a prisoner of circumstances than an independent actor. This impression of causality is associated more with his name than with any Sulṭān before or since: whatever course Fayṣal took, the outcome was determined by events beyond his control.

Fayṣal was born in 1864 of an Abyssinian mother. His education was rudimentary and he never mastered literary Arabic; indeed, his strongest language was Gujerati rather than even colloquial Arabic.[1] His apprenticeship as Heir Apparent consisted of several stints as wālī (governor) in Samā'il and Nizwā; he also led military campaigns into the interior in 1883 and against the Banī Baṭṭāsh tribe in 1886. His succession to the throne was peaceful, his status as Heir Apparent relatively unchallenged. This was to be the first time since the mid-nineteenth century decline of the Sultanate that transfer of power had been orderly; it was to mark a trend that would last until 1970.

Although young when he became Sulṭān, the first phase of his reign was marked by his self-confident manner, apparently born of his successful activity in the interior as Heir Apparent. A contemporary observer noted that

> Seven years ago, when we first saw him, he was but a beardless boy, timid and shy, and now that he has reached man's estate, he still retains the nervous manner of his youth; he lives in perpetual dread of his elder brother Mohammed, who, being the son of a negress, was not considered a suitable person to inherit the throne, and the two brothers, though living in adjacent houses, never meet without their own escorts to protect them from each other.[2]

His relations with the 'Azzān bin Qays branch of the Āl Bū Sa'īd, estranged from the Muscat Sulṭāns since 1784, were good—he married a daughter of Ibrāhīm bin Qays in 1898—and likewise he was on good terms with Ṣāliḥ bin 'Alī al-Ḥarithī, the leading personality of the interior. But this apparently successful beginning rapidly deteriorated. By the early 1890s, his authority over the interior had evaporated and he found himself derided by the tribal *tamīmas* (paramount shaykhs or leaders) and religious leaders alike because of his dependence on the British. Their attitude crescendoed with the siege of Muscat in 1895 when Fayṣal was compelled to seek refuge in Fort Jalālī.

In addition, the Sulṭān was threatened from another quarter in a two-horned dilemma: Fayṣal was equally an object of scorn for most of the Political Agents in Muscat (PAM) in the 1890s and the first decade of the twentieth century, who were inclined to speak disparagingly of him and looked down on him as if he were a child. To an empire in full splendour of its raj, Fayṣal and his problems were a 'petty bother about dates and marauding Beduin and an impecunious potentate bereft of his dominions . . .'[3] His attempts to recapture Muscat after it had been over-run in 1895 were frustrated by a British ruling that any damage to property incurred as a result of his efforts would be his responsibility and not the rebels'. Subsequently, Fayṣal was held responsible for compensation on all damages due to the entire episode.

It was not surprising that Fayṣal felt himself increasingly isolated: his subjects had become enemies and his protectors had become punitive. In his view, the only course of action remaining was to seek assistance elsewhere. Coincidentally, the French were at that time in the process of formulating a challenge to British supremacy in the Gulf and sought the collaboration of the now complaisant Sulṭān.[4] Consequently, the appointment of a French Consul to Muscat in 1894 was well-received by the Sulṭān. This would provide him with an opportunity to escape an unprofitable as well as demeaning position of dependence. Fayṣal readily consented to French proposals over the next few years, including the cession of a coaling station at Bandar Jiṣṣa, not far from Muscat, and the acquiescence in French flag privileges given to Ṣūrī *dhows* (wooden sailing craft). Eventually, Fayṣal felt secure enough to omit proper recognition of the annual salute to the Queen–Empress. However, he had gone too far. The British viewed the increasing French influence in the Sultanate with concern and would not brook any change in the Sulṭān's status. Any further intransigence he may have intended was dismissed by the ultimatum of 1899 whereby he was ordered to appear on board the British flagship or see his palace and capital bombarded. Fayṣal gave in and was subsequently forced to renounce the Bandar Jiṣṣa action in a public speech.

It was unfortunate for Fayṣal to have all his major policy endeavours end in disaster. But the public display of his disappointments in such a humiliating manner was to have severe effects on the Sulṭān. Given to periodic fits of despondency, he was morose enough by the turn of the century to believe that the only solution was abdication.[5] He broached the subject with Lord Curzon, the Viceroy of India, who visited Muscat in November 1903, but was brusquely turned down. As a result, what was left of his fitful determination and drive vanished and the ensuing decade and a half of power was unmarked by any initiative on his part. Affairs of state in Muscat were left to Sa'īd bin Muḥammad Āl Bū Sa'īd, who had been wazīr (principal government official) to Turkī bin Sa'īd. During his active period, Fayṣal had completely rejected Sa'īd but by the turn of the century he no longer cared. Responsibility for what residue of authority was left in the interior fell to an ex-slave, Sulaymān bin Suwaylim. The latter's assassination in 1907 was the beginning of a transformation of the relationship between the Sultanate and the loosely-governed interior into politically distinct areas. Gradually all control over the interior was lost and by 1913 the newly-reconstituted Imamate was in a position to pose a threat to Muscat.

Almost as if this last crisis was too much for the Sulṭān to bear, he fell ill and died on the evening of 5 October 1913.[6] His son and successor, Taymūr bin Fayṣal, was only marginally better equipped to handle the Sultanate's problems. But where Fayṣal had met only hostility and disdain, Taymūr was to benefit from increased British responsibility for internal affairs. Moreover, he possessed a highly obstinate character, which allowed him to escape Muscat on a periodical basis up to 1931 and then permanently thereafter.

Although both his contemporaries and later writers spoke disparagingly of Fayṣal, it is only fair to point out that many of the failures of his reign were due as much to circumstances as to his personal shortcomings. It may be true that a stronger Sulṭān might have mitigated the situation but it is unlikely that he would have been able to change the outcome. After all, the deterioration in the interior resulted, in part, from the dictation of unpopular policies by the British and the circumstances of Fayṣal's unenviable position between competing Great Powers made him little more than a pawn in a wider game than Oman.

Taymūr Bin Fayṣal

The reign of Taymūr bin Fayṣal was characterised by a kind of tug-of-war between the Sulṭān and his British protectors over who should rule the Sultanate. Although this had also been a central concern of Fayṣal's reign, the difference at this time was that Taymūr and the Government of India were both determined that the other party should govern. In consequence, the Sultanate existed in something of a vacuum, especially for the period between 1921, when the British began concerted attempts to improve the administration, and 1929, when Sa'īd bin Taymūr became President of the Council of Ministers and re-established firm Omani control over the state.

Taymūr's candidacy to succeed his father was doubly assured by his being the oldest son of Fayṣal and his parentage.[7] Since he was recognised as Heir Apparent from early life, the British were determined that he would become a capable Sulṭān. In their view, 'capable' meant being well-educated, able to deal with affairs of state, and, of course, pro-British. Consequently, his education was emphasised by sending him to Mayo College in Ajmer, India.[8] In further recognition of the responsibilities to come, Taymūr represented his father on a state visit to India in 1903 and was received by the Viceroy there. When the interior rebellion broke out in 1913, Taymūr continued to justify the trust placed in him, serving as wālī in Bidbid which was located in the line of the rebel thrust towards Muscat.

Taymūr became Sulṭān on 9 October 1913, in the midst of the dynasty's most serious threat to date and it was patently clear to him that his continued survival depended absolutely on British support. Even the declaration he was forced to sign on ascending the throne reflected this dependence.[9] Given the unpromising milieu of Taymūr's reign, including such aspects as the dismal financial and political situation that the Sultanate was in, the humiliating attitude displayed to the Sulṭān by the British and Taymūr's own upbringing (which failed to prepare him for a Sulṭān's role in Muscat at that time), there can be little wonder that Taymūr's abiding goal was abdication. This conviction was the product of a number of interrelated factors. One of these was Taymūr's resentment over the high-handed British attitude towards him. This was exhibited in the requirement of his letter of accession and the Government of India's refusal to allow him to buy a house in Dehra Dun, India, or even to transfer it to his name after he had purchased it.[10] He was also intimidated by the manner of some of the PAMs, particularly Haworth and Wingate.[11] Undoubtedly, he found the outcome of the British-conducted negotiations at al-Sīb in 1920, whereby tribal autonomy was recognised in the interior, as a blow to his pride and position.

Never enthusiastic about administration or the affairs of state, Taymūr felt that he had inherited a rather insignificant and certainly troubled throne. The government in Muscat was chaotic at best and corruption was rife. Its territorial authority was rapidly shrinking and its treasury was deeply in debt. Even the continued survival of the state was in doubt, following the outbreak of hostilities on the part of the interior tribes and, later, as a result of Saudi expansionism and intrigues in the 1920s. The Sulṭān's personal position was also in considerable jeopardy, due to threats of assassination by interior tribesmen on one hand and the hostility and venality of Āl Bū Sa'īd family members on the other.[12] Furthermore, Taymūr developed a taste for the 'civilised' life, an experience not to be gained in the Muscat of that period. This was expressed first in his marriage to a Circassian woman from Istanbul, for whom he bought the cottage in Dehra Dun,[13] and later appeared in his frequent sojourns in Karachi and Bombay. As the years wore on, Taymūr developed a psychological complex against residence in Muscat and tried to justify his continued absence on grounds that his health would not permit him to return to Muscat's oppressive climate.

Taymūr's desire to abdicate was a tendency ingrained in twentieth-century Sulṭāns. As mentioned above, Fayṣal had sought to abdicate in 1903, and Sa'īd was to retreat to Dhufar when he felt pressured. Qābūs bin Sa'īd also found solace in Dhufar, particularly since he was born and raised there. Taymūr expressed his desire during an interview on his first visit to India as Sulṭān in November 1920. When his request was rejected, the Sulṭān returned to Muscat but went off again to India the next February 'in a sulk' and

> openly said he would be an unwilling Sultan in name because we [i.e. the British] wanted it. It was however gradually brought home to him that we expected him to assume some responsibility and to take some interest in his state. He realised that personal supervision could not but benefit his revenues, and that if he played the game now Government would be far more likely to listen to him later if he could put up a reasonable case, such that his son was of age and well educated and that the state revenues were flourishing.[14]

As it turned out, pursuance of that course would have achieved the desired result if Taymūr's resolve had lasted long enough for Sa'īd to reach a suitable age. After a few years of genuine effort to rule conscientiously, Taymūr had had enough. He left the state in the hands of his wazīr, Muḥammad bin Aḥmad al-Ghashshām—which, in actuality, meant leaving the administration to British advisers—and went off to enjoy himself in the cosmopolitan atmosphere of Bombay and Karachi. The situation was not to the Government of India's liking but Taymūr was obstinate. When, in desperation, the PAM wrote to the Sulṭān telling him that his allowance would be cut from Rs. 10,000 monthly to Rs. 5,000 and that the Arms Traffic Subsidy would be discontinued if he did not return to Muscat, Taymūr grudgingly accepted a compromise that he need spend only three months of each year in Muscat. But this understanding was only temporary. Taymūr effectively made his escape from Oman in 1929 when Sa'īd turned eighteen and became old enough to assume Presidency of the Council of Ministers. The Sulṭān would accept no more compromises, claiming his health would not allow him to return, and dodged meetings with PAMs across India. The Government of India finally issued an ultimatum: if he abdicated, his allowance would be cut to Rs. 2,000 monthly and the Sultanate would lose the Arms Traffic Subsidy.[15] Taymūr's answer was prompt, coming in the form of a letter of abdication naming Sa'īd bin Taymūr as his successor and stating he absolutely could not return to Muscat.[16]

The man who never wanted to be Sulṭān finally got his way. Over the next three decades, he celebrated his freedom by indulging in frequent nightclub adventures, dabbling in business throughout the Orient and pursuing his interest in women. His travels took him to Karachi, Bombay, Calcutta, Singapore, Tokyo and Kobe, always travelling under the name, T. F. T. Alsaid. In the course of his varied life, he received a son from each of five women and a daughter from a sixth.[17] Taymūr later expressed a desire to return to Muscat but the jealousy of his son Sa'īd was an instrumental obstacle. The only visit he made came at the end of World War II—September 1945 to January 1946—when his presence and insistence on holding regular family councils irritated Sa'īd immensely. Thus, after the Sulṭān had promised his father a home in Ṣalāla, Sa'īd continually put him off, claiming that it was not ready yet. Consequently, Taymūr spent the last years of his life in Green's Hotel, Bombay, awaiting Sa'īd's call. However, the message never came and when Taymūr died in 1965, he was buried in Bombay.

Although this was the period of the strongest British influence in Oman, it was a presence by default, unlike the 1890s when the Government of India actively sought more control in Oman. It is indeed ironic that one of the policies pursued by the British at the turn of the century, i.e. the attempt to ensure that Fayṣal's successor should more closely identify himself with British interests, resulted in a successor whose exposure to India and other parts of the world made him reluctant to remain confined to Muscat. It is also something of a paradox that this era of heavy British influence should mask a period of declining British interest in the purely domestic affairs of Oman. The nineteenth-century belief that imperial interests were best served by close watch over every corner of the British sphere had been replaced by a twentieth-century reassessment that called for circumspect retreat from such undertakings. Nevertheless, that call had not been heard in the Sultanate until the century was nearly a third spent.

Sa'id Bin Taymur

To a British establishment disappointed over the attitude and actions of Sulṭān Taymūr, Sa'īd bin Taymūr represented the 'great British hope'. It was thought that he would be the first ruler since his namesake of the previous century, Sa'īd bin Sulṭān (r. 1807–56), to present a character strong-willed enough to reverse the trend of decay in the Sultanate:

> . . . we now have in Muscat a young Sultan who, if tactfully handled, should, I think, turn out a good ruler. He should, I think, be given every chance to administer his State on Arab lines, and every effort should be made to free him from those relics of the past which are galling to him, while we should try, at the same time, to build up a facade of independence in the eyes of the world.[18]

In retrospect, it seems that Sa'īd's character was too dominant for British sensibilities: the streak of obstinacy which Taymūr had displayed but deprecated was to reach full flower in his son and heir.

Like his father, Sa'īd was sent abroad for schooling, first at Mayo College and then in Baghdad. Soon after he returned to Oman, he was chosen to replace the late Muḥammad bin Aḥmad al-Ghashshām as President of the Council of Ministers, and thereby inaugurated a three-year regency. Sulṭān in all but name, Sa'īd was careful not to exhibit too prominent a profile in those years, leaving many details of state to the British establishment in Muscat. Nevertheless, he managed to consolidate his control over the family, as exemplified by the dramatic showdown with his uncle, Ḥamad bin Fayṣal, then the semi-independent wālī of Ṣuḥār.[19] When he formally received the title of Sulṭān in 1932—his accession was announced on 2 Shawwāl 1350/10 February 1932—he was forced to sign the same humiliating letter that had been required of his father.[20] Furthermore, necessity compelled him to accept the presence of British advisers for military and financial affairs until he was able to extricate the state from its overwhelming debts, a feat he accomplished by the forthright expedient of simply not spending beyond his income.

This phase of dutiful, if reluctant, co-operation gradually shifted into another phase, an active attempt to cultivate his own independence. In his eyes, one way to accomplish this was by a world tour. In late 1937, the Sulṭān set off to the east, first to meet his father in Kobe, Japan, and then on to the United States, where he visited 'various places of interest including Hollywood—a most important place in the eyes of the Sultan who is a keen critic of the cinema . . . ',[21] and received an audience with President Roosevelt in March 1938. His next stop was England, where he took in a film of *Snow White and the Seven Dwarfs* among other engagements, followed by visits to France, Italy, India and then home to Muscat.[22] A few years later he undertook a similar trip to Egypt, where he struck up a friendship with King Farūq almost immediately, and Jerusalem, where he met his old friend, Bertram Thomas.[23]

Despite these enjoyable diversions, Sa'īd's grand strategy of independence could not succeed unless he first brought the interior back into the Sultanate. The financial and military help tendered to the Sultanate during World War II, in combination with concession payments by the Iraq Petroleum Company, allowed him to pursue his hope of regaining control there. Even though Sa'īd's obsession with complete independence was manifested both in the financial field and the awaited reconquest of the interior, the two goals were not incompatible. If the Sultanate were to remain financially independent, then it needed oil revenues. For the concession-holder to find oil, it needed to explore the interior of its concession territory. If Sa'īd could regain the interior by his own machinations, then the circle of independence would be complete.

To achieve this end, the Sulṭān relied on the twin methods of reasserting his pre-eminent authority in settling tribal disputes and seeking rapprochements with the important tamīmas. In October 1937, he hosted 'Īsā bin Ṣāliḥ al-Ḥārithī and two of his sons, Muḥammad and Ṣāliḥ and, a week later, sent them on their way with Rs. 4,000.[24] Almost exactly a year later, 'Alī bin 'Abd Allāh Āl Ḥamūda of the Banī Bū 'Alī visited Muscat, stayed two weeks and departed with Rs. 14,000.[25] 'Īsā bin Ṣāliḥ returned in February 1940, was treated for pneumonia by Dr Wells Thoms of the Arabian Mission and then sought additional treatment in al-Baḥrayn before returning to the interior in June.[26] By 1945, the Sulṭān's activity had come to a head. Many of the Ghāfirī and Hināwī (the two major tribal confederations) leaders, including ʻĪsā bin Ṣāliḥ and Sulaymān bin Ḥimyar al-Nabhānī, gathered at al-Kāmil in the Sharqīya in March.[27] Following this, ʻAlī bin ʻAbd Allāh Āl Ḥamūda and Sulaymān bin Ḥimyar met with Saʻīd in Muscat in April.[28] As a result,

> (a) Both Sheikhs had declared that they would take no part in election of Imam's successor, (b) Both had placed themselves under the 'Orders' of the Sultan, (c) A declaration similar to (a) had been received from Sheikh Isa bin Saleh of Sharqiyah, (d) Sultan had received letter from Imam informing him of despatch of emissary to discuss 'important questions'.[29]

A further triumph for the Sulṭān came when he successfully mediated in a dispute between ʻĪsā bin Ṣāliḥ and ʻAlī bin ʻAbd Allāh Āl Ḥamūda at Muscat in October 1945.[30] Not only had he increased his own prestige but he had shown that he could successfully arbitrate between the Hināwī and Ghāfirī factions. The co-operation between the Banī Bū ʻAlī and the Sulṭān is all the more striking in view of the tribe's intransigence in the 1928–31 period and further bellicosity in the later years of Saʻīd's reign.[31]

Thus by late 1945, Saʻīd had achieved the co-operation of the Ghāfirī faction and the neutrality of the Hināwīs. In Ṣalāla, he was particularly anxious to acquire any supplies that the Americans might leave behind in order to build up his military potential.[32] He was also willing to bind himself to accept advisers exclusively from the British in return for their help. This was suggested at 1,000 rifles with 100 rounds each, six mortars and two sections of machine guns, the unrestricted purchase of tenting, medical supplies and signalling equipment, along with a British officer to train the levies, who was to be seconded along with several retired Indian officers and NCOs.[33] The necessity of a military back-up force, especially RAF cover, despite the agreement of the tribal leaders, was underscored with the death of ʻĪsā bin Ṣāliḥ *c.* 13 March 1949.[34] His death would complicate matters.

Although London was also eager for the Sulṭān to regain control over the interior, as it would facilitate British oil exploration, they were unwilling to sanction the use of the RAF to support Saʻīd's ground operations, a condition that the Sulṭān felt was absolutely necessary as he could not face the possibility of any prolonged struggle.[35] Instead, HMG suggested, as an alternative, that 'suitable financial inducements in Sultan's name might succeed in securing co-operation of tribal chiefs'.[36] Even though this setback was a major disappointment to Sa'īd, the primary obstacle proved to be the continued survival of Imām Muḥammad bin 'Abd Allāh al-Khalīlī until 1954, despite his poor health and near blindness. Then on top of the Sulṭān's careful plans came a renewed Saudi threat, appearing in 1952 as it had periodically over the last century and a half. The Saudis' occupation of al-Buraymī and their subsequent intrigues with certain figures of the interior, principally Sulaymān bin Ḥimyar al-Nabhānī and Ṭālib bin 'Alī al-Hinā'ī, were a severe check to Sa'īd's programme and once again threatened to bind him to British intervention: to raise money to counter the revolt of 1957-9, he was forced to sell the Gwadar enclave on the Pakistan coast and accept British military and development subsidies.[37]

The solution as he came to see it was retreat to Ṣalāla. Dhufar was a mistress his father had flirted with but Sa'īd courted her ardently and finally 'married' her. The courtship had begun early in Sa'īd's reign, as he had made a number of improvements to his palace and fields there by 1935.[38] It deepened with the Sulṭān's almost constant presence there during World War II and was kept alive afterwards by periodic reunions through the late 1940s and early 1950s.

There are a number of explanations behind Sa'īd's permanent withdrawal from Muscat in 1958.[39] The reintegration of the interior into the Sultanate had produced a steady procession of tribal shaykhs to Muscat to profess their allegiance and receive their subsidies. If Sa'īd were absent from Muscat, then he could not receive them and thus reduce his cash outflow significantly. Furthermore, Ṣalāla was more secure than Muscat: a bomb had destroyed a Land Rover belonging to the Minister of External Affairs in 1958 and the Minister of the Interior barely escaped death from another bomb in 1959.

Sa'īd had also married Dhufari wives and adopted the province as his own 'personal estate'.[40] It was one place where he could truly be free of official British interference.[41] In addition, Sa'īd had developed a possibly psychosomatic sinus condition which allegedly prevented his return to the climate of Muscat.[42] Finally, Dhufar seemed to be a place where he could hold time back forever because of the physical isolation of the country; it was to be his personal preserve which he could run with impunity.[43] In Dhufar, he could show his generosity in simple things, such as a gift of dates or of a rifle to a shaykh. He felt comfortable there because the people were kept on a simple level and because his popularity continued for some time. His aura of independence depended on his obsession that he could stop time and thereby exercise his form of patriarchy to the utmost.[44] As it turned out, this last assumption proved incorrect and it eventually became the major reason why Sa'īd lost his throne. Because he tried to keep the twentieth century out of Dhufar, he forced the Dhufaris into open rebellion. Since Dhufar really was a part of Oman and not his 'own private estate', his attitude presented a threat to the security of the rest of the country. His idiosyncrasies finally betrayed him: because he refused Dhufaris the rights and privileges they felt they deserved, he provoked a revolution that was dedicated to the complete overthrow of the Sultanate. Because he did not trust his son with responsibility, Qābūs turned against his father and worked with others to prepare the ground for a *coup d'état*. Finally, after Sa'īd had entrusted his administration to inadequate officials—one prominent official under Sulṭān Qābūs described them as being 'incapable of guiding the destiny of a bicycle, let alone a country'—the expatriates in Muscat co-operated in his downfall.

Particularly in the latter part of his reign, the peculiarities of Sa'īd's personality came to dominate the political structure of the Sultanate.[45] His major obsession was a complex concern with position. Included in this trait was his drive for complete independence for the Sultanate and correct status for himself. This was manifested in a sensitivity towards what he regarded as the dignity and respect due an independent sovereign.[46] It also appeared in his extreme frugality, which was at first a means to secure independence but later became an end in itself. Externally, this complex appeared in such activities as the concentration of financial decisions in his own hands—for example, he eschewed British help in the preparation of budgets—and in his retreats to Dhufar when pressure grew intense. Internally, it resulted in what might be termed his 'maharaja' complex. Traditional Arabian concepts of social democracy, the *majlis* (a council where advice is offered to the shaykh or ruler), and salutations on a first name basis between shaykhs and their tribesmen, were anathema to Sa'īd. He sought to isolate himself from his countrymen, mistrusted his family, felt more at home with expatriates, found relaxation in India and London and trusted only his slaves. He was comfortable in Western company and Westerners were generally impressed by him.[47]

In addition to the part that Sa'īd's upbringing and education in India played in shaping his personality is the impression left on Sa'īd by his father's rejection of homeland and family, since Sa'īd just as firmly rejected his father and refused to allow him to settle in the Sultanate later. His relations with the rest of his family were something of a paradox. On one hand, he exhibited almost a total lack of feeling for anyone, including his son. Yet he also attempted to exercise complete domination over relatives. One explanation of the almost complete isolation he ordered for Qābūs after the latter's return from Europe lies in Sa'īd's past: he had been thrust into virtual power without preparation. Even more importantly, Sa'īd had undercut his father's position as Sulṭān and he was not about to see that happen again.

The Sulṭān was particularly adept at manipulating situations to suit himself. After the British had prevented his campaign to regain al-Buraymī in 1952, he shrewdly acquired British support in 1958 without committing himself to anything more than an additional subsidy for development.[48] Although not particularly religious, he had courted the muṭawwi's before the death of Imām Muḥammad bin 'Abd Allāh al-Khalīlī, with the result that his name was mentioned in the nomination process for a new Imām in 1954. An impression often held by the outside world that Oman was a 'colony' of the British suited him because he knew who controlled the country and the resultant isolation helped him to keep it under control.[49] He was also careful to implement his unpopular policies through such officials as Ismā'īl bin Khalīl al-Raṣāṣī and Shihāb bin Fayṣal Āl Sa'īd so that some of the unpopularity would be associated with them.

His parsimonious nature grew out of his realisation that there could be no independence while the Sultanate was in debt to Britain and consequently his policy during the 1930s was successfully directed towards eradicating that debt. This frugality was to serve him well for the next several decades as the state continued to be mired in poverty. But the question arises as to whether his rejection of any capital outlay was absolutely due to financial necessity or was simply his manner of looking at the world.[50] In other words, did Sa'īd prevent the outside world from encouraging impossible hopes in Omani hearts by keeping the country isolated, or did he keep the country isolated so that he would not have to answer to rising expectations? According to his own logic, the seeming conclusion was that he could not afford to allocate funds for development without having firm assurances that he would be able to cover all future expenditures arising from such decisions—and his ability to make that guarantee simply did not exist until 1968. Against that, it may be argued that the British development subsidy of 1958 had given him the opportunity to set up development programmes which he resisted. Sa'īd's probable counter to this would have been that the development subsidy ended before the state began receiving oil revenues (a matter of months): 'Had there been no economy in expenditure we would have had no financial reserves, and we would not have been able to bear the burden of what we spent those months.'[51] In this regard, it is significant to note that when the oil revenues were finally realised, Sa'īd started his own capital development programme and a fairly ambitious one at that. The problem was that it was too slow to obtain results: development efforts had become obvious only by 1970, which was too late.

The reasons for Sa'īd's downfall are rooted in perceptions that others held about him, ranging from convictions that he would never change and had simply outlived his time,[52] to the belief that he was changing, but for the worse. A significant charge levelled against him was that he had forsaken his country for his palace in Ṣalāla. Certainly, he had not visited Muscat for twelve years and since the attempt on his life in 1966, he had rarely ventured out even from the palace itself.[53] Nevertheless, his physical absence was not comparable to the studied unconcern shown by Taymūr: Sa'īd continued to rule the Sultanate with a strong hand by means of an efficient spy network and a radio-telephone link. There was little that went on in Muscat that he did not know about, just as there was little that any official could do without express permission from the Sulṭān.[54]

A more serious allegation against Sa'īd was not only that he was isolated but that his control of the country was disintegrating, and his critics pointed to increased success by the Dhufari rebels, the rising tide of unfulfilled expectations in Muscat and the NDFLOAG attack on Izkī in 1970.[55] Beyond these criticisms were charges that Sa'īd's mind was beginning to degenerate: the retreat of government control in Dhufar cannot be denied but there has been no hard evidence in favour of the latter allegations. The most persuasive argument for this thesis of mental decline is the fact that the *coup d'état* caught Sa'īd by surprise, despite the wide scope of the plotters and the ominous danger signals that had been flashing for nearly a year.[56]

The final question to be raised deals with the problem of how to assess Sa'īd bin Taymūr in comparison to the other rulers of the area who found themselves confronted by new-found wealth and the intrusion of Western ideas and technology. Sa'īd did not become a profligate like Shaykh Aḥmad bin 'Alī Āl Thānī of Qatar; nor was he even ostentatious.[57] It is clear that Sa'īd was not a miser in the pattern of Shaykh Shakhbūt bin Sulṭān Āl Nuhayyān of Abu Dhabi, since he had begun to spend, however cautiously, on development after he had received additional revenues. The safest conclusion that can be made is that the situation in which the Sultanate had found itself in 1932 had radically altered by 1970: Sa'īd, by contrast, had not.

The Ruling Family

Although the present dynasty of Sulṭāns is commonly referred to by the name of Āl Bū Sa'īd, it should be explained that there are several levels of stratification within this group. In its broadest sense, Āl Bū Sa'īd refers to the tribe, centered in Oman province and particularly found in the towns of Ādām, Izkī and Nizwā. In addition, there is the Āl Bū Sa'īd family, i.e. all the descendants of Aḥmad bin Sa'īd, the first Āl Bū Sa'īd ruler of Oman. The final distinction is between the Āl Bū Sa'īd and the Āl Sa'īd. This final category consists of the descendants of Sa'īd bin Sulṭān (r. 1807–56). The Sulṭāns of the twentieth century and their close relatives belong to this group.

Although the tribe is essentially rooted in the interior, Āl Bū Sa'īds were apparently employed as wālīs throughout Oman by the Ya'rubī dynasty (1625–1737). After Aḥmad bin Sa'īd's assumption of power in *c.* 1744, members of the tribe were employed in the service of the country's new rulers and migrated to Muscat. This is especially true of the Āl Bū Sa'īd family, while the Āl Sa'īd have lost all contact with the ancestral home of Ādām. As a consequence, the Āl Sa'īd and the Āl Bū Sa'īd family became one of the strongest sources of support for the Sultanate. Their identification with the secular rulers of the country allowed them to transcend the Ghāfirī–Hināwī tribal dichotomy, as witnessed by their value as wālīs in areas where either Ghāfirī or Hināwī identification would be a handicap. The disadvantage of their removal from the tribal system was their absolute dependence on the Sulṭān. Although undesirable or politically inadequate Āl Bū Sa'īd individuals could be ignored to some extent, provisions were necessary for all the Āl Sa'īd.[58] Able members of the clan had to be given jobs, whether the reason was to help alleviate the state's shortage of officials or simply to keep the relatives busy and out of trouble. Non-productive members still received allowances from the state—thus approximately one third of the Sultanate's budget during the crisis years of the 1920s and 1930s was devoted to the Civil List.

In addition to the genealogical divisions, there are several categories of political roles played by the Āl Sa'īd and the Āl Bū Sa'īd family. Historically, these have been either roles taken in opposition to the Sulṭān as petty fiefs, as assistants in the Sultanate's 'bureaucracy', or the assumption of a politically inactive status. The extent of these roles has been largely determined by limitations on the Sultanate's authority. The concept of the Sultanate as a comprehensive central government over much of geographical Oman has rarely been an actuality. Not only did the rulers of Muscat prior to 1970 lack control enough to prevent the interior from following its own autonomous way, they frequently were unable to exercise full control over even much of the Bāṭina coast. Consequently, relatives have frequently held towns such as Ṣuḥār and al-Rustāq in virtual independence of the Sulṭān. The case of al-Rustāq is unique, as it was held in hereditary fief by a collateral line of the family in Muscat, the descendants of 'Azzān bin Qays, a grandson of the first Āl Bū Sa'īd ruler. Although this line of Āl Bū Sa'īd lost control of al-Rustāq in 1917, the town was not incorporated into the Sultanate until 1955. Ṣuḥār, although held by the Āl Sa'īd—not necessarily on a hereditary basis as al-Rustāq was—also retained its semi-independent status until well into the twentieth century. It was politically incorporated into the Sultanate when Sa'īd bin Taymūr personally led an expedition to Ṣuḥār in 1929 and brought back his strong-willed uncle, Ḥamad bin Fayṣal, who had been wālī. Despite the political annexation, the Ṣuḥār treasury continued to receive local revenue and handle expenditure for the old *wilāya* (territory controlled by a wālī), including Ṣuḥār, Ṣaḥam, Līwā and Shināṣ, until 1941.

By the time of the accession of Sa'īd bin Taymūr, the threat of family fiefdoms had disappeared permanently. Consequently, opposition to the Sulṭān became limited to intrigues in the capital and fruitless schemes to supplant the Sulṭān. The potential success of any such scheme had waned by the beginning of the twentieth century: the days of Sālim bin Thuwaynī, 'Azzān bin Qays, Turkī bin Sa'īd and 'Abd al-'Azīz bin Sa'īd all marshalling their respective forces in a showdown for the throne were irretrievably gone.[59] When Taymūr became Sulṭān on the death of his father Fayṣal, the objections of his brother Muḥammad were limited to a visit to the PAM followed by acquiescence; there was no dissent when Sa'īd bin Taymūr came to the throne. The major reason for this aura of legitimacy and stability was the British presence; likewise, British dissatisfaction with Sa'īd was the single most important factor that allowed Qābūs to succeed in overthrowing him.[60]

The declining role of opposition was matched by an emerging role of assistance. This aspect goes back to the nineteenth century when various members of the Āl Bū Sa'īd family had served as wazīrs. Sulṭān Fayṣal had relied on his sons, principally Taymūr, Muḥammad and Nādir, as wālīs and field generals. Taymūr also relied on his brothers in much the same manner during the early years of his regime. Furthermore, when the Council of Ministers was created in 1920, Nādir bin Fayṣal was named President.

Taymūr's full-brother Shihāb was to become a prominent example of this role of assistance. Shihāb first acted as Sa'īd's representative on several occasions during the Sulṭān's absences in the 1930s. In August 1939, he was named Minister of External Affairs (Nāẓir al-Shu'ūn al-Khārijīya) and given rank just behind Nādir bin Fayṣal.[61] Since the latter dropped out of politics after 1926, Shihāb was effectively left in charge of Muscat during the World War II period when Sa'īd was in Ṣalāla. That his execution of government affairs was less than adequate is indicated by Sa'īd's reaction to the situation in the capital on his return from Dhufar in 1945: 'in his fury at the chaotic state of affairs existing in the most important office of his State, the Sultan immediately dismissed Saiyid Shihab, halved his allowance and, to make quite certain that his displeasure was fully understood, cut off the water supply of his house.'[62] Shihāb was not restored to grace until Sa'īd permanently retired to Dhufar and left his uncle in Muscat as his representative (*wakīl*) and Governor of the Capital (Muḥāfiẓ al-'Āṣima), posts which Shihāb filled until his retirement in the summer of 1970.

Sa'īd attempted to employ another uncle, Ḥamad bin Fayṣal, in a similar manner. After he was removed from Ṣuḥār, Ḥamad became wālī of Maṭraḥ in 1931 and then a member of the somewhat inert Council of Ministers in 1933. However, his poor performance caused his removal in 1935 from the position of wālī and another stint

(1937–9) was equally unsatisfactory.[63] Efforts to use other uncles were failures as well, largely owing to either their mental incapacity or simple lethargy.

A more common role was that of wālī or clerk. Certain lines of the Āl Bū Sa'īd established reputations for producing generations of faithful wālīs.[64] Even after the more remote towns of the Sultanate were consolidated under central control in the twentieth century, Sulṭāns used brothers and sons as wālīs.[65] Fayṣal bin 'Alī, a grandson of Sulṭān Fayṣal, and Thuwaynī bin Shihāb, son of the Governor of the Capital, both served long apprenticeships as school-teachers and clerks.[66] One of the Āl Bū Sa'īd wālīs who later assumed a more prominent role was Aḥmad bin Ibrāhīm, a nephew of Imām 'Azzān bin Qays. Aḥmad had become the independent ruler of al-Rustāq in 1916. Driven out by the forces of the Imamate in 1917, he temporarily took up residence in nearby al-Ḥazm. When he was once again attacked by Imamate forces, he called upon Sulṭān Taymūr for assistance, thus healing the century-old breach between the Āl Sa'īd and the descendants of 'Azzān bin Qays bin Aḥmad. Aḥmad bin Ibrāhīm later served as wālī for the Sultanate in several locations in the Bāṭina, principally at al-Suwayq, until 1939 when he was appointed Minister of the Interior (or Internal Affairs: Nāẓir al-Shu'ūn al-Dākhilīya). Since the Sultanate lacked control over the interior at this time, Aḥmad's position was essentially one of liaison and correspondence with the leading shaykhs.[67] His jurisdiction was considerably expanded after the interior was reoccupied in late 1955, and Aḥmad remained an important figure in Muscat until his retirement in 1970.

The third pattern to emerge from this analysis concerns that category of individuals who remained politically inactive. Their reasons are varied, ranging from the suspicions of the Sulṭān—as in the attitude of Sulṭān Taymūr towards his half-brother Muḥammad—to protest (Nādir bin Fayṣal resigned as President of the Council of Ministers in 1926 over a dispute about his allowance and never returned to political activity although he lived until 1971)—to simply inability to handle political roles:

> Brought up as they are among the women in the hideous position and climate of Muscat, it is little to be wondered at that at a very early age they develop into the most useless and vicious types of degenerates, possessed of childish ideas of their own importance, difficult to deal with, a justifiable cause of annoyance to the tribes

of the interior, and a continuous drain on the slender purse of the state.[68]

Of the ten sons of Sulṭān Fayṣal, seven spent much or all of their lives in isolation from politics.

The lack of adequate numbers of capable people among the ruling family was a constant irritant to various British officials in Muscat. In addition, the resident British extended their criteria for inadequacy to many of those who did hold positions. This problem was painfully obvious to Sulṭān Sa'īd, who complained of the situation to the PAM on more than one occasion, and it was the reason he dismissed Shihāb in 1945 in the display of fury mentioned above. Many of these inactive individuals spent their lives in Muscat receiving state allowances and engaging in favourite pastimes. Others, whose leisure was enforced, left. Some went to Zanzibar, where a direct descendant of Sulṭān Thuwaynī bin Sa'īd reigned until the revolution of 1963.[69]

One of those in the latter category of forced inactivity was Sa'īd's son Qābūs. Son of a Qarā mother and raised in Ṣalāla, Qābūs was sent to school in England and later graduated from Sandhurst. After a brief period of service with the British Army in Germany and some training in municipal administration in England, he returned to Ṣalāla and was kept busy there studying Islamic law. After a lengthy period of diligent effort, he began to send visitors on to his father—since Qābūs had his own house and rarely saw his father more than once or twice a year—to ask if he might be given a responsible position. The answer was always no. Eventually, the Heir Apparent felt that he could not accept a position even if one had been offered to him and so began to plot Sa'īd's removal.[70]

In possible recognition of their potential threat to him, Sa'īd developed the habit of keeping people in minor offices or none at all when their education, experience and position demanded more. His half-brothers, Ṭāriq and Fahr, in addition to Qābūs, are prime examples of this. Both were educated in India and then came back to fill minor jobs or do nothing until they individually decided to go into self-exile.

Ṭāriq bin Taymūr was born in Istanbul in 1922 and lived there until the age of twelve when he was sent to live with an uncle in Frankfurt-am-Main. In 1937, he was brought to Muscat for the first time where his inacquaintance with the ways of the Sultanate prompted the observation that he 'does not take kindly to walking backwards out of his brother's presence'.[71] After a brief period spent in the Muscat Infantry, he was sent to a police training school in Vellore, near Madras, India, in 1942 and then served with the Zhob Militia on the North-West Frontier before engaging in administrative studies in Quetta. He returned to Muscat amid speculation that he was to be named Minister for External Affairs, replacing Shihāb bin Fayṣal, but on his return he was named head of the Muscat/Maṭraḥ Municipality until 1957.[72] When the 1957–9 revolt broke out, he accompanied the military expedition into the interior, personally pushing the plunger that blew up Tanūf in 1957, and remained there as liaison between the military and the local population for a time. After Aḥmad bin Ibrāhīm returned to Muscat in 1958, Ṭāriq was put in charge of the interior as sort of a 'super-wālī' until leaving for medical treatment in India in the spring of 1959.

His return to Muscat included hopes of an important position at last—he had been promised the job of Inspector of Wālīs—but Sa'īd's mistrust of close relatives, combined with a certain jealousy of Ṭāriq's accomplishments in the interior, prevented him from holding any position at all. Finally, broke and frustrated, Ṭāriq decided to leave in 1962 for self-exile in Europe. Sa'īd was unable to comprehend why Ṭāriq had left, in the same way that he was later unable to understand Qābūs's role in his overthrow. Part of Sa'īd's attitude towards Ṭāriq, paralleling as it did his attitude towards Qābūs, undoubtedly sprang from the potential threat that Ṭāriq posed for him as Sulṭān: Tāriq had been named Heir Apparent at a meeting between Taymūr, Sa'īd and himself in a hotel room in Japan in November 1937, a position he forfeited when Qābūs was born in late 1940.[73]

The case of Fahr bin Taymūr was similar. He was first sent to school in Baghdad, where he did poorly and dropped out, subsequently being enrolled in Mayo College. After his return to Muscat, he was employed in various ways, including that of radio operator for the Bāṭina wālīs. Having been received in the same manner as Ṭāriq, he chose the same path. In 1964, he left for other parts of the Middle East, including Abu Dhabi, Libya and Cyprus, only returning after the 1970 *coup d'état* to become Deputy Minister of Defence, as well as Minister of the Interior and then Youth.

In many ways, the Āl Bū Sa'īd were the essential ingredient in the Omani government of the last two centuries. At various times, the state's territorial extent grew to include overseas possessions in Asia and Africa; at other times it shrank to constitute barely the core of Muscat/Maṭraḥ. An elective Imamate was transformed into a secularised Sultanate; while the title of the rulers changed from Imām to Sayyid to Sulṭān. The constant factor throughout has been the presence of Āl Bū Sa'īd rulers, contenders and associates. Their importance in the development of the Sultanate has been as considerable in the middle of the twentieth century as it was at any time in the past.

Notes

1. A Political Agent of that time, Percy Cox, remarked that much of Fayṣal's 'anti-British' attitude could be traced back to misunderstandings arising out of Fayṣal's language difficulties. Cox became a friend of the Sulṭān partly because the pair engaged in lengthy conversations in Gujerati. Philip Graves, *The Life of Sir Percy Cox* (London: Hutchinson, 1941), pp. 66–7.

2. J. Theodore Bent, 'Muscat', *The Contemporary Review* (London), vol. 68, no. 360 (Dec. 1895), p. 873. Muḥammad was also considered unsuitable as Sulṭān because of his demonstrated inability to govern while wālī of Ṣuḥār from 1878 to 1884.

3. *The Times*, 18 Sept. 1913.

4. For extensive discussion of the French challenge, see Briton Cooper Busch, *Britain and the Persian Gulf, 1894–1914* (Berkeley: University of California Press, 1967); and Firouz Kajare, *Le Sultanat d'Omân: la question de Mascate* (Paris: A. Pedone, 1914). See also Chapter 5.

5. Fayṣal's principal concern was that his son Taymūr should succeed him and not his older brother Muḥammad. IO, R/15/3/51; PAM Cox to the Foreign Secretary of the Government of India, No. 598, 27 Oct. 1903.

6. Major S. G. Knox, PAM at that time, wrote that 'A much abused man, while he lived, Syud Faisal bin Turkī has, in many quarters, been deeply regretted since his death. He was undoubtedly a weak ruler but his pleasant genial manners and his accessability won him some popularity. He never wanted personal courage and was undoubtedly kindly and humane. He could never, at least so far as the writer could observe, find it in his heart to punish anybody (sic) and the natural result, in a place like Muscat, was chaos in the administration.' IO, R/15/3/337; Annual Muscat Administration Report for 1913.

7. Taymūr's mother was an Arab, unlike most of Fayṣal's other sons, who were the offspring of concubines and slaves. Moreover, Taymūr's mother, 'Āliya bint Thuwaynī, was the daughter of a former Sulṭān. Thus Taymūr's accession strengthened ties between the descendants of Sulṭān Turkī bin Sa'īd and Sulṭān Thuwaynī bin Sa'īd, from whom most of the Sulṭāns of Zanzibar were descended.

8. Mayo College, also known as 'Chief's College', was established in 1875 by Viceroy Lord Mayo as an 'Eton of India' for sons of Indian aristocracy. See V. A. S. Stow, *A Short History of the Mayo College, 1869–1942* (Ajmer, India: Fine Art Printing Press, 1942).

9. For the text of an identical statement signed in 1932 by Sa'īd bin Taymūr on his accession, see Appendix E.

10. IO, R/15/3/188; PAM Wingate to PRPG Trevor, Demi-official enclosure to letter No. 15–C, 24 March 1923.

11. Wingate described him as 'incredibly weak and incurably vain. Both these characteristics have not made him a successful ruler of an Arab state. His weak-

ness has resulted in his being exploited by his family and unscrupulous persons and in his being unable to make any headway against the rebellion, while his vanity in an Arab country where geniality and good manners towards high and low alike are obligatory, has alienated many of those who are by conviction of his supporters.' Wingate goes on to mention his 'cavalier treatment of sheikhs and his general pomposity', as well as his 'absurd ideas about his position and his independence'. IO, R/15/3/52; Wingate to Civil Commissioner in Baghdad, No. 898, 28 April 1920. Later PAMs such as Murphy and Fowle, had better opinions of Taymūr.

12. Taymūr faced opposition in particular from a number of his half-brothers, the 'wicked uncles' who later challenged Sa'īd bin Taymūr during the early part of the latter's reign.

13. When it was made clear to him that he would not be allowed to abdicate nor keep the Dehra Dun property, he divorced his wife. She returned to Istanbul, took the name of Kâmile Ilgiray and bore the Sulṭān's son, Ṭāriq bin Taymūr. Years later, she wrote to the British Consul General in Ankara and then to Sulṭān Sa'īd asking for financial support. IO, R/15/3/230 and R/15/3/231.

14. IO, R/15/3/188; Wingate to PRPG Trevor, No. 15–C, 24 March 1923.

15. IO, R/15/3/53; E. B. Howell, Foreign Secretary to the Government of India, Simla, to the PRPG, No. F.40–N/31, 25 Sept. 1931.

16. IO, R/15/3/53; Taymūr bin Fayṣal, Karachi, to PRPG, 6 Rajab 1350/ 17 Nov. 1931. Despite the ultimatum cited above, the Arms Traffic Subsidy was continued through 1935 due to the financial plight of the state.

17. His first son, Mājid, was the result of a union with a Negro palace slave. Mājid was to become a long-time wālī in his half-brother's service. Taymūr's first wife, Fāṭima bint 'Alī bin Sālim, was a daughter of the ruling family and bore him Sa'īd. The second wife, Kâmile Igray, was a Circassian whom he divorced before the birth of his son, Ṭāriq, who later became Prime Minister under Sulṭān Qābūs. The fourth son, Fahr, Deputy Minister of Defence under Sulṭān Qābūs, was born of a Dhufari slave. The fifth son, Shabīb, an Ambassador under Sulṭān Qābūs, was born to Taymūr's last wife, a daughter of his childhood tutor, K. B. Ṣādiq Ḥasan, and divorced while still pregnant. Another wife whom he married *c.* 1936 was Japanese; she bore him a daughter, Buthayma, who later came to live in Muscat.

18. Public Records Office, Foreign Office Records (hereinafter cited as FO), 371/15998 of 1932, Arabia E1963/4/91; PRPG Biscoe to the Government of India, No. 215–S, 7 Apr. 1932; included as enclosure in S. F. Stewart, IO, to FO, 20 Apr. 1932.

19. Sa'īd was described as setting off for Ṣuḥār 'with a detachment of the Muscat Infantry and a set of irons which he said he would place on his uncle if he proved recalcitrant!' IO, R/15/3/216; PRPG Fowle, al-Baḥrayn, to A. E. B. Parsons, Foreign Secretary to the Government of India, Demi-official No. C/166, 16 Aug. 1937.

20. See Appendix E for complete text.

21. IO, R/15/3/338; Annual Muscat Administration Report for 1938. Sa'īd's visit to the US is described in Wendell Phillips, *Unknown Oman* (London: Longman, 1966), pp. 18–19; and Richard H. Sanger, *The Arabian Peninsula* (Ithaca: Cornell University Press, 1954), p. 194.

22. IO, R/15/3/338; Annual Muscat Administration Report for 1938.

23. FO, 371/39896 for 1944, Arabia E888/252/91; Muscat Intelligence Diary for 16–30 June 1944.

24. IO, R/15/3/338; Annual Muscat Administration Report for 1937.

25. Ibid.; Annual Muscat Administration Report for 1938. These cash gifts

were only made possible by the 1937 concession payment, discussed in the following chapter, n. 54.

26. IO, R/15/3/338; Annual Muscat Administration Report for 1940.

27. IO, R/15/3/242; PAM Galloway to PRPG Prior, No. S.434–8/62, 17 March 1945.

28. IO, R/15/3/470; Assistant PAM Hallows to PRPG at Camp Karachi, Telegram R.1, 28 May 1945.

29. Ibid. Actually, 'Īsā bin Ṣāliḥ only promised to remain neutral. This shaky alliance was one reason why the Sulṭān refused to allow teams from the Anti-Locust Control Group to travel through the interior in the 1945–8 period.

30. FO, 371/45181 for 1945, Arabia E7890/150/91; Muscat Intelligence Diary for 1–15 Oct. 1945.

31. The Banī Bū 'Alī are discussed in the last part of Chapter 4.

32. IO, R/15/3/470; Assistant PAM Hallows to PRPG Galloway, Demi-official No. S.933–8/62, 18 July 1945. See also Hallows to Galloway, S.1126, 19 Aug. 1945. A US Army Air Force unit was based in Ṣalāla during the war

33. IO, R/15/3/470; PRPG Prior to Foreign Secretary of the Government of India, No. 84–S, 15 Jan. 1946; Foreign Department of the Government of India, New Delhi, to the Secretary of State for India, Telegram No. 2343, 8 March 1946.

34. Ibid.; PAM to PRPG, No. C.251–8/62, 19 March 1946.

35. Sa'īd's confidence in the RAF was conditioned by their successful activities against the Banī Bū 'Alī during his regency. The revolt of 1957–9 was to prove airpower somewhat less than effective against tribesmen who had become more acquainted with the applications and limitations of Western technology.

36. IO, R/15/3/470; Secretary of State for India to Government of India, Telegram 7741, 18 April 1946; PAM to PRPG, Telegram C 226, 30 April 1946; Secretary of State for India to PRPG, Telegram 12479, 7 July 1946. The decision against use of the RAF came in spite of the PRPG's action in pointing out that the Sulṭān had allowed the RAF to establish bases in his territories over a number of years and had co-operated in gaining tribal acceptance of their existence.

37. The events of the 1950s are discussed in Chapter 7.

38. IO, R/15/3/338; Annual Muscat Administration Report for 1935.

39. His retirement to Ṣalāla at that time was not necessarily meant to be permanent, as he made plans to return at least twice but changed his mind at the last minute both times. Interview with Sultanate official of the late 1950s.

40. He had one daughter by a concubine, then another daughter from a 1933 marriage to a member of the Bayt Ma'ashānī clan of the Qarā tribe, subsequently divorcing her and marrying her first cousin in 1936, who bore him Qābūs in 1940. Interview with Sayyid Ṭāriq bin Taymūr Āl Sa'īd, 28 Dec. 1974.

41. Certainly he accepted pressure to appoint British advisers in the late 1960s but they were completely isolated in Muscat with little contact with the Sulṭān in Ṣalāla.

42. This is reminiscent of his father's assertion that his health required him to forsake the humidity of Muscat for the mountain air of Kashmir.

43. The personal nature of the Sulṭān's reign in Dhufar is illustrated by the statement of Bertram Thomas: 'Although my position was that of Wazir to His Highness the Sultan, and I had introduced the copper currency of Muscat into the Province in 1926 . . . I had no jurisdiction in Dhufar, nor indeed had the Muscat and Oman Council of State, of which I was a member. The Sultan treated Dhufar as a Royal Domain. His rule through the Wali was personal and untrammelled by any foreign influence.' *Arabia Felix: Across the Empty Quarter* (London: Jonathan Cape, 1932), p. 36n.

44. Interview with Sayyid Ṭāriq bin Taymūr.

45. Detailed assessments of Sa'īd's character have been written by Ian Skeet, *Muscat and Oman: The End of an Era* (London: Faber and Faber, 1974), pp. 163–203; and David Holden, *Farewell to Arabia* (London: Faber and Faber, 1966), pp. 214–22.

46. For example, he was careful to refer to the British PAM as Consul and nothing else.

47. One PAM wrote that 'The present Sultan is one of the most capable Arab rulers of his time; he is young, well educated, has broadened his vision by extensive travel, possesses strength of character, is supremely shrewd, and enjoys a high degree of natural prestige. Given the opportunity he could, in my opinion, be capable of holding his own amongst any of the tribal leaders and, by the sagacious handling of the tribes, might bring an era of enlightenment to the people whose self-imposed isolation has precluded all advance.' IO, R/15/3/242; PA Hallows to PRPG, No. S.1126, 19 Aug. 1945.

48. Another example of Sa'īd's ability to make the best of a bad situation is given in Holden, *Farewell to Arabia*, p. 207. When the British decided to prevent the army that Sa'īd had assembled at Ṣuḥār from marching on al-Buraymī in 1952, the British Consul General in Muscat, F. C. L. Chauncy, was sent to Ṣuḥār with the message. The Sulṭān agreed to bow to the British decision but he requested Chauncy to give him the message in full view of the army 'so that they would understand that the British Government, not the Sultan, was responsible for the cowardly withdrawal.'

49. Interview with Sayyid Ṭāriq bin Taymūr Āl Sa'īd.

50. As the first Director of Development later wrote about his arrival in 1959, 'It wasn't the most auspicious moment to inaugurate a brand new Development Department, the more so since the Sultan was, I felt, very half-hearted about plans for health, education, agriculture and so on. My first job was a road, something the Sultan really was keen about: but before I could start on anything, I had to organize the Department and find trained staff.' Sir Hugh Boustead, *The Wind of Morning* (London: Chatto and Windus, 1972), p. 219. See also Skeet's comments in *Muscat and Oman*.

51. 'The Word of Sulṭān Sa'īd bin Taymūr, Sulṭān of Muscat and Oman, About the History of the Financial Position of the Sultanate in the Past and What It Is Hoped It Will Be in the Future, After the Export of Oil' (1968). An English text of this statement is given in John Townsend, *Oman: The Making of a Modern State* (London: Croom Helm, 1977), pp. 192–8. The Arabic text is contained in Riyāḍ Najīb al-Rayyis, *Ṣirā' al-Wāḥāt wa-al-Nafṭ: Humūm al-Khalīj al-'Arabī Bayna 1968–1971* (Beirut: al-Nahār, al-Khidmāt al-Ṣiḥāfīya, 1973), pp. 380–8.

52. 'Oman is famous for its fossils; until July 1970 the biggest of them all was to be found in Salalah.' R. P. Owen, 'The Rebellion in Dhofar—A Threat to Western Interests in the Gulf', *The World Today*, vol. 29, no. 6 (June 1973), p. 382.

53. Rumours were rife inside as well as outside the country that he was actually dead and that the British ruled Oman in his name.

54. Since Sa'īd was prone to ignore requests from his officials, Francis Hughes, the General Manager of PDO, became an influential if unofficial individual in Muscat. Since he was one of few people to have regular, generally monthly, contact with the Sulṭān, he was frequently recruited to bring up non-oil matters on his trips to Ṣalāla.

55. The National Democratic Front for the Liberation of Oman and the Arabian Gulf was an outgrowth of the Dhufari rebel organisation. For a fuller account of NDFLOAG and its activities, see Chapter 7.

56. Indeed, Sa'īd apparently never suspected Qābūs of planning his overthrow,

and, even in exile later, he still refused to believe that his son had had anything to do with the *coup*.

57. His allowance,according to the Civil List in 1968, when oil revenues began, was Rs. 12,00,000 per annum, or about $250,000. His most extravagant deed was to stay at the Dorchester when in London—although he had deposited a fair amount of cash in foreign banks as well. 'I knew that only recently the State of Gwadar in Pakistan, which had belonged to Oman, had been sold by the Sultan to the Pakistan Government for three million pounds, the interest of which accumulated in Swiss and American Banks.' Boustead, *The Wind of Morning*, p. 222.

58. This, of course, did not include those members of the Āl Sa'īd who chose to reside in pre-revolutionary Zanzibar.

59. The last credible challenge to the Sulṭān from a member of the family, excluding 1970, was the short-lived regency of 'Abd al-'Azīz bin Sa'īd in 1875. See *Lorimer's Gazetteer*, vol. 1, pt. 1, pp. 502–3.

60. It was presumably this presence as well which limited succession to the throne in the line of Turkī bin Sa'īd and Fayṣal bin Turkī, and not Thuwaynī bin Sa'īd and Sālim bin Thuwaynī, in the interest of stability in Muscat.

61. IO, R/15/3/216; PAM Tom Hickinbotham to PRPG, No. C/562, 15 Oct. 1940.

62. FO, 371/45181 for 1945, Arabia E150/150/91; Muscat Intelligence Diary for 1–15 May 1945.

63. He apparently became bitter towards the Sulṭān and retired from political life, dying a few years later. The situation was complicated by his violent feud with Shihāb, which nearly split the family apart as evidenced by the events of 'Id al-Fitr, 1935, when the family was forced in Sa'īd's absence to choose between paying respects to Ḥamad or Shihāb. IO, R/15/3/355; Muscat Diary of 1–15 Jan. 1935.

64. A particularly good example comes from the al-Sammār branch: in the twentieth century, Hilāl bin Ḥamad, his son Ḥamad and his grandsons Hilāl and Sulṭān. The latter Hilāl became Minister of Justice under Sulṭān Qābūs. Another example is the family of Ḥamad bin Sa'ūd Āl Bū Sa'īd. Ḥamad was wālī of Ṣuhār, then al-Buraymī and finally Nizwā—which he surrendered to the rebel forces in 1957. His brother Hilāl had also been wālī of al-Buraymī and had then succeeded their father, Sa'ūd bin Ḥārib, as wālī of 'Ibrī. By coincidence, Ḥamad bin Sa'ūd's great uncle, Sayf bin Ḥamad, had been wālī of Niẓwā when he was killed defending the city against the Imamate forces in 1913.

65. Good examples are Fayṣal's employment of Taymūr, Muḥammad and Nādir; and the role played by Mājid bin Taymūr as long-time Bāṭina wālī and part-time Passport Officer for his half-brother Sa'īd. For more information on the system of wālīs, see the following chapter.

66. Fayṣal was later to join the 'Imamate of Oman' headquarters set up in Cairo, although he returned to Muscat after 1970 to take posts as Minister of the Economy, Ambassador to the US and UN, Minister of Education and Minister of Cultural Heritage. Thuwaynī, first a school-teacher and then a clerk in his father's office, succeeded Shihāb as Governor of the Capital after the latter retired in 1970 and was also appointed Personal Adviser to Sulṭān Qābūs and often served as Acting Sulṭān during Qābūs's journeys abroad.

67. A report on Aḥmad made by the PDO representative in Muscat in the early 1950s noted that 'he himself entertains every traveller and messenger from the interior, and he knows personally nearly all the shaikhs of importance. He corresponds directly with the chiefs of the interior (the shaikhs of Harth, Bani Riyam, etc.) and also with the Imam's administration. Hence he has sources of

information which are undoubtedly unique.' PDO, E. F. Henderson to R. A. T. Codrai, 2 March 1953.

68. IO, R/15/3/55; PA Wingate to Deputy PRPG, No. 1392, 25 June 1920. To this indictment can be added the effects of venereal disease, which was prevalent in the family and caused mental problems in more than one member.

69. This was the course of action taken by Ḥamūd bin Fayṣal prior to World War II; he later wrote to his nephew the Sulṭān, complaining that his allowance had been discontinued, a plea that bore no fruit with parsimonious Sa'īd. IO, R/15/3/237; Ḥamūd bin Fayṣal bin Turkī to British Resident, Zanzibar, 18 July 1942; Sa'īd bin Taymūr, al-Ḥusn, Dhufar, to PAM, 15 Oct. 1944.

70. Ṭāriq bin Taymūr was later to remark that Sa'īd had been quite skilled at keeping people totally inactive and engaged in meaningless routine until they became completely resigned to their positions. Interview with Sayyid Ṭāriq bin Taymūr, 28 Dec. 1974. Unfortunately for Sa'īd, Qābūs's experience abroad evidently had protected him against these techniques, which were also applied to expatriate employees who frequently spent their first year in Muscat in idleness.

71. IO, R/15/3/230; PAM Hickinbotham to PRPG Prior, Demi-official No. C/444, 15 Aug. 1940.

72. A British report noted that his 'determination to clean up the towns of Muscat and Mutrah shows no signs of abating. His ferocious appearance, enhanced by the large stick which he usually carries when engaged on his duties, appears to have struck terror into the hearts of property owners who are now busily engaged in obeying his orders to either repair or dismantle delapidated house property which had been left to decay.' IO, R/15/3/359; Muscat Intelligence Survey for 1–15 Nov. 1945.

73. Interview with Sayyid Ṭāriq bin Taymūr.

CHAPTER 3

Development of the Administration

The impact of government administration in Oman on the politics of the country over the last century has been far less than would appear at first glance. Despite the occasional minor reforms of the twentieth century, virtually all decision-making remained in the hands of the Sulṭāns—or a direct surrogate, as in the case of Taymūr bin Fayṣal—until 1970. Furthermore, those few administrative responsibilities as existed were frequently pre-empted or short-circuited by various PAMs, British advisers and even Sulṭān Sa'īd bin Taymūr. These limitations were compounded by the chronic situation of lack of physical control over much of the territory of Oman through the late 1950s and even into the early 1970s in some areas. Tribal authority was supreme not only in regions falling under the Imamate but also in various other parts ostensibly included in the Sultanate, such as al-Sharqīya, Ja'lān, al-Ẓāhira, Musandam and the mountains of Dhufar.

Until the *coup d'état* of 1970 radically altered the course of Omani history, the term 'government' in the Sultanate always had a nebulous ring to it. The skeletal nature of the administrative structure tended to serve as both the cause and effect of this situation. Administration generally consisted of little more than the Sulṭān, a few officials in Muscat and a fluctuating number of wālīs scattered around the countryside. Before World War I, there were no real departments and successive Sulṭāns placed routine affairs in the hands of a wazīr, who was generally but not necessarily from the Āl Sa'īd or Āl Bū Sa'īd family. Even after the First World War, only two departments—customs and the military—provided any semblance of organisation in a sea of chaos. For the actual administration of the country, the Sulṭāns were forced to rely upon the British PAMs and 'advisers', members of the ruling family, religious figures, Indian merchants, a few tribal notables, slaves and ex-slaves, and occasional foreign eccentrics who happened to wander into Muscat.

Traditional Structure of Government

Until the British-instigated reforms began to make their mark in the 1920s, the Sulṭāns' principal advisers were almost always chosen from the Āl Bū Sa'īd family although the PAMs increasingly began to interfere in internal policy as the Sulṭāns' control became accordingly weaker. Sulṭān Thuwaynī's principal adviser had been a cousin, Thuwaynī bin Muḥammad Āl Bū Sa'īd, who served for a number of years until dismissed for fraud.[1] However, Thuwaynī later served as wazīr for Sulṭān Turkī bin Sa'īd until dismissed once again in 1873 and replaced by his brother Sa'īd who remained in the position until exiled in 1888. However, he also resumed the post in 1896 under Sulṭān Fayṣal bin Turkī.[2] But an even closer relative—thus one with more immediate chance of occupying the throne—had served as wazīr in the latter half of the nineteenth century: 'Abd al-'Azīz bin Sa'īd. When increased illness forced Sulṭān Turkī to vacate Muscat for the temporary confines of Gwadar in August 1875, his uncle 'Abd al-'Azīz became regent until the Sulṭān's abrupt return in December.[3] The principal wazīr to Sulṭān Fayṣal, in the early part of his reign, was Muḥammad bin 'Azzān Āl Bū Sa'īd, who lost his post for treating with the rebels in 1895. Another long-time assistant had been Badr bin Sayf Āl Bū Sa'īd who served as general in various campaigns and intermittently as wālī of Ṣuḥār (1873–8) and Maṭraḥ (after 1879). After the turn of the century, the most important adviser and wazīr was Muḥammad bin Aḥmad al-Ghashshām, a capable member of the Āl Bū Sa'īd family who continued to wield considerable influence until his death in 1929 and who served as Acting Sulṭān during Sulṭān Taymūr's numerous absences from Muscat.

A major exception to this familial pattern was the three-year reign of 'Azzān bin Qays Āl Bū Sa'īd (r. 1868–71). Since 'Azzān ruled as Imām and had conquered Muscat from the outside and not inherited it, his power base was different from that of his predecessors and successors. The majority of the Āl Bū Sa'īd family opposed 'Azzān as ruler, so little help could be expected from that quarter. Consequently, 'Azzān's advisers came from interior politics. His wazīr was the leader of the muṭawwi' party, Sa'īd bin Khalfān al-Khalīlī, while the third member of the ruling triumvirate was the tamīma of the Ḥirth, Ṣāliḥ bin ʻAlī.[4] But there were also a number of non-family advisers who served the Sulṭāns. A Persian merchant by the name of Ḥajjī Aḥmad had been employed by both Sulṭāns Thuwaynī bin Saʻīd and Sālim bin Thuwaynī, then later made himself an independent ruler of Bandar ʻAbbās after ʻAzzān captured Muscat.[5] A slave, Sulaymān bin Suwaylim, achieved prominence as an official of Sulṭān Turkī in 1879 when he was appointed wālī in Dhufar.[6] Sulaymān was to continue to serve Sulṭān Fayṣal who relied upon him extensively as his trouble-shooter and personal emissary in interior Oman until the former's assassination in 1907. Fayṣal also relied upon Rāshid bin ʻUzayyiz al-Khusaybī, whom he generally employed as wālī of Samā'il. During Sulṭān Fayṣal's French flirtation in the 1890s, his confidential secretary, ʻAbd al-ʻAzīz al-Ruwāḥī, became an important go-between with the French as he also served as dragoman for the French Consul, Paul Ottavi. Another of Fayṣal's unofficial but influential advisers was Yūsuf al-Zawāwī, an emigrant from the Ḥijāz who set up shop as a merchant in Muscat.[7]

The two major functions of government in the nineteenth century were collection of revenues and the keeping of the peace and/or paramouncy of the Sulṭān's authority. As early as 1829, customs had been farmed out to a Banyan (Indian Hindu) merchant in return for cash advancements. As the economic fortunes of the Sultanate fell, this dependence on merchants became increasingly more important and consequently the merchants acquired a greater potential for influence over government policy. Initially, the British were not adverse to this development as much of their involvement in Oman had been to protect the interests of the Hindu merchants—who held British citizenship—and the merchants were frequently the only educated group in the country. But as the state sank farther into debt to these merchants, British apprehensions were correspondingly raised, resulting in the reforms discussed below.

The Sultanate's authority was maintained by a loosely-organised army which maintained a relatively large garrison in Muscat and smaller garrisons in the forts of the major towns along the Bāṭina, as well as in the interior whenever the reigning Sulṭān exercised control there. Since these *ʻaskarīs* were intended to be responsible to the Sulṭān alone, few of them were recruited from the tribes—with the exception of standing levies from certain tribes long regarded as allies, such as the Ḥawāsina, the Banī ʻUmr and the Banī Bū Hasan.

Instead, most were mercenaries deliberately recruited among non-Omanis.

World War I and Post-war Reforms

By the second decade of this century, the Sultanate's political fortunes and the quality of its administrative structure and officialdom—from the Sulṭān on down—had declined so precipitously that the existing British policy of non-interference in Muscat routine was forced to undergo re-evaluation. Early in 1913, the Imamate was re-established in the interior and full-scale revolt broke out, resulting in the rapid loss of the Sultanate's control over interior forts and towns. The state suffered a second blow in the autumn of that year when Sulṭān Fayṣal died and was succeeded by his son Taymūr. The latter had proved competent as wālī for his father in several locations and had also led military campaigns in the field, most recently having held the fort at Bidbid against the rebels. Despite his reluctance at becoming Sulṭān, Taymūr applied an initial diligence to his job:

> Saiyid Taimur appears to have grasped the reins of Government firmly and to be inclined to work through his brothers, Saiyid Nadir and Muhammad and his cousin Dhiyab-bin-Fahad-bin-Turki. Great reforms are promised, especially in the Customs; public smoking and drinking are to be prohibited and prostitutes are to leave the town, the local authorities at Matrah have received warnings against the taking of bribes and justice has been promised to high and low. Most of these reforms are in deference to the presumed wishes of Shaikh Abdullah-bin-Hamaid As-Salimi, one of the moving spirits of the rebellion.[8]

But even though the beginning was auspicious, Taymūr soon lost interest in the hard work of ruling and consequently the British were forced to take increasingly strong control of the internal affairs of state.

Their immediate concern was to prevent a military victory by the Imamate forces. This aim carried the realisation that the military capability of the Sultanate must be expanded. In the short run, this could only be done by stationing Indian Army troops in Muscat: this step was taken in July 1913, and Indian troops remained there until April 1921. But the British, wary of continued external control of the regime and being particularly concerned about the financial cost of the garrison there, were adamant that the long-term solution required that the Sultanate defend itself. But in order to achieve this objective, basic reforms in the structure of the Muscat government were required. Financial reorganisation was at the crux of the matter: the practice of farming out the customs was stopped in December 1913 and the department was put under the control of a Director of Customs directly responsible to the Sulṭān. In order to pay off the debts incurred by the Sulṭān, the Arms Traffic Subsidy, originally granted in 1911, was continued to Taymūr even though it had been first granted only for the duration of Fayṣal's reign. The PAM began to exercise a stronger voice in the councils of the Sulṭān, whether the concern was financial or not. Additional British goals were to assure continued trade with India on favourable terms, through the prolongation of the Commercial Treaty of 1891, and eventually to extricate the Indian military presence from Muscat. Thus the possibility of a levy corps was an early proposal, first advanced by PAM S. G. Knox in December 1913—who suggested that such a force be financed half by an advance on the Zanzibar Subsidy and half by the British government as an additional subsidy.[9] The Government of India tentatively gave their approval in March of the next year and in June the new PAM, R. A. E. Benn, submitted a detailed scheme which called for two British officers, seven native (i.e. Indian) officers and 291 NCOs and rank-and-file, to consist of Baluchis from Baluchistan, Baluchis from Oman, Omani Arabs and Somalis. All this was to be done at a cost of Rs. 1,40,518 with an initial outlay of Rs. 35,042.[10]

Like his father before him and his son Sa'īd after him, Sulṭān Taymūr resented his dependence on the British. He was irritated by the idea of spending half his Zanzibar Subsidy on a new set of troops when the Indian Army was already defending the capital. His solution was to raise an 'independent force' on his own in order to forestall one that might be nominally his but actually under the operation of the British. Unfortunately, this organisation would have been of dubious value in any combat.[11] In the end, both the British proposal for a levy corps and Taymūr's response to it came to nought as a result of the outbreak of World War I. Indian Army troops saved Muscat from capture during the tribal assault in 1915 and those troops continued to defend the Sultanate throughout the war. Yet even before its end, PAM L. B. H. Haworth was submitting proposals on a new military force—although his suggestions proved both premature and excessive.

Even though the establishment of a local military organisation was an essential keystone of British policy, a solid financial and administrative base to support the military was necessary for the over-all policy to succeed. Accordingly, a British adviser, locally known as a wazīr, was sent to Muscat in April 1920. R. C. McCollum, previously PAM in al-Kuwayt, received precise instructions from PAM Wingate on his 'delicate' role in Muscat:

> The very skeleton of reform of the administration is necessary. We only want to make the state pay its way and our loan and if possible make it stand on its own legs without continual propping from us. Make the customs pay and remove the more glaring faults and let the rest rip. Go very slow, be very tactful and try and remove any feeling the people may get that your coming is only the prelude to British occupation. In addition to the fact that this is not true such a rumour cannot but have a bad effect on our policy and our prestige elsewhere. Pay the greatest respect to local prejudices and above all to religion. It is not a difficult matter nowadays to raise anti-Christian sentiment, and the Omani fanatics are next door with whom we want to get some kind of agreement.[12]

In addition, Wingate counselled the new adviser to

> Officially wear some native uniform or dress, never British uniform of any kind which is never worn by a British officer in the service of another state. Sink your individuality as a British officer and take on that of an oriental wazir in a medieval Arab state. Entertain the ashraf. Concentrate on making your reforms such as are popular with the people. Muscat under the last few Sultans has been famous even in Arabia for bad government and needless oppression.[13]

In addition to the 'wazīr', Wingate arranged for a Council of Ministers (or Deputies: al-Majlis al-Niyābī) to be set up, ostensibly to assist the Sulṭān but more accurately to administer the state during Taymūr's frequent and lengthy sojourns in Dhufar and India. This Council was inaugurated by a letter from Taymūr to his local 'wazīr', Muḥammad bin Aḥmad al-Ghashshām.[14] Consequently, a four-man cabinet was formed in 1920, consisting of the Sulṭān's elder brother, Nādir bin Fayṣal, as President (Ra'īs) and Acting

Sulṭān (Nā'ib Sulṭān) in Taymūr's absence; the above-mentioned Muḥammad bin Aḥmad, the wālī of Maṭraḥ for many years, as head of financial affairs; Zubayr bin 'Alī al-Hūtī, a Baluchi immigrant, as head of justice and the courts; and the old retainer, Rāshid bin 'Uzayyiz al-Khusaybī, as head of religious affairs.[15] The council was of necessity largely ceremonial since none of its members displayed particular qualifications for the administration of a modern state.[16]

The duties of the council and its functions were fully described by Wingate who had been responsible for its creation: nevertheless the PAM entertained no delusions regarding the gap between the theoretical responsibilities of the organisation and its actual capabilities.[17] In spite of the ceremonial functioning of the council, these venerable individuals held the nominal reins of state for a lengthy period.[18] Major decisions were made by McCollum during the six months he spent in Muscat and later by successive PAMs and Financial Advisers.

The declining financial position of the state during this period resulted in the temporary loan of an Imperial Customs expert named Bower to reorganise the Sultanate's department. Although this provided a good start, it was recognised at the time that only a full-time Financial Adviser could hope to overhaul fully the antiquated system. Therefore, on the recommendation of Sir Arnold Wilson, then Managing Director of the Anglo–Persian Oil Company, Bertram S. Thomas was selected for the position of Financial Adviser (FA). Before his transfer to the Transjordan administration, Thomas had served under Wilson in Mesopotamia. Arriving in February 1925, Thomas was to spend six years in Muscat as an official of the Sultanate while simultaneously pursuing his interest in exploration, with the latter preoccupation at times being at the expense of the former duties. In spite of his wandering interests, Thomas gradually accrued more and more power in the state's politics. At first he was simply titled Financial Adviser but permission was subsequently received from the Government of India for him to use the title of Wazīr and serve on the Council of Ministers, which he soon dominated.

The objections of Indian officialdom to his activities finally reached the point of no return in connection with Thomas's preparations for his epic crossing of the Rub' al-Khālī, and arrangements were made for his replacement by a Mesopotamian official, S. E. Hedgcock, at the end of 1930.[19] Clearly inadequate in the position, Hedgcock was eased out after he had been in Muscat for but a few months. The duties of the FA were then temporarily taken over by the Military Adviser—and frequently Officiating PAM as well—R. G. E. W. Alban. When Alban was invalided home soon afterwards, the new Sulṭān, Sa'īd bin Taymūr, refused to accept a replacement. The period of direct British supervision over the Sultanate's administration had come to an inconsequential close.

Administration under Sa'īd bin Taymūr

Although Sa'īd's formal investiture as Sulṭān did not take place until 1932, he had ruled in essence as Sulṭān *de facto* since becoming President of the Council of Ministers in 1929. Taymūr had rarely visited Muscat after that and final authority was almost without exception vested in Sa'īd. Even during his regency, Sa'īd was fully cognizant of the state of dependency for which the Sultanate's dismal financial state was responsible. In addition, the squabbles of the last few years between various British advisers and Government of India officials had left him confused and suspicious. As a consequence, Sa'īd was determined to assert his own authority, including redress of the financial imbalance and reliance on his own counsel. One of his first actions was formally to abolish the Council of Ministers and replace it with three clearly subordinate offices: finance, under Alban; internal affairs, under his uncle, Ḥamad bin Fayṣal, then wālī of Maṭraḥ; and justice, under Zubayr bin 'Alī.[20]

Despite Sa'īd's reluctance to delegate authority, he was far more responsive to improvements in and additions to the administrative structure of the state than any of his predecessors had been. Although the scope of Sa'īd's government was modest when compared to the proliferation of agencies and personnel after 1970, three distinct phases of administrative expansion in addition to a compact nucleus merit examination here. By the time that Sa'īd had assumed the title of Sulṭān, the British-instituted reforms of the 1920s had coalesced into a truncated set of responsibilities handled by a small number of offices. Typically, these consisted of the respective 'minister' and perhaps a clerk or two—two exceptions being the customs and the military. This state of affairs continued almost unchanged until three separate periods of modest expansion in the late 1930s, the 1950s and the late 1960s wrought equally modest structural alterations.

The first set of these offices may be described as 'continuing': those which Sa'īd inherited and continued to the end of his reign.

Foremost among these was finance, the province of European advisers or 'wazīrs' during Sa'īd's regency and thereby a province ultimately outside Sa'īd's control since these advisers, despite protestations to the contrary, were subordinate to the orders of the Government of India or its representatives. When R. G. E. W. Alban finally left Oman in June 1933, Sa'īd refused the offer of a new FA and steadfastly claimed the responsibilities and work of the office as his own, including the preparations of budgets which he continued through the late 1940s. He had always been keenly interested in economics since his school days in India and he continued to supervise personally this aspect of administration until 1970. The day-to-day routine was handled by a number of Indian 'fonctionnaires', the first being R. S. Malik Duli Chand. He held the title and duties of Director of Customs and Revenue from October 1932 to March 1939, when he left Muscat under suspicious circumstances.[21] For the next few years, the Sulṭān relied on British help and his own hard work until he was able to secure the services of the Political Agency's treasury officer, K.S. (later K.B.) Maqbul Husayn, as Financial Officer in October 1941. Husayn served in that capacity —in addition to many other positions—until his retirement in July 1966. He became a chief aide to the Sulṭān, accompanying him on his trips to London and seeing to numerous details of government. The post of Treasury Officer was filled by a number of civil servants, the longest-serving being Harichand Kothari between the years 1945 and 1959, although he had also been Treasury Officer previous to World War II.

Customs was the only area of the government that was relatively well organised, primarily due to the state's overwhelming need for revenue. The system whereby customs had been farmed out to Indian merchants in repayment of state and personal loans was abruptly ended by British pressure in December 1913 and thereafter a Director of Customs was directly appointed by the Sulṭān.[22] Despite this action, customs remained a haphazard process until a British customs expert was loaned from Egypt for six months in the early 1920s to overhaul the department. Following this initiative, the post of director was filled by a succession of trained and seconded officials from Egypt and then India, a policy that has continued into the reign of Sulṭān Qābūs. The only adequately controlled customs facilities were at Muscat and Maṭraḥ. Customs fees at Ṣuḥār were traditionally left in the treasury of the Ṣuḥār wilāya—where they generally found their way into the wālī's pocket until stronger control over Ṣuḥār was exercised by Sa'īd bin Taymūr. The other ports of the Bāṭina were scarcely better controlled. The situation in Ṣūr was chaotic as importers generally ignored the customs post; and on several occasions the Banī Bū 'Alī tribe set up their own post in the suburb of al-'Ayqa.[23] The duties of the director ranged far afield. In the 1940s, the PAM wrote that the director of that time had dealt with:

> (a) Zakat, which we may parallel with land revenue and
> (b) Bait-al-Mal, which we may parallel with Crown lands. He has also been President of the price control committee, and has in general advised and been consulted on commercial and economic matters. He also drew up the existing Customs Regulations during his tenure of office.[24]

The customs department had long been responsible for the collection of zakāt along the Bāṭina coast, using a staff of several hundred in the 1960s scattered through a dozen villages.

The third continuing office was internal affairs. Since the 'interior' of the Sultanate consisted at that time of little more than the Bāṭina coast and the Ru'ūs al-Jibāl (or 'Musandam') region, Sa'īd had little trouble in handling it himself. The requirements of the office were not much more than a matter of correspondence with the Imām and the representatives of the Ghāfirī and Hināwī tribal factions as well as a few other important shaykhs, while the wālīs along the Bāṭina were still somewhat independent in their daily routines as they had long been. For a brief period soon after Sa'īd's accession, his uncle Ḥamad bin Fayṣal had been placed in charge of the office but quickly proved unsatisfactory, and the appointment of the Libyan, Sulaymān al-Bārūnī, in 1938 was little more than a sinecure.

Sa'īd's goal had always been integration of the interior into the Sultanate's administrative network, but only the oil concession royalties and British financial aid on the eve of World War II allowed him to take the first step of appointing Aḥmad bin Ibrāhīm Āl Bū Sa'īd as Minister of Internal Affairs (Nāẓir al-Shu'ūn al-Dākhilīya) in August 1939—a position he held until 1970. From that time, and frequently in tandem with Shihāb bin Fayṣal, Sa'īd's uncle, Aḥmad served as 'the government' in Muscat when the Sulṭān was absent. After inner Oman was reintegrated into the Sultanate between 1955 and 1957, and after Sa'īd retired permanently to

Ṣalāla in 1958, Aḥmad bin Ibrāhīm became the principal liaison between the shaykhs and wālīs in Oman and the Sulṭān in Ṣalāla. He heard their requests and disputes and frequently referred them to Ṣalāla for final decisions, in addition to dispensing the Sulṭān's largesse to the shaykhs from Muscat. At the same time, as part of Sa'īd's practice of not allowing anyone to acquire too much power, several counterbalances were established against Aḥmad. First, Ismā'īl bin Khalīl al-Raṣāṣī, who had been wālī of Maṭraḥ since January 1939, was made Inspector of Wālīs and the recipient of appeals from the *sharī'a* (Islamic law) courts. Then in 1968, John D. Shebbeare was appointed Secretary for Internal Affairs, a post which he relinquished in 1970 and which largely consisted of providing an independent opinion on internal affairs to the Sulṭān and exercising a judicial check on the work of the wālīs and qāḍīs.

Although foreign relations were handled by the British and direct contact with neighbouring states or rulers was extremely rare, Sa'īd also appointed Shihāb bin Fayṣal as Minister of Foreign Affairs (Nāẓir al-Shu'ūn al-Khārijīya; later referred to in English as External Affairs) in August 1939. The post was not necessarily a sinecure, however, as Sa'īd also made Shihāb his Ceremonial Representative in his absence. This meant that often Shihāb served as the official channel of communication between the British representative in the Sultanate and the government, i.e. Sa'īd. Nevertheless, Shihāb was summarily fired in May 1945 when the Sulṭān returned from Ṣalāla and discovered the chaotic state of affairs existing in Muscat. After that Sa'īd turned to Europeans: Basil Woods-Ballard served from 1948 to 1953 and then Neil McL. Innes took over from 1953 to 1958. After Innes's departure in April 1958, the post lay vacant until 1971; the office was turned into a Department of External Affairs and put under the charge of Col. P. R. M. Waterfield, the Military Secretary, for a time. Provision was made for a Secretary but none was ever appointed and the department barely continued to exist.[25]

Through this office, the Sultanate's minor international contacts were maintained.[26] The only foreign affairs conducted on a heads-of-state level occurred on Sa'īd's frequent, almost yearly, visits to London—although they were private visits, audiences with the Queen and/or Prime Minister were not unusual. Otherwise, Sa'īd's only official contact with another head of state was during the visit of Shaykh Zāyid bin Sulṭān Āl Nuhayyān of Abu Dhabi to Ṣalāla in 1968. A communiqué released at the end of that visit seemed to indicate, perhaps prematurely, to the British that the era of stagnation in this part of the world was over: Shaykh Shakhbūt of Abu Dhabi was gone and Sulṭān Sa'īd appeared to be changing.[27] The Sultanate had only one Consul: C. E. Kendall in London, who was appointed in 1963.[28]

Another sphere of government activity was the administration of justice. Traditionally, this was meted out by a *qāḍī* (religious judge) whose responsibility covered not only strictly religious affairs, but also matters in the criminal and civil realm. One or more qāḍīs were assigned to each wālī and their decisions could be appealed to a chief qāḍī residing in Muscat. Generally speaking, these qāḍīs had broad jurisdiction over most Muslims, especially Ibāḍīs and Sunnīs. Major exceptions were the Shī'īs and Khojas, who were responsible for their own religious and judicial affairs, and those Indian Muslims who were British subjects. Foreigners were normally subject to the Muscat Orders-in-Council, which authorised a civil court with the PAM on the bench.[29] In the twentieth century, various attempts were made to establish independent civil courts. Nādir bin Fayṣal Āl Sa'īd was placed in charge of civil cases after his brother Taymūr had come to the throne and generally continued to act in that capacity despite criticism until the Council of Ministers was created in 1920 and Zubayr bin 'Alī al-Hūtī was given responsibility for justice and the courts.[30] At that time, proper civil (*'adlīya*) and commercial (*tijārīya*) courts were set up to complement the religious (*sharī'īya*) court.[31] Their ineffectiveness matched the general level of government during this period and the commercial court seems to have faded away soon after.[32] The civil court had a longer life: when Zubayr bin 'Alī finally retired in 1936, Ismā'īl bin Khalīl al-Raṣāṣī took his place as head of justice until the civil court was abandoned on al-Raṣāṣī's assumption of duties as wālī of Maṭraḥ in 1939.[33] Thereafter, judicial duties were handled on an *ad hoc* basis until 1970.

The first phase of expansion was made possible by an improvement in the Sultanate's financial position and was primarily directed at instituting basic social services in the Muscat/Maṭraḥ region. Sa'īd had first advanced a scheme for a municipality (*baladīya*) in 1937. This would have provided a joint committee for Muscat and Maṭraḥ, including a president and eight members, an annual budget and financing to come from a special municipal tax.[34] The scheme was finally put into operation in 1938 with Hilāl bin Badr Āl Bū Sa'īd as President and was primarily concerned with public health and sanitation.[35] By 1941, the municipality included a public health department and was also responsible for electricity. Sa'īd's brother Ṭāriq was appointed Municipal Administrator in October 1945, a post he held until 1957 when he was succeeded by Martin G. Wynne, who had spent the previous ten years as governor of the Gwadar enclave. On Wynne's departure in October 1961, the organisation reverted to a municipal council of eleven or twelve members with the wālī of Maṭraḥ, Ismā'īl bin Khalīl al-Raṣāṣī, as chairman but with daily responsibility resting with the Executive Officer, Muhammad Sayyid Qurayshi, a Pakistani who remained in that office until August 1970.

Almost coterminous with the municipality was the development of a police force. Although rudimentary police functions had been assumed as early as 1936, the force was reorganised in 1940.[36] A properly-constituted force was established eventually with a havildar, a naik, three lance naiks and thirty constables in the ranks.[37] Unfortunately, these auspicious beginnings failed to take root: by the mid-1960s, the only function of the extant force was to garrison Fort Mīrānī while a new police corps was established, and was in turn itself superseded by another force created after the 1970 *coup*. A temporary organisation also created during the war period was the committee to regulate the price of foodstuffs and other essentials and to arrange for their distribution. The membership of this committee was composed of merchants and was under the chairmanship of the Director of Customs.[38]

The brief outburst of wartime activity was followed by a lull of more than a decade. Finally, the permanent retirement of Sa'īd bin Taymūr to Ṣalāla in 1958 and an increase in British involvement in the Sultanate after their assistance in the 1950s rebellion provoked several adjustments in the structure of government. Foremost of these was the necessity to delegate authority in Muscat. For a variety of reasons, the Sulṭān's choice was Shihāb bin Fayṣal, the uncle disgraced in 1945 and removed from public life. But by 1960, Shihāb had resumed his former title of Ceremonial Representative of the Sulṭān as well as that of Governor of the Capital (Muḥāfiẓ al-'Āṣima).[39] Sa'īd also was to work through his Personal Adviser, F. C. L. Chauncy, appointed in 1960 after having served as Consul General in Muscat from 1949 to 1958.

The newly-instituted British development subsidy resulted in the creation of a Development Department in September 1959, with the first Director being H. R. D. Boustead, previously the Resident Adviser at Mukallā in the East Aden Protectorate.[40] This department was the direct result of British pressure on Sa'īd; therefore it never had his private approval and its effective life-span was only as long as the subsidy was paid, that is, until March 1968. It was always kept administratively separate from the other sections of the government and its budget was subject to the review of the British Consul General as well as the Sulṭān.

The obstinacy of Sa'īd towards anything connected with the department's efforts resulted in the resignation of the first director: the second director's incumbency was even briefer. It was left to the third appointee to see it out: D. N. R. Ogram arrived in November 1963 and remained through to the dissolution of the remnants of the department in early 1971. At its peak, the department had an annual budget of approximately a half million rupees and was responsible for health, with a chain of ten health centres, twelve dispensaries and a maternity centre at Samā'il; roads in a programme which included the first Bāṭina coast road to Ṣuḥār as well as another through the Wādī Samā'il; agriculture, with the establishment of experimental farms at Nizwā and Ṣuḥār; and educational administration, which included responsibility for the salaries of teachers, the sending of students to Aden and Mukallā for teacher training and the construction of an unused boarding house in Muscat for the sons of shaykhs. Maximum staff level was approximately 300 with seventy to eighty of those being expatriates.[41] When the subsidy was discontinued, the department's activities were naturally curtailed and gradually slowed down—it was even rumoured that salaries had to be paid out of loans procured in the Maṭraḥ sūq—until final disbandment in 1971. Nevertheless, the four operational areas of the department were to provide the nucleus for the establishment of various modern ministries after 1970.

This phase also saw the introduction of several miscellaneous functions. In January 1958, Mohammed Lisanul Haq was seconded from India to direct the Audit Office and found himself holding a number of other positions as well during his career in Muscat, often in collaboration with Maqbul Husayn. Other innovations of this period included the Sultanate Printing Press in 1958; a power plant begun with four generators in April 1961 with additional generators added in 1963 and 1964; and in April 1966, the Sultanate's own post office which took over from the British GPO which had handled the mail since 1948.[42]

The final period of pre-1970 expansion was a result of the oil discoveries of the late 1960s. As it soon became the dominant source of income, the British subsidies begun in the 1950s were ended and Sa'īd was inspired to issue 'The Word of the Sulṭān' in 1968 to explain the new situation.[43] Since the financial surplus which the Sulṭān had always claimed was necessary for development was at hand, the new oil revenues were channelled into a special development budget. The role of the old Development Department was superseded by a new Development and Planning Board, this time with Sa'īd's approval and, indeed, his relative enthusiasm. C. J. Pelly, a former PAM, was engaged as Director of Planning and Development and William Heber-Percy was brought in as Secretary.

While the old Department gamely tried to continue its responsibilities in health, roads, agriculture and education, the new Board began to plan and, in some cases, implement a number of major projects, including the new Maṭraḥ port, now known as Mīnā' Qābūs; the girls' school in Muscat; Ruwī Hospital, later renamed al-Nahḍa Hospital; the paved road to Ṣuḥār; the new power station in Riyām, originally under the private ownership of Muscat Power Company Ltd; a water scheme for the capital and the Khawr government office building in Muscat, later the Ministry for Foreign Affairs.[44] The only problem with this approach was Sa'īd's extreme chariness. The state's chronic poverty had taught him to be careful about spending money and consequently he was overly cautious: when the *coup d'état* came, these projects were just beginning to show results and consequently were a step behind the rising expectations of the country's people.

In addition to the Development Board, a public works department was founded in July 1968 with a director seconded from India and a new police force was organised in 1969. The Oman Currency Board was also set up with the help of the British Bank of the Middle East (BBME), an established institution in Muscat since 1948, and the Sa'īdī *riyāl* was issued on 7 May 1970, thus putting an end to the complicated system whereby at least three different currencies had been in use for three different parts of the country.

In response to continued British pressure on him to expand his top-level 'cabinet', Sa'īd hired a number of expatriate advisers during this period. Generally, their influence was negligible: their function, in Sa'īd's eyes, or so it seemed to those who served him, was to appease the British by their presence in the capital while Sa'īd was saved from their interference by his isolation in Ṣalāla. He reserved for himself the authority for most decisions and issued his orders through Chauncy, Aḥmad bin Ibrāhīm and Shihāb bin Fayṣal. Most of the new posts created were occupied by men who had either previously served in Muscat for the Government of India or who were retired personnel from the Foreign Office, Colonial Office, War Office, etc. That these new officials were all expatriates was no coincidence: the only group that Sa'īd mistrusted more than capable Omanis in general were members of his own immediate family. Of these expatriates, the first to arrive was L. B. Hirst, who had been Military Adviser in the 1940s and who became the rarely consulted Secretary for Petroleum Affairs in 1965. Pelly was appointed in 1968 and, with the help of Lisanul Haq, produced the first budget in two decades. He was closely followed by John D. Shebbeare, the Secretary for Internal Affairs.

Following the overthrow of Sa'īd bin Taymūr in July 1970, almost the entire hodge-podge system of administration was scrapped. Along with the change in rulers had come a commitment to 'modernisation' and, although the major emphasis was to be on socio-economic development, any change would invariably affect the existing government structure. Within a month of the *coup d'état*, Ṭāriq bin Taymūr Āl Sa'īd, an uncle of the new Sulṭān, was named Prime Minister and he immediately set about creating the nucleus of a more systematic government. Ministries for the interior, education, health and justice were established almost immediately and within a year there were additional ministries for information, social affairs and labour, economy and foreign affairs. Only the Defence Department weathered the change without any great difficulty. Simultaneously, this institution of a new order resulted in the abolishment of the old 'secretary' posts and the British incumbents departed with them. The new ministers, and, indeed, nearly all high-level government officials, were henceforth to be Omanis and, within that qualification, almost entirely Arab.

The Sultanate's Finances

Finance has been perhaps the single most pervasive determinant of the Sultanate's policies over the last century. With Oman's general economic decline in the latter half of the nineteenth century came a corresponding fiscal malaise in the state treasury: the division of Oman and Zanzibar served to separate the Omani Sultanate from most of Sa'īd bin Sulṭān's merchant fleet as well as Zanzibar's rich customs revenues. Furthermore, the Sulṭān's inability to maintain an adequate administration in the countryside led to a further decline in zakāt and customs revenues in Oman—yet futile efforts to reclaim lost authority over the interior and such ports as Ṣūr added to the drain on the treasury. Continued indiscriminate spending by the ruling family only compounded the problem: there being no distinction between state and crown property, debts of individual members of the family had to be paid or guaranteed by the state.[45] Eventually, the Sulṭāns found themselves ensnared in a mass of debt owed to various Indian merchants of Muscat. Loans were secured against future revenues: since customs provided the only dependable source of income, it was regularly farmed out.

British attempts to persuade Sulṭān Taymūr to pursue a stricter policy were to no avail. Consequently, the Government of India initiated a phase of active control over the Sultanate's finances. The debts to Muscat merchants were paid off by Indian loans and extended subsidies. As discussed above, the customs department, rescued from the hands of the merchants in 1913, was reorganised in the early 1920s and a tradition of directors seconded from Egypt or India begun. Nevertheless, the Indian loans were not paid off until after Sa'īd bin Taymūr had taken the reins of state. Knowing well the power that the Government of India exercised over the Sultanate as a result of its insolvency, Sa'īd took personal charge of the state's finances while still only President of the Council of Ministers, supervising the budgets, adding customs posts in Ṣuḥār and Ṣūr, and restricting the profligate spending of his relatives by cutting allowances under the civil list. By the 1940s, the Sulṭān had erased both public and private debt and had managed to begin a modest programme of investment in Newfoundland stock and Government of India war bonds.[46]

According to Sa'īd's version of financial orthodoxy, the initiation of any substantial undertaking was automatically ruled out unless funds to complete it were already in hand. Consequently, capital projects were necessarily modest and limited to municipal improvements in Muscat and Maṭraḥ. In this manner, Sa'īd had been able not only to place the state on a solid financial footing, but also to pursue an independent domestic policy free of British supervision. However, the crises of the 1950s were to upset his careful financial manipulations. Although the Sulṭān was able to finance the recapture of inner Oman in late 1955 through his own funds, albeit with the help of Petroleum Development (Oman), the rebellion of 1957–9 was financially beyond his resources. As a result, he was forced to sell the enclave of Gwadar on the Makrān Coast to Pakistan for £3,000,000 sterling,[47] and accept British military and financial subsidies.[48]

Until 1968 when the Sultanate first began receiving a regular oil income, the Muscat treasury had been dependent on four basic sources of revenue: loans and subsidies, customs, zakāt and periodic payments from oil concessionaires.[49] The most plentiful of these, and the most dependable, was also the least indigenous: British contributions, transmitted to Muscat first *via* the Government of India and then *via* the Foreign Office, were in the form of either loans or subsidies. Yet because they were almost entirely granted on an *ad hoc* basis and withdrawn after the disappearance of the political and/or economic crises that had made them necessary, these funds were clearly unsuitable for long-range economic planning.[50]

Customs provided the largest indigenous income, despite the laxity in collection and corruption in the department which plagued the Sultanate throughout most of the twentieth century. In 1931, customs collection brought in some Rs. 4,21,000 or 57 per cent of the total budget receipts. By the late 1960s, the customs share of government income had risen to approximately 90 per cent.[51] The predominant role of customs in the state's finances was responsible for the attention paid to the department's reform in the 1920s as well as the efforts of the late 1920s and early 1930s to bring the ports of Ṣūr and Ṣuḥār under the Sulṭān's firm control.

Collection of zakāt formed the third revenue source. Essentially a tax applied to property and production, zakāt revenues yielded on average between Rs. 15,000 and 20,000 in the period before World War II, while during the War the average jumped to Rs. 60,000 and 75,000.[52] Until the interior was reintegrated into the Sultanate in 1956, sole responsibility for zakāt rested with the customs department, largely because it was the only administrative agency capable of handling the job. Between 1956 and 1971, zakāt collection was split between the military, responsible for the interior region, and the customs department, retaining collection duties at Muscat/Maṭraḥ and along the Bāṭina. In the late 1960s, the latter agency collected approximately Rs. 2,00,000 annually from its area.[53] In 1971, the collection and administration of zakāt revenues for the entire Sultanate were entrusted to the newly-created Ministry of Awqāf and Bayt al-Māl, later renamed Awqāf and Islamic Affairs.

The final source was oil, although in an indirect sense. Despite the granting of a two-year exploration licence to the D'Arcy

Exploration Company—a subsidiary of the Anglo–Persian, later Anglo–Iranian, Oil Company—in 1925 and the despatch of an expedition team into inner Oman at that time, the basic groundwork for an oil concession in the Sultanate was not laid until the mid-1930s. Negotiations between the Sulṭān and B. H. de R. Lermitte, acting for Petroleum Concessions Ltd (PCL)—a new subsidiary of the Iraq Petroleum Company—were concluded in July 1937 and the Sulṭān was awarded a payment of Rs. 1,78,000 at that time.[54] PCL sent exploration parties to al-Buraymī *via* Sharjah and Ṣuḥār in November/December 1938 but suspended further operations in the area until after the Second World War, at which time the options on both the Oman and Dhufar concessions acquired in 1937 were taken up. Although the PCL payments for the Oman concession were treated as state income, Dhufar payments were considered private by Sa'īd bin Taymūr and were used for improvements on his property there.

One of the major effects of the modest 1920s reforms was the institution of regular budgets, beginning with the one prepared by McCollum in 1921 and continuing to the late 1940s.[55] For the majority of the years in this period, items of receipt covered a standard field of approximately a dozen heads. Chief among these were customs, with approximately 73 per cent of the total budget over the quarter century; subsidies, which varied according to British policy; zakāt, with an average of 1.5 per cent; brokerage tax, 2 per cent; and landing charges, 1 per cent. In the early part of the budget period, the income from the wilāya of Ṣuḥār formed a major head: the treasury of Ṣūḥār had been kept separate from Muscat until Sa'īd finally incorporated it into the Sultanate treasury in 1929. Average receipts were approximately ten lakhs until the depression hit and consequently fell to approximately seven lakhs. With the beginning of World War II, receipt totals began to grow quite rapidly, reaching a peak of over thirty-one lakhs in 1945 and then starting to decline in post-war years.

On the expenditure side of the ledger, items were concentrated in five major areas: the civil list, with approximately 32 per cent share of the average total; the *dīwān* al-Sulṭān or central administration, with 3.5 per cent; defence, consisting of the Muscat Infantry and the Sultanate yacht, 13 per cent; customs and revenues department, with some 13 per cent of the total; and wālīs and their staffs, 12 per cent. Other steady items were for Fort Jalālī (the prison), Fort Mīrānī (headquarters for the police and Muscat 'askarīs), the municipalities and public works, quarantine, education, loan repayments, subsidies to shaykhs and other miscellaneous items. The total level of expenditure was set at approximately ten lakhs until Sa'īd bin Taymūr became President of the Council of Ministers. He deliberately cut expenditure to less than seven lakhs for a number of years until increased income during the war allowed him to gradually increase expenditure—this reached a total of nearly thirteen lakhs by 1947.

The net result was a budgetary deficit running at an annual average of two lakhs from 1925 until after Sa'īd took control. His draconian measures served to put the budget into the black by half a lakh in 1931. This modest surplus continued until the substantial inflows during World War II and afterwards, when the Sultanate piled up reserves of twelve lakhs in 1943, nearly nineteen lakhs in 1944 and over twenty-one lakhs in 1945. Even by 1947, there was a surplus of nearly thirteen lakhs. Consequently, the financial position of the state was favourable until the events of the 1950s. By the time that the budget was reinstated in 1968—as a result of the combined efforts of the new Financial Adviser, C. J. Pelly, and the Director of the Audit, Mohammed Lisanul Haq—the totals of both expenditures and revenues had been inflated quite dramatically. The 1968 budget had an expenditure total of Rs. 5,92,58,900. The column heads by this time had grown more sophisticated and detailed, the major ones being: Defence Department, 75.1 per cent; civil list, 2.4 per cent; dīwān al-Sulṭān, 1.3 per cent; Governorate of the Capital (i.e. Muscat), 0.6 per cent; Internal Affairs Department, 0.4 per cent; Department of Financial Affairs, 0.4 per cent; wālīs, 3.3 per cent; police departments—including 'askarīs—3.3 per cent; customs, 0.9 per cent; health, 1.3 per cent; education, 0.8 per cent; agriculture, 0.8 per cent; ceremonial purposes, 0.8 per cent; and Sa'īd's capital improvement programme, 4.3 per cent.[56]

Evolution of the Military

Traditionally, military capability in the Sultanate was limited to two basic forces. On a permanent basis, the Sulṭāns only had need of garrisons for the forts of the capital and in the towns of the Bātina and the interior where the wālīs were appointed. The composition of these garrisons, staffed by 'askarīs, was frequently diverse. In some cases, particularly in the interior, they were recruited from the dominant tribe of the area. More frequently, however, they were mercenaries, chosen especially because their lack of involvement in

Omani politics assured a certain degree of loyalty to the Sulṭān. Most were recruited among non-Omanis. During Sulṭān Turkī's reign, it has been estimated that approximately 400 were Muwaḥḥidūn (Wahhābīs) from the Najd and al-Aḥsā' (Hasa), another 250 were Ḥaḍramīs, 100 were Baluchis from the Makrān Coast and others were Negro slaves and freedmen.[57] Such artillery as existed was serviced by Persian gunners. In 1917, Taymūr bin Fayṣal even attempted to raise a short-lived force of Negroes and Baluchis with a Turkish commandant.

On the other hand, when specific campaigns were undertaken or when Muscat came under attack, the Sulṭān was obliged to seek temporary help from tribes loyal to him. These levies were frequently motivated as much by the promise of loot as they were by loyalty and their effectiveness was frequently decried: on several occasions, they melted away at the time of battle. The most notable levies were from the Banī 'Umr and the Ḥawāsina tribes of the Bāṭina who frequently provided 'askarīs for wālīs, even up to the present. At certain periods, the Shiḥūḥ, the Banī Bū Ḥasan, the Banī Bū 'Alī and the Banī Ghāfir have all rallied to the Sulṭāns' aid.

But by the turn of the century, it was obvious that these traditional means of support would not protect the Sultanate or even the capital. The spectacle of rebellious tribes running through Muscat in 1895 and the necessity of stationing troops from the Indian Army at Bayt al-Falaj in 1913 to prevent a repetition served to put the Government of India on notice that the slow but steady increase of Muscat's dependence on India had to be reversed. Certain steps were necessary to accomplish this, taking the form of economic, political and military reorganisation. In the latter field, proposals were first advanced in 1913 and 1914 by PAMs Percy Cox and R. A. E. Benn, suggesting that a levy corps be recruited from the Makrān Coast with a British officer or two in command and annual expenses in the range of about one-and-a-half lakhs of rupees.[58] Although Government of India opinion on the project was essentially favourable, the idea was forgotten until brought up again in 1917 by PAM L. B. H. Haworth. Haworth's proposals were much more elaborate than those previous: he recommended a thousand men at double the cost.[59] Furthermore, his proposals were for an offensive force which would have carried the attack back to the interior. As this aggressive plan held the potential for conflict with the Government of India's desire to extricate itself from the Sultanate's problems, it was duly rejected. Consequently, the actual birth of the Muscat Levy Corps (MLC) was delayed to April 1921 when Captain E. R. McCarthy and the redundant Seistan Levy Corps disembarked in Maṭraḥ, made their way to Bayt al-Falaj and relieved the Indian Army troops there. Its limitation as a garrison force was essentially because of its size—never more than 300 men in strength and generally closer to 200 or less—and due to the state of peace arranged by Wingate in the Agreement of al-Sīb (1920). For the next several decades, the MLC's functions were concerned with providing armed guards for the Sulṭān's Palace, the British Political Agency and the Sultanate Treasury, and, in addition, building new roads in the Muscat/Maṭraḥ area. Its role in deterring tribal assaults is hard to assess in light of the Sīb negotiations and the generally pacific nature of the interior after 1921. Nevertheless, the MLC remained the sole military force in the Sultanate until the early 1950s and despite complaints as to its viability and effectiveness, it served as a model and source of recruits for the Baḥrayn Levy Corps (later known as the Baḥrayn Police Force).[60]

As the first Commandant, Capt. McCarthy was generally responsible for the broad organisation of the MLC and for the somewhat unsuccessful attempt to 'Arabise' the Corps which actually resulted in little more than replacing Seistan Baluchis by either Gwadar or Bāṭina Baluchis; few Arabs actually enlisted. In 1932, McCarthy handed over to Captain R. G. E. W. Alban—a familiar figure in the Oman establishment over the next two decades—and a precedent of two-year tours for commandants was set.[61] Over the years, the MLC suffered from a lack of adequate arms and a steadily declining roster—both direct consequences of the economic malaise of the Sultanate. The ruling family disliked the force because a larger proportion of the state's meagre treasury was thus directed away from their allowances. The state's FA reported the misuse of funds by the MLC in 1931 but his charges were later dismissed.[62] When Alban returned as Commandant in late 1931, he severely criticised the low level of discipline and preparedness to which his predecessor had allegedly allowed the Corps to deteriorate; yet he apparently did little to rectify the situation.[63] By 1939, its strength had been cut to 150 men, the requirement for a British commandant had been dropped and the Muscat Infantry—as it came to be known—was riddled with nepotism, bribery and intrigue. In addition, the soldiers were underpaid and chronically ill with malaria; the guns were old and many were unworkable.[64] The situation on the outbreak of World War II was not much of an improvement over the status of the defence of Muscat twenty-five years earlier. Fortunately, the interior remained quiet.

During World War II, the Sultanate proved to be a consistent if peripheral supporter of the Allies, and Sa'īd bin Taymūr was almost enthusiastic in his loyalty to the British. In return, the British sought the security of a tranquil Oman and achieved this by offering the Sulṭān a package of financial and military support in return for his offer of facilities within Oman, such as the use of airfields at Ṣalāla, al-Maṣīra Island and Ra's al-Ḥadd. British commitments were to relinquish wartime facilities at the end of the war, to ensure a steady supply of foodstuffs from India to Muscat, to seek the Sulṭān's approval before entering into correspondence with tribal leaders, to pay a war subsidy of Rs. 20,000 per month as well as an initial Rs. 50,000 for the repair of fortifications, and to provide various military supplies, when available, such as lorries, rifles, machine guns, cannon and ammunition.[65] Major A. O. C. Pettyfer was brought in as Military Adviser and the Infantry was regrouped into a headquarters company and two rifle companies, increased in size to 355 men, a training camp organised and facilities at Bayt al-Falaj improved.[66] But the interior remained quiet throughout the war and its only direct effects on Muscat were the shortage in rice and the torpedoing of a Norwegian freighter in Muscat harbour.[67] With the abandonment of the war subsidy, the Muscat Infantry was reduced in size and capability. The British Officer/Commandant was retained but his duties dealt with foreign affairs in addition to the military.

But the emerging demands of a changing twentieth century would not leave the Sultanate alone and the need arose for greater strength.[68] The armed Saudi occupation of al-Buraymī oasis in 1952 pointed up the need for something more than a garrison force. Consequently, the Batinah Force, with headquarters at Ṣuḥār, was hurriedly organised that same year.[69] The creation of a third unit was also due to impetus from outside: the Sultanate's petroleum concession holder, Petroleum Development (Oman) Ltd (PDO), had been making plans to renew exploration deep in the interior and consequently required escort protection. With this in mind, PDO funds enabled the raising of the Muscat and Oman Field Force (MOFF) near Ṣuḥār in 1953. The major criterion used in the assembly of this force was to reach the minimal number of 400 men—when this happened, the MOFF, under the command of Lt. Col. Percy Coriat, was whisked off to al-Duqm, on the Gulf of al-Maṣīra, in early 1954 and from there accompanied the PDO expedition to Jabal Fahūd. A MOFF detachment travelled on from Fahūd to 'Ibrī, against Sa'īd's direct orders, where it captured the town in the name of the Sulṭān and expelled the wālī of Imām Ghālib bin 'Alī.

Following the expulsion of the Saudis from al-Buraymī in 1955, the MOFF took charge of the capture of Nizwā that December and a permanent camp was established at nearby Firq. But the fact that the MOFF had been sent into the field without proper training was to prove disastrous when Ghālib and his supporters rose in rebellion in June and July of 1957. The MOFF's attempt to lay siege to Ghālib bin 'Alī's village of Bilād Sayt not only proved unsuccessful but the force's subsequent retreat to Firq was turned into a rout when Banī Riyām snipers appeared. As a result, the totally demoralised MOFF had to be withdrawn from the field to Fahūd and then disbanded, with part of its troops going to the new Northern Frontier Regiment (NFR).

As of 1955 Sa'īd bin Taymūr possessed three separate military forces in need of some co-ordination. This he accomplished by the creation of an administrative headquarters at Bayt al-Falaj in 1955 with Col. P. R. M. Waterfield, formerly the Commandant of the Muscat Infantry, as Administrative Commandant.[70] A training centre was established at the same time at nearby al-Ghalla. In March 1957, the forces were all designated regiments: Muscat Infantry became Muscat Regiment; Batinah Force became Frontier Regiment; and Muscat and Oman Field Force became the short-lived Oman Regiment. The next major step was the consolidation of these loosely-organised groups into the Sultan's Armed Forces (SAF) in 1958.[71] This reorganisation was made possible by the military assistance and subsidy granted by the British government according to an exchange of letters with the Sulṭān in August. Col. David deC. Smiley, a British Army officer, was seconded as Commander of SAF and Col. Colin Maxwell, a contract officer, was appointed Deputy Commander. Waterfield, meanwhile, became Military Secretary and the head of the newly-created Defence Department; as such he served as liaison and a channel of communication between SAF and the Sulṭān. He continued to hold the post until retirement in early 1970 when the post went to a former SAF commander, Col. Hugh Oldman.

The 1958 agreement with the British allowed a steady expansion of the military, and their commitment was reaffirmed as a result of a report submitted in 1960 by War Office representative, Brig. M. R. J. Hope-Thomson. The first product of this expansion was the Oman Gendarmerie, established in mid-1959 with headquarters first at Ṣuḥār, then at al-'Adhayba (Azaiba) and finally at al-Sīb. Originally, it was conceived of as a sort of rural police with the responsibility of patrolling the northern borders of the Sultanate but was later reconstituted as a regular regiment. Soon afterwards, the Sulṭān of Oman's Air Force (SOAF) was created with a nucleus of three Provost T52 and two Pioneer aircraft. The increasing size of SAF and the gradual appearance of guerrilla war in Dhufar requiring air support meant a steady growth in SOAF's size and sophistication. Another addition was the Sulṭān of Oman's Navy (SON), begun with a motorised dhow. SAF expansion included another group, the Desert Regiment, which was raised in 1965–6 with headquarters at Bidbid.

By the summer of 1965, it had become obvious that a serious rebellion existed in Dhufar. Sa'īd bin Taymūr had earlier entrusted St John Armitage with the formation of the Dhofar Force in 1955, using principally *Jibālī* (i.e. Qarā) soldiers in a regiment that was kept completely independent from SAF. However, it had proven inadequate to meet the guerrilla challenge as it developed, and as early as May 1965, SAF units—principally from the Muscat and NFR regiments—were operating in Dhufar. A further doubt as to the effectiveness of the Dhofar Force came on 26 April 1966, when a number of jibālī members of the force attempted to assassinate the Sulṭān during a parade at the Force's headquarters in 'Ayn Arzāt outside Ṣalāla.[72] Eventually the suspect force was absorbed into the new and predominantly Baluchi Southern Regiment of SAF. Another group was formed in 1971 expressly for service in Dhufar: the Frontier Force which originated as Sa'īd's Baluchi counter-balance to his bodyguard of slaves.

Following the *coup d'état* of 1970, SAF continued to increase its ranks and acquire sophisticated materiel. The prevailing ratio of 70 per cent Baluchi rank-and-file to 30 per cent Arab was gradually reversed and the Baluchis were, in addition, concentrated in the Dhufar units (Southern Regiment and Frontier Force). In 1971, the Jabal Regiment was established at Nizwā in order to free the Muscat Regiment for duties in Dhufar. Diversification into more specialised units also marked this period, with the creation of a Training Regiment, with a number of seconded Jordanian officers, an Artillery Regiment, a Signal Regiment, an Armoured Car Squadron, a Garrison detachment and an Engineers' Unit. By the mid-1970s, SAF strength had grown to over 13,000 personnel.[73] This was a direct consequence of the bitter war in Dhufar, which forced military expenditure regularly to consume between 40 per cent and 60 per cent of the Sultanate's budget during this period. SAF's expansion was aided by a number of governments in addition to the British: Pakistani officers and NCOs—mostly retired personnel on private contract—have long been employed, particularly in the Dhofar Force; a few Indian military doctors were seconded in the early stages of the Dhufar Rebellion; Iranian troops and support played an important part in the latter stages of the rebellion; Jordanian officers served in the administrative and training fields and Jordanian aircraft were given to the Sultanate, in addition to the brief loan of Jordanian combat troops in 1975; and the Saudis promised financial support in 1971 and then offered use of their training facilities. By the conclusion of the war in Dhufar in late 1975, Oman possessed a large and efficient military establishment.

Recruitment of Officials

One of the major problems faced by the government of Oman has been procuring qualified personnel. The constraints of service within the Sultanate have been legion and the advantages few. The tribes were generally eliminated as a potential source on grounds of doubtful loyalty and the increasing incapability of the ruling family in general made serious inroads on that traditional source. The employment of expatriates was severely hampered by a number of factors: the unsuitability of Muscat as a place to live for sanitary and climatic reasons, the inability of the state to pay adequate salaries and the necessity of approval by the British establishment ruled out many nationalities. One of the few positive factors was the exotic appeal of living in a generally unknown locale: this was the attraction for Bertram Thomas and only a proviso restricting exploration in the interior prevented Wilfred Thesiger from accepting a post.[74]

The primary source of officials up to 1970 was naturally the ruling family. Two subdivisions, the Āl Sa'īd (i.e. the descendants of Sulṭān Sa'īd bin Sulṭān, r. 1807–56) and the Āl Bū Sa'īd (i.e. variously referring to the tribe and the descendants of Imām Aḥmad bin Sa'īd, r. 1744–83), each played distinct roles within that group. The reservation of positions for the Āl Sa'īd was frequently dictated more by political necessity than the ability of the candidate to fill the functions of his post: uncles, brothers, sons and cousins had to be kept occupied. After the British had implicitly ordained succession by primogeniture along with the designation of heir apparents in the late nineteenth century, there was little reason for the Sulṭāns to doubt the loyalty of close relatives since the family was too fragmented to do other than accept the choice of the Government of India as Sulṭān. There would be little chance of a successful plot. Consequently they occupied important positions and were largely co-opted into the existing framework.[75]

The Āl Bū Sa'īd had always been considered more trustworthy: they were genealogically too far removed to assume power in a palace *coup d'état*, yet stood to gain more by service under the Sulṭān than in opposition to him in alliance with the tribes.[76] Consequently, the Āl Bū Sa'īd tended to fill the lower positions in the hierarchy, such as wālī, and were kept out of the inner circles of authority to prevent their amassing enough political power from force of personality to jeopardise the Sulṭān. This phenomenon is well illustrated by the career of Aḥmad bin Ibrāhīm.

Although a nephew of 'Azzān bin Qays, the last member of the family to challenge successfully the ruling dynasty, at least temporarily, Aḥmad could be trusted not to appeal to the interior tribes for support since they had driven him out of al-Rustāq in 1917. On the other hand, his loyalty to the Sulṭān had been proven by two decades of service as wālī in the Bāṭina, although there were suspicions of his involvement in disturbances at Ṣūr in 1928.[77] When he was appointed Minister of the Interior in 1939—thereby becoming one of the two or three most powerful individuals in Muscat after the Sulṭān—his loyalty was more or less assured. Nevertheless, as discussed above, the Sulṭān was careful to keep him under control by dividing his responsibilities with Shihāb bin Fayṣal, Ismā'īl bin Khalīl al-Raṣāṣī and, in the late 1960s, J. D. Shebbeare. This system of checks and balances assured that no intriguer had control over all the necessary government/family apparatus needed to supplant the Sulṭān, as well as ensuring that the work of incompetent officials was also covered by more competent ones working in overlapping fields. The remarkable part of this intricate balance-of-power system in Muscat was the manner in which it was orchestrated, in combination with the balance of tribal power in the interior, by a Sulṭān who never left Ṣalāla, except for visits to London, for the last twelve years of his reign.

Throughout the half century from 1920 to 1970 the British Government was a major source of personnel, either directly or indirectly. In the 1920s, the Government of India arranged for British 'advisers' and Egyptian customs officials in addition to successive Commandants of the Muscat Levy Corps, both British and Indian, along with NCOs. In the 1950s and 1960s, the Foreign and Commonwealth Office was instrumental in arranging for the British 'secretaries' and was the go-between in acquiring directors of audit, customs, public works and health from India and Pakistan. The expansion of the military in the mid-1950s and after owed much to Britain and to Pakistan for equipment and financial assistance, as well as the more obvious aspect of seconded and contract officers.

Another prominent source, if only because of the small size of the total government, was the odd individual who somehow managed to work his way into the confidence of the Sulṭān. One of these was Sulaymān al-Bārūnī al-Nafūsī, a Libyan Ibāḍī author, ex-member of the Ottoman Senate and a friend of King Fayṣal of Iraq. Al-Bārūnī originally came to Oman as financial supervisor for the Imamate and later became the Sulṭān's 'adviser on internal affairs', a largely honorific position.[78] Other examples are Ismā'īl bin Khalīl al-Raṣāṣī and Malik Duli Chand. Originally recruited from Palestine in 1928 by Bertram Thomas as a school-teacher, al-Raṣāṣī stayed on after the school was closed and over the next half-century served in such positions as wālī of Maṭraḥ, president of the appeals court, inspector of al-Bāṭina wālīs, director of passports, chairman of the Muscat/Maṭraḥ municipal council, director of education, director of the Development and Planning Board and, finally, Oman's first ambassador to Iran. For many years the lone Palestinian in Oman, he was later joined by a small number of fellow Palestinians, who were also recruited as school-teachers in the 1960s. The Indian, R. S. Malik Duli Chand, Director of Customs when Sa'īd bin Taymūr became Sulṭān, wielded a considerable amount of influence ranging far beyond customs and succeeded in arousing the ire of successive PAMs who perceived him as being distinctly anti-British, an opinion also assessed of al-Raṣāṣī. His character was sullied when he left Muscat quite abruptly in March 1939.[79]

The sources of military personnel differed markedly from the civilian. The forerunners of the Muscat Levy Corps had been composed of mercenary troops, mostly Ḥaḍramīs (i.e. from the

Ḥaḍramawt), Muwaḥḥidūn (Wahhābīs) from al-Aḥsā' (Hasa), and an occasional Turk who served the Sulṭān after desertion from the Ottoman army in Yemen. The majority of the MLC and SAF personnel were Baluchis from either the Bāṭina or the Makrān—even though Baluchis rarely entered civilian government service. Following the events of 1970, the composition of the Sultanate's military forces—like those of the civilian administration—changed drastically. Indeed, the civilian field was marked by the emergence of high-level government officials on non-ascriptive terms.[80]

Local Government

Even though the government in Muscat was anything but extensive during the period under review, there did exist a somewhat fragile organisation for local administration. Wālīs were posted in nearly every village of consequence and each wālī was generally assisted by a qāḍī. There were several criteria for the selection of wālīs, depending on how important the village was and the status of the tribes inhabiting and surrounding it. Although wālīs, particularly those from the ruling family, were frequently transferred from one wilāya to another, they constituted a recognisable corps of 'professional civil servants' who made being a wālī a career. Most of these were members of the Āl Bū Sa'īd family; in general, the larger the town the more closely related to the Sulṭān was the wālī. For example, Muscat and Ṣuḥār always had as wālīs members of the Sulṭān's immediate family, either an uncle or a brother. But a wālī could also be chosen from an important tribe, such as the sons of Zāhir bin Ghuṣn al-Hinā'ī, who served Sa'īd bin Taymūr in Samā'il, and al-Sharqīya, or 'Alī bin 'Abd Allāh al-Khalīlī, the wālī of Bawshar during the time his brother Muḥammad was Imām. Other wālīs could come from outside the traditional paths, either as expatriates, in the manner of al-Raṣāṣī, or as slaves, such as Sulaymān bin Suwaylim, the wālī of Dhufar under both Turkī bin Sa'īd and Fayṣal bin Turkī. Furthermore, although wālīs frequently were shifted from place to place, the positions of some became almost hereditary, as in the case of al-Rustāq where the descendants of Imām 'Azzān bin Qays retained control until 1917; or Bawshar, where Hilāl bin 'Alī al-Khalīlī automatically succeeded his father as wālī. Some of the more trustworthy wālīs were the products of generations of dependable service, a good example being the Sammār branch of the Āl Bū Sa'īd: the tradition being handed down from the grandfather, Hilāl bin Ḥamad, to the father, Ḥamad bin Hilāl, to the son, Hilāl bin Ḥamad, who also became Minister of Justice in the 1970s. Another example is that of the above-mentioned Sulaymān bin Suwaylim who was often employed as a trouble-shooter in northern Oman until his assassination in 1907. His son Muẓaffar was thereafter wālī in various towns along the Bāṭina as was the grandson, ʻAlī bin Muẓaffar.

Since the extent of territory which the Sultanate actively controlled has fluctuated greatly over the last century, the number of wilāyas has also fluctuated. Generally speaking, the appointment of wālīs up to 1955 was limited to Muscat and its hinterlands, the Bāṭina coast, Khaṣab, Ṣūr, Gwadar and Ṣalāla. The last location, however, was a special case since the Sulṭān was often in residence there and took a special interest in local affairs. Furthermore, the wālī there has been more in the tradition of a provincial governor since he was responsible for all the province (*minṭaqa*) of Dhufar. After the reassertion of authority over interior Oman, wālīs were posted to various towns in the Ḥajar, Ẓāhira and Oman provinces and were subject to the control of Aḥmad bin Ibrāhīm, the Minister of the Interior, whereas Bāṭina wālīs were subordinates of al-Raṣāṣī. Deputy (*nā'ib*) wālīs were attached to Nizwā wilāya to administer the Banī Riyām settlements of Sayq and Birkat al-Mawz and deputy wālīs were later introduced in outlying areas of Dhufar.

Despite the numerical increase in wilāyas in the mid-1950s, several areas of the Sultanate, such as al-Sharqīya province and part of the Ru'ūs al-Jibāl region, were not incorporated into the wilāya system until 1970, and of course, the wilāya of Gwadar ceased to be a concern of the state after 1958. Wālīs of this period were often underpaid, corrupt, incompetent and/or uninterested. A report in 1934 by the Muscat Political Agency is typical:

> . . . most of the walis have no influence at all unless it be entirely due to their personality. They have to keep in with both sides—i.e., placate His Highness and to keep in with the local people. Their offences are rarely punished, justice is seldom done and many prohibited practices are carried on with the knowledge of the Wali.[81]

Government on the local level, however, was a dual system. The wālī served as the Sulṭān's representative and was responsible for a geographical area, generally the village. Depending on which village, the wālī may have served as adjudicator in local disputes or he may have been secure enough in his position to exercise absolute jurisdiction over the area. Furthermore, since the wālī was rarely appointed to the area in which he lived, he was theoretically considered impartial in his dealings between various tribes.

But in contrast to the wālī was the institution of the shaykh. Representative of a tribe, the latter's authority flowed up from the people and not down from the Sulṭān—although the Sulṭān did appoint the shaykhs of some tribes on occasion. The shaykh's jurisdiction consisted of the tribe, or a group of people without regard to their location and therefore not necessarily a physical area. For example, although settled tribes occupied well-defined areas, badū dīras (territories) were frequently modified over time, expanding or contracting as tribal influence grew or declined. Theoretically, the shaykh was chosen by members of his tribe but frequently became hereditary in practice.

The wālī, as the Sulṭān's representative, was the proper intermediary between the people and Muscat, *via* either Aḥmad bin Ibrāhīm or al-Raṣāṣī—after 1958, these officials would act independently on minor problems and pass more serious requests or grievances on to the Sulṭān in Ṣalāla. But this link could be short-circuited *via* the tribal shaykh and frequently if a tribe felt that its case in a dispute had been unsatisfactorily dealt with by the wālī, the shaykh would go to Muscat to seek personal action by either Aḥmad bin Ibrāhīm or al-Raṣāṣī. If the shaykh was important enough or determined enough, he could also travel overland to Ṣalāla to seek redress from the Sulṭān in person. The decline in importance and influence of the tribe after 1957 as a result of the active presence of the Sulṭān's authority in the interior, backed up by SAF, meant a corresponding decline in the role of the shaykh. The authority of most shaykhs became strictly limited to intra-tribal affairs and, after 1970, that final bastion of authority became increasingly eroded as well. Most of the shaykhs to escape the effect were of the badū tribes and even there change slowly transformed authority patterns.

Imamate and Sultanate

It is debatable whether the Imamate of the twentieth century should be considered a proper government in the same sense as the Sultanate. Unlike the Imamate of the centuries up to 1793, the twentieth-century institution was largely an instrument of legitimation for the exercise of tribal politics by a handful of powerful tamīmas. While it can be argued that an 'Imamate' existed as a political entity in a restricted sense, it is more difficult to claim similar political status for the Imām. His position originally sprang from his religious and spiritual authority, and under the classical Imamates, he was the absolute temporal leader as well, although subject to the continued approval of the Ibāḍī population. But his position in the revivals of the Imamate of the nineteenth and twentieth centuries owed much to the appearance of the Imām as a symbol to rally the tribes behind a few powerful tamīmas in opposition to the Sulṭān. The Imāms elected in 1868, 1913 and 1920 were chosen by a coalition of Ghāfirī and Hināwī tribal leaders who, at least initially, dominated the rebel movements. The Imām of 1954, however, failed to gain allegiance even from most tribes loyal to the previous Imām. These Imāms were chosen primarily for their religious stature and not for political ability, although some displayed such ability after taking office. Conversely, some were woefully inadequate to the political demands of the office, as witness the assassination of the Imām in 1920 and the expulsion of the Imām from Nizwā in 1955 with the subsequent unrest arising from his activities.

In the political realm, the authority of the Imām was limited to mediation between tribes—a responsibility also assumed by the Sulṭān. The affairs of the more important tribes were definitely outside his jurisdiction and any major political or military activities were subject to the approval and support of the leading tamīmas. By way of illustration, the independent expedition of Imām Muḥammad bin 'Abd Allāh al-Khalīlī against al-Ẓāhira province in 1925 turned into a fiasco when the leader of the Ghāfirī tribal confederation voiced his disapproval. Furthermore, the concept of a standing army went against Ibāḍī principles.[82] Indeed, the tribes were generally on their own and the Imām's function remained restricted to religious and judicial affairs except when disputes arose or when threats materialised from outside, such as the Saudi movement into al-Buraymī in 1952.

The 'capital' of the Imamate was wherever the Imām happened to be, since central administration usually consisted of no more than the Imām, his scribe and his chief assistant/qāḍī. Under Muḥammad bin 'Abd Allāh al-Khalīlī, the latter position was first filled by 'Āmir bin Khamīs al-Mālikī, who died in 1928, and then by Manṣūr bin Nāṣir al-Fārisī.[83] In the mid-1920s, a counterpart to the Sulṭān's Council of Ministers was established, consisting of

Sulaymān al-Bārūnī as head, Sa'īd bin Nāṣir al-Kindī, 'Āmir bin Khamīs al-Mālikī, then wālī of Nizwā, and Mājid bin Khamīs al-'Ibrī.[84] Al-Bārūnī served as financial director with the assistance of Muḥammad bin 'Īsā al-Ḥārithī until 1928 when dissatisfaction with his zeal reached a crescendo and he prudently left for Muscat.[85] Another of the Imām al-Khalīlī's advisers during the latter part of his Imamate was the director of *bayt al-māl* (public treasury), Ghālib bin 'Alī al-Hinā'ī, who was to succeed him as Imām.

A nebulous form of local administration also existed in the form of wālīs appointed by the Imām. Serving in more or less the same capacity as those of the Sulṭān, these wālīs were appointed for towns within the area defined as the Imamate, i.e. the territory enclosed by the individual dīras of tribes which considered themselves loyal to the Imām. Wālīs of the Imām were chosen from these tribes but with the same criteria as the Sulṭāns': they served in areas away from their tribe to minimise partiality and their authority over tribal shaykhs suffered from the same or even greater limitations. As was the case in the Sultanate's wilāyas, each wālī was assisted by a qāḍī.

Although the Imamate disappeared in 1955, the foundations of the Sultanate's administration, so haphazardly laid over the course of the twentieth century, remained. Although clearly inefficient and frequently ineffectual, the various officials and agencies in Muscat and the countryside represented the first faltering steps of the Sultanate towards meeting the challenge of the twentieth century. Being political innovations largely without concomitant social, economic and educational transformation, these hesitant attempts were for the most part doomed to an insulated existence alongside the traditional Omani way of life until they became the major building blocks of the post-1970 society.

Notes

1. Robert G. Landen, *Oman Since 1856: Disruptive Modernization in a Traditional Arab Society* (Princeton: Princeton University Press, 1967), p. 289.
2. Ibid., pp. 343–4.
3. *Lorimer's Gazetteer*, vol. 1, pt. 1, p. 502. Lorimer states that the only thing preventing 'Abd al-'Azīz from declaring himself Sulṭān was probable non-recognition by the Government of India.
4. Sa'īd bin Khalfān was killed with the fall of the Imamate but Ṣāliḥ bin 'Alī returned to Muscat later briefly to direct municipal affairs during the regency of 'Abd al-'Azīz.
5. IO, R/15/3/1; Acting PAM Atkinson to PRPG Pelly, 6 May 1867.
6. *Lorimer's Gazetteer*, vol. 1, pt. 1, p. 511.

7. Al-Zawāwī was later to build one of the principal Sunnī mosques of Muscat. His son 'Abd al-Mun'im served as purchasing agent for the Sultanate in Karachi and his grandson Qays became Minister of State for Foreign Affairs under Sulṭān Qābūs bin Sa'īd.

8. IO, R/15/3/253; Muscat News, No. 1008 for the week ending 11 Oct. 1913.

9. IO, R/15/3/253; PAM to PRPG, Telegram P, No. 215, 11 Dec. 1913.

10. IO, R/15/3/66; Submitted with Benn to PRPG Knox, No. 145, 27 June 1914.

11. The PAM submitted a concise report on the new force: 'His Highness seems to be extraordinarily keen at present on his "troops", which consist mostly of about 50 young Sidi and Baluch boys. They have been fitted out with quite serviceable looking uniforms and accoutrements and are almost "smart". They have done a great deal of musketry practice and ordinary drill under Fuwad, the Turkish instructor, and handle the machine guns fairly well. Whether they can hit a mark or not I do not know.

All this is costing H.H. a considerable amount of money which may perhaps bring him in some return in the future in the shape of greater security—theoretically, if not practically!

His latest innovations are a Police Force under a Turk, Ali Effendi (H.H. calls him a Bagdadi Arab), and a brass band of 22 men. The latter are being trained by a Goan Bandmaster imported from Bombay and are still in the most embryo stage. I am glad to say a place at the opposite end of Muscat has been selected for their practice.' IO, R/15/3/43; Benn to PRPG Knox, Demi-official no., 15 Dec. 1914.

12. IO, R/15/1/417; Memorandum from Wingate to McCollum on his arrival as wazīr, 20 April 1920. McCollum left that same autumn.

13. Ibid.

14. Taymūr wrote that his health required him to live in India and that the Council of Ministers was being formed to conduct his government except in regard to certain matters, *i.e.* he retained ultimate authority. IO, R/15/3/29; Sulṭān Taymūr bin Fayṣal Āl Sa'īd to Sayyid Muḥammad bin Aḥmad al-Ghashshām, 8 Sept. 1920.

15. Zubayr's son, Muḥammad bin Zubayr, subsequently became Minister of Trade and Industry under Sulṭān Qābūs. The tolerant nature of Omani society is here illustrated by the inclusion of a Baluchi and a Baysarī, Rāshid bin 'Uzayyiz, on the state's highest official body.

16. An indication of its quality is shown in the Annual Muscat Administration Report for 1923: 'It functions with delatoriness [sic] and during the absence of His Highness to Dhofar found a new excuse for procrastination by reserving decisions in important matters pending his return. Saiyid Nadir the President when remonstrated with averred that it was impossible for the Council to arrive at a unanimous decision as the second member, the Member for Finance, invariably opposed any suggestion he made and the third member, the Minister of Justice, not being an Arab is treated by the other three as a nonentity, but has to be tolerated by them as he is the only one who can read or write.' IO, R/15/3/337.

17. 'The Council meets twice a week, on Mondays and Thursdays. At the meetings all political matters and other affairs of importance are discussed and decided. The ministers continue throughout to carry out their own specific duties, and within certain roughly defined and understood limits are fully responsible in their own spheres. The fact that any extraordinary or unauthorized action by them will at once be known and will be liable to be discussed and possibly reversed by the Council is sufficient check against the abuse of their separate authorities.

The President has no more power than the other ministers. His chief function is to represent the Sultan on all official occasions. In addition he has been entrusted by the Council with the authority to sign all passports and permits for travellers and dhows.

The appointment of a member of the Royal family as President was necessary in order to retain the prestige of the family in Muscat. It cannot be said that Saiyid Nadir possesses any great qualifications but he is the best the family can do, and under the late regime he had not been treated very well. The personalities of the members of the Council very largely curtail any powers for evil that he may have.

The Council acts as a court of appeal in the place of the Sultan in the few instances when appeals are made.' IO, R/15/1/417; Wingate to PRPG Trevor, No. 2091, 15 Oct. 1920.

18. Nādir resigned in 1926 in a huff and never again held an official position; Muḥammad bin Aḥmad died in August 1928 and his position was subsequently filled by Sa'īd bin Taymūr; Zubayr bin 'Alī finally retired in 1936 and served the Sulṭān in Dhufar as part-time wālī and director of his building projects—he also married there and his son Muḥammad is half Dhufari.

19. For a more detailed account of the impact of these two individuals on the Sultanate, see Chapter 5.

20. IO, R/15/3/54; PAM Fowle to Secretary to PRPG, No. 200, 24 Feb. 1932.

21. Much of the detailed information given in this section on various officials of the Sultanate up to the end of World War II has been collected from issues of the fortnightly Muscat Intelligence Diaries, scattered throughout the Foreign Office and India Office, particularly Muscat Agency (R/15/3), records. Mohammed Lisanul Haq was extremely helpful for the period 1958–70 while treatment of the years between these two periods relies principally on interviews with various Omanis and expatriates in Muscat.

22. Customs at Gwadar, however, continued to be farmed out until much later.

23. Wingate reported in 1920 that customs revenue from these outlying ports never reached Muscat and that bribery and smuggling were rampant. IO, R/15/416; Wingate to Civil Commissioner in Baghdad, No. 25, 3 Jan. 1920. For more information on the Banī Bū 'Alī, see the following chapter.

24. IO, R/15/3/199; PAM Howes to PRPG, No. C/78, 19 Jan. 1942.

25. K. B. Maqbul Husayn, Martin G. Wynne and F. C. L. Chauncy all acted as Secretary at times and an Indian official, M. G. Mohieuddin, presided over a tiny staff of four or five throughout this period. Interview in 1975 with a long-time official of the Department of Foreign Affairs.

26. These included an abortive attempt to join the Food and Agricultural Organisation (FAO) in the late 1940s and another attempt in 1962 to join the World Health Organisation (WHO): Ismā'īl bin Khalīl al-Raṣāṣī was even sent to Geneva as an observer but Arab League lobbying prevented Omani membership. Interview with ibid. Another abortive initiative came in 1967 when Sa'īd announced that he was sending an application for membership to OPEC but nothing seems to have come of it. *The Times*, 3 Oct. 1967.

27. See *The Times*, 5 Apr. 1968.

28. UN General Assembly, 19th Session, 22 Jan. 1965, *Question of Oman; Report of the Ad Hoc Committee on Oman*, A/5846 (the Jiménez Report), p. 172.

29. These British extra-territorial rights were gradually disposed of, beginning with the Anglo–Sultanate treaty of 1951. For more information on the Orders-in-Council and the exercise of extra-territorial rights, see Chapter 5.

30. IO, R/15/3/337; Annual Muscat Administration Reports for 1913 and 1919. Some of Taymūr's other brothers, Ḥamad, Ḥamūd and his son Mājid, intermittently acted in the same capacity.

31. IO, R/15/1/417; Wingate to Deputy PRPG Trevor, No. 815, 16 Apr. 1920.

32. This was probably because most merchants were British subjects and thus came under the PAM's jurisdiction.

33. It may be possible that subsequent references to qāḍīs of an appeals court in Muscat, who were distinct from the chief qāḍīs, may have dealt with civil cases. For example, when chief qāḍī Sayf bin Ḥamad al-Aghbarī died in 1945, he was replaced by Ibrāhīm bin Sa'īd al-'Ibrī, the qāḍī of the appeals court (Ibrāhīm subsequently became Oman's first *muftī* in 1971). Al-Raṣāṣī continued to hear appeals until 1970 as one of his many duties.

34. IO, R/15/3/253; PRPG to Secretary of State for India, Telegram Q, No. 1024, 26 Oct. 1937; and R/15/3/338; Annual Muscat Administration Reports for the years 1936–41.

35. For example, new drainage ditches were built along with a vegetable market in Muscat which is still standing and a fish market in Maṭraḥ, likewise still in operation.

36. A retired Indian policeman was first engaged as chief. However, he proved unsuitable and responsibility for police functions and discipline was thereupon split between the Military Adviser and the Minister for External Affairs. IO, R/15/3/338; Annual Muscat Administration Report for 1940.

37. Ibid.; Annual Muscat Administration Report for 1941.

38. IO, R/15/3/357; Muscat Diary for 1–15 Sept. 1939.

39. The capital at that time consisted of little more than Muscat and so complemented the wilāya of Maṭraḥ: the two boundaries met at the village of Riyām. Sa'īd's purpose in creating the additional post of governor for Shihāb may have been meant in part as a counterbalance to Ismā'īl bin Khalīl al-Raṣāṣī, since the wālī of Maṭraḥ and Shihāb had never gotten along.

40. Boustead describes his Omani experiences in his book, *The Wind of Morning*, pp. 219–26. For the background of this British subsidy, see Chapter 5.

41. Interview with D. N. R. Ogram, Muscat, 21 Dec. 1974.

42. Interviews with Mohammed Lisanul Haq, Muscat, Dec. 1974; and the 'Jiménez Report', p. 175. The GPO had itself replaced the Indian post office which had established a branch at Muscat in 1864. See *Lorimer's Gazetteer*, vol. 1, pt. 2, pp. 2448–9.

43. For complete text, see John Townsend, *Oman: The Making of a Modern State* (London: Croom Helm, 1977), pp. 192–8.

44. Early roles in this process were played by Sir Gawain Bell, who produced an apparently moribund development survey, and John Harris, whose architectural firm has long been active in the Gulf region. Interviews with Lisanul Haq and others involved with development in that period, Dec. 1974 and Jan. 1975.

45. In essence, the distinction was first made by Sa'īd bin Taymūr. Following his abdication in 1970, he sent a request to Muscat for the return of his property to him in London and carefully distinguished in his note between his and the state's property. Interview with Sultanate official in Muscat, Jan. 1975.

46. According to the Sultanate's financial position of 1 January 1940, total reserves were more than three lakhs and the state's last debts, to K. B. Nasib and Sons, had been paid off. As of 12 December 1946, the state showed assets of Rs. 46,94,208/– and MT$ 2,86,000. This was divided among War Loans of Rs. 20,00,000/–, a Muscat Treasury balance of Rs. 18,37,313/– and MT$ 2,86,000,a Lloyd's Bank (Bombay) balance of Rs.7,29,745/–, a loan to the Government of India of Rs. 92,600/– and Newfoundland stock of Rs. 34,450/–. IO, R/15/3/196.

47. *New York Times*, 9 Sept. 1958. Pakistan had pressed the British Foreign Office for the return of Gwadar by the Sultanate ever since Pakistan's independence. See IO, R/15/3/183.

48. In 1961, the civil subsidy was set at £1,058,750, while the military subsidy was £477,175. *The Times*, 25 March 1961.

49. There were in addition to these sources a number of minor ones, such as

passport fees, landing charges, court fees and postage stamps after 1966. In addition, a tax was levied on all products exported from the interior to Muscat until after 1970. See Skeet, *Muscat and Oman*, pp. 185–91.

50. The British loans and subsidies are covered in greater detail in Chapter 5.

51. The 1931 figure is taken from the budget for that year—see note 55 below. The latter figure is based on a 1975 interview in Muscat with a customs official at that time.

52. Figures according to annual budgets discussed below.

53. Interview with customs official cited above.

54. IO, R/15/3/424; PRPG to Secretary of State for India, Telegram Q, No. 730, 13 July 1937. Two concessions were actually agreed upon: one for Oman and one for Dhufar. Payment for the first was to be one lakh immediately and Rs. 5,000 monthly for the option period. For Dhufar, the arrangement was for an initial sum of Rs. 30,000 plus Rs. 3,000 a month. In the event of the option being taken up, additional lump sums and increasing annual payments were agreed upon. IO, R/15/3/424; PAM Watts, Karachi, to PRPG, Express Letter R-82/10, 5 July 1937. Gwadar was specifically excluded from these concessions and the Sulṭān held unsuccessful negotiations with Burmah Oil Company in 1939 regarding a possible concession there. IO, R/15/3/432–R/15/3/434. Prior to granting the two concessions to PCL, Sa'īd had been attempting to interest Standard Oil of California in the Sultanate, but the firm apparently did not feel that the British would approve of any American concession. See correspondence between Sa'īd and Standard in R/15/3/424.

55. Details of the Sultanate's budgets for this period are given in Appendix G.

56. General Abstract of the Sultanate Budget for 1968, unpublished. The totals for receipts have since disappeared.

57. Landen, *Oman Since 1856*, pp. 355–6.

58. IO, R/15/3/215; PRPG Cox to Foreign Department of the Government of India, Telegram M–15, 14 Oct. 1913; R/15/3/253; PAM Benn to Cox, Telegram 215, 11 Dec. 1913; R/15/3/66; Benn to PRPG Knox, No. 145, 27 June 1914; R/15/3/66; Sir Henry McMahon, Foreign Secretary of the Government of India, to Knox, No. 1292–D, 12 March 1914.

59. IO, R/15/3/48; Haworth to Deputy PRPG, No. 37–C, 24 Apr. 1918.

60. See IO, R/15/1/437.

61. For a complete list of Commandants, see Appendix C.

62. See the following chapter for Hedgcock's allegations.

63. Alban's criticism is contained in IO, R/15/1/429; Alban to PRPG, No. C–202, 15 Sept. 1931. Later comment on Alban's term as Commandant is contained in IO, R/15/1/454; PAM Bremner to PRPG Fowle, No. 248–C, 26 Dec. 1933.

64. Government of India, General Staff, *Military Report and Route Book: The Arabian States of the Persian Gulf, 1939* (New Delhi: Government Printing, 1940), pp. 216–18.

65. FO, 371/24545 for 1940, Arabia E635/509/91; PAM Hickinbotham to Sulṭān Sa'īd bin Taymūr, No. C/514, 13 Feb. 1940.

66. IO, R/15/3/338; Annual Muscat Administration Report for 1940.

67. Reports on this event are contained in IO, R/15/3/451 through R/15/3/453.

68. The remainder of this section is largely based on Colin C. Maxwell, *Short History of the Sultan's Armed Forces* (mimeographed, Bayt al-Falaj, Oman, Nov. 1969), and interviews with members of SAF prominent during much of this period.

69. The first commander was Colin C. Maxwell who was to serve in a number of positions for the Sultanate in the course of the next quarter century.

70. Waterfield owed his appointment as Commandant of the Muscat Infantry in 1953 to a chance encounter with Neil Innes at the latter's farewell party in England. When Innes arrived in Muscat, he mentioned Waterfield to the Sulṭān as a suitable Commandant. Interview with Innes, Uplyme, Dorset, 17 Apr. 1975.

71. In Arabic, Quwāt al-Sulṭān al-Musallaḥa.

72. For a fuller account of this attempt, see Chapter 7.

73. By way of comparison, SAF's strength was reported to be 2,333 in the early 1960s. UN General Assembly, 18th Session, 8 Oct. 1963, *Report of the Special Representative of the Secretary-General on his Visit to Oman*, A/5562 (the 'de Ribbing Report'), Annex 8.

74. Thesiger was offered the position of Minister of External Affairs in 1948 but turned it down since he would have been expected to remain in Muscat. Letter from Wilfred Thesiger to the author, 6 June 1975.

75. This phenomenon seemed to reverse itself during the latter part of Sa'īd bin Taymūr's reign. He tended to refuse to trust the most qualified of his relatives, such as Ṭāriq bin Taymūr, Fahd bin Taymūr and even his own son Qābūs, and so was forced to rule with the aid of less-qualified family members and eventually with non-Omanis.

76. The one major exception to this generalisation was the cadet branch of the Āl Bū Sa'īd, descended from 'Azzān bin Qays bin Imām Aḥmad bin Sa'īd, at al-Rustāq which saw 'Azzān bin Qays, grandson of the above 'Azzān, erect the 1868–71 Imamate in Muscat with tribal backing.

77. In a report on the problem in Ṣūr in 1928, the PAM, G. P. Murphy, mentioned the probable involvement of Aḥmad bin Ibrāhīm and stated that 'Last July he obtained a passport from the Council of Ministers for the ostensible purpose of proceeding to Bahrain for medical treatment . . . It appears that instead of obtaining medical treatment at Bahrain, he has gone to Nejd to visit Ibn Saud.

It would seem that he is either the head or the catspaw of the present movement.' R/15/3/65; Murphy to PRPG, No. 128, 29 Oct. 1928. Murphy also quotes 'Īsā bin Ṣāliḥ al-Ḥārithī as saying, 'As you know, Saiyid Ahmad went to Nejd with a view to instigate King Ibn Saud. We are afraid that his going there might lead to some disturbances! ' Ibid.

78. More information on the pre-Oman period of Sulaymān al-Bārūnī's life is to be found in Laura Veccia Vaglieri, 'Sulaymān al-Bārūnī, *Encyclopedia of Islam*, 2nd edn, vol. 1, pp. 1070–1; and Veccia Vaglieri, 'Il tripolitano ibadita Suleiman el-Baruni e sue notizie sull''Oman', *Oriente Moderno*, vol. 14, no. 8 (Aug. 1934), pp. 392–6.

79. The British maintained that he absconded with funds entrusted to him and apparently a warrant was issued for his arrest in India. Another story is that he left due to trouble over another man's wife, which would tend to be substantiated by the fact that he visited Muscat the following year without any problems. A lengthy account of alleged extortion, intrigues and nepotism on his part is contained in IO, R/15/1/454; PAM Bremner to PRPG, No. C/26, 15 Jan. 1935.

80. Post-1970 recruitment of officials is discussed in Chapter 8.

81. IO, R/15/1/424; report on Bāṭina tour by Mirza Ismail Barduli of the Political Agency, contained as enclosure to letter of PAM Bremner to PRPG, No. C/298, 17 Dec. 1934.

82. 'Since it is the absolute obligation of every true Muslim to support the just Imām and render aid against the community's enemies, the Imām has no need for a standing army; indeed he may not have such a force under his command for that way lies the slippery path to despotic power [*sulṭān al-jawr*].' J. C. Wilkinson, 'The Ibādī Imāma', *BSOAS*, vol. 39, pt. 3 (1976), p. 536. Wilkinson

mentions in a note that 'The association of these two words in Ibāḍī doctrine explains why the Āl Bū Sa'īd sultans were reluctant to adopt this title by which the British designated them in official correspondence' (p. 548, n. 5).

83. A sympathetic description of the Imamate of Muḥammad bin 'Abd Allāh al-Khalīlī is contained in the Arabian American Oil Company, *Oman and the Southern Shore of the Persian Gulf* (Cairo: Aramco, 1952), pp. 70–4 and 87–8.

84. IO, R/15/3/337; Annual Muscat Administration Report for 1927. The council was known in Arabic as Hay'at Kibār al-'Ulamā' wa-al-Ru'asā'. See Muḥammad bin 'Abd Allāh al-Sālimī, *Nahḍat al-A'yān bi-Ḥurrīyat Ahl 'Umān* (Cairo: Dār al-Kitāb al-'Arabī, 1380/1961), p. 382.

85. IO, R/15/3/337; Annual Muscat Administration Report for 1928; and al-Sālimī, *Nahḍat al-A'yān*, pp. 379–84.

CHAPTER 4

Tribal Politics

The Traditional System

Tribalism has been a dominant force in Omani politics since the beginning of Arab migrations into the area nearly two millenia ago. Furthermore, despite powerful pressures originating in the eighteenth century and exerted by the Āl Bū Sa'īd dynasty and the spread of the British Empire, the sway that tribal politics held over inner Oman was not seriously upset until 1955 and its definite decline dates only from the events of 1970.

With the notable exception of the last quarter century, the interplay between various shaykhs and muṭawwi's has determined the shape of the political system of the interior since the appearance of Islām in the seventh century AD.[1] Religion has essentially played a supporting role to tribalism, inasmuch as the development of Ibāḍism as a sub-sect of Khārijism owed much to Omanis resident in eighth-century al-Baṣra. The establishment of the Ibāḍī Imamate in Oman was due to a combination of religious factors superimposed on the political organisation of the tribes. Even the provisions for the election and office-holding of the Imām derive their origins from the institution of the tribal shaykh; and since the extent of the shaykh's political authority was generally limited, so the Imām has traditionally resembled a *primus inter pares* in the political arena.[2]

The formalisation of a supra-tribal system under the institution of the Imamate, with all its inherent tendencies towards anarchy and instability, has provided the philosophical basis for the background of much of Omani history.

> This decentralization of physical power has been one of the important factors which has led to the continuation of an active

tribal structure in the sedentary community of Oman and why its leaders have tended to remain in their villages in direct contact with the source of their power. The structure of this society has militated against the development of feudal power within the villages.[3]

In the political sphere, the location of the residence of the Imām, generally at Nizwā or al-Rustāq, has followed practical requirements: only by his physical presence there was the Imām able to retain his power among the tribal units and retain the active support of the shaykhs in such functions as tax collection and military operations. This phenomenon owes a great deal to the historical development of Oman, whereby the interior provinces of Oman proper and the Western Ḥajar (known from Persian times as al-Mazūn) provided the focal point of Arab and tribal opposition to Persian control of the coastline in pre-Islamic times and later Ibāḍī and tribal opposition to Sunnī (primarily 'Abbāsid) control of southeastern Arabia.[4] Since the foundation of the first Imamate in the mid-seventh century, this area has been the core of the Ibāḍī heartland and the ultimate source of resistance to external threats posed by Persians, Portuguese, British, Saudis and, of course, even the Āl Bū Sa'īd.

The creation of the Āl Bū Sa'īd dynasty in the mid-eighteenth century began as a manifestation of a new dynastic cycle of which the history of Ibāḍī Oman is replete.[5] However, the natural demise the dynasty would have suffered according to the usual cycle was prevented by active intervention on the part of the British, as in the defence of Muscat in 1915. Consequently, the process of cyclical regeneration was limited to the interior fastness and was subordinated to a rearguard action against the new and formidable alliance between a coastal-based dynasty and a seemingly omnipotent external force.[6]

In the context of the nineteenth and twentieth centuries, the essentially autonomous tribal regime of the interior was marked by several inter-related characteristics. The assumption of ultimate authority by tribal tamīmas meant the subordination of the recrudescent Imamate to inter-tribal manipulations and alliances.[7] The manner in which tribal alliances were formed, with the object of electing their own candidate as Imām, was dictated by the exigencies of the Ghāfirī-Hināwī dichotomy. These alliances, combined with the sedentary nature of tribal settlement in Oman, have consequently resulted in a highly complex balance-of-power system operating on three levels: the country as a whole, the province and the local arena of the village or wādī.

The Ghāfirī-Hināwī Dichotomy

The dichotomy has its immediate origins in the civil war of the early eighteenth century fought over the succession to the Ya'rubī Imamate.[8] The intervention of the Banī Ghāfir tamīma, Muḥammad bin Nāṣir, widened its scope from simply a dynastic struggle to a country-wide alignment of inter-tribal forces. Muḥammad's success in naming his candidate Imām apparently resulted in rebellion by the Banī Hinā tribe against the Imamate. The escalation of the battle by Muḥammad's attack on allies of the Banī Hinā and the latters' subsequent retaliation against allies of the Banī Ghāfiri was the beginning of the polarisation into Hināwī and Ghāfirī confederations respectively. To some extent, this polarisation has even deeper roots in ethnic and religious cleavages. Ethnically, it has been noted that many of the Hināwī tribes are South Arab (Yamanī or Qaḥṭānī) in origin while the Ghāfirīs tend to be North Arab ('Adnānī or Nizārī). However, much of the explanation for this lies in the nature of the balance-of-power system described below; opposing alignments on North Arab/South Arab lines have their roots in historical rivalries dating from the arrival of North Arab tribes in Oman after the settlement of South Arab tribes there. In the religious sphere, the apparent recruitment of Sunnī tribes by Muḥammad bin Nāṣir al-Ghāfirī against the Hināwī faction seems to have introduced the beginnings of a semi-valid distinction that the Hināwī faction is Ibāḍī and the Ghāfirī is Sunnī. It should be stressed that these distinctions are not rigid since important ethnic and religious anomalies occur across confederation lines.[9]

The prolongation of the formal dichotomy over the last two centuries is largely due to its easy application to the centrifugal political system of the tribal interior. Disparities in tribal size and fighting strength could be ameliorated by the ability of a weak tribe to call for help from its Ghāfirī or Hināwī allies to resist the activities of an aggressive tribe. Conversely, the dichotomy provided a defence against attempts by predominant tribes towards hegemony: any such tribe would find itself opposed by the collective weight of the opposing confederation. It could, of course, call upon its allies but the net effect would be simply to achieve a rough balance between opposing sides. If, however, a tribe were to call for help from other members of its confederation and those tribes failed to respond, the first tribe would have the option of changing sides: that is, a Ghāfirī tribe could become Hināwī or *vice versa.*

As a consequence of these political foundations, the Ghāfirī–Hināwī dichotomy evolved into an intricate series of balance-of-power systems. On a country-wide level, the system has been most obvious in the deliberations for the election of an Imām. No Imām was able to secure election—or what was usually more accurate, no tribal shaykh was able to secure the election of his candidate—unless the leaders of the opposing faction agreed to it. Attempts made in the late nineteenth century to elect Ibrāhīm bin Sa'īd Āl Bū Sa'īd, the nephew of Imām 'Azzān bin Qays (r. 1868–71), failed due to Ibrāhīm's perceived candidacy as a protégé of the Hināwī leader, Ṣāliḥ bin 'Alī al-Ḥārithī. Similarly, Ṣāliḥ's occupation of Muscat in 1895 was seen as a Hināwī activity; his failure to depose the Sulṭān and establish an alternative government was once again due to lack of Ghāfirī support. On the other hand, the elections of Imāms Sālim bin Rāshid al-Kharūṣī in 1913 and Muḥammad bin 'Abd Allāh al-Khalīlī in 1920 succeeded because both factions had agreed on the candidate, even though the first was a protégé of the Ghāfirī leader and the second of the Hināwī leader. The reason why only an Imām could over-ride factional rivalry was due to religious identification: the Imām had become primarily a religious figure and any candidate for the office had to possess the necessary religious qualifications—even to the point of neglecting political criteria to be elected. Even Ghālib bin 'Alī al-Hinā'ī, elected in 1954, possessed the essential religious qualifications, which included long service as a qāḍī in al-Rustāq and Nizwā, followed by administration of the Imamate's *bayt al-māl* (public treasury). Nevertheless, his political credentials were lacking and he proved to be easily manipulated by his brother Ṭālib and the Banī Riyām tamīma, Sulaymān bin Ḥimyar al-Nabhānī.

Even more important than these Ghāfirī–Hināwī interactions on the country-wide level is their effect on the province. This is principally because Omani provinces possess natural limitations and are not artificially created to serve political purposes. Geography, in the form of mountains and deserts, has dictated that the primary focus of political attention has been the immediate area. Wider involvement was discouraged by the considerable amount of time required to inform other areas of events and to assemble conventions of notables or armies. The tribes of one province generally had little to do with tribes of another, even those from their own confederation. Indeed, some of the provinces were so isolated that they were rarely active in Omani politics, as in the case of the Ru'ūs al-Jibāl and Dhufar. Others were geographically vulnerable to outside influences and thus their inhabitants tended to shy away from involvement in Omani tribal politics, as in al-Bāṭina and al-Ẓāhira.

The province was thus in many ways a microcosm of the political system for the country as a whole. The Ghāfirī–Hināwī struggle was therefore replicated on the provincial level: the role of the Imām would frequently be assumed by the tamīma of a dominant tribe, such as the tamīma of the Ḥirth in al-Sharqīya province. The rivalry assured stability in most provinces: neither side commanded enough resources to warrant waging war against the other. It was a rare occasion when local or tribal disputes embroiled an entire province. More often, the threat of partisan response predisposed tribes to settle their disputes through recourse to mediation and acceptance of blood money.

The physical effects of the dichotomy are most readily seen in the settlement patterns of the larger towns and wādīs. These are generally divided into two separate parts: *'alāya* (upper) and *sifāla* (lower), each controlled by one faction. Prominent examples of this development are in Nizwā—where Ghāfirī tribes, such as the Banī Riyām and the Kunūd, dominate al-'alāya and Hināwī tribes, such as the Banī Hinā and the Āl Bū Sa'īd, are found in al-sifāla—and Samā'il, where the settled area of Wādī Samā'il, which is abundantly watered and cultivated, actually consists of two towns separated by approximately five miles, the upper inhabited by the Hināwī Banī Ruwāḥa and the lower largely by the Ghāfirī Siyābīyīn.

The Predominance of the Tamīmas

The key figure in this political system was the tamīma. Although the word is frequently translated as paramount shaykh, the tamīma's function went beyond that of shaykh: he was at the head of a unified tribe and his decisions were binding on members of that tribe. According to some sources, the definition of a tamīma includes the authority to impose the death penalty on tribesmen guilty of wrongdoing. Nevertheless, the institution was limited to a few tightly-knit tribes; there were only a half-dozen tamīmas at any one time.

The ability of some tamīmas to extend their influence beyond the tribe was a direct result of the forcefulness of their personalities. In consequence, the strength of a tribe depended not only on its degree of cohesiveness but on the character of its tamīma—that is, if it was cohesive enough to generate a tamīma in the first place. An illustrative example is that of the Ḥirth whose influence in the twentieth century was far greater than its size would have indicated. Under its last tamīma, Aḥmad bin Muḥammad, the Ḥirth became the most powerful tribe of the interior during the period from 1956 to 1971, despite having been implicated in the revolt of the 1950s. On the other hand, the decline of the Banī Riyām and its regression into a multitude of small sub-tribal units is a direct result of the defection of tamīma Sulaymān bin Ḥimyar al-Nabhānī to Saudi Arabia in 1959.

An important function of the tamīma was serving as guardian of the peace. Just as the Imām had often served as arbiter of tribal disputes at the country-wide level, the tamīma of an important tribe was frequently the arbiter of disputes in his province, as in the case of ʻĪsā bin Ṣāliḥ al-Ḥārithī who skilfully played that role in the chronic Banī Bū ʻAlī–Banī Bū Ḥasan rivalry. The tamīma's personal stature, as well as his ability to call forth an impressive number of fighters, made him the only recognisable figure of authority in an otherwise fragmented interior.[10] In addition, the title of tamīma was frequently hereditary—through the immediate family, if not in a father–son sequence—and the tamīmaships of many tribes tended to support minor dynasties.

When the tamīmas found themselves in agreement, they were often strong enough to threaten the coast. The problem in achieving that degree of unity, however, lay in overcoming the rivalries engendered by either personal ambition or the Ghāfirī–Hināwī rivalry. The only solution to these difficulties was recourse to a supra-tribal religious institution: the Imamate. Elections for the position of Imām were marked by extensive manoeuvring among the leaders of both the Ghāfirī and Hināwī confederations on behalf of their candidates. The trick was not only to secure the election of one's candidate but to have him accepted by the other faction. In practice, this meant that candidates became recognised as Imāms only after the other faction had agreed to co-operate with the first faction: in other words, the principal tamīmas had to reach a prior understanding.

As a consequence, the recent Imāms were very much dominated by the tamīmas in the political realm; their religious supremacy served to help blur the political struggle behind the election. Indeed, any political activity pursued by the Imām was likely to be perceived as partisan. Thus the 1925 attempt by Imām Muḥammad bin 'Abd Allāh to draw 'Ibrī into the fold of the Imamate was seen as a Hināwī action and was thwarted by the gesture of Sulaymān bin Ḥimyar al-Nabhānī, the Ghāfirī leader, who expressed support for the Ghāfirī inhabitants of 'Ibrī, principally the Ya'qūbī tribe.[11] Muḥammad learned his lesson well and his only overtly political activity thereafter was as a neutral arbiter. In this manner, the office of Imām gradually acquired a stature of its own apart from being a figurehead for the tamīmas.

Whereas the tamīmas had originally picked Muḥammad bin 'Abd Allāh, by the 1940s they could no longer dominate him. Even though he had grown old, infirm and nearly blind by the 1950s, his personal reputation and the potential of a political vacuum along Ghāfirī–Hināwī lines prevented any attempt to depose him. As a result, although all the major tribal leaders had participated in discussions with Sulṭān Sa'īd bin Taymūr in the 1940s and had agreed to acknowledge the extension of Sa'īd's control over the interior on the death of the Imām, no action could be taken until Muḥammad died.

By the time the Imām passed away in 1954, the situation had changed drastically. 'Īsā bin Ṣāliḥ, one of the major tamīmas who had supported Sa'īd's proposal, had died; the second of the two major figures, Sulaymān bin Ḥimyar, had been in contact with the Saudis who could pay far more than the Sulṭān for Sulaymān's acquiescence; and Sa'īd's stature had been weakened by the prevention of his ejection of the Saudis from al-Buraymī as the result of British pressure. The opportunity for a peaceful transfer of power from the tamīmas to the Sultanate was lost and Sa'īd's eventual occupation of the interior was accompanied by violence which was to last nearly a decade.

The Transformation of the Political Structure

Tribal political power in the twentieth century has been in a continual state of flux, reaching its apex in the 1920 Agreement of al-Sīb and then entering a terminal decline after the events of 1970. The first major phase was an era of loose subordination to the Sulṭān during the period prior to 1913: the Sulṭān's wālīs were accepted in the major villages as a result of the inability of the tamīmas to agree on an Imām. Their problem was solved by 1913 with the choice of

Sālim bin Rāshid al-Kharūṣī, and a combined Ghāfirī–Hināwī offensive removed the Sulṭān's authority from all of Oman with the exception of the capital region and the Bāṭina coast. This shift was marked by the sharing of ultimate power by the leaders of the Ghāfirī and Hināwī factions and was legitimised by the Sīb document.

The beginning of the following phase of temporary stability in interior politics is difficult to date precisely but its genesis lies in the decline of Ghāfirī influence following the death of Ḥimyar bin Nāṣir and the subsequent rise in stature of Imām Muḥammad bin 'Abd Allāh al-Khalīlī. By the mid-1940s, this phase had reached its dénouement in a delicate balance shared among Ghāfirī and Hināwī leaders, the Imām and the Sulṭān. Its termination began with the death of Imām Muḥammad and was completed by the occupation of the interior by the Sulṭān's forces.

The events of 1955 entailed a marked disintegration of tribal power in Oman. Henceforth, the supreme authority was to be the government of the Sulṭān as exercised through his representatives and enforced by his relative military power. Even the Jabal al-Akhḍar revolt can be seen as an unsuccessful attempt to circumvent this authority. Nevertheless, Sa'īd bin Taymūr tended to work through the tribal system rather than supplant it, implementing his policy primarily through two individuals. The first of these was his Minister of the Interior, Aḥmad bin Ibrāhīm. After being named Minister in 1939, Aḥmad's principal function had been that of liaison between the Sulṭān and the principal shaykhs of the interior. As the Sulṭān had exercised no direct control over them, Aḥmad's role was largely confined to sending and receiving communications on behalf of the Sulṭān, receiving tribal visitors and doling out shaykhly subsidies. With the reincorporation of the interior into the Sultanate in 1955, Aḥmad's responsibilities naturally grew to include supervision of newly-established wālīs. He was deputed as the Sulṭān's personal representative in the interior after Nizwā was reoccupied following the revolt of 1957 and served as governor, based in Nizwā, until the Sulṭān's removal to Ṣalāla in 1958 necessitated Aḥmad's return to Muscat. Thereafter, Aḥmad continued to exercise primary control over the tribal shaykhs and tamīmas until his retirement in 1970, even though his authority was limited by the responsibilities given to Aḥmad bin Muḥammad al-Ḥārithī and the Secretary for Internal Affairs, J. D. Shebbeare.

Of the Sulṭān's two deputies, Aḥmad bin Muḥammad was the more influential in interior politics. Tamīma of the Ḥirth after his uncle, Ṣāliḥ bin 'Īsā, fled the country in 1956, Aḥmad had long cultivated friendship and loyalty to the Sulṭān. With this in mind, Aḥmad was made temporary wālī of Nizwā after the Sultanate asserted control in late 1955, and later installed his cousin, Khalīfa bin 'Alī, as his successor as wālī. His loyalty through the events of 1957–9 enhanced his position and after Aḥmad bin Ibrāhīm returned to Muscat, Aḥmad bin Muḥammad served as a direct link between the tribes of the interior and the Sulṭān in Ṣalāla, bypassing Aḥmad bin Ibrāhīm and steadily increasing his personal influence and that of his tribe. Aḥmad bin Muḥammad continued to manifest much of his power after the *coup d'état* of July 1970, but his failure either to comprehend or acknowledge the regime's fundamental shift in its power base and source of legitimacy resulted in his downfall: in mid-1971, Aḥmad was placed under house arrest in Muscat and the era of the supremacy of the tamīma had come to an end. Although a few tamīmas continued to exist following this, their influence was severely circumscribed by the new composition of government. The importance of tribal unity for economic purposes (e.g. maintenance of the falaj system) was replaced by the role of the government in the distribution of social services made possible by oil income. The shaykh and the tamīma were increasingly becoming an anachronism in a situation where political power was centralised in Muscat and tribal loyalty was increasingly superseded by the identification of many tribesmen with larger political entities.

Political Decline of Six Principal Tribes

The nature of the basic and irreversible transformation from tribal autonomy into nation–state can best be shown by examination of the disintegration of the tamīmas' power on a tribe-by-tribe basis. The six tribes selected for review have all been influential in the twentieth-century politics of the interior. The circumstances of their integration into the Sultanate differ, yet they all owe their subordination to the state's authority to the decline of the tamīma system, regardless of whether or not this decline was prompted by internal factors, as in the case of the Banī Ruwāḥa, or external factors, as in the case of the Durū'. It should be noted that all of the tribes discussed below are located in the heartland of geographic Oman and are Ibāḍī, with the exceptions of the Banī Bū 'Alī and the majority of the Durū'; thus they can safely be assumed to present an accurate portrayal of the decline of tribal power in the Sultanate.[12]

al-Ḥirth

Although the Ḥirth constitute a relatively small tribe, their domination of al-Sharqīya province is stronger than that of any tribe over the other provinces, with the possible exception of the Shiḥūḥ tribe in the Ru'ūs al-Jibāl. The principal Ḥārithī settlements include al-Qābil (the headquarters of the tribe), Ibrā, Izz, al-Darīz, al-Mintarib and al-Muḍaybī. An important facet of the tribe is its historical relationship with Zanzibar. Ḥārithīs played perhaps the greatest role in that island of any Omani tribe, both in the numbers of tribesmen who migrated there and in the predominance of Ḥārithī political figures in the pre-revolutionary Zanzibar regime.

Much of the reason for the powerful position which the tribe enjoyed in Oman was due to the aggressive and astute politics pursued by successive Ḥārithī tamīmas. Perhaps the most notable was Ṣāliḥ bin 'Alī bin Nāṣir, who exercised his control during the latter half of the nineteenth century.[13] Ṣāliḥ had been involved in an 1859 plot against the life of Mājid bin Sa'īd, the Āl Bū Sa'īd Sulṭān of Zanzibar, in company with Mājid's brother, Barghash, and the ruler of Oman, Thuwaynī bin Sa'īd—who later withdrew when he realised that his goal, the annexation of Zanzibar to Oman, was not the ambition of Ṣāliḥ. The affair erupted into open revolt in Zanzibar and when it was suppressed, Ṣāliḥ returned to al-Qābil empty-handed. His next step was to forge an alliance with the prominent muṭawwi', Sa'īd bin Khalfān al-Khalīlī, and the pair subsequently became the power beind the Muscat regime of Imām 'Azzān bin Qays. The three years that Ṣāliḥ spent in Muscat stoked his ambition and he later attempted to regain his influence there by resorting to attacks on several occasions. His forces occupied Maṭraḥ in January 1874 and again in 1877. He led a six-day siege of Muscat in 1883 and in 1895, with the help of his son 'Abd Allāh, the Ḥārithī tamīma succeeded in capturing all of Muscat by stealth except for the Portuguese-built forts overlooking the harbour. Despite the success indicated by the rebels' hold over the city for a period of two months, they were driven out after the Sulṭān had received tribal reinforcements, principally from Ghāfirī tribes.[14]

Ṣāliḥ was killed in a tribal skirmish in 1896 and was succeeded by his son 'Īsā.[15] His claims to leadership of the Hināwī faction were uncontestable but his attempts to replace the government of the country after the 1871 regime had been defeated were failures primarily due to his inability to obtain Ghāfirī participation. By way of contrast, it will be recalled that his principal partner in the 1868–71 Imamate, Saʻīd bin Khalfān, was a Ghāfirī even though the Imām was Hināwī. In his subsequent activities, Ṣāliḥ promoted members of the same Āl Bū Saʻīd branch for the office of Imām,[16] but the Ghāfirī element was always lacking. Even in his most notable attempt, the near success of 1895, the Ghāfirīs stood aloof; although Ṣāliḥ captured the town, he could not gain the forts—where the Sulṭān had taken refuge. Consequently, the offensive quickly turned into a stalemate and eventually Ṣāliḥ was forced to withdraw.

The death of Ṣāliḥ a year later caused the advantage in the Ghāfirī–Hināwī dichotomy to shift to the other side under the leadership of Ḥimyar bin Nāṣir al-Nabhānī, and the *status quo ante* was restored only on Ḥimyar's death in 1920. That it did return to the previous balance was largely due to the strength and personality of ʻĪsā bin Ṣāliḥ. ʻĪsā had first established his name and claim to authority by the obstruction of a party of geologists sent to explore coal-fields near Ṣūr in 1901. Two years later, he made a cursory attempt to elect the nephew of ʻAzzān bin Qays, Saʻīd bin Ibrāhīm, as Imām—using the same techniques as his father had and obtaining the same results. ʻĪsā further antagonised the Muscat regime when he proved unco-operative in avenging the murder of Sulṭān Fayṣal's roving wālī and trouble-shooter, Sulaymān bin Suwaylim.[17]

The next attempt to re-establish the Imamate was initiated by the Ghāfirī bloc and ʻĪsā remained detached from the movement at first. His subsequent acceptance of the election probably owed much to his sons' tutor, theologian ʻAbd Allāh bin Ḥumayd al-Sālimī, who was a driving force behind the revival. In any case, ʻĪsā soon became an important addition to the movement and, in turn, sought unsuccessfully to involve young Aḥmad bin Ibrāhīm Āl Bū Saʻīd, successor to his brother Saʻīd as semi-independent ruler of al-Rustāq in 1916, in the Kharūṣī Imamate. When Ḥimyar bin Nāṣir eventually passed away, ʻĪsā took over the reins of interior leadership. He was the leading figure behind the siege of Muscat/Maṭraḥ in 1915, and he achieved the election of his candidate, Muḥammad bin ʻAbd Allāh al-Khalīlī, the nephew of Saʻīd bin Khalfān, as Imām in 1920.[18] ʻĪsā remained the leading and most respected figure of the interior until his death in 1946. His son and successor, Muḥammad, however, lacked the aggressive qualities of his forebears and consequently failed to provide the same standard of leadership. In addition, he was in ill health and his death two years later attracted little attention.[19]

The death of Muḥammad provoked a long-standing internal struggle among the contenders to his position, the foremost claimants being Muḥammad's son, Aḥmad, and Muḥammad's brother, Ṣāliḥ. The struggle between these two divided the loyalty of the tribe and of 'Īsā's other sons. Nāṣir, born of a black mother and not considered suitable for the tamīmaship himself, supported Aḥmad, as did Khalīfa. Ibrāhīm, a full brother to Ṣāliḥ, supported Ṣāliḥ. The sequence of events following Muḥammad's death is confused but it is clear that Ṣāliḥ eventually came out on top. At the insistence of the new tamīma, Aḥmad was named wālī of Bilād Banī Bū Ḥasan by the Imām, far enough from al-Qābil to hamper his activity in the Buldān al-Ḥirth. In consequence, Aḥmad turned to the Sulṭān for help and continued to plot against Ṣāliḥ. Aḥmad's machinations were singularly unsuccessful until Ṣāliḥ fled the country after the collapse of the Imamate in late 1955. Aḥmad's position was then paramount and recognised by the Sulṭān who appointed him tamīma of the Ḥirth. Nāṣir returned from self-exile in Zanzibar and was appointed wālī of Bilād Banī Bū Ḥasan for the Sulṭān, although he later broke with Aḥmad and left for exile in Abu Dhabi until 1970. Ibrāhīm, meanwhile, continued to resist Aḥmad although he remained in al-Qābil and covertly led the pro-Ṣāliḥ faction of Ḥirth. In 1957, as part of a planned country-wide uprising, Ibrāhīm engineered a revolt in al-Sharqīya in May. However, the leader of the other arm of the campaign, Ṭālib bin 'Alī al-Hinā'ī, was delayed in his return to Oman and Ibrāhīm's effort ended in disaster when he accepted an invitation from the Sulṭān to talk at Bawshar (near al-Sīb). On his arrival, he was promptly escorted to Fort Jalālī prison where he was kept until freed in 1970, his mind broken.

Ṣāliḥ's fortunes outside the country were better. Residing in Cairo as the self-styled 'Deputy Imām', he became a major spokesman for the 'Imamate of Oman', and lobbied for that cause in the capitals of the Arab world, as well as in the People's Republic of China and the Soviet Union. His relations with the other rebel leaders led to an open clash in 1961, allegedly over his diversion of Imamate funds for personal ends. He continued to reside in Egypt after the fall of Sa'īd bin Taymūr in 1970 although an abortive offer was made by the Ḥirth for him to return to Oman.

The career of the last of the Ḥārithī tamīmas, Aḥmad bin Muḥammad, has already been discussed. By reason of his political acumen, Aḥmad was able to extend his influence beyond that exercised by Ṣāliḥ bin 'Alī nearly a century before. Indeed, Aḥmad's position in the late 1950s and through the 1960s was unprecedented in recent tribal history: by striking an alliance with the Sulṭān and foregoing a pact of dubious value with the Ghāfirī party, the Ḥārithī tamīma was able to overcome such obstacles as a numerically small power base of Ḥārithī tribesmen and the involvement of a substantial section of his tribe in the 1950s rebellion. Clearly, Aḥmad's machinations were the best possible course for a tamīma to chart at the twilight of the traditional tribal political system. Nevertheless, even Aḥmad proved unable to adapt to the next step in Oman's political evolution and his authority was consequently swept away for essentially the same reasons as his erstwhile ally, Sulṭān Sa'īd bin Taymūr: inflexibility in the face of changing circumstances. Following Aḥmad's removal from al-Qābil, the Ḥirth found themselves in a vastly inferior political situation: the leading shaykh of the tribe was Aḥmad's son, Muḥammad, whose authority was limited by his youth, the reputations of his father and uncles and the deliberate policy of Sulṭān Qābūs.

Banī Riyām

Over the course of the last century, the Banī Riyām (singular, Riyāmī) have established the reputation of being the premier Ghāfirī tribe in Oman. With a total of approximately 15,000 members, the tribe is actually a loose grouping of a number of heterogeneous sub-tribal units held together up to 1959 by the shaykhs of the Āl Nabāhina, a group which had also furnished Oman with a famous line of medieval Imāms. The tribe is largely concentrated on the central plateau of al-Jabal al-Akhḍar and around its bases in Oman proper. Major settlements include Nizwā, Izkī, Muttī, Birkat al-Mawz and Qarūt, as well as the villages of Sayq, Sharayja, Minākhir and Wadī Banī Ḥabīb on the plateau—and formerly the town of Tanūf.

The tribe achieved prominence at the beginning of the twentieth century when Ḥimyar bin Nāṣir al-Nabhānī began to acquire enough strength to pose a counterbalance to Ṣāliḥ bin 'Alī al-Ḥārithī. As his position grew, he was able to join with the theologian, 'Abd Allāh bin Ḥumayd al-Sālimī, in re-establishing the Imamate in an election held at Tanūf, Ḥimyar's headquarters, in 1913. That the conclave of shaykhs and muṭawwi' s present—with the notable exception of 'Īsā bin Ṣāliḥ—should elect Sālim bin Rāshid al-Kharūṣī Imām is hardly surprising: the Banī Kharūṣ of the 'Awābī area have traditionally had a very close relationship with the Banī Riyām. Despite Ḥimyār's success in manipulating the election, leadership of the resurgent movement gradually began to shift to 'Īsā. By 1920, Hināwī domination was assured as Imām Sālim, 'Abd Allāh bin Ḥumayd al-Sālimī and Ḥimyar bin Nāṣir all died within a few months of each other.

Ḥimyar's successor was his son Sulaymān, then a boy of about sixteen, who was no match for the experienced Hināwī leaders.[20] Consequently, the new Imām was Muḥammad bin 'Abd Allāh al-Khalīlī. Sulaymān was forced to be content with gradually rebuilding the Ghāfirī power base. His first test came as a result of the joint operation by the Imām and 'Īsā bin Ṣāliḥ against 'Ibrī in 1925, ostensibly for the purpose of keeping a line of communications open with Shaykh Sa'īd bin Maktūm of Dubay. The Hināwī overtones of the expedition aroused the hostility of the Ghāfirī Ya'āqib of 'Ibrī who called on Ghāfirī support. Sulaymān's action in condemning the operation and threatening to move on Nizwā resulted in the rapid withdrawal of the Imām back to Nizwā and 'Īsā to al-Qābil. As a result of the perceived Ghāfirī victory, the Imām allegedly threatened to resign over the disgrace.[21] To further his influence, Sulaymān entered into correspondence with Sulṭān Sa'īd bin Taymūr in the late 1930s, in connection with the latter's plan to regain control of the interior and prevent the election of another Imām. Accordingly, Sulaymān journeyed to Muscat in 1945 and again in 1948 and reached agreement with the Sulṭān, as did 'Īsā bin Ṣāliḥ, that there was to be no election after Muḥammad's death. But the first to die was 'Īsā bin Ṣāliḥ and as his death caused a split in Hināwī ranks, Sulaymān bin Ḥimyar consequently became the strongest figure in the interior and in a good position to further his own plans.

Long known as being extremely ambitious,[22] Sulaymān was prominent in establishing a relationship with Saudi Arabia and in attempting to secure a favourite candidate to succeed Muḥammad bin 'Abd Allāh as Imām. His first choice was 'Abd Allāh bin Sālim al-Kharūṣī, son of the 1913–20 Imām. However, this candidacy was precluded by 'Abd Allāh's arranged marriage to a Riyāmī girl, his tribe's close relationship with the Banī Riyām and fears that he would be dominated easily by Sulaymān. By this time, Sulaymān's involvement with the Saudis had advanced to the point of accepting cash presents, as had the Imām's wālī of al-Rustāq, Ṭālib bin 'Alī al-Hinā'ī. The two apparently decided to join forces and back the candidacy of Ṭālib's brother, Ghālib bin 'Alī, then a qāḍī of Nizwā.

When Ghālib was eventually elected, Sulaymān became the major power behind the new Imamate. But his increased status suffered when the Sulṭān entered Nizwā in December 1955 and received a subdued Sulaymān in an audience there. The Riyāmī leader's supposed sincerity on that occasion was exposed as a ploy by the events of 1957–9. Upon the clandestine return of Ṭālib bin 'Alī from Saudi Arabia in June 1957, Sulaymān slipped from house arrest in Muscat and led his tribesmen against the Sulṭān's troops. After the reverses following the initially successful uprising in the towns of Oman proper, Sulaymān and his cohorts retreated to Banī Riyām territory on the Jabal al-Akhḍar plateau. As a consequence, when the Sultanate and British troops captured the Jabal in the spring of 1959 and the rebel leaders fled the country, the Banī Riyām were placed under a military governor, forbidden to make improvements in their villages—for example, no shops were allowed on the mountain plateau, forcing the inhabitants to make frequent trips down the mountain for their supplies—the town of Tanūf was completely destroyed and Sulaymān's 'castles' in Birkat al-Mawz and Sayq were reduced to rubble.

As a result of Sulaymān's exile in Saudi Arabia, the Banī Riyām were left leaderless and, predictably, split up into the nearly three dozen original sub-units. The Sulṭān deliberately prevented the emergence of a successor to Sulaymān. The tamīma's two sons had supported the uprising along with their father: Sulṭān, the eldest, was captured and placed in Fort Jalālī while Ḥimyar joined Sulaymān in exile. But even if more suitable successors had existed, the wrath of Sa'īd bin Taymūr would have prevented the emergence of any new Riyāmī tamīma, whether Nabhānī or otherwise. Consequently, control of tribal affairs reverted to a Nā'ib wālī of Nizwā stationed at Birkat al-Mawz and a military governor at Sayq; and, in addition, Riyāmī prerogatives were frequently encroached upon by Aḥmad bin Muḥammad al-Ḥārithī.

Apart from the Āl Nabāhina, the most prominent Riyāmī shaykh of the twentieth century was Muḥammad bin Sālim al-Ruqayshī. Muḥammad was also influential in the establishment of the Kharūṣī Imamate and later served as wālī of 'Ibrī, beginning in 1940, for

Imām Muḥammad bin ʻAbd Allāh for many years—although he left the post prior to its occupation by Sultanate forces in 1954. His presumed connection with the Imamate of Ghālib bin ʻAlī earned him the enmity of the Sultanate and he was incarcerated in Fort Jalālī until May 1970. Several of his sons served as wālīs and qāḍīs under the regime of Sulṭān Qābūs bin Saʻīd.

The political declines of the Banī Riyām and the Ḥirth exhibit a number of similarities. The last tamīmas of both tribes had sought to upgrade their positions by concluding alliances with powers outside the Imamate, although only Aḥmad bin Muḥammad was successful in his choice of partners. Furthermore, the removal of both Sulaymān and Aḥmad bin Muḥammad, even though separated by more than a decade, resulted in the fragmentation of their respective tribes and accelerated the disintegration of the Ghāfirī and Hināwī blocs as cohesive forces in Omani politics.

Banī Hinā

The Banī Hinā have been in the forefront of tribal politics ever since they gave their name to the Hināwī faction. Part of this position derives from the large size of the tribe but of greater importance is its strategic location at the northern rim of the Oman province. From that vantage point, the Banī Hinā command the inland approaches to the Oman heartland: through al-Ẓāhira and then along a course parallel to the Jabal al-Akhḍar. The spread of Hinā'ī settlements around al-Ghāfāt (the tribal headquarters), Bilād Sayt and Nizwā, effectively gives the tribe control over a band of territory stretching from the desert to the mountains. In view of their geographic location, it is not surprising that the Banī Hinā have been involved in a number of serious disputes over the last century.

The present line of tamīmas began with the rise of Hilāl bin Zāhir in the late nineteenth century; he successfully wrested the tamīmaship away from Saʻīd bin Muḥammad and then took control of Nizwā from the Sulṭān's wālī.[23] Saʻīd, however, turned to the ʻIbrīyīn, causing Hilāl to request help from rivals of the ʻIbrīyīn, the Banī Riyām. This Hinā'ī/Riyāmī alliance was successful although it soon ended in hostility.[24] Hilāl was killed when the forces of Sulṭān Fayṣal bin Turkī recaptured Nizwā in 1894 and was briefly succeeded by his son Badr and then by another son, ʻAbd Allāh, one of the signatories to the Agreement of al-Sīb in 1920. The tamīmaship became firmly established in the line of Hilāl bin Zāhir and the title eventually passed to Zāhir bin Ghuṣn, a nephew of 'Abd Allāh bin Hilāl. Zāhir's sons, the 'Awlād Zāhir', were to exert considerable influence on the contemporary political scene of the interior.[25]

However, another branch of the family was also to become prominent in the mid-twentieth century. 'Alī bin Hilāl, the father of Ghālib and Ṭālib, had served as wālī for the Khalīlī Imām, first in al-Rustāq and then in Ja'lān, and his sons were educated by Imām Muḥammad. Ṭālib succeeded his father as wālī of al-Rustāq, a post he held until the town was captured by the Batinah Force in 1955, while Ghālib had been qāḍī at al-Rustāq until the Imām brought him to Nizwā *c.* 1950 to be a qāḍī there and also to handle the Imamate's bayt al-māl. The Imām's high opinion of Ghālib was apparently a major factor in his subsequent election.

Despite Ghālib's religious reputation, political leadership of the tribe was firmly retained by the tamīma, 'Abd Allāh bin Zāhir, who consolidated his position in 1954 by travelling to Ṣalāla to see the Sulṭān and declare his allegiance: he continued to remain loyal to the Sulṭān and did not participate in Ghālib's Imamate or the revolt of 1957–9. Primarily because of his professed loyalty, the Banī Hinā escaped the retribution suffered by the Banī Riyām, even though many of the 1950s rebels were from the Banī Hinā and the major supply route to the encircled rebels on al-Jabal al-Akhḍar led through Hinā'ī territory.

Although unable to command the wide influence that Aḥmad bin Muḥammad al-Ḥārithī exhibited, 'Abd Allāh displayed a similar astuteness in seeking good relations with the Sulṭān. In addition, he understood the changed circumstances after 1970 and so retained his position—as well as securing a cabinet post for his tribe—long after Aḥmad had chosen confrontation and lost.

Banī Bū 'Alī

The Ghāfirī tribe of the Banī Bū 'Alī (singular, 'Alawī), along with the Hināwī Banī Bū Ḥasan, dominate the province of Ja'lān. The tribe is centred around its capital at Bilād Banī Bū 'Alī, although another major 'Alawī settlement is the 'Ayqa section of Ṣūr. The Banī Bū 'Alī differ from many of the other tribes of Oman in that they are Sunnī (of the Hanbalī school of Islamic jurisprudence) and have frequently been regarded as Muwaḥḥidūn (Wahhābīs) since the Saudi invasion of Ja'lān in 1812–13.[26]

The tribe has long had a reputation for truculence and xenophobia, which extended to the Sultanate and Imamate alike. Following British accusations of acts of piracy by the Banī Bū 'Alī in the early nineteenth century, a joint expedition was undertaken by Sulṭān Sa'īd bin Sulṭān and Captain Thompson of the British Residency in Muscat in 1820. The venture ended in catastrophe after being ambushed in Ja'lān with British casualties exceeding 270 men. The defeat was avenged the following year when a stronger force of two brigades succeeded in razing Bilād Banī Bū 'Alī and capturing the tribe's tamīma.[27]

They refused to support the Imamate of 'Azzān bin Qays and when 'Azzān sent an expedition against them, the Banī Bū 'Alī forged an alliance with the main branch of the Āl Bū Sa'īd. This unlikely connection proved to be fortunate for Sulṭān Fayṣal bin Turkī as it was 'Alawī tribesmen who helped drive the Hināwī invaders from Muscat in 1895. 'Alawī levies were also instrumental in the revolt of 1913–20 when they held many forts for the Sulṭān and some were even garrisoned in Muscat during the siege of 1915.

The Banī Bū 'Alī's tamīmas in the twentieth century have come from the Āl Ḥamūda section. The tamīma for the period up to 1913 was 'Abd Allāh bin Sālim, who had begun his career as the only notable 'Alawī shaykh to escape capture by 'Azzān bin Qays. After his death in 1913 and the gradual assumption of power by his son, 'Alī, and his grandson, Muḥammad bin Nāṣir, relations between the Sultanate and the tribe began to weaken.[28] As early as 1923, the tribe claimed that Ṣūr was outside the Sultanate's jurisdiction and, therefore, the state had no right to tax cargoes landed there. The Banī Bū 'Alī also sought to extend their control over Ṣūr to the 'Arāma and Makhāna sections of the Janaba tribe resident there. In support of 'Alawī claims to Ṣūr, the tribe revived the Saudi connection and briefly flew the Saudi flag at al-'Ayqa in 1928.[29] The situation concerning the Sulṭān's customs post in Ṣūr deteriorated by 1930 to the point that the PAM felt strong action was necessary and so the RAF was ordered to bomb al-'Ayqa. The end result was the levelling of a customs post set up there by the Banī Bū 'Alī and the restoration of firmer Sultanate control over Ṣūr. But by 1945, the estrangement had healed sufficiently for Sa'īd bin Taymūr to visit Ṣūr. There he received 'Alī bin 'Abd Allāh and received his promise of co-operation in the Sulṭān's scheme to regain future control of the interior.[30]

Despite this short-lived understanding, Banī Bū 'Alī–Sultanate relations remained strained until 1970. The tribe continued to reject Sultanate control over their territory. Even after the events of 1955, military parties travelling through the area, on their way to Ra's al-Ḥadd, did so at their own risk. The military was restricted from taking action against 'Alawī hostility by the personal order of the Sulṭān. Consequently, the tribe's integration into the Sultanate did not come about until after the accession of Sulṭān Qābūs. Their acquiescence then in accepting a wālī and other government services came only as a result of the action of government health teams during a cholera epidemic.

Banī Ruwāḥa

One of the largest tribes of Oman, with estimated numbers of more than 8,000, the Banī Ruwāḥa (singular, Ruwāḥī) have lost much of the influence their size would indicate due to a lack of cohesion among the heterogeneous units. The tribe occupies the upper or western part of the Wādī Samā'il (also known as Wādī Banī Ruwāḥa), as well as parts of the nearby Wādī 'Andam and Wādī Ḥalfayn. Major settlements include Upper Samā'il, al-Khudra, Upper Qarūt and part of Izkī. The tribe's disunity during the last century resulted in numerous feuds and was exacerbated by encroachment on the part of the neighbouring Banī Riyām, traditional Ghāfirī rivals of the Hināwī Banī Ruwāḥa. In order to reverse this situation, an offer was made to the Awlād Khalīlī of the Banī Kharūṣ tribe to provide the tamīma of the Banī Ruwāḥa. The Khalīlī acceptance resulted in a satisfactory arrangement which continues to function.

One of the first of the new Khalīlī tamīmas was Sa'īd bin Khalfān, who possessed a reputation as a fanatical muṭawwi' and was a principal adviser to Imām 'Azzān bin Qays. When Turkī bin Sa'īd recaptured Muscat in 1871, Sa'īd bin Khalfān was taken prisoner and walled up alive in Fort Mīrānī along with his son Aḥmad. His other son, 'Abd Allāh, had previously joined forces with Turkī and subsequently remained in the service of the Sulṭāns. After 'Abd Allāh was killed in the Bāṭina, the state assumed responsibility for the upbringing of his son 'Alī, who was later appointed wālī of Bawshar. Another son, Muḥammad, had remained in Samā'il and assumed a vacillating role in the 1913–20 struggle between the Sultanate and the newly formed Imamate.[31] His ambivalence had no effect on his religious stature, however, as he was elected Imām following the assassination of Imām Sālim in 1920. He was considered a protégé of 'Īsā bin Ṣāliḥ al-Ḥārithī during the early period of his office and was related to him by marriage. Nevertheless, as the years passed, he acquired something of a political reputation matching his religious stature. One result was that the renewed Saudi interest of the early 1950s had no effect on the Imām who remained completely opposed to any foreign influences in Oman, whether Saudi, British or purely oil-related.

In his last years, Muḥammad was nearly blind and often infirm, and various attempts were made to select a successor. His three nephews—the sons of 'Alī: 'Abd Allāh, Hilāl and Sa'ūd—sought to place one of them, Hilāl, in line to succeed Muḥammad, a move that received the consent of a number of shaykhs but was rejected outright by the Imām. When Muḥammad finally passed away and Ghālib bin 'Alī was elected Imām, the three brothers contrived to play the same ambivalent role as their uncle had nearly forty years previously. Nevertheless, 'Abd Allāh was perceived to be leaning towards the Imamate when the interior was taken over by the Sultanate, and Hilāl, although wālī of Bawshar for the Sulṭān since the death of his father in 1943, was reported to be in al-Riyāḍ in 1954 as ambassador for the Imām and interested in getting an oil concession from Aramco.[32] Sa'ūd, however, had remained in Samā'il and assisted Aḥmad bin Ibrāhīm and Ṭāriq bin Taymūr in the administration of the interior after 1955; although 'Abd Allāh had succeeded his uncle Muḥammad as tamīma of the Banī Ruwāḥa, Sa'ūd was the *de facto* leader. After the *coup d'état* in 1970, Hilāl was named Ambassador to Saudi Arabia and Sa'ūd became Minister of Education and then Ambassador to Egypt. In this way, the Awlād Khalīlī, along with 'Abd Allāh bin Zāhir al-Hinā'ī, were representative of that part of the traditional tribal community that correctly perceived the changed criteria of political power in the Sultanate after 1970 and acted accordingly.

al-Durū'

There are three major nomadic tribes which inhabit the desert fringes of Oman: the Durū', the Janaba and the Yāl Wahība. The range of the Durū' (singular, Dara'ī) extends from the settled areas of Oman proper on the east to the sands of the Rub' al-Khālī and the Umm al-Samīm on the west. To the north and the south, their boundaries are restricted only by the relative strength of other tribes: the Āl Bū Shāmis and the Banī Qitab to the north (i.e. on the south side of al-Buraymī oasis) and the Janaba and the Ḥarāsīs to the south (near Wādī Ḥalfayn and Jiddat al-Ḥarāsīs). Apart from their predominant economic trait of pastoralism, the Durū' also mine salt and manufacture charcoal for sale to settled tribes. They also own date palms in villages such as 'Ibrī and Ādām—in which they gather during the summer harvest. Their ties to 'Ibrī are especially close and they have an almost 'client' relationship with the Ya'āqib tribe there, as both are Ghāfirī.[33] However, the majority of the Durū' are Sunnī rather than Ibāḍī—a factor which has become increasingly important over the last quarter century.

In common with most badū tribes, the Durū' possess a very loose-knit tribal organisation and there is no tamīma. At best, there is a senior shaykh who may be *primus inter pares* but is forced continually to vie for influence in competition with other shaykhs of the Maḥāmid clan.[34] The lack of a tamīma has proved recently to be an important factor in the development of the tribe's relations with the oil company, PDO, as discussed below.

In the last quarter century, the tribe has been caught in the midst of some of the most important developments in Oman. Early in the 1950s, the Ya'āqib of 'Ibrī threw off the control of the Khalīlī Imām's wālī and thus acquired a semi-independent status. After the accession of Imām Ghālib bin 'Alī, an army was sent to recapture 'Ibrī. Since the Durū' viewed this action against 'Ibrī, where many Durū' owned property, as a threat, a Dara'ī delegation visited Muscat and met with Aḥmad bin Ibrāhīm and the representative of the oil company, Edward Henderson.[35] Their purpose was to seek help from the Sultanate against the aggressive new Imamate. The Sultanate, for its part, needed Dara'ī approval and help for PDO which was preparing to move an exploratory party into the interior. The meeting ended satisfactorily for both sides.

Early in 1954, PDO had established a base camp at al-Duqm on the southern coast of Oman and had awaited the build-up of its armed escort, the new Muscat and Oman Field Force (MOFF), to an arbitrary figure set at 400 men. The PDO group and its MOFF escort, accompanied by Dara'ī shaykhs, finally set off for the interior in summer 1954 and reached Jabal Fahūd in October, where another base camp was established. Subsequently, the MOFF proceeded north, entered 'Ibrī and evicted the Imām's wālī; the Sulṭān later appointed his own wālī. This marked the beginning of a special relationship between PDO and the Durū'. PDO needed the co-operation of the tribe because all of their drilling took place in Dara'ī territory and the Durū' insisted that all local labour be recruited from their tribe. This had the effect of somewhat expanding the Dara'ī political system to encompass the local equivalent of a labour union. The traditionally loose confederation of Dara'ī sub-units were gradually brought together through the labour requirements and methods of recruitment. The shaykhs saw their traditionally insubstantial authority grow in stature as they evolved into an Arabian equivalent of 'shop stewards'. PDO gradually adopted the expedient of using the shaykh as 'labour supervisor' on drilling sites to prevent wild-cat strikes by the Dara'ī labour force. 'Alī bin Hilāl was able to increase his prestige in the tribe after organising such a strike in 1955, as all labour had to be recruited through him, and his rival, Musallim bin Ḥamad, lost considerable ground. But despite this early shift in power, the dispute was not settled. In order to co-ordinate clans and shaykhs effectively, 'Alī bin Hilāl was recognised as the pre-eminent shaykh by the oil company, a position that was resented by many members of the tribe because it eroded the old social order. Consequently, internal power struggles developed and by 1964, PDO was forced to institute a 'duty shaykh' system, whereby three of the more prominent shaykhs each served three-month periods in rotation as 'duty shaykh', with their duties including liaison between the labour staff and PDO, prevention of strikes and defusing grievances.[36]

The next step in the transformation of the social order involved the elimination of the go-between. In a strike at Fahūd in August 1970, intervention by the shaykhs proved ineffective and so their place was gradually assumed by an 'employees' representative committee'. The role of the 'duty shaykhs' was thereafter limited to work on geophysical and other outlying parties. A footnote to this evolution in tribal development is the role of the Sulṭān. In November 1968, one of the shaykhs, Maṭar bin Muḥammad, went to see Sa'īd bin Taymūr in Ṣalāla to complain of the way in which 'Alī bin Hilāl had been distributing the government subsidy. Although he returned empty-handed in July 1969, his chosen avenue of appeal from PDO decisions bore fruit: in April 1971, the new Sulṭān recognised him as senior shaykh in place of 'Alī.

The relationship of the Durū' with PDO should be contrasted with the situation of the two other major nomadic tribes. All 'client' relationships forged between badū and ḥaḍar tribes have been altered by recent events. In the case of the Durū', PDO has proven to be a much more resourceful and beneficial partner than the Ya'āqib. Since the fall of Aḥmad bin Muḥammad, the Ḥirth's clients, al-Janaba, have also turned to direct negotiations with PDO rather than relying on Ḥārithī leaders to take care of their interests.

Up to 1970, the tribes of Oman still exercised many of the traditional rights and prerogatives which other Arabian tribes had already surrendered to various national governments. Although the Omani tribes' political powers, both individually and collectively, had been steadily eroded since the halfway mark of the twentieth century, the rapid political, social and economic change of the 1970s served to accelerate the decline of the ancient tribal structure.

Notes

1. The following discussion of the origins of the tribal system relies heavily on J. C. Wilkinson, 'The Origins of the Omani State', in Derek Hopwood (ed.), *The Arabian Peninsula: Society and Politics* (London: George Allen and Unwin, 1972), pp. 67–88.

2. The tamīmas, discussed below, constitute an exception to the limitations of the shaykhs.

3. Wilkinson, 'The Origins of the Omani State', p. 78. This helps to explain why the stratified village society found elsewhere in Arabia, as in the Ḥaḍramawt, is not found in Oman, where the only stratification seems to be between tribesmen and unassimilated minority groups such as ex-slaves and the Bayāsira and Bayādīr.

4. J. C. Wilkinson provides an introduction to the pre-Islamic arrangements made in al-Mazūn and other areas of modern Oman between the Arab tribes and the Persian Government, in 'Arab–Persian Land Relationships in Late Sasānid Oman', *Proceedings of the Sixth Seminar for Arabian Studies* (1972), pp. 40–51.

5. See Chapter 1, note 12.

6. In explanation of the blindness of traditional groups to external forces, W. Montgomery Watt has mentioned the concept of 'noyau' or 'a society of inward antagonism' whereby 'members are so engrossed in their mutual rivalry that they pay slight attention to external enemies . . .' so that consequently Great Powers are able to gain the upper hand in an area by supporting one of the contending sides. 'Traditional Arab Communities in the Modern World', *International Affairs* (London), vol. 44, no. 3 (July 1968), p. 496.

7. By the nineteenth century, the Imamate as a political institution owed its legitimacy to the consent of the tribal leaders and not simply to the collective members of the Ibāḍī community as prescribed by Ibāḍī tenets.

8. For a short history of the Ya'rubī dynasty and the civil war which led to its downfall, see R. D. Bathurst, 'Maritime Trade and Imamate Government: Two Themes in the History of Oman to 1728', in Derek Hopwood (ed.), *The Arabian Peninsula: Society and Politics* (London: George Allen and Unwin, 1972), pp. 89–106.

9. Indeed, a good example is that of the Banī Ghāfir themselves, who, although North Arab, are Ibāḍī in religion and have fluctuated from the Ghāfirī side to the Hināwī side and back during the past two centuries.

10. It may be argued that the Imām was the supreme authority, but events show that he generally acted in the same manner as a tamīma in political affairs, since he served as the tamīma of his own tribe as well as Imām, as in the case of Imām

Sālim bin Rāshid and the Banī Kharūṣ and Imām Muḥammad bin 'Abd Allāh and the Banī Ruwāḥa. The failure of Imām Ghālib bin 'Alī to wrest leadership of his tribe, the Banī Hinā, away from its tamīma, 'Abd Allāh bin Zāhir, is one more indication of the fragility of his claims to leadership of Oman.

11. See IO, R/15/3/39; PAM Crosthwaite to PRPG, No. 96, 29 Dec. 1925; R/15/3/337; Annual Muscat Administration Report for 1925; J. B. Kelly, 'A Prevalence of Furies: Tribes, Politics and Religion in Oman', in Derek Hopwood (ed.), *The Arabian Peninsula: Society and Politics* (London: George Allen and Unwin, 1972), pp. 123–4; and G. J. Eccles, 'The Sultanate of Muscat and Oman, With a Description of a Journey into the Interior Undertaken in 1925', *JRCAS*, vol. 14, pt. 1 (1927), p. 23.

12. The analyses presented here are largely limited to discussion of the role of the tamīmas partially because of the general scarcity of information relating to tribes in this area. Much of the information used in the following section was gleaned from the records of the India Office Library and Petroleum Development (Oman) Ltd (PDO), as well as from interviews with members of the families and tribes concerned, supplemented by Muḥammad bin 'Abd Allāh al-Sālimī, *Nahḍat al-A'yān bi-Ḥurrīyat 'Umān* (Cairo: Dār al-Kitāb al-'Arabī, 1380/1961). The only anthropological studies of eastern Arabian tribes fall outside the Oman heartland. Principal among these are: Bertram Thomas, 'Among Some Unknown Tribes of South Arabia', *Journal of the Royal Anthropological Institute*, vol. 59, pt. 1 (1929), pp. 97–111; ibid., 'The Musandam Peninsula and Its People the Shihuh', *JRCAS*, vol. 16, pt. 1 (1929), pp. 71–86; Wilfred P. Thesiger, 'The Badu of Southern Arabia', *JRCAS*, vol. 37, pt. 1 (1950), pp. 53–61; Walter Dostal, 'The South Arabian Tribes: al-Qarā and al-Ḥarāsīs', *Arabian Studies*, vol. 2 (1975), pp. 33–41; ibid., 'The Shiḥūḥ of Northern Oman: A Contribution to Cultural Ecology', *GJ*, vol. 138, pt. 1 (Mar. 1972), pp. 1–7; and Donald Powell Cole, *Nomads of the Nomads: The Āl Murrah Bedouin of the Empty Quarter* (Chicago: Aldine, 1975). There is no study of village life comparable to Abdalla S. Bujra, *The Politics of Stratification: A Study of Political Change in a South Arabian Town* (Oxford: Oxford University Press, 1971), although important information is contained in J. C. Wilkinson, *The Organisation of the Falaj Irrigation System in Oman*, Research Paper, No. 10 (Oxford: School of Geography, University of Oxford, July 1974). An all-too-brief look at the social changes brought about in the area's badū tribes is found in Frauke Heard-Bey, 'Social Changes in the Gulf States and Oman', *Asian Affairs*, vol. 59, pt. 3 (1972), pp. 309–16; and the same author's 'Development Anomalies in the Beduin Oases of al-Liwa', *Asian Affairs*, vol. 61, pt. 3 (1974), pp. 272–86. Some tribal information is contained in Arabian American Oil Company, Relations Department, Research Division, *Oman and the Southern Shore of the Persian Gulf* (Cairo: Aramco, 1952), although it should be used cautiously due to the difficulties that the Aramco researchers faced in gathering material from a distance. The work is also demonstrably pro-Saudi and pro-Imamate. In addition, Aramco researchers provided articles on the area's tribes for the *Encyclopedia of Islam*, 2nd edn, as given in the bibliography.

13. Detailed information on the career of Ṣāliḥ bin 'Alī and on the early part of his son 'Īsā's career is contained in 'Sketch of the Careers of Saleh bin Ali and his son Isa bin Saleh, the Stormy Petrels of Oman Politics', written by PAM G. P. Murphy, *c*. 1928; contained in IO, R/15/3/243. See also *Lorimer's Gazetteer*, vol. 1, pt. 1. For genealogical data on the Ḥārithī tamīmas, as well as for the other tribes discussed here, see Appendix D. The Ḥārithī connection to East Africa is discussed in the sources cited on p. 40.

14. This event is discussed in Chapter 6.

15. 'Abd Allāh, his eldest son, had died of wounds incurred during the 1895 occupation of Muscat.

16. He supported Ḥamūd bin 'Azzān bin Qays in 1874, Ibrāhīm bin Qays in 1877, and even 'Abd al-'Azīz bin Sa'īd of the mainline Āl Sa'īd in 1883 when Ṣāliḥ briefly occupied a position in Muscat as adviser during 'Abd al-'Azīz's brief regency.

17. Although the murder had occurred in Siyābīyīn territory, Sulaymān had just left al-Qābil after an unfruitful meeting with 'Īsā.

18. A visitor to the interior a few years later remarked that 'The present Imam of the interior, Muḥammad bin 'Abdillah al-Khalili, of the Bani Ruwaiḥah, is merely a puppet in the hands of Shaikh 'Isa bin Ṣaliḥ of the Ḥirth.' G. C. Eccles, 'The Sultanate of Muscat and Oman', p. 23.

19. According to Aramco's *Oman and the Southern Shore of the Persian Gulf* (p. 81), Muḥammad 'earned himself an unsavory reputation as a minor despot.' In addition, the work states that Sulṭān bin Taymūr arranged for Muḥammad's medical treatment in India in 1946. He died at al-Qābil in 1947.

20. A short biographical sketch of Sulaymān, together with notes on his ancestry, is to be found in Aramco's *Oman and the Southern Shore of the Persian Gulf*, pp. 75–9.

21. See note 11 above.

22. He had stationery printed in English and Arabic proclaiming him 'King of the Jabal Akhdar' and requested the explorer Wilfred Thesiger to transmit a message to British authorities requesting recognition of his independence. Thesiger, *Arabian Sands* (London: Longman, 1959), p. 305.

23. S. B. Miles, who was the guest of Hilāl during one of his journeys in Oman, describes him in 'On the Border of the Great Desert: a Journey in Oman', *GJ*, vol. 36, no. 2 (Aug. 1910), pp. 175–6.

24. The 'Ibrīyīn constitute a Ghāfirī tribe prominent at that time under the leadership of tamīma Muḥsin bin Zahrān and traditional Hinā'ī rivals. Despite being Ghāfirī, the 'Ibrīyīn were also estranged from the Ghāfirī Banī Riyām, then under the leadership of Sulaymān bin Sayf al-Nabhānī.

25. Of Zāhir's eight sons, Muḥammad was to become the Sulṭān's wālī in Samā'il, 'Abd Allāh became tamīma of the tribe, 'Alī became wālī of al-Muḍaybī, and al-Walid served as Minister first of Education and then of Awqāf and Islamic Affairs in the post-1970 regime.

26. Much of the background information used in this section is based on a 'Report on Sur', by G. P. Murphy in Oct. 1928, and contained in IO, R/15/3/65.

27. A detailed account of these campaigns can be found in J. B. Kelly, *Britain and the Persian Gulf, 1795–1880* (Oxford: Clarendon Press, 1968), pp. 167–92.

28. One explanation for the disintegration of this relationship was given in a letter to the present writer from Muḥammad bin 'Abd Allāh al- Sālimī, 7 Ṣafar 1395 (19 Feb. 1975): the leader of the Ghāfirī bloc in the early twentieth century, Ḥimyar bin Nāṣir al-Nabhānī had sought 'Alawī support for the Imamate of Sālim bin Rāshid al-Kharūṣī. 'He wished to contact the Banī Bū 'Alī and persuade them to come to his side and so spoke to the Shaykhs Muḥammad bin Nāṣir and 'Alī bin 'Abd Allāh, the two Amīrs of the Banī Bū 'Alī, but they delayed in giving their support. Then he [Ḥimyar] asked them to quit their support for the Kings [sic] of Muscat and because he was their guest, they did not wish for him to leave without having achieved any of his requests so they acquiesced. This was in Dhū al-Qa'da 1331 (Oct. 1913). They fulfilled their promise and did not knock on the door of the Sulṭān for twelve years' [my translation].

29. 'Alī bin 'Abd Allāh allegedly visited al-Riyāḍ at this time, and Aḥmad bin Ibrāhīm, who was also supposed to have travelled to the Saudi capital, was

implicated in the intrigue. IO, R/15/3/63; Murphy to PRPG, No. 128, 29 Oct. 1928.

30. Sa'īd bin Taymūr was also a successful mediator during this period in several disputes between the Banī Bū 'Alī and the Ḥirth. See Chapter 2.

31. Entrusted with Samā'il fort by the retreating Sultanate forces, Muḥammad subsequently turned it over to the Imamate army.

32. PDO, 'Note of E. F. Henderson's Visit to Duru' Shaikhs in Muscat—4th–11th August 1954.'

33. This symbiotic relationship between badū and ḥaḍar (settled) tribes seems to have been a common feature in Oman, as it allowed both tribes to benefit from their combined strength. Two other prominent examples are that of the Yāl Wahība/Ḥirth—Wahībī fortunes flourished while Aḥmad bin Muḥammad was tamīma of the Ḥirth—and the Janaba/Banī Riyām—whose relationship suffered when the Banī Riyām became leaderless and the Janaba lost territory to the Yāl Wahība.

34. The Maḥāmid constitute the shaykhly clan while other major clans include the Lābāt, Najāda and the Mafāfī—each with its own *rashīd* or leader. The best source of information on the Duru' is an unpublished, 32-page study produced *c.* 1970 by PDO in combination with other studies on the Janaba and the Yāl Wahība. The tribe is also discussed in Aramco, *Oman and the Southern Shore of the Persian Gulf*, pp. 92–4.

35. Members of this delegation included the senior Dara'ī shaykh, 'Alī bin Hilāl, his brother Ḥumayd, his chief rival, Musallim bin Ḥamad, the latter's brother Ḥārib, and several others. PDO, 'Note of E. F. Henderson's Visit to Duru' Shaikhs in Muscat—4th–11th August 1954'.

36. These three shaykhs were: 'Alī bin Hilāl; Maṭar bin Muḥammad, son of the shaykh, Muḥammad bin Sa'īd, whom 'Alī had ousted as senior shaykh in 1949; and Ḥārib bin Ḥamad, brother of Musallim bin Ḥamad, 'Alī's chief rival during the 1950s, who died in 1960.

CHAPTER 5

External Influences on Omani Politics

The twentieth century has largely been a time of isolation for Oman. Suffering political fragmentation and economic stagnation, the country's contacts with the outside world have been few and far between, consisting in the main of occasional steamer calls at Maṭraḥ and radio broadcasts monitored on the few sets available locally. Even traditional trade markets, such as Germany and the United States, were lost by mid-century and Muscat's historical role as a regional entrepot centre was lost to other ports, such as al-Kuwayt and Dubay. Only India remained as competition for Japanese exports.

On the political level, only Britain (and India in the post-independence period) maintained resident Consuls in Muscat between 1915 and 1970. Consequently, Britain's dominance and guiding interest in the Sultanate has been obvious. Her influence on the state's last three rulers has been equally evident: two were educated at the so-called 'Eton of India' and the present Sulṭān is a Sandhurst graduate.

Oman has only recently begun to emerge from the cocoon spun around it by its European mentors, a state of affairs that was largely accepted by its rulers and inevitable given the historical circumstances. Yet one of the consequences of this policy by mid-century was the apprehension that all non-British states, whether European, Asian or Arab, were either enemies or of little concern to Muscat. This line of thought was altered only with the accession of Qābūs bin Sa'īd when international contacts were rapidly expanded and long-hostile or dormant relations with neighbours were exchanged for closer ties. Within a few years, Oman had fully entered the international arena and was on friendly terms with all but a few of her fellow Arab states.

Roots of Britain's Interest in Oman

Britain's presence in Oman, as well as her interest in the Gulf and eastern Arabia in general, was the result of an evolving series of goals and perceived needs, linked only by the strong concern over the defence of India. Consequently, British actions in the eighteenth century, designed to exclude other European states from activity in the Indian Ocean, were based on different objectives than those of the nineteenth century, when the predominant need was to protect the lines of communication to India, or the twentieth century, with the necessity of a secure cordon around the subcontinent.

The role that the Arabian Peninsula played is demonstrated by the fact that, until 1947, British representatives in the Peninsula were almost exclusively appointed by the Government of India, which also decided British policy towards the area. Delhi's preoccupation with security throughout the Indian sphere of influence resulted in its increasing assumption of responsibility for the Sultanate. This policy was only reversed with Indian independence, when Britain, caught up in the denunciation of 'imperialism', sought to extricate herself from a potentially embarrassing situation in Oman and the Arabian Gulf.[1]

Britain first became interested in the area as a consequence of her drive for paramouncy in the Indian Ocean: British factories competed with French, Portuguese and Dutch establishments and eventually supplanted them. The Gulf held interest due to its trade potential, particularly on the Iranian littoral. The Arab coast was less promising since the Āl Bū Sa'īd refused to allow a factory to be established in the important entrepot centre of Muscat and Gulf settlements were viewed as little more than pirates' lairs.

The beginnings of a British relationship with the Sultanate, arising in the early nineteenth century, were based largely on the need to prevent piracy against British shipping, as Arab maritime activities were perceived to be.[2] The Sultanate's value to the British in this regard was its pre-eminent position in Arabia and its willingness to work with the British. This factor contributed to the Āl Bū Sa'īd drive to consolidate control over outlying parts of geographical Oman, as well as enclaves on the Iranian coast such as Hormuz and Bandar 'Abbas. Then towards the middle of the century, British activity began to coalesce around the campaign to repress slavery. Thereafter, her policy in Oman was directed increasingly toward the prevention of slave transport in Omani vessels, as well as gun-running by sea, and then slave-trading in Omani market-places.

By the process of introducing demands on the states and rulers of the Arab coast, Britain found herself committed to a vested interest in the continued survival of those dynasties. Particularly in Oman, the Government of India was forced to interrupt a centuries-old process of cyclical regeneration of politico-religious power in order to protect its relationship with the Āl Bū Saʿīd dynasty. As the political and financial bases of the Muscat regime deteriorated, India became more and more involved in Omani politics, as evidenced by the Canning Award of 1861, the Zanzibar Subsidy and the defence of Muscat between 1913 and 1921.

Eventually, when it became obvious that even the preservation of the *status quo* would leave the Sultanate perpetually dependent on India, the British sought to restructure the Muscat regime, particularly in the financial realm, in order to relieve themselves of the burden that Oman entailed in terms of manpower, subsidies and loans. This policy came at a time of general retrenchment from the view of imperial omnipotence and its success in Oman was eventually due to the appearance of a seemingly vigorous Sulṭān on the throne in Muscat: Saʿīd bin Taymūr. Nevertheless—despite the continuing British efforts at disentanglement from Arabian internal affairs, achieved in the Gulf by the official withdrawal in 1971—ties with Oman were not so easily severed. This was primarily a consequence of the need for British assistance in combating the rebellions on the Jabal al-Akhḍar and in Dhufar. Although the freedom of the Sultanate to assume an independent stance *vis-à-vis* the British on some matters had led a fragile existence since the early part of Saʿīd bin Taymūr's reign, the special relationship between Britain and the Sultanate had not disappeared completely by the mid-1970s.

In addition to the over-all policy outlined above, there were also a number of special interests in the Sultanate. Some were commercial, such as securing facilities for British steamers stopping at Muscat and the encouragement of British oil concessions, beginning with one of 1937 granted to a subsidiary of the Iraq Petroleum Company. In the course of the last two centuries or more, a sizeable community of Indian merchants has settled in Oman, primarily in Muscat and Maṭraḥ but also along the Bāṭina coast and, to a lesser extent, in Ṣūr and Ṣalāla. After the creation of the Government of India in 1857, members of this community were offered British registration—although this was to apply later primarily to the Hindus and not Muslim Indians, such as the Khojas. As a result, many Indians living in the Sultanate were entitled to British protection under clauses of extra-territoriality, a factor which exacerbated British–Sultanate relations under Sulṭān Fayṣal bin Turkī and which was to result in British pressure on the Muscat regime on frequent occasions when tribal incursions caused damage to Indian property.

Another British concern lay in the field of communications, beginning with the Indo–European Telegraph in 1864. The cable passed through Sultanate territory at Gwadar and across the Maqlab Isthmus in the Musandam—with a short-lived station on nearby Telegraph Island—and was extended to Muscat in 1901. The Telegraph Department (of the Government of India) was eventually to become the firm of Cable and Wireless, which continues to handle public communications in the Sultanate as well as in several Arab states of the Gulf.[3]

Oman also figured in the development of air routes to India, for both Imperial Airways and the RAF. The period of 1929–32 saw the creation of the Persian Gulf route, with bases established at Ṣuḥār, Shināṣ and Muscat—an airstrip was built at Bayt al-Falaj, seaplanes were anchored in Muscat harbour and the old American Consulate in Muscat was taken over by the RAF as a resthouse and wireless station.[4] The South Arabian route was also established at this time with facilities at Ṣalāla, Mirbāṭ, al-Maṣīra Island, Ra's al-Ḥadd and Gwadar.[5] The base at al-Maṣīra remained an important staging post for the RAF up to the mid-1970s, while the Ṣalāla base proved to be important to the Sultanate in the course of the Dhufar rebellion. The reciprocal relationship between the RAF and Muscat is illustrated by the base privileges that the RAF were given in Oman during World War II in return for a substantial military subsidy, and the permission given by Sulṭān Sa'īd bin Taymūr for continued use of al-Maṣīra as a *quid pro quo* for RAF assistance during the Jabal al-Akhḍar revolt and their agreement to keep Ṣalāla Air Base open for the Sulṭān's military needs.[6]

Formal Anglo–Omani Bonds

The changing nature of British interests in Oman was chronicled by a succession of treaties, agreements and demands, both written and verbal, as well as various types of financial assistance.[7] Their origin was in an Anglo–Omani treaty of 1798, largely prompted by apparent French interest in Oman. This treaty was backed up by a similar agreement two years later, which laid the basis for the first British representation in Oman.

British attention subsequently focused on prevention of the slave trade.[8] Theoretically, slavery had been abolished under British law as early as 1772 but final liberation of all slaves under the British flag was not effected until 1838. The first British action taken which involved Oman was the 'Moresby' treaty of 1822 between the two countries which was intended to stop the Africa-to-India trade in Omani vessels by drawing a line across the Indian Ocean, south of which slave vessels were prohibited. By a modification of this treaty in 1839, the restrictive line was moved north, bisecting the Indian Ocean along a course from the island of Suquṭra (Socotra) to a point on the Makrān coast, so closing Gwadar to the slave trade. Then in August 1845, Sulṭān Sa'īd bin Sulṭān agreed to help the British apprehend British subjects engaged in the trade. A few months later, in October 1845, Sa'īd signed an even more restrictive treaty, by which he agreed to prohibit any slave trade whatsoever between his possessions in Africa and those in Arabia and giving the East India Company the right to seize any Omani vessels which might be in violation.[9] This was a serious step for Sa'īd to take, as slave-trading formed a substantial part of the economic base of his empire, a reason which helps explain why the treaty was never seriously enforced. A later treaty of 1873 was far more drastic, absolutely prohibiting the importation of slaves into Oman, closing all public slave markets, and stipulating the freedom of all people thereafter entering the Sultanate. Needless to say, these treaties were not popular in Oman, where slavery was legal under Islām and a profitable trade for shipowners on the coast and dealers in the interior; eventually the treaties proved to be one more point of dissatisfaction and contributed to the interior uprising in the late nineteenth and early twentieth centuries.

The changing nature of these anti-slavery treaties illustrates the increasing influence that Britain exercised over Muscat. By the time of the arbitration over the successors to Sa'īd bin Sulṭān as rulers of the Āl Bū Sa'īd dominions, the predominance of Britain was obvious. As a result of the recommendations of the Coghlan Commission, the Canning Award of 1861 formalised a permanent division between the African and Arabian parts of the state, with Mājid bin Sa'īd ruling Zanzibar and Thuwaynī bin Sa'īd ruling Oman. Thirty years later, in March 1891, Sulṭān Fayṣal bin Turkī agreed to 'pledge and bind himself, his heirs and successors never to cede, to sell, to mortgage or otherwise give for occupation, save to the British Government, the dominions of Muscat and Oman or any of their dependencies'.[10] By the terms of this agreement, the British adopted a legally paramount position in Muscat and it was the closest that Oman came to being formally part of the British Empire.[11]

The following four decades were to witness a number of measures which served to bind British interests more closely to the Sultanate. Discussions were initiated in the early 1890s between the India Office and the Government of India on the possibilities of establishing a protectorate in Oman. This would have been a desirable position from the British point of view due to the seeming inability of Āl Bū Sa'īd rulers to control their own affairs satisfactorily, as well as because of the French challenge of that time. But ironically enough, it was precisely the renewal of French interest in Oman that prevented the establishment of a protectorate. According to an Anglo–French declaration signed in Paris in 1862, any compromise in Omani independence would require the consent of the French, a step that Paris would be unlikely to take in the 1890s and which the British were consequently wary of requesting. Thus, the Government of India was resigned to bolstering the existing regime as best as possible and employing generally subtle methods of persuasion to achieve its ends.

The first step in this 'policy of resignment' was the guarantee given to the Sulṭān after the 1895 rebellion that no further attacks on the Muscat/Maṭraḥ region would be tolerated, an undertaking that was directly responsible for the posting of Indian Army troops for the defence of the capital area from 1913 to 1921. The sharp British reaction to the hostile activities of Fayṣal bin Turkī during this period, culminating in the 1899 ultimatum to the Sulṭān to renounce his agreement for a French coaling station at Bandar Jiṣṣa, fell under the guidelines of this policy.[12] To prevent the reoccurrence of any such ambivalence in the future, the British demanded a written commitment from Taymūr bin Fayṣal on his accession to the throne, to seek British advice 'in important matters'.[13] The new Sulṭān had no choice but to accede to this pressure.

Another part of the problem was the establishment of Muscat as a centre for the re-export of arms, mainly to Afghanistan and the Northwest Frontier of India, although it also was responsible for the re-arming of tribes in inner Oman. The elimination of the arms traffic was sought by the British not only because of repercussions on the Northwest Frontier, but also for the reason that the trade was controlled in Oman by the French, out to undermine British influence.[14] The British solution was to force Fayṣal to require all imported arms to be placed in a guarded warehouse. In return for this concession, the Sulṭān was awarded an Arms Traffic Subsidy of Rs. 1,00,000 annually. The warehouse was as disastrous a policy for the Sulṭān as his restrictions on slavery: both policies contributed greatly to tribal disgruntlement.

When Sa'īd bin Taymūr ascended to the throne in February 1932, he too was forced to sign a supplicatory statement for the British, identical to the one his father had signed.[15] However, unlike his father, Sa'īd insisted on a good deal more independence and the vague clause in the statement which required the Sulṭān to seek British guidance in 'important matters' was easily circumvented by Sa'īd when so desired. Indeed, he developed a knack for turning agreements to his advantage. He agreed to extend use of airfields in Sultanate territory to the RAF, the US Army Air Force and BOAC, in exchange for a monthly subsidy for the duration of World War II.[16] The exchange of letters of August 1958 between the Sulṭān and the Secretary of State for Foreign Affairs procured British assistance for the development of his military; assistance which included financing, matériel and personnel, and which cost Sa'īd nothing.[17]

More 'regular' relations were maintained by a series of Commercial Treaties, the first being signed in 1839, and followed by the Customs Agreement of 1846 (which fixed duties at 5 per cent) and various commercial arrangements of the 1870s. The 1839 treaty was superseded by one of 1891 which recognised the most-favoured-nation status of Britain and provided the basis for the extra-territorial rights of British subjects, primarily Indian merchants, in the Sultanate.[18] This treaty was to remain valid for twelve years. On its expiry, it was renewed for five-year and then one-year periods until finally revised in a new treaty of 5 February 1939. This treaty retained the provisions for extra-territorial rights although somewhat restricting the jurisdiction of the British Consul in Muscat.[19] It was replaced by another treaty in December 1951, notable in reflecting the changing relationship between Britain and the Commonwealth countries, which were no longer included in the provisions of Anglo–

Omani treaties.[20] An accompanying exchange of letters placed numerous restrictions on the concept of extra-territoriality, especially in court cases involving the Sultanate or Omani nationals.[21]

The British position in Oman was also maintained by financial means. Their first activity in this regard was the assumption of the Zanzibar Subsidy of Rs. 86,400 annually. Soon after its payment by the Sulṭān of Zanzibar was stipulated by the Canning Award, the Sulṭān defaulted: its subsequent issuance became a charge on the Government of India in 1883 after being passed back and forth between India and the Foreign Office. This was the only permanent subsidy lasting throughout the twentieth century up to its abolition in 1970. Other subsidies granted in the twentieth century were generally given in response to specific situations. The first of these was the Arms Traffic Subsidy of Rs. 1,00,000 annually. Originally granted only for the period of Fayṣal's reign, it was extended until 1 January 1935, due to the economic position of the state. It was succeeded by the defence subsidy of World War II, whereby payments were made to the Sulṭān ostensibly to refurbish defences in case of attack by interior tribes. Fear of such attacks represented a misconception on the part of New Delhi officials whose grasp of the Muscat situation was some twenty years behind the times but one that Sa'īd was careful not to correct. Consequently, he received a monthly grant of Rs. 20,000 for the duration of the war (actually ending in 1946) in addition to an initial sum of Rs. 50,000 for the repair of fortifications and modernisation of the Sultanate's military establishment.[22]

When a genuine threat did appear in inner Oman, i.e. the rebellion of the 1950s, British subsidies were once again forthcoming. These consisted partly of an annual cash payment for military support—amounting to £477,175 in 1961[23]—supplemented by a programme of secondment of British officers and military equipment, and partly of a development subsidy—£1,058,750 in 1961[24]—which never received the support of the Sulṭān.

In addition to the subsidies, it was occasionally necessary in the early part of this century and before to advance loans to the Sultanate. These were used either to pay off Indian merchants who were charging excessive interest on debts incurred by the Sulṭān and members of the ruling family, or to meet essential expenses of the state (such as salaries) which otherwise would not have been met. The first loan was of five and a half lakhs of rupees (i.e. Rs. 5,50,000) advanced in 1918, with an additional lakh added in 1919. The latter was made conditional on the repayment of the entire sum by December 1929.[25] However, the appearance of the world depression had its effect on Muscat as elsewhere and repayment was extended until Sa'īd included the final two lakhs in his budget for 1932.

British Representation in Muscat

The means by which Britain extended its control over the Sultanate was the Political Agent in Muscat (PAM). The Political Agency there was part of a complicated system covering eastern Arabia and the Gulf, and administered by the Government of India as part of its Residency system. This included a Political Resident in the Persian Gulf (PRPG), who was based at Bushire until just prior to Indian independence when the Residency was shifted to al-Manāma in the state of al-Baḥrayn.[26] Subordinate to the PRPG at one time or another were Political Agents in Muscat, al-Dawḥa (Qaṭar), al-Manāma (prior to the relocation of the Residency there), al-Kuwayt, al-Baṣra (then Turkish Arabia), and Political Officers variously at Sharjah, Dubay and Abu Dhabi (generally subordinate to the Political Agent in al-Manāma).[27] Following Indian independence in 1947, the Gulf officers were placed under the jurisdiction of the Commonwealth Office for a year until the Foreign Office was given permanent charge. The PAM subsequently became a Consul General, reporting directly to the Foreign Office although responsibility for 'general political considerations' rested with the PRPG.[28]

The first British representative to reside in Muscat was a Political Resident under the control of the Bombay Presidency. However, the difficulties of life in Muscat—the climate claimed the lives of the first three officers—accounted for the short duration of this post (1800–10) and Muscat affairs were thereafter handled from Bushire for the next thirty years. Nevertheless, the increasing importance of the Sultanate, a result of the dynamism of Sulṭān Sa'īd bin Sulṭān, called for the resumption of a local agent and so Captain Atkins Hamerton was appointed in 1840. Once again, the appointment was short-lived as Sa'īd soon moved court to Zanzibar: the Resident followed soon after and British affairs in Muscat were left to a Native Agent.

The permanent return of the British representative to Muscat came after the division of the Omani empire when a representative was reposted there in 1860.[29] This, however, resulted in an ambiguous situation whereby the PAM generally reported directly to Bombay and not to the PRPG. The problem was compounded by the PRPG, Lewis Pelly. During that period, Pelly was assiduously consolidating his hold on British policy in Arabia through his aggressive use of the position which he held for over a decade and through his belief in a British 'mission civilatrice'. Pelly's unique position in the Gulf was due to his close relationship with the Governor of Bombay, Sir Bartle Frere, and consequently the PRPG remained subordinate to Bombay for several years.

Soon after Pelly's departure, however, the Government of India in Delhi assumed direct control over Bushire and thus over Muscat. The line of authority was thereby set for the following three-quarters of a century (1873–1947): thus the PAM reported to the PRPG who in turn reported to the Government of India in Delhi. Although the chain of command theoretically extended from Delhi to the India Office in Whitehall, London was rarely up to date on events in Muscat. There, little interest was displayed in Muscat affairs except on the rare occasions when HMG served as a go-between in the Sultanate's international relations, such as when the revision of the Commercial Treaty of 1891 required the assent of France and the US because of their earlier treaties with the Sultanate.[30]

At times, the PAM was also placed over subordinates who were assigned as the need arose. When the construction of the Indo-European Telegraph necessitated closer contact with the Sultanate's enclave of Gwadar, an Assistant PAM for Gwadar was appointed in 1863, with responsibility divided between the PAM on matters regarding local affairs in Gwadar and the Commissioner of Sind on affairs concerning the Makrān hinterland. Soon after, the PRPG assumed the role that the Commissioner of Sind had played, and then as Gwadar seemed to diminish in importance, the Assistant PAM was replaced by a Native Agent.[31] Another Assistant PAM was appointed for Ṣalāla during World War II, when Sa'īd bin Taymūr's presence there and the construction of the South Arabian air route, along with the RAF and US Army Air Force bases in Ṣalāla, required closer attention than the PAM could give to Dhufar. Nevertheless, the post was abandoned after the end of the Second World War when Sa'īd returned to Muscat in 1945.

One concession that the Agency was forced to make to the climate of Muscat was the annual summer recess. During this season, the PAM would retire to India, usually either Quetta or Ziarat (now in Pakistan), and return to Muscat for the 'cold weather'. There the PAM continued to direct his correspondence to the Sulṭān and the

PRPG and paid visits to the Foreign Department in Simla.[32] During these periods of recess, the Agency was left in the care of the ranking subordinate. In the nineteenth century, this was the Sub-Agency Surgeon, A. S. G. Jayakar, who also served as Acting PAM between permanent appointments. In the twentieth century, the Military Adviser to the Sultanate was frequently left in charge in Muscat or, during World War II, the Assistant PAM was shifted from relatively pleasant Ṣalāla to the capital.

With India's assumption of independence in 1947, the PAM was placed directly under the Foreign Office. Formally, the shift was not unusual, as the PAM had officially held the dual title of 'Political Agent and His Britannic Majesty's Consul, Muscat', since 1863. This set of circumstances was unique for a Political Agent in the area, the result of the Sultanate's position as a nominally independent state, although the PRPG also held the rank of Consul for Fars while the Residency was located in Bushire. The post was upgraded to Consul General in 1951. Then, in conjunction with the British official withdrawal from the Gulf and the Sultanate's entry into a wider international arena after 1970, the British appointed their first Ambassador in July 1971. Although Ambassadors had been appointed for Oman in the past, Donald Hawley was the first actually to reside in Muscat. The Sultanate's only representative abroad was C. E. Kendall, whom Sulṭān Sa'īd bin Taymūr had appointed in October 1963 to look after his affairs in London.

Since the greatest British impact on the Sultanate was through the Political Agents in Muscat, a closer look at these individuals seems warranted. They generally held their appointments in Muscat for short periods of time, due to the climate, although the appointments of a few were renewed. Others held commissions in the Indian Army so their services were frequently required elsewhere. Although most members of the Indian Political Service (IPS) and the Indian Civil Service (ICS) viewed Muscat as a distinctly undesirable post, some found themselves pursuing entire careers in Muscat and the Gulf, as Agents and Residents—and the PAM occasionally served as Acting PRPG in the latter's absence. Some notable exceptions to the rule of quick turnover in Muscat were S. B. Miles, serving a total of twelve years as PAM, P. Z. (later Sir Percy) Cox, serving five years, and F. C. L. Chauncy, who spent nine years there.[33]

The wide variance in the capability of various PAMs was often a matter of the particular attitude of each individual. In the early twentieth century, several, especially Haworth and Wingate, displayed obvious characteristics of the 'Raj' and saw their role in Muscat as agents of a 'mission civilatrice'. Later PAMs were to complain of the unimportance of Muscat. Consequently, the presence of British officials with antagonistic attitudes often aroused the resentment of individual Sulṭāns and the populace of the Sultanate in general. On the other hand, the work of Cox, as exemplified by his discovery that Sulṭān Fayṣal's favourite language was Gujerati, and the keenness on exploration and travel throughout the country, as displayed by Miles and Cox, secured the co-operation, respect and friendship of the rulers.[34]

In contrast to the high example set by the handful of Government of India officials who policed Arabia in the nineteenth century, the twentieth century was frequently marked by a procession of little-known names interrupted at intervals by exceptionally good or woefully inadequate individuals. The reassignment of Cox to Bushire in 1904 resulted in a marked decline in the general quality of the PAMs, a situation equally applicable to the Gulf in general. Most of the PAMs subsequently served either as Agents elsewhere in the Gulf throughout their careers until retirement or decided to join the area's oil companies. Some, however, were highly qualified as their later careers indicate. Cox was to become Foreign Secretary of the Government of India and High Commissioner for Mesopotamia. R. E. Holland later became a Member of the Council of India. E. B. Howell became Foreign Secretary and R. E. L. (later Sir Ronald) Wingate also acted in that capacity. Tom (later Sir Tom) Hickinbotham became Governor of Aden and then joined the board of directors of the Chartered Bank. A. C. Stewart became Ambassador to Iceland and then Libya; while several others culminated their careers with the post of PRPG.

Nevertheless, these officials had their opposites in men who proved completely unsuitable. Some were unable to speak Arabic—many members of the ruling family spoke nothing else—while others indulged in reckless derision of the Āl Bū Sa'īd and other indigenous inhabitants, a habit that even appeared in official and demi-official correspondence. Some, perhaps feeling that their presence in Muscat was a waste of time, displayed acute disinterest in the state's problems and consequently the PRPG was frequently compelled to deal with the Sulṭān when the PAM was unable to act on his own. In defence of those PAMs who had to deal with Sa'īd bin Taymūr, the latter's sensitivity regarding his sovereignty frequently required PAMs to tread carefully. In retrospect, it seems that Sa'īd's increasing competence in Sultanate administration more than offset the inability of the PAMs to control affairs in Muscat.

The British Impact on the Muscat Government

The peak of British influence in the Sultanate was reached during the reign of Taymūr bin Fayṣal. That it had become so pervasive was due to a combination of the state's financial status, the inability to control its hinterlands and the indifference towards politics exhibited by Taymūr. By 1920, the British had acquired extra-territorial rights, forbidden the cessation of territory to any other power, dictated the terms of a peace settlement with the interior tribes, and assumed financial control of the Sultanate by loans and subsidies, military control by a battalion of the Indian Army and political control by the introduction of an Englishman as *de facto* ruler of the state.

Decisions to introduce taxes or to initiate punitive measures against recalcitrant tribes were all subject to review by the PAM. Until Sa'īd bin Taymūr assumed the role of President of the Council of Ministers in 1929, British officials not only had the last word on matters of state, they also initiated them. They decided when Taymūr was finally allowed to abdicate and they exercised final approval of his successor. Sa'īd was subsequently required to present the same letter of supplication to the British as had his father when he acceded.

The British officials seconded to the Sultan's government not only served as instruments of British policy and standards but also exercised personal influence on the society of Muscat. In particular, the arrangements made for a Financial Adviser (FA) to the Sultanate provide a vivid example of the calibre of British employees of local states in the Peninsula at that time, and constitute an episode which was to have great impact on the formation of Sulṭān Sa'īd bin Taymūr's personality.[35] The first of the three incumbent FAs was the explorer, Bertram S. Thomas, who apparently regarded the position as an excellent opportunity to conduct exploration in a largely unknown corner of Arabia.[36] In the five years (1925–30) that Thomas held the position, he was the most important figure in the Muscat government—both in a *de facto* as well as a *de jure* sense, due to his membership in the Council of Ministers. This fact, along with his apparent disregard of the duties of the FA in favour of his travels, gave rise to frustration and a certain enmity among contemporary PAMs and PRPGs. In addition, his successor was to raise allegations of financial laxity and mismanagement against him. Nevertheless, if the regional Government of India hierarchy had been uncomfortable with Thomas, they were to find S. E. Hedgcock impossible to deal with.

Hedgcock held the position of FA for only the first six months of 1931. Yet in that period of time, he managed to alienate the Commandant of the Muscat Infantry, the PAM, the PRPG, and the Foreign Secretary of the Government of India. Furthermore, he succeeded in turning Sa'īd bin Taymūr's opinion against Thomas and British advisers in general, and drove a wedge between the ruling family and the British establishment. In addition, he made several charges of corruption and lies against British officials in the area and then personally conducted an inconclusive investigation of his own charges. As a result, he was pressed to resign his position and left Muscat in the early autumn of 1931. Unfortunately, this was not to be the last incident concerning the post of FA. Hedgcock's temporary successor was R. G. E. W. Alban, the Commandant of the Muscat Infantry, who also proved inadequate in judgement in several matters and was soon invalided home.

Hedgcock's departure and Alban's heavy workload—since he was Acting PAM and MLC Commandant as well as Financial Adviser—had allowed Sa'īd bin Taymūr, as President of the Council of Ministers, to take control of the state's finances. He was not eager to relinquish this new-found fragment of independence. When Alban left, Sa'īd rejected a suggestion that his brother, E. C. H. Alban, replace him. As a consequence, there was no replacement and Sa'īd remained unimpeded in that department until 1968.[37] Nevertheless, the activities of Thomas and Hedgcock left an indelible impression on Sa'īd. Hedgcock's attacks on Thomas were echoed in the 1968 'Word of the Sulṭān': 'Whilst hopes were pinned on Mr Thomas to repair what others had destroyed he completely ruined the finances and left them in an even sorrier state.'[38] Finances, in Sa'īd's opinion, were a strictly personal business.

In contrast to the apathy displayed by Taymūr, Sa'īd was determined to reverse the situation of the Sultanate's dependence on expatriate officials and Britain's policy of dictation. His efforts, however, were met by staunch resistance in the British hierarchy. When he made the arrangements for a world tour in 1938 without consulting the PAM or the latter's superiors, Whitehall officialdom engaged him in a 'tempest in a teapot' but eventually were forced to conclude that they were powerless to prevent Sa'īd's trip through the US.[39] Saʿīd was victorious in another 'tilt' with Whitehall in 1944 when he refused to acknowledge a routine communication from the Saudi Sharīʿ Court of Mecca, which had been addressed to HMG. The Sulṭān was satisfied only when a second note was addressed to him and merely forwarded *via* the British, as there was no direct Saudi–Omani channel of communication.[40]

Officialdom in the field was much better prepared to recognise the nominal nature of the Sultanate's independence. PAMs communicated with the Sulṭān as 'His Majesty's Consul' and not as Political Agent. When one objected to Saʿīd's pretensions with the remark that the Sultanate was only a 'six lakh state', he was duly reprimanded and speedily replaced. The Government of India seemed willing to humour Saʿīd, if only because the Sultanate retained its strategic value, partially due to the necessity for secure air routes in the World War II era and after.

Although the post-war years saw the steady dissolution of the British Empire in the Indian Ocean, Oman continued to hold high priority in the eyes of 'East of Suez' policy-planners. Its importance had increased in an age when the role of airpower was predominant. Furthermore, Oman was located in an oil-abundant area which held the key to Britain's economic well-being. The RAF viewed al-Maṣīra Island as an important link to Singapore, while the possibility of oil deposits under Omani soil encouraged London to back the Sultanate against Saudi claims during the Buraymī crisis. In addition, the Sultanate controls the southern shore of the Strait of Hormuz, through which all tankers entering and exiting the Gulf must pass.[41]

The threat to the British position in the Middle East, as posed by the rise of Arab nationalism and exemplified by the Suez crisis of 1956, also served to turn Oman into a pawn between opposing camps. Even though the rebellion waged by the 'Oman Revolutionary Movement' in the latter half of the 1950s ranked as little more than a skirmish in military terms, its implications heightened tension in Anglo–American relations, brought sharp debate to the House of Commons on British involvement and was responsible for the introduction of the crack Special Air Service (SAS) into the fray in early 1959, as Britain attempted to put a quick end to an embarrassing situation with the best means at her disposal.[42]

Following the administrative integration of the interior into the Sultanate, British interest in the area diminished considerably: British activity, primarily on the military side, was limited to guaranteeing the security of the state in its existing form. But even this tranquil relationship was soon disturbed: the Labour Government's decision to abrogate Britain's special treaty relationship with the Arab states of the Gulf was overshadowed by the apparent failure of the Sultanate to combat insurgency in Dhufar effectively, primarily the result of refusal by an anachronistic Sulṭān to meet the challenge of changing expectations in the country.

The Anglo-Omani relationship was altered dramatically by the beginning of the 1970s as Oman took steps to expand its role in the international arena. Although British interests continued unabated, Britain's influence was subject to increasing competition. British contractors were in the forefront of the state's newly-emphasised development, but close behind were American, Cypriot, French, German, Lebanese, Swedish and Swiss firms. Although British officers continued to provide the backbone of the Sultan's Armed Forces, Jordanian and especially Iranian troops also contributed greatly to the victory in Dhufar. Finally, with Britain's growing economic troubles, Oman was forced to look to its neighbours, including its arch rival Saudi Arabia, for financial support. In short, Britain's paramount position of centuries past was dramatically transformed: she remained a friend and an ally but she was no longer the only one.

Relations with Other Countries

The Sultanate's era of isolation had lasted nearly a century. When the political centre of the Āl Bū Sa'īd moved to Zanzibar in the mid-nineteenth century, Oman's ties to the outside world were severely checked and then almost completely severed by the division of Sa'īd bin Sulṭān's realm. The economic decline which plagued Oman prevented the resumption of the state's European ties in Muscat—always with the exception of Great Britain, of course—and when the Sultanate finally got its house back in economic order much later, Sa'īd bin Taymūr emphatically refused new bonds, whether political, cultural or economic, European or Middle Eastern.

Originally, treaty relationships had been initiated with the United States (1833), France (1844) and the Netherlands (1877), but when the Zanzibar connection was broken, only the US felt that the Sultanate was important enough to warrant a Vice-Consul.[43] Nevertheless, the Consulate, established in 1880, saw its function gradually reduced to invoicing several dozen date shipments and looking after the American missionaries in Oman: it was abruptly closed in 1915.[44] Official contacts were sparse between then and the signing of a new treaty in 1958: brief visits were made by American diplomats in 1923, 1934 and 1946; while Sa'īd visited the US in 1937.

A joint Franco–Russian challenge had been mounted in the 1890s to British supremacy in the Gulf; and a French Vice-Consul was appointed for Muscat in 1894. The machinations of the Vice-Consul, Paul Ottavi, and his successors, although initially successful, eventually withered in the face of British steadfastness, whether the project was support of slave-running dhows carrying French flags, the Muscat arms trade or the abortive arrangement for a coaling station at Bandar Jiṣṣa. The French withdrew from Muscat at the beginning of World War I.[45] Russian activity was limited to establishing a short-lived steamship line for the Gulf, calling at Muscat, and arousing British suspicions regarding their actions at Bandar 'Abbas and Gwadar. Germany, already engaged in building the Berlin-to-Baghdad railway, also sent steamers into the Gulf.[46] During World War I, German agents in German East Africa (later Tanzania) were reportedly subverting Omanis there to agitate against the Sultanate during the 1913–20 revolt.[47] Nevertheless, these challenges proved ineffective and by the end of World War I, only Britain had active relations with Oman.

Closer to home, ties with the rest of Arabia had disintegrated with Oman's decline. The state's tenuous control over the Arabian Gulf coast of Oman had disappeared with construction of the Trucial system. The role of Oman as aggressor in Arabia was reversed by the mid-nineteenth century. Indeed, Saudi incursions had threatened the Sultanate as early as 1803, when a Saudi army surged through the Bāṭina.[48] In combination with the Qawāsim, the Saudis established bases at Khawr Fakkān and Shināṣ; a joint Anglo–Omani expedition against them in 1810 ended in failure with the Saudis pursuing the attackers to the outskirts of Muscat. In the next few years, under the leadership of Muṭlaq al-Muṭayrī, the invaders were able to sack Izkī, after the defeat of a joint Sultanate–Persian army and Maṭraḥ, as well as range through al-Sharqīya and Ja'lān with impunity. The death of al-Muṭayrī, the death of the Saudi amīr in Dara'īya, and the expansion of Muḥammad 'Alī's Egyptian state all played a role in the withdrawal of the Saudis from this highpoint of their designs on Oman. Even so, they continued to threaten the country, *via* the gateway of al-Buraymī, on numerous occasions until they were decisively driven from al-Buraymī by

'Azzān bin Qays in 1869. Once again, sagging Saudi fortunes in central Arabia prevented them from countering. The potential of the Saudi threat was renewed only by the revival of the Saudi state after 1902.

Undoubtedly, the architect of the modern Saudi state, 'Abd al-'Azīz bin 'Abd al-Raḥmān (also known as Ibn Sa'ūd) envisaged control over all of Arabia: he was successful in adding 'Asīr and the Ḥijāz to the Saudi dominions of the Najd and al-Aḥsā' (Hasa).[49] But expansion in the east was precluded by the presence of the British. In Oman, therefore, the Saudis were limited to intrigues with various tribes against the Sultanate, and Saudi tax collectors were reported to be at al-Buraymī in 1925.[50] The Banī Bū 'Alī tribe of the Ja'lān proved to be willing partners. Their traditional truculence had flared up again in the 1920s with a dispute over the Sulṭān's custom post at Ṣūr. Saudi arms and money were allegedly passed to the rebels at this time and the latter constructed their own customs station at the nearby suburb of al-'Ayqa and raised the Saudi flag in 1928. However, a display of gunboat diplomacy by the British brought the dispute to a quick end and the Saudis had no significant influence in Oman until the early 1950s.[51]

The next occasion of Saudi irredentism surfaced with the expectation of oil deposits under the sands of the Rub' al-Khālī, provoking the Saudis to extend their territorial claims in eastern Arabia. In October 1952, they backed these claims with the armed occupation of al-Ḥamāsa village in the Buraymī oasis.[52] The occupation of this strategic point enabled the Saudis to extend their influence among the tribes of al-Ẓāhira. Furthermore, the liberal supply of cash and, later, arms helped win allies for them among the leaders of the post-1954 Imamate; indeed, the resultant Oman Revolutionary Movement set up its headquarters in exile in al-Dammām and its 1957 uprising was financed and armed by Saudi Arabia. Al-Riyāḍ continued to grant asylum to the ex-Imām, Ghālib bin 'Alī, and loosely supported his cause until a rapprochement was reached with Sulṭān Qābūs in 1971.

The uneasy alliance forged by Saudi Arabia in the 1950s with the Arab nationalist camp, primarily Egypt, only reinforced Sa'īd bin Taymūr's determination to keep the external world at bay. He not only attempted to prevent travel to and from the Sultanate but official international relations were almost non-existent. Only Britain and India maintained Consulates in Muscat; while several other countries, such as the US and the Netherlands, updated treaties but maintained no offices in the country. Sa'īd was equally aloof to his Arab neighbours. Although many of the Trucial Rulers had developed the habit of visiting the hospitals in Muscat and Maṭraḥ, the Sulṭān would not receive them. His only concession had been two widely-publicised meetings with successive Rulers of Abu Dhabi: he greeted Shaykh Shakhbūt bin Sulṭān Āl Nuhayyān at al-Buraymī in late 1955 and then invited Shaykh Zāyid bin Sulṭān to Ṣalāla in 1968.

Omani relations with Iran were equally distant until the 1970s. As is the case among the peoples of the Arab littoral of the Gulf, Iran has traditionally been viewed with suspicion by Omanis. Persian intrusions have periodically menaced Oman for millenia, the last being in the mid-eighteenth century. Although the Persian presence at that time was originally in response to a request for help by a contending faction to the Imamate, and despite Iran's role as co-defender of Izkī for the Āl Bū Sa'īd state against a Saudi army in 1812, Iran has generally been seen by Omanis as more of a threat than an ally.[53] In like manner, the substantial Iranian help offered to the Sultanate after 1970, in the course of the Dhufar rebellion, was viewed with suspicion in some quarters. Coming as it did on the heels of Iranian occupation of Abū Mūsā and the Ṭunb islands in the Gulf, leftist groups and states in the Arab world voiced their disapproval and charged the Shah with attempting to extend his hegemony in the manner of his predecessors. What is often overlooked are the constraints on the Iranian position: whatever influence Iran may have gained in the Sultanate was subordinate to that of the British, as well as to that of the United States. Iran's troops in Dhufar were kept rigidly isolated from politics and from even casual contact with most Omanis.

The tacit wariness between the Sultanate and its ideological opposites in the Arab world continued on into the post-1970 regime. Even though Oman became substantially liberalised, it was still plagued by rebels backed by Arab regimes whose ideological stance remained far to the left of the Sultanate's. The gradual evolution of opposition to the Sultanate along the ideological spectrum from religious xenophobia to radical Marxist–Leninism gave notice to the Sultanate that change was absolutely necessary. The state's response to these stimuli forms the basis for the following chapters.

Notes

1. The revolt of the 1950s in Oman did catch Britain in the ire of Arab nationalism, whose proponents accused Britain of subjecting a 'colonialist

regime' to a war with a so-called 'nationalist movement'. For more information on this revolt, see the following chapter.

2. Another spur was Napoleon's abortive dream for the conquest of India, which included the despatching of a letter to the 'Imam of Muscat' but which was intercepted by British agents. For more information on Napoleon's contacts with Arabia, see J. B. Kelly, *Britain and the Persian Gulf, 1795–1880* (Oxford: Clarendon Press, 1968), pp. 62–78.

3. See the appendix in *Lorimer's Gazetteer* on the telegraphs of the Gulf, vol. 1, pt. 2, pp. 2400–38; and Christina Phelps Harris, 'The Persian Gulf Submarine Telegraph of 1864', *GJ*, vol. 135, pt. 2 (June 1969), pp. 169–90.

4. For more information on the creation of the Persian Gulf air route, see G. W. Bentley, 'The Development of the Air Route in the Persian Gulf', *JRCAS*, vol. 20, pt. 2 (1933), pp. 173–89; Lt. Col. Gordon Dalyell of the Binns, 'The Persian Gulf', *JRCAS*, vol. 25, pt. 3 (1938), p. 359; Robin D. S. Higham, *Britain's Imperial Air Routes 1918–1939* (London: G. T. Foulis, 1960), pp. 122–33; and John Marlowe, *The Persian Gulf in the Twentieth Century* (London: Cresset Press, 1962), pp. 249–51.

5. The major source on the development of aviation in the Sultanate is the IO files from the Muscat Political Agency, R/15/3/72 through R/15/3/121. These facilities largely consisted of unmarked landing strips and were—except for Ṣalāla and al-Maṣīra—abandoned after the war. Ra's al-Ḥadd and Ṣalāla had also been used by the US Army Air Force.

6. The necessity for this arrangement was ended by the conclusion of the Dhufar rebellion in late 1975. Accordingly, the British government made the announcement in July 1976 that it would withdraw from both bases.

7. The texts of the treaties and agreements concluded between the British and the Muscat government, up to 1929, are contained in C. U. Aitchison (ed.), *A Collection of Treaties, Engagements and Sanads relating to India and Neighbouring Countries*, 5th edn (Calcutta: Government of India, 1933), vol. 11, pp. 269–322. For the period between 1930 and 1970, see the Treaty Series of the League of Nations and United Nations. Some of the principal agreements are discussed in Husain Albaharna, *The Arabian Gulf States: Their Legal and Political Status and Their International Problems*, 2nd edn (Beirut: Librairie du Liban, 1975), pp. 47–54; as well as in UN General Assembly, 19th Session, 22 Jan. 1965, *Question of Oman; Report of the Ad Hoc Committee on Oman*, A/5846 (the 'Jiménez Report'), pp. 113–33 and 165–6.

8. For a good account of activities in this regard, see *Lorimer's Gazetteer*, vol. 1, pt. 2, pp. 2475–503.

9. This treaty was duplicated by a British agreement with the independent ruler of Ṣuḥār, Sayf bin Ḥamūd, in May 1849.

10. Agreement regarding the Cession of Territory by the Sultan of Oman, dated 20 March 1891, as quoted in Aitchison, *Treaties*, vol. 11, p. 318; and *Lorimer's Gazetteer*, vol. 1, pt. 1, p. 628.

11. The agreement was formally terminated by an exchange of letters in 1958. See the 'Jiménez Report', pp. 122–3.

12. For a detailed study of the French challenge in Oman, see Briton Cooper Busch, *Britain and the Persian Gulf, 1894–1914* (Berkeley: University of California Press, 1967), pp. 49–93 and 154–86.

13. The PAM, Percy Cox, reported to his superiors that 'I had informed [Taymūr] that I considered that he should address a supplementary communication to British Agency saying that he realised that he could not hold his own without our material and moral support and begging Political Agent to assure Government that he accepted all the obligations which his father bore towards the British Government and intended to pursue his father's policy, in regards to

the arms traffic as well as other matters, and undertook to be guided by our advice in all important questions (of course without prejudice to his independence). Then in conclusion he was to say that he hoped that Government would strengthen his hands for the difficult task before him by according him official recognition as speedily as practicable. The natural corollary of such recognition being in our case the continuance of the subsidies paid to his father.' IO, R/15/3/215; Cox to Foreign Department, Government of India, Telegram M–12, 14 Oct. 1913.

14. The Anglo–French crisis over the Muscat arms trade is discussed by Busch, *Britain and the Persian Gulf*, pp. 270–303.

15. For the complete text, see Appendix E.

16. He also succeeded in turning a profit in Ṣalāla while providing the British and US bases there with labour and water. IO, R/15/1/425; Asst. PAM Bird to PAM Metcalfe, Demi-official No. C/1185, 13 July 1944.

17. The background for this exchange of letters is discussed in the latter part of the following chapter.

18. The application of extra-territorial rights, primarily relating to rights of trial by a court sitting under the PAM, was handled under a series of Muscat Orders-in-Council, principally those of 1915 and 1939, contained in IO, R/15/3/252 and R/15/1/298 respectively.

19. Jasper Y. Brinton discusses the treaty in 'The Arabian Peninsula, the Protectorates and Sheikdoms', *Revue Egyptienne de Droit International*, vol. 3 (1947), pp. 29–30.

20. For a comparison of the 1939 and 1951 treaties, see Richard Young, 'United Kingdom–Muscat Treaty of 1951,' *American Journal of International Law*, vol. 46, no. 4 (Oct. 1952), pp. 704–8.

21. The exchange of letters provided for the retention of extra-territorial privileges for ten years, later partially renewed in 1961 and relinquished on 1 Jan. 1967. Albaharna, *The Arabian Gulf States*, p. 53; and the *Persian Gulf Gazette*, Supplement No. 53 (Jan. 1967), Appendix 1. Between 1961 and 1967, the only jurisdiction Britain exercised was over members of its armed forces in Oman. See Jiménez Report, pp. 173–4.

22. FO, 371/24545 for 1940, Arabia E635/509/91; PAM Hickinbotham to Sulṭān, No. C/514, 13 Feb. 1940.

23. *The Times*, 25 Mar. 1961.

24. Ibid.

25. IO, R/15/1/419; PAM to Secretary, PRPG, No. K/73, 24 Aug. 1927.

26. The Government of India also maintained a Residency at Aden for much of the nineteenth and early twentieth centuries. Indian control was transferred to the Colonial Office when the Crown Colony of Aden was created in 1937.

27. For a good discussion of the development of the British position in eastern Arabia, see J. B. Kelly, 'The Legal and Historical Basis of the British Position in the Persian Gulf', *St Antony's Papers*, No. 4; Middle Eastern Affairs, No. 1 (London: Chatto and Windus, 1958), pp. 119–40. An excellent summation of where British representatives in Oman stood in the imperial hierarchy was prepared by Penelope Tuson as the introduction to the Muscat Agency Records in the India Office. See also Tuson's 'Forthcoming India Office Records Relating to the Middle East', *British Society for Middle Eastern Studies Bulletin*, vol. 2, no. 1 (1975), pp. 46–50.

28. Interview with FO official with long service in the Gulf. A complete list of British representatives in Muscat is given in Appendix F.

29. A Political Agent remained in Zanzibar under the authority of the Government of India until 1883 when the post was transferred to the jurisdiction of the Foreign Office.

30. The paperwork required in this process took the better part of two decades simply to obtain agreement to raise tariff rates in Muscat from 5 per cent to 10 per cent and involved a line of communication from the Sulṭān to the PAM to the PRPG to the Government of India to the India Office to the Foreign Office to the British Embassies in Washington and Paris and on to the State Department and the Quai d'Orsay, and then the exact reverse. See IO, R/15/3/49.

31. The title was later changed to Pro-Consul; the long-serving incumbent, K. B. 'Abd al-Qayyūm, retired in 1958 when Gwadar was transferred to Pakistan. *Persian Gulf Gazette*, vol. 6, no. 16 (Oct. 1958).

32. Although it may be assumed that the PAM found himself removed from the centre of action for these months, it will be noted that Muscat generally slumbered through its summers of 115° heat and high humidity. As a consequence, offices were closed and the well-to-do deserted the capital. Sulṭāns Taymūr and Sa'īd generally spent the summers in India and London, the PRPG generally was in recess himself; even the Government of India transferred operations from oppressive Delhi to Simla.

33. Miles took advantage of his appointment to travel extensively in the interior and recounted his experiences in various articles and his book, *The Countries and Tribes of the Persian Gulf*, 2nd edn (London: Frank Cass, 1966). Chauncy returned to Muscat later as Personal Adviser to the Sulṭān from 1961 to 1970. It should also be noted that Foreign Office appointees (i.e. those serving in Muscat after Chauncy) generally held appointments for two years or more, in distinction from Government of India officials who averaged approximately nine months per posting in the twentieth century.

34. A detailed account of the period Cox spent as PAM is found in Philip Graves, *The Life of Sir Percy Cox* (London: Hutchinson, 1941), pp. 64–91. Cox himself recounted his travel experiences in 'Some Excursions in Oman', *GJ*, vol. 66, no. 3 (Sept. 1925), pp. 193–227.

35. The role of this office in the Muscat government and the problems which arose from it are discussed in greater detail in the present writer's forthcoming article, 'British Financial Advisors in Muscat During the Interwar Period', *Arabian Studies*, vol. 5 (1978).

36. During his residence in Muscat, Thomas reported on such notable exploits as his stay in the Ru'ūs al-Jibāl region of the northern extremity of Oman and his epic journey across the Rub' al-Khālī desert, the first Westerner to accomplish this feat.

37. Even when C. J. Pelly was appointed Secretary for Financial Affairs in that year, his writ was considerably less than what Thomas's and Hedgcock's had been several decades earlier.

38. 'The Word of Sulṭān Sa'īd bin Taymūr, Sulṭān of Muscat and Oman, About the History of the Financial Position of the Sultanate in the Past and What It Is Hoped It Will Be in the Future, After the Export of Oil' (1968).

39. FO, 371/20781 for 1937, Arabia E6332/1023/91; Memorandum by W. E. Beckett, Legal Adviser, FO, 3 Nov. 1937; and ibid., Arabia E6946/1023/91; Memorandum from T. V. Brennan and Lacy Baggallay, FO Eastern Department, to Gibson, IO, 21 Dec. 1937.

40. FO, 371/39925 of 1944, Arabia E5534/5534/91; Eldon Ellison for HM Minister, Jedda, to Anthony Eden, FO, 30 Aug. 1944, No. 84/1714/785/8; ibid., C. A. F. Dundas, FO, to F. A. K. Harrison, IO, 25 Sept. 1944; and ibid., C. W. Baxter, Head of Eastern Department, FO, to S. R. Jordan, British Legation, Jedda, No. 127, 19 Oct. 1944.

41. In the 1970s, Iranian concern over the safety of the Strait of Hormuz led Iran to conclude a joint-policing pact with the Sultanate for the area. See Chapter 7.

42. A more detailed look at this rebellion is to be found in the following chapter. Its impact on over-all defence policy is treated in Phillip Darby, *British Defence Policy East of Suez, 1947–1968* (London: Oxford University Press for the Royal Institute of International Affairs, 1973), pp. 128–33. Col. David Stirling, the founder of SAS, wrote a letter to *The Times* (10 April 1959) soon after the SAS activities in this rebellion, asserting that the group had by this operation achieved their 'true peace-time role'.

43. Albaharna briefly discusses treaties with France (1844), the Netherlands (1877), India (1953) and the US (1958), in *TheArabian Gulf States*, pp. 54–7.

44. When the order came from Washington to close the Consulate and send its files to al-Baṣra, the Sulṭān was caught completely by surprise and he enquired of the PAM whether he had done anything to displease the Americans. IO, R/15/3/147; PAM Benn to PRPG Cox, No. 96, 11 Apr. 1915.

45. Unlike the American Consulate, the French had purchased their Consulate property in Muscat. However, the building was continually in need of repair—supervised by the PAM at the request of the nearest French Consul in Bombay. During World War II, Sulṭān Sa'īd sent a message to the de Gaulle government, offering use of the building to the Free French. In reply, the French stated that 'it would be no longer required and might be occupied by the [Sultanate]'. IO, R/15/3/151; PAM A. C. Galloway to PRPG Prior, No. S–244–6/4, 19 Feb. 1945. It was subsequently taken over by Cable and Wireless, then the Imperial Bank of Iran (later British Bank of the Middle East) and then by Petroleum Development (Oman) Ltd.

46. These attempts to supplant the British are described in Busch, *Britain and the Persian Gulf;* and Firouz Kajare, *Le Sultanat d'Oman: la question de Mascate; étude d'histoire diplomatique et de droit international* (Paris: A. Pedone, 1914). The arms trade is also treated in *Lorimer's Gazetteer*, vol. 1, pt. 2, pp. 2556–93.

47. German agents were also alleged to have travelled from Dar al-Salaam to Ṣūr and from there, to have journeyed through al-Sharqīya, distributing money. IO, R/15/3/45; PAM Benn to PRPG Knox, No. 31, 25 Jan. 1915.

48. This subject is covered by M. Morsy Abdullah, 'The First Sa'udi Dynasty and Oman, 1795–1818', *Proceedings of the Fourth Seminar for Arabian Studies* (1970), pp. 34–40; and Muḥammad Sa'īd al-Sha'fī, 'al-'Alāqāt al-Sa'ūdīya—al-'Umānīya 1800–1818', *Majallat Kullīyat al-Ādāb li-Jāmi'at al-Riyāḍ*, vol. 1 (1970), pp. 206–29.

49. 'As long as we paid him the subsidy [during World War I] he kept his hands off the Hejaz; since it ceased he has extended his authority over that country, and I have little doubt but that in the course of time he will seek to extend his authority over the interior of 'Oman.' Comment by Sir Percy Cox following lecture given by G. J. Eccles on 27 Oct. 1926, before the Royal Central Asian Society, London. See Eccles, 'The Sultanate of Muscat and Oman, With a Description of a Journey into the Interior Undertaken in 1925', *JRCAS*, vol. 14, pt. 1 (1927), p. 40.

50. IO, R/15/3/337; Annual Muscat Administration Report for 1925.

51. More information on the Banī Bū 'Alī is contained in the previous chapter.

52. The oasis consists of nine villages, of which three, including al-Buraymī proper, have traditionally been under Omani sovereignty. The other six have been claimed by the State of Abu Dhabi, which frequently refers to its territory by the name of the second largest village, al-'Ayn. For detailed accounts of the Buraymī dispute and the historical factors leading up to it, see J. B. Kelly, *Eastern Arabian Frontiers* (London: Faber and Faber, 1964); David Holden, *Farewell to Arabia* (London: Faber and Faber, 1966), pp. 201–13; and Albaharna, *The Arabian Gulf States*, pp. 196–238. The connection of the Buraymī problem with the Imamate revolt of the same period is discussed in the following

chapter. See also the memorials prepared by Saudi Arabia and the United Kingdom (on behalf of the Sultanate and Abu Dhabi) and presented to an arbitration tribunal established to consider the conflicting claims. In 1938, a British official, J. B. Howes, accompanied a party of geologists from PCL on a visit to al-Buraymī, being the first Europeans to visit the oasis since Percy Cox in 1905. In his report to his superiors, Howes noted that 'The influence of Ibn Saud is practically nil, though he remains in the back of people's minds as a possible offset to Muscat, and I have heard his name used for this purpose.' IO, R/15/3/426; Howes, Assistant Political Agent in al-Baḥrayn, to the Political Agent there, H. Weightman, 21 Dec. 1938.

53. By way of illustration, a number of Omanis, including 'Īsā bin Ṣāliḥ al-Ḥārithī and Sulaymān bin Ḥimyar al-Nabhānī, voiced concern to the PAM and the Sulṭān about fears of an Iranian invasion during the early days of World War II. IO, R/15/1/425; PAM Hickinbotham to PRPG Prior, Demi-official No. C/546, 9 Oct. 1940.

PART TWO

Challenges to the Sultanate

CHAPTER 6

Imāms, Tribes and the Changing Nature of Challenges

Although the Āl Bū Sa'īd Sultanate[1] in Oman has existed for more than two centuries, rarely has it been able to exercise more than a precarious hold on the political dynamics of the country. The manner of its evolution from religious Imamate into a secular dynasty was common enough in the history of Oman, but its perpetuation and then transformation into a legitimate base for a modern 'nation–state' was certainly alien to the traditional political milieu. As a result, the institution of the 'Sultanate' has been continually resisted in a number of quarters, ranging from individual schemes simply to replace the Sulṭān in the Muscat palace to a protracted struggle to tear down the entire political system in the region, including not only the trappings of the Sultanate but also the traditional hierarchy of tribal social organisation. In a somewhat different and more recent sense, the Sultanate has also been faced with the threat of disintegration under the pressure of social and economic change. This is a challenge that cannot be met, contained and conquered; rather, the state must accept and adapt—fully recognising that in so doing it may be participating in its own demise. This is by far the most profound of all the challenges that have confronted the Sultanate in the past.

A Variety of Challenges

An examination of these challenges reveals not only that their appearances have been prompted by different stimuli but also that their roots display various characteristics which can be classified in several distinct groups. Prominent among these have been the external threats—encroachments on the state by military force, which must be met by military force. This phenomenon long antedated the appearance of the Sultanate and can best be described as a threat to the entire country. In the last two centuries, such a threat has come primarily from Iran or the Saudis. Its effect has been greatest in uniting diverse political elements against the intruder. The Saudi occupation of al-Buraymī is a good example: the Sulṭān immediately began raising a force to recapture the oasis while the Imām likewise called for support and sent elements to join the Sulṭān's men at Ṣuḥār—a futile gesture as the British pressured the Sulṭān to drop his plans.

Although external threats have often been of considerable force, the hardiest threat to the Sultanate *per se* has always been internal. It began when the Āl Bū Sa'īd rulers dropped the title of Imām and thus gave rise to the question of legitimacy of rule and opened the dynasty to threats of replacement as temporal rulers of the country. The Āl Bū Sa'īd were thereby perceived by some as antithetical to Ibāḍism. Consequently, opposition to the dynasty arose in the form of religious indignation over the course followed by the Muscat rulers and was frequently combined with a purely political disavowal of Āl Bū Sa'īd claims to sovereignty or even primacy. After all, the Āl Bū Sa'īd tribe lacked importance in both terms of numbers and geographical location.

The institution of a central government, whether the secularised Sultanate or the Ibāḍī Imamate, has earlier been shown to be at odds with the development and maintenance of the tribal system of politics in Oman. Only the vitality of various resurgent Imamates was able to hold the natural state of tribal autonomy in check. As a threat to the established political order, this natural centrifugal tendency was only effective when the Imamate reached a stage of decadence. But another aspect of tribal politics, the Ghāfirī–Hināwī dichotomy, not only limited the effect of natural autonomy but also was able to channel the energy of tribal politics into a determined assault on the institution of the Sultanate. Although the late nineteenth century is illustrative of Hināwī offensives in particular, the tribal threat was most effective under the Ghāfirī–Hināwī alliance of the early twentieth century and when harnessed in tandem with the religious feeling engendered by the restoration of the Imamate in 1913. The combination of a religious regeneration and a major tribal alliance had served in the past to set new historical cycles into action. But the process was interrupted in the twentieth century by the presence of the British, who proved to be a factor more durable than the traditional cycle, even when the latter was allied with an external threat. If the 'British factor' was responsible in one sense for the continued survival of the Sultanate, it was also symbolic of a new threat: the challenge of 'development', the Pandora's box which has frequently spelled the end of traditional politics throughout the world. For much of the twentieth century, this new spectre was kept at bay by the poverty of the state and the deliberate policy of Sa'īd bin Taymūr. Nevertheless, increasing awareness of the outside world crept in. A small number of transistor radios were tuned into Cairo's 'Ṣawt al-'Arab' and the many Omani workers employed in the newly affluent states of the Gulf returned home with new dreams and hopes for the future. The failure of Sa'īd bin Taymūr to respond to this drive, coming as it did on top of the military threat from Dhufari rebels, resulted in his deposition.

The characteristic roots of the challenges to the Sultanate have evolved over the course of the twentieth century in a more or less linear movement of ideology from right to left. The conservatism of the traditional challenge, a mixture of religious fanaticism and tribal xenophobia, was tempered by the introduction of Arab nationalism in the 1950s, an introduction provided *via* the external threat posed once again by Saudi Arabia.[2] After the moderately leftist threat fell victim to tribal aloofness and prompt military response, another nationalist insurrection arose in Dhufar and contact with the same Arab nationalist elements provided the means for transition to the radical brand of Marxist–Leninist beliefs which characterised the Popular Front for the Liberation of the Occupied Arabian Gulf (PFLOAG) and its successors. This ideological evolution, from traditional challenge to nationalism to radicalism is well illustrated by the three major rebellions of the twentieth century, each of which will be examined in detail in the following pages.

The possibility of a traditional challenge had been opened by the Āl Bū Sa'īd as early as 1784 when the title of Imām was dropped. Consequently, Muscat faced the continual probability that tribal rivalries and discontentment with Sultanate policies would be organised under the banner of a religious campaign against the Sulṭāns of the coast. In some cases, this double opposition could join with yet a third force: rival branches of the Āl Bū Sa'īd. Among these, the most persistent opponents were the descendants of 'Azzān bin Qays, grandson of Aḥmad bin Sa'īd, founder of the dynasty. This particular collateral branch was headquartered in the environs of al-Rustāq and periodically allied itself with major tribes of the interior in order to increase its territorial influence at the expense of the Sulṭāns. It was a strategy most successfully pursued by 'Azzān bin Qays, grandson of the 'Azzān mentioned above, who threw in his lot with the Hināwī leaders and managed to capture Muscat in 1868 where he ruled for three years as Imām.[3]

Although 'Azzān was clearly the leading figure in the Imamate triumvirate of 1868–71, a number of less successful attempts to restore the Imamate later in the nineteenth century owed their impetus to the ambitions of Ṣāliḥ bin 'Alī al-Ḥārithī, who had formed part of the earlier trio of 1868–71.[4] Ṣāliḥ was successful in enlisting as his candidates for Imām relatives of 'Azzān and even 'Abd al-'Azīz bin Sa'īd, the son of Sulṭān Sa'īd bin Sulṭān. Yet his efforts were doomed to failure because of the narrowness of his power base: he relied solely on the Hināwī faction and even lacked significant support among the Hināwīs; the Ghāfirīs, meanwhile, generally rallied to the Sulṭān. The zenith of nearly a half-century of attempts to supplant the Sulṭāns came with the 1895 sack of Muscat. The failure of this attempt illustrates the weakness of an essentially tribal approach spurred on by secular ambition.

The 1895 Siege of Muscat

Although Ṣāliḥ's desires in regard to Muscat had long been obvious, his final offensive in the mid-1890s was prompted by several immediate factors. One was the accession of Ḥamad bin Thuwaynī, the son of the former Sulṭān of Oman, to the Rulership of Zanzibar in 1893. When Ṣāliḥ's son, 'Abd Allāh, and several of his associates visited Zanzibar soon after, they were warmly received and sent back to Oman with gifts of field pieces and gunpowder.[5] Encouraged by this support, Ṣāliḥ at the same time witnessed the growing estrangement of Sulṭān Fayṣal and the British. Indeed, Fayṣal seemed to face the problem of worsening relations on all sides. He had lost much of his influence in the interior due to his vacillating policy and lack of interest. He had also poisoned momentarily good relations with Ṣāliḥ by throwing his support behind a rival Ḥārithī shaykh. In addition, the sight of Muscat left nearly defenceless by the financial plight of the Sulṭān's treasury and general sloppiness on the part of the Muwaḥḥidī (Wahhābī) and Ḥaḍramī guards, was in itself enough to tempt tribesmen bent on loot. Accordingly, Ṣāliḥ set his plans in motion.[6] In early 1895, 'Abd Allāh bin Ṣāliḥ was sent to settle a major tribal dispute at Nizwā and he then journeyed to Muscat, ostensibly to announce the return of control of the interior town to the Sulṭān. Meanwhile, Ṣāliḥ moved north out of the Buldān al-Ḥirth under the pretext of settling some minor disputes among the Hināwī tribes of the Western Ḥajar. When 'Abd Allāh arrived at Ruwī on 11 February, he was admitted to Muscat without any problems, along with Muḥsin bin 'Amr al-Ḥārithī and forty followers, and was there received by the Sulṭān. The following day, Ḥamūd bin Sa'īd al-Jahafī also arrived with some followers and the three shaykhs received presents from the Sulṭān and announced their imminent departure for that evening. However, small groups of tribesmen quietly began to enter Muscat at nightfall and at four a.m., those tribesmen already inside the walls rushed the gates and admitted the rest of the Hināwīs. Most of the town was over-run, including the new palace of the Sulṭān. The fight was carried to the old palace, which the Sulṭān and his family were forced to abandon by fleeing over the roofs of Indian merchants until they reached the British Agency. Fayṣal then went on to Fort Jalālī. By mid-morning, Muscat was in rebel hands, with the exception of the Agency and its surroundings (the Waljāt quarter), Fort Jalālī (held by Sulṭān Fayṣal) and Fort Mīrānī (held by Fayṣal's brother Muḥammad). The attack gave way to stalemate as the PAM, Major J. Hayes Sadler, indicated his neutrality to Fayṣal and warned the rebels against damage to Indian property. On the seventeenth, the Sulṭān's first reinforcements arrived by boat. These were to consist primarily of the Banī Jābir, the Banī Bū 'Alī and other Ghāfirī contingents, further indicating the strictly Hināwī nature of the assault.

The British were quick to assume the role of referee in the fray. Ṣāliḥ bin 'Alī and Ḥamūd bin 'Azzān bin Qays, the rebel leaders, were informed that the Government of India disapproved of their action and rejected their contention that the Hināwīs should be allowed to choose a new leader of Oman. They were also held responsible for all damage. Meanwhile, the Sulṭān was told that he could expect no help from the British—even though British demands on Fayṣal had been responsible for much of the considerable hostile mood among the interior tribes. Furthermore, after the rebels had occupied the town without major incident for five days, Fayṣal was dissuaded from employing his newly-arrived tribal levies in an all-out offensive. He received a British warning that since the *status quo* had changed, the Sulṭān would be liable for damages incurred during any attack his forces made on the town.

The remainder of February and the early part of March were marked by minor skirmishes and periodic consultations by the opposing sides with the British representatives, PRPG H. A. Wilson and Major Hayes Sadler, the only result of which was to convince both sides that they could expect no British help and were only liable to incur more financial damages through any occurrence of looting. The deadlock was finally eased by compromise. The rebels agreed to withdraw in exchange for a payment of MT$ 12,000 and the continuation of allowances to the tribal leaders and the al-Rustāq branch of the Āl Bū Sa'īd, in addition to a complete amnesty. On 10 March, the rebels withdrew to Ruwī and the Sulṭān's allies surged through Muscat. Between the two forces, much of the town had been looted and several fires broke out.

It is easy to understand Fayṣal's bafflement and later rebellion against the British after viewing their official attitude towards the attack. Lord George Hamilton, the Secretary of State for India, remarked that 'I observe with satisfaction that the policy towards Muscat laid down in 1886, of non-interference in dynastic struggles or internal administration, was carefully observed by the British political officers who were at Muscat during the disturbances.'[7] In truth, the British had forced the Sulṭān to commit himself to British policy yet felt themselves free from any obligation in return. Indeed, the Sulṭān was subsequently made responsible for compensation to British subjects arising from the rebellion. Although he was allowed to tack an additional 10 per cent on the export tax for Hināwī commodities moving from the interior to the coast, it was made clear to Fayṣal that he had to pay the full amount of the compensation in quarterly instalments over three years or have the amount deducted from the Zanzibar subsidy.[8] The petty insistence on compensation is all the more remarkable when it is recalled that Muscat teetered on the edge of financial ruin and the entire ruling family—which, in effect, meant the state as well—was put deeper in debt to the same merchants they were forced to compensate, and whose clutches the state only later escaped by the expediency of British loans.

The only benefit arising to the Sulṭān from this close call to his throne was a British guarantee to defend Muscat/Maṭraḥ against tribal incursions in the future.[9] But even this measure was taken not as a gesture of support for the Sulṭān, but because of British commercial interests in Muscat and since other alternatives, such as annexation of Muscat/Maṭraḥ or the establishment of a protectorate, were precluded by nature of the Anglo-French rivalry. As a result of the British attitude towards Fayṣal and the Sultanate's impotence, the Government of India was obliged to play the pivotal role in the next major challenge, the revolt of 1913–20.

The Restoration of the Imamate and De Facto Division of Oman

There were two factors which made the first major revolt of the twentieth century a deadly menace to Muscat and gave it as good a chance of wresting control of the entire country away from the Sulṭān as the movement of 1868–71 had. The first was the revival of the Imamate, without which little tribal co-operation could have been expected and, at best, the revolt could have only repeated the attack of 1895. The second factor was the development of a Ghāfirī–Hināwī compact, a situation that even 'Azzān's movement had been unable to achieve. Thus the combination of forces set in motion in the spring of 1913 posed the most dangerous threat to the regime in Muscat since it had become capital of the country. On this occasion, the British would become more involved in the defence of the Āl Bū Sa'īd regime than at any other time in Omani history, with the possible exception of the suppression of the Jabal al-Akhḍar revolt in 1959.

Their support followed from both moral and practical obligations to the Sultanate. Morally, they had been responsible for much of the dissatisfaction in the interior since they had forced the Sulṭān's hand in the suppression of the slave trade and the arms trade while upholding the rights and commerce of various British subjects up and down the coast. In practical terms, they could not afford to allow the Sultanate to disappear, since the Sulṭān had proven so malleable to their interests—either through the use of financial inducements or persuasion through the use of force. This situation would certainly have changed under a fanatically religious, xenophobic and inward-looking Imamate. Thus the British hand was forced to the extent of providing troops for the defence of the capital. Eventually, in order to allow the removal of those troops, the British introduced the Sulṭān's own armed force of regular troops—as distinct from the small garrisons of Wahhābī and Ḥaḍramī mercenaries or doubtful tribal levies.

The immediate causes of the Imamate's revival in 1913 are several. There was a swelling of religious feeling, as emphasised by the increased influence of the muṭawwi' movement led by the blind theologian, 'Abd Allāh bin Ḥumayd al-Sālimī. A second factor was the unrest due to the gradual economic decline of the country, especially as manifested in the loss of Oman's superior trading position. It was also brought on by the inability of the Sulṭān to continue the monthly stipends to important shaykhs, and by his failure to take an active role in the affairs of the interior. A further cause was growing public indignation at the position of influence the British were assuming over Fayṣal. Their action forbidding slave trading and in the compulsory establishment of an arms warehouse in Muscat in 1912 struck tribesmen not only as restricting activities that were perfectly legal under Islām, but also dealt a blow to their economic prosperity. A final factor, indeed, the most important one, was the secular ambitions of the two major tamīmas: Ḥimyar bin Nāṣir al-Nabhānī, the leader of the Ghāfirī faction, and 'Īsā bin Ṣāliḥ al-Ḥārithī, the leader of the Hināwī faction and son of Ṣāliḥ bin 'Alī, the mastermind of the 1895 attack.

At the beginning, the role played by Ḥimyar was by far the most important.[10] He was responsible for calling an assembly of notables at his headquarters in Tanūf in May 1913. The upshot of this convention was the election of Sālim bin Rāshid al-Kharūṣī as Imām. His selection was due to a combination of his personal character and religiosity, his impeccable lineage from a line of medieval Imāms, his relationship as son-in-law of al-Sālimī, and the close connections that his tribe, the Banī Kharūṣ, held with the Banī Riyām, the tribe of Ḥimyar. It is significant to note that 'Īsā bin Ṣāliḥ was not present at this assembly, and his—and consequently Hināwī—participation did not come until the capture of Izkī a month afterwards.

With the election of an Imām, an army was raised and Nizwā was chosen as the first objective. It fell on 5 June 1913 after the Sulṭān's wālī committed suicide. By this time, Muscat had become thoroughly alarmed. The Imām's forces, consisting of levies from nearly a dozen tribes, captured Izkī and al-'Awābī in late June, were threatening Nakhl and Samā'il and had received significant support from 'Isā bin Ṣāliḥ and the Banī Ruwāḥa. Fayṣal had good cause to be worried: his sons, Nādir, Ḥamad and Taymūr—defending Samā'il, Nakhl and Bidbid, respectively—were short of supplies and commanded untrustworthy tribal levies. Consequently, Fayṣal was forced to address a plea to the Government of India which then despatched troops to defend Wādī Bayt al-Falaj at the gateway to Maṭraḥ and Muscat beyond. Despite the suggestions for an attack advanced by PRPG Percy Cox, the Government of India indicated that the Indian Army (IA) detachment was to be used for purely defensive purposes, a decision which was to keep them at Bayt al-Falaj for eight long years.[11]

Soon after the arrival of IA troops, Nādir bin Fayṣal was forced to withdraw from Samā'il all the way to Muscat, since Bidbid had already fallen. Although left in neutral hands, the Samā'il fort was soon occupied by the rebels. At the same time, a rebel offensive on the coastal side of al-Jabal al-Akhḍar was designed to lure Aḥmad bin Ibrāhīm Āl Bū Sa'īd, the nephew of 'Azzān bin Qays and the ruler of al-Rustāq, to the Imamate's side and was successful in capturing the town of Nakhl, although not the fort.

The outlook at this point was extremely bleak. The safety of the capital depended on the IA troops and some 250 tribesmen, drawn variously from the Banī Bū 'Alī, Banī 'Umr, Shiḥūḥ, Na'īm and Banī Yās, and an attack was expected at any time. But the days stretched into weeks and then months of waiting without the threat materialising; the Indian troops were reinforced and a picket line was set up along the hills surrounding the capital area. In case Muscat should have relaxed its vigil, the Imām sent a haughty letter to the PAM in October, proclaiming 'that the people of Oman have agreed by common consent to depose their Sultan, and have assembled to rise against him . . .'[12]

In the midst of all these troubles, Sulṭān Fayṣal took ill. His condition gradually worsened: he lost consciousness and finally passed away on 5 October 1913. On 8 October, his son Taymūr announced his accession to the throne, which was agreed to by all the family except his uncle, Muḥammad bin Turkī. But Muḥammad eventually came into line after Taymūr agreed to an adjustment of his allowance. Fayṣal's death was soon followed by the death of al-Sālimī towards the end of January 1914. The new Sulṭān's position was far from enviable. Taymūr was in the unfortunate position of being beset on all sides and having precious few allies he could count on. Even there, his allies were prone to desertion at crucial times; several coastal cities had to be bombarded by the British navy to dislodge rebels and the Sulṭān had to undertake a minor campaign to quell Banī Baṭṭāsh raids.

By the end of 1914, the rumours were persistent that forces of the Imamate were gathering in preparation for an attack on Muscat. In early January 1915, the Imām advanced from Bidbid to Bawshar and then on to al-Waṭayya where he met a contingent of Imamate supporters under 'Īsā bin Ṣāliḥ. They were opposed by 750 IA troops commanding the hills fronting Bayt al-Falaj and Ruwī. In the early hours of 11 January 1915 the Imām's forces attacked the IA picket line and were finally driven back after hours of hand-to-hand fighting.[13] British casualties were later determined to be seven killed and fifteen wounded, while the Arabs had 186 killed out of some 350 casualties.[14]

In spite of the victory, the British urged caution on the Sulṭān. The elated Taymūr had expressed his desire to send a force of his 'askarīs and the Banī 'Umr on the heels of the defeated rebels. His intention was to recapture the forts of Bidbid and Samā'il but he was dissuaded by the PAM who argued that the risks of losing the fruits of the recently gained victory were too great. When the Viceroy, Lord Hardinge, visited Muscat on 11 February, he warned the Sulṭān that he should reach a settlement with the Imām as he could not count on having British troops forever.[15] Consequently, Taymūr sent an emissary to the shaykhs of the Wādī Samā'il, unsuccessfully seeking the return of the forts of the wādī. In May, Ḥumayd bin Sa'īd al-Fulaytī arrived in Muscat to discuss a list of fanciful demands with the PAM, which were speedily refused.[16] A month later, the Imām's qāḍī, 'Abd Allāh bin Rāshid al-Hāshimī, wrote to the PAM about the rebels' grievances, including a complaint against the British for 'permitting the forbidden, such as the sale of wine and tobacco, and forbidding the permitted, such as the trade in arms and slaves'.[17] The Imām himself wrote to the Sulṭān in late August, agreeing to negotiations with 'Īsā bin Ṣāliḥ as his representative. These abortive talks took place at al-Sīb on 15 and 16 September, between 'Īsā and the PAM, Major R. A. E. Benn.[18] The major obstacle was the obstinacy of the muṭawwi' faction who were indisposed to make any concessions. Consequently, the rebels turned their attention to consolidating control over the interior and no further discussion took place for another four years. In the meantime, the Imām's army captured Bahlā in June 1916 and then 'Īsā bin Ṣāliḥ led an attack against Aḥmad bin Ibrāhīm in al-Rustāq. Aḥmad's vacillation between the two sides was abruptly halted as he had no choice but to appeal to the Sulṭān for help. Despite Taymūr's positive response, a number of the Sulṭān's tribal levies deserted during the battle and the fort fell in August 1917. This was to create a situation of peripatetic warfare in the immediate area for the next several years, with Nāṣir bin Rāshid al-Kharūṣī, brother of the Imām, commanding al-Rustāq and Aḥmad bin Ibrāhīm newly entrenched in al-Ḥazm, just down the wādī.

These periodic sieges were the only activities in an otherwise peaceful interlude. Indian Army troops had been stationed at Bayt al-Falaj for more than four years, the Sulṭān was still unable to rely upon his tribal allies as they had deserted him more than once, and the Imām's position seemed to be growing stronger. In mid-1917, the new PAM, Major L. B. H. Haworth, produced a number of proposals designed to put the Sultanate on a proper financial footing, allowing the establishment of a local levy corps and thereby opening the way for the withdrawal of the British troops. These proposals were an elaboration on the idea of the Muscat Levy Corps (MLC) originally raised and presented to the Sulṭān by PAM Benn and PRPG Cox in early 1914, and were the forerunners of the steps taken by the British at the beginning of the 1920s. Haworth's scheme involved a European superintendent of customs, a British Adviser to be replaced by an Indian or Egyptian as soon as possible, a programme of education to allow Āl Bū Sa'īd family members to replace the Indian or Egyptian official in the future, and a military force, with a strength of 600–1,000 men, to take the offensive to the interior tribesmen.[19] The Government of India found these proposals too elaborate for the situation as it existed.

In 1919, the immediate need was to reopen negotiations with the Imamate. These were begun between Haworth and 'Īsā bin Ṣāliḥ at al-Sīb on 15 and 16 September 1919.

> The situation was discussed with considerable frankness by both sides. The proposal of the Political Agent that the Sultan should be the temporal and the Imam the spiritual head of a united Oman was however immediately negatived by the Omani chiefs. It was realised that a settlement on the basis of the Status Quo was the only possible solution, the Omanis ruling their country, and the Sultan his, with freedom of travel and intercourse, and guarantee on the part of both sides against attack.[20]

These discussions and the use of another channel, instituted through the medium of Sa'īd bin Nāṣir al-Kindī, a respected jurist who acted as a go-between for Haworth's successor, R. E. L. Wingate, and the Imām, showed the beginnings of a willingness on both sides to compromise. Nevertheless, the fierce opposition of the muṭawwi' faction prevailed. The first step considered essential by the Sultan, i.e. the return of certain date gardens in Wādī Samā'il, was never agreed to—thus deadlocking any further attempts at peace.

The breakthrough for the successful negotiations of September 1920 came about earlier that year as the result of a series of unrelated events. Wingate urged the Sulṭān to put pressure on the tribes by raising the zakāt from 5 per cent to 25 per cent on interior date exports to the coast and up to 50 per cent on pomegranates. Then in May, Ḥimyar bin Nāṣir al-Nabhānī, one of the three leading figures in the Imamate, passed away and was succeeded by his son Sulaymān, barely sixteen years old at the time. A month later, the Imām's unpopular brother, Nāṣir bin Rāshid, launched an ill-judged attack on Aḥmad bin Ibrāhīm at al-Ḥazm. Its failure was compounded by the Imām's loss of prestige after receiving no answers to his appeals for help from the Ghāfirī and Hināwī leaders. The final event in this string of setbacks came on 23 July 1920, when Imām Sālim bin Rāshid was assassinated in his sleep in the Wādī 'Andam by a Yāl Wahība tribesman.[21]

Contrary to the election of 1913, when Ḥimyar bin Nāṣir had taken the lead by securing the election of a candidate favourable to him, the election of 1920 was dominated by 'Īsā bin Ṣāliḥ. Consequently, his choice, his father-in-law Muḥammad bin 'Abd Allāh al-Khalīlī, the tamīma of the Banī Ruwāḥa, was elected. The new Imām's first action was to relieve a counter-attack on al-Rustāq by Aḥmad bin Ibrāhīm, which proved successful for the Imām who followed up by replacing Nāṣir bin Rāshid with a member of the Āl Bū Sa'īd as his wālī there.[22]

With the more conciliatory 'Īsā bin Ṣāliḥ now obviously in control, the long-blocked negotiations were able to come to a swift conclusion; the ascendancy of the obstinate muṭawwi's had been considerably checked. Talks were again initiated with the PAM at al-Sīb on 23 September 1920, and concluded on 26 September. Wingate wired the PRPG that the 'Agreement takes the form of two identical letters addressed to me by Sultan Government and Oman tribes accepting and guaranteeing terms arranged by mediation of P.A. and giving terms in full. There is no mention of recognition of Sultan or Imam.'[23] The letters of agreement were identical in the body of the text, although necessarily differing in the preambles and signatures. The body spells out the four conditions binding on each party:

What concern the Omanis are these:

Firstly—On all commodities brought from Oman of all kinds to Muscat, Matrah, Sur and all the coast towns nothing more should be taken than 5 per cent.

Secondly—For all the Omanis there should be safety and freedom in all the coast towns.

Thirdly—All restrictions on entry to and exit from Muscat, Matrah and all the coast towns should be removed.

Fourthly—The Sultan's Government should not protect criminals who flee from the justice of the Omanis and that they may be returned to them if asked for and that the Sultan's Government should not interfere in their internal affairs.

The four which concern the Government of the Sultan are stated as follows:

Firstly—All the tribes and Shaikhs should remain in peace and amity with the Government of the Sultan and that they should not attack the coast towns and should not interfere in his Government.

Secondly—All travellers to Oman on their lawful business should be free and there should be no restrictions on trade and travellers should be safe.

Thirdly—All criminals and evil men who flee to them should be turned out and should not be protected.

Fourthly—The claims of merchants and others against the Omanis should be heard and decided as is just according to the Sharah [*sic*].[24]

Muḥammad bin Aḥmad al-Ghashshām signed the Sulṭān's copy in his capacity as acting wazīr; while the tribes' copy was signed by eighteen shaykhs and muṭawwi's, including the Imām, 'Īsā bin Ṣāliḥ and Sulaymān bin Ḥimyar al-Nabhānī.

The implications of the agreement have been treated extensively elsewhere, usually in attempts to apply it to the rebellion of the 1950s. This contention would allege that it was the basis for the creation of an independent 'Imamate of Oman' in the interior as opposed to a 'Sultanate of Muscat' on the coast.[25] By close examination of the articles of the agreement, it would appear, however, that the first three articles binding on the Sulṭān and those numbered one, two and four, binding on the Omanis, are nothing more than a return to conditions existing prior to the outbreak of hostilities in

1913. The only part of the document that introduces a new element is the exchange of fugitives from justice. This is hardly a solid foundation on which to build the case that a separate government existed in the interior. Indeed, it is similar to informal agreements between friendly tribes by which a fugitive from one tribe would be returned by a second tribe to the first, if for no other reason than to prevent hard feelings between the tribes.

It seems conclusive that if the 'people of Oman' had regarded the Imamate as constituting an independent and sovereign government, they would not have continued to rely upon the Sulṭān for the issuance of passports and for mediation in tribal disputes, even those involving the Imām as a party. Nor would they send him armed men to contest the Saudi occupation of al-Buraymī in 1952, to cite only a few examples. The use of the agreement some thirty-five to forty years later to attack the British as 'colonialists' and 'imperialists' adds nothing to understanding the purpose for which the agreement was signed: an attempt to restore peace to a war-torn countryside by a method of compromise in a manner which recognised the *status quo ante bellum*. It happened that the *status quo* before 1913 and after 1920 was a situation whereby the Sulṭān had been weakened enough so that his control over the interior was tenuous at best. Given the circumstances existing in Muscat in 1920 and the several preceding decades, the freedom from day-to-day responsibility over the interior was probably beneficial. The Sultanate simply did not have the resources, either financially or in terms of manpower, to administer the interior properly. It was only with British aid, both military and financial, immediately before and following the Jabal al-Akhḍar war of the 1950s, that Sulṭān Sa'īd bin Taymūr was able to secure and control the interior.

In the following decades, it seemed almost as if all the interior's rebellious energy had been consumed by the uprising of 1913–20. After a brief attempt to expand its influence in the mid-1920s, the Imamate slumbered in isolation, with the tribes basking in relative independence and their leaders' ambitions held in check by the increasing respect commanded by Imām Muḥammad bin 'Abd Allāh and the political ascendancy wielded by 'Īsā bin Ṣāliḥ al-Ḥārithī. Correspondence between the Sulṭān and major tamīmas was maintained during this period and on the rare occasions that tribal notables ventured forth from Oman, they did so *via* Muscat and on Sultanate passports.[26]

Although Sa'īd bin Taymūr had granted an oil concession covering all Oman as early as 1937, and despite his attempts in the mid-1940s to arrange for the eventual reabsorption of the interior under active Muscat control,[27] inner Oman's isolation was threatened only by the death of the two principal figures of the interior. The death of 'Īsā bin Ṣāliḥ in 1946, followed by the brief succession of his son Muḥammad as the Ḥārithī tamīma, meant a temporary eclipse of the fortunes of the Ḥirth and thus of the strong and stabilising effect that the Hināwī faction exercised on tribal politics. But it was the death of the Imām in 1954 which removed the last restraint on the formidable new combination of internal and external ambitions and prompted the reunification of Muscat and Oman.

Notes

1. The term 'Sultanate' is used here to refer to the entire Āl Bū Sa'īd dynasty, as a matter of convenience, although the first Āl Bū Sa'īd rulers were Imāms and the term Sulṭān was first applied by the British in the mid-nineteenth century and not generally accepted in Oman until the beginning of the twentieth century or later.

2. This is not to say that the Jabal al-Akhḍar revolt of the 1950s was a nationalist struggle—it clearly was not. However, the continuation of discontent in the interior of Oman after the events of December 1955 was only possible due to the support given the rebels by Saudi expansionism and the strident pan-Arab nationalism of Egypt, Syria and Iraq.

3. For a detailed account of this episode, see Ravinder Kumar, 'British Attitudes towards the Ibadiyya Revivalist Movement in East Arabia', *International Studies*, vol. 3, no. 4 (April 1962), pp. 443–50.

4. For additional biographical data on Ṣāliḥ bin 'Alī, see Chapter 4.

5. *Lorimer's Gazetteer*, vol. 1, pt. 1, pp. 536–7.

6. Accounts of the offensive are to be found in *Lorimer's Gazetteer*, vol. 1, pt. 1, pp. 536–43; IO, R/15/3/37; PAM J. Hayes Sadler's diary, and the source of Lorimer's information; 'Abd Allāh bin Ḥumayd al-Sālimī, *Tuḥfat al-A'yān bi-Sīrat Ahl 'Umān*, 5th edn (al-Kuwayt: Dār al-Ṭalī'a, 1394/1974), vol. 2, pp. 294–5; and J. Theodore Bent, 'Muscat', *The Contemporary Review* (London), vol. 68, no. 360 (Dec. 1895), pp. 871–82.

7. IO, R/15/1/394; Hamilton to Governor-General of India in Council, No. 26, 2 Aug. 1895.

8. IO, R/15/1/394; Deputy Secretary of the Government of India in the Foreign Department, Fort William, to PRPG, No. 641E, 27 March 1896. The debt was actually terminated by October 1900.

9. This guarantee was covered by a letter from PRPG Wilson to Sulṭān Fayṣal bin Turkī, on 4 Nov. 1895, contained in IO, R/15/1/394. Fayṣal was also informed that he must take all measures possible for the defence of his capital notwithstanding the guarantee.

10. The following account of the course of the rebellion is drawn from several sources, primarily the present writer's article, 'The Revival of the Ibāḍī Imamate in Oman and the Threat to Muscat, 1913–1920', *Arabian Studies*, vol. 3 (1976), pp. 165–88; Muḥammad bin 'Abd Allāh al-Sālimī, *Nahḍat al-A'yān bi-Ḥurrīyat 'Umān* (Cairo: Dār al-Kitāb al-'Arabī, 1381/1961), pp. 137–247; Lt. Col. C. C. R. Murphy, *Soldiers of the Prophet* (London: John Hogg, 1921), pp. 128–36; and

various records of the Muscat Political Agency in the India Office Library, London. Al-Sālimī is the son of 'Abd Allāh al-Sālimī, the muṭawwi' mentioned above; while Murphy was Intelligence Officer for the British troops in Muscat during the rebellion.

11. IO, R/15/3/42; Cox to Foreign Department, Government of India, and to PAM, Telegram No. 1294, 19 July 1913. After surveying the suggestion, the Government of India replied that 'Nevertheless we adhere to our opinion that our action should be limited to the Coast, as we are convinced that intervention in hinterland is fraught with dangers greater than any advantages that may be expected to follow.' IO, R/15/3/42; Foreign Department to PRPG, repeated in Assistant PRPG to PAM, Telegram No. 1411, 13 Aug. 1913.

12. IO, R/15/3/42; translation of letter from Imām al-Muslimīn, Sālim, in PAM Knox to PRPG Cox, No. 181, 9 Oct. 1913.

13. A detailed account of the actual assault is given in Major J. T. Gorman, *Historical Record of the 2nd Battalion, 4th Bombay Grenadiers (King Edward's Own), formerly 192nd King Edward's Own Grenadiers, 1776–1933*, new edn (Weston-super-Mare, Somerset: Lawrence Brothers, 1933), pp. 89–95. Murphy, *Soldiers*, also gives many details on pp. 135–6.

14. IO, R/15/3/45; PAM Benn to PRPG Knox, No. 31, 25 Jan. 1915.

15. IO, ibid.; PAM Benn's 'Memorandum on Interview of the Viceroy with the Sultan on board the H.M.S. Northbrook', 11 Feb. 1915.

16. Gertrude Bell, 'The Rebellion Against the Sultan of Muscat, May 1913 to July 1916', *The Arab War: Confidential Information for General Headquarters from Gertrude Bell; being Despatches reprinted from the Secret 'Arab Bulletin'* (London: Golden Cockerel Press, 1940), p. 24.

17. Ibid., p. 25.

18. IO, R/15/3/46; Enclosure in Benn to Cox, 28 Sept. 1915. Cox was acting as High Commissioner in Baghdad at this time.

19. IO, R/15/3/48; PAM Haworth to Denys Bray, Deputy Foreign Secretary to the Government of India, No. 1–T, 30 Oct. 1917; and Haworth to Deputy PRPG, No. 37–C, 24 Apr. 1918.

20. IO, R/15/3/337; Annual Muscat Administration Report for 1919.

21. Wingate contended that '. . . it is quite certain that he was killed because the tribes were utterly sick of his rule and that of his brother's, which was a combination of utter religious bigotry combined with shameless selfishness and oppression and a complete disregard of politics or government . . . ' IO, R/15/3/204; Wingate to Deputy PRPG, Demi-official, 4 Aug. 1920.

22. Nāṣir swiftly faded into obscurity and years later became a qāḍī for Sulṭān Sa'īd bin Taymūr on the Bāṭina.

23. IO, R/15/3/204; Wingate to PRPG, Telegram No. 1990, 7 Oct. 1920. Wingate's account of the negotiations is contained in Wingate to Deputy FRPG, No. 2052, 14 Oct. 1920; and his autobiography, *Not in the Limelight* (London: Hutchinson, 1959), pp. 88–91.

24. As Wingate emphasised to the present writer, the agreement itself was discussed, written and signed solely in Arabic, and thus the copies in English are only translations for information. Wingate's translation (used above), along with an explanation of the events leading up to the successful agreement, is found in IO, R/15/3/204; Wingate to Deputy PRPG, No. 2052, 14 Oct. 1920. Other English texts are to be found in IO, R/15/3/337; Annual Muscat Administration Report for 1920; David Holden, *Farewell to Arabia* (London: Faber and Faber, 1966), pp. 249–50; Robert G. Landen, *Oman Since 1856: Disruptive Modernization in a Traditional Arab Society* (Princeton: Princeton University Press, 1967), pp. 403–404n; Husain Albaharna, *The Arabian Gulf States: Their Legal and Political Status and Their International Problems*, 2nd edn (Beirut: Librairie du

Liban, 1975), pp. 367–8; *The Question of Oman: An Analysis of the British Oman Dispute* (New York: Arab Information Centre, 1960); *et al.* The Arabic text has been printed in al-Sālimī, *Nahḍat al-A'yān*, pp. 345–9. Wingate also notes in his despatch to the Deputy PRPG that originally there were only three obligations accruing to the Sulṭān: numbers two and three were then split from a single one in order to save face for the Omanis for conceding four terms.

25. See the Arab Information Centre pamphlet cited above in support of this contention. For rebuttals, see J. B. Kelly, 'Sultanate and Imamate in Oman', *Chatham House Memoranda* (London: Royal Institute of International Affairs, 1959); and ibid., 'A Prevalence of Furies: Tribes, Politics, and Religion in Oman and Trucial Oman', in Derek Hopwood (ed.), *The Arabian Peninsula: Society and Politics* (London: George Allen and Unwin, 1972), pp. 107–41.

26. Even the Sulṭān and the Imām maintained a regular correspondence—although the Sulṭān did not recognise Muḥammad as Imām, referring to him instead as "alāma' (learned scholar).

27. By 1945, Sa'īd had extracted promises of support from both the Hināwī leaders, such as 'Īsā bin Ṣāliḥ al-Ḥārithī, and the Ghāfirī leaders, notably Sulaymān bin Ḥimyar al-Nabhānī and 'Alī bin 'Abd Allāh Āl Ḥamūda. IO, R/15/3/339; Muscat Administration Report for 1945. These negotiations are also discussed in Chapter 2.

CHAPTER 7

The Mountain Rebellions: al-Jabal al-Akhḍar and Dhufar

The near absolute isolation which had enveloped southeastern Arabia and the Gulf for centuries began to disappear by the 1950s. No longer would internal disruptions in Oman occur without notice elsewhere, nor would British activity in the Sultanate escape outside attention. The two rebellions taking place in Oman in this half of the twentieth century have been the focus of debate and opinion in various Arab and other international councils and the rebelling factions in both cases have relied on considerable outside support for their armed struggle. As a consequence, the Oman government found it increasingly necessary to seek outside support of its own to counter the rebels.

Despite certain similarities between the events of the 1950s in northern Oman and the rebellion in Dhufar, they were characterised by fundamental differences. Although both began as essentially tribal insurrections directed against a central authority, only the Dhufar revolt forsook its tribal nature and was transformed into an increasingly radical subversive organisation. Because of the more systematic ideological threat posed in Dhufar, the eventual success of the government there required considerably more time and effort to achieve, and resulted in substantial changes in the political structure of the Sultanate.

The Demise of the Imamate and the Jabal al-Akhḍar War

The nearly complete sense of quiet which settled over inner Oman after the Agreement of al-Sīb in 1920 came to an abrupt halt in the 1950s. During that decade, a succession of inter-related events not only shattered the heretofore peaceful relationship between the Sultanate and the autonomous tribal regime of the interior, but also threatened the territorial integrity of eastern Arabia and focused international attention on Oman. The dispute concerning sovereignty over the interior of Oman was soon submerged in a wider struggle regarding the long-standing British role in Arabia and the opposition to it by the proponents of pan-Arab nationalism, particularly the 'progressive' states of Egypt and Iraq. The crisis was precipitated by the question of succession to Imām Muḥammad bin 'Abd Allāh al-Khalīlī. By the beginning of the 1950s, whatever genuine co-operation there had been with the Sulṭān on the part of the tamīmas had given way to co-operation with the muṭawwi' faction in a search for Muḥammad's successor. The interior notables were particularly anxious to select a new Imām before the death of Muḥammad in order to forestall any possible advance into the interior by the Sulṭān.

In this process of selection and sifting, four names have frequently been mentioned as having arisen: 'Abd Allāh bin Sālim al-Kharūṣī, son of Imām Sālim bin Rāshid, who held office from 1913 to 1920; Ghālib bin 'Alī al-Hinā'ī, previously the qāḍī of al-Rustāq and then a qāḍī at Nizwā with responsibility for the Imamate's bayt al-māl; Muḥammad bin 'Abd Allāh al-Sālimī, son of the blind theologian, 'Abd Allāh bin Ḥumayd, who had been a principal figure in the establishment of the 1913 Imamate; and Sulṭān Sa'īd bin Taymūr.[1] Another individual under consideration at one point was Hilāl bin 'Alī al-Khalīlī, the wālī of Bawshar for the Sulṭān and a nephew of Imām Muḥammad. Hilāl's name was perhaps the first to appear when the Awlād Khalīlī, the shaykhly clan of the Banī Ruwāḥa, presented his candidacy to Imām Muḥammad sometime between 1950 and 1952. The Imām, however, rejected the idea outright, not wishing to transform the Imamate into yet another dynasty.[2]

Soon afterwards, the selection process began in earnest between the Imām, the tamīmas and the muṭawwi's. Muḥammad bin 'Abd Allāh al-Sālimī was never a serious candidate, possibly due to his lack of an aristocratic background and his close relationship with Ṣāliḥ bin 'Īsā.[3] The candidacy of 'Abd Allāh bin Sālim al-Kharūṣī had been advanced particularly by Sulaymān bin Ḥimyar. Eventually, this proved to be one of the strongest arguments against his candidacy: the Banī Kharūṣ were largely a client tribe of the Banī Riyām and coupled with 'Abd Allāh's betrothal to a Riyāmī girl, it was felt that he would be too much under the influence of Sulaymān bin Ḥimyar, especially as doubts had been raised about his weakness of character. Sulṭān Sa'īd bin Taymūr was not a serious candidate: it seems certain that he never sought election—since it would have cast doubts on his legitimacy as Sulṭān—and his mention by some shaykhs during the actual election is a measure of the success of his outward attempts at religious conformity and the confusion surrounding the interior at that time.[4]

In view of the rejection of 'Abd Allāh bin Sālim because of his weak character, the eventual choice of Ghālib bin 'Alī is surprising. But adverse considerations of his personality were outweighed by other factors. Ghālib was respected as a muṭawwi' through his work as qāḍī and financial administrator. He apparently was the personal choice of Imām Muḥammad, who had personally supervised his education in Nizwā.[5] In purely political terms, Ghālib being a Hināwī, there would be little objection from that faction. Meanwhile, Ghāfirī objections were eased by the strong support from the head of the party, Sulaymān bin Ḥimyar, who was acting in tandem with Ghālib's brother Ṭālib, the wālī of al-Rustāq for the Imām. Already this alliance was being bolstered by Saudi patronage.[6]

The death of Imām Muḥammad bin 'Abd Allah al-Khalīlī finally came in May 1954, at the age of approximately 70. The tribal shaykhs and muṭawwi's quickly gathered in Nizwā to formally nominate Ghālib bin 'Alī as his successor.[7] Ghālib's domination by Sulaymān and Ṭālib soon became apparent, as the Imamate raised an expedition to recapture the northern town of 'Ibrī. The Ya'āqib tribe there had turned out the Imām's wālī several years previously; consequently, the object of this expedition was to return the town to the authority of the Imamate and thereby keep open the line of communications to the Saudi outpost at al-Buraymī.[8] At the same time, a Petroleum Development (Oman) Ltd (PDO) exploration team, accompanied by the newly-formed Muscat and Oman Field Force (MOFF), began to move north from al-Duqm on the Gulf of al-Maṣīra. After a short halt at Jabal Fahūd, south of 'Ibrī, the PDO and MOFF groups went on and occupied 'Ibrī in late 1954. Although this hindered communication between the Imamate leaders and the Saudis, direct contact was not severed until the Trucial Oman Scouts (TOS) occupied al-Buraymī in October 1955 and displaced the Saudi garrison there.[9]

A few months later, the Sultanate launched a two-pronged operation against the interior. The MOFF moved south and easily captured Nizwā on 15 December 1955. Meanwhile, the Sultanate's Batinah Force, supported by tribal contingents, laid siege to al-Rustāq and captured it after four days of fighting. The reactions of the leaders of the interior alliance were varied. Imām Ghālib posted a notice of abdication on the Masjid al-Jāmi' (community mosque) of Nizwā and prudently retired to his home in nearby Bilād Sayt. Sulaymān bin Ḥimyar returned to his home in Tanūf. The Imām's brother, Ṭālib bin 'Alī, escaped from al-Rustāq and made his way to Saudi Arabia, where he began to train an army in anticipation of his return; meanwhile, the tamīma of the Ḥirth, Ṣāliḥ bin 'Īsā, departed for Zanzibar.[10] The Sulṭān capped the reunification of the country with an epic journey across the desert from Ṣalāla: after visiting the oil installation at Fahūd, he arrived in Nizwā on 24 December.[11] Sa'īd completed his display of authority by appointing Aḥmad bin Muḥammad al-Ḥārithī, nephew of Ṣāliḥ bin 'Īsā, as tamīma of the Ḥirth and wālī of Nizwā.[12]

The interior remained quiet for eighteen months. Nevertheless, plans were being made by Ṭālib bin 'Alī in Saudi Arabia for an invasion by his new Oman Revolutionary Movement (ORM). Ṭālib and some of his men were transported by dhow to the Bāṭina, where they landed on 14 June 1957, and subsequently made their way to Oman province.[13] There, Ṭālib joined forces with his brother Ghālib in defence of Bilād Sayt against a siege by the Sulṭān's Oman Regiment (formerly the MOFF). The siege, however, failed when the regiment found itself outnumbered and was forced to withdraw to Firq, near Nizwā. The retreat turned into disaster when the Banī Riyām joined in the revolt and subsequently the regiment was pulled back to Fahūd where it was disbanded. The rebel forces then moved into Nizwā and Bahlā without opposition, having taken control over virtually all of Oman province. Faced with a major insurrection, the Sulṭān had no choice but to call on the British for support. His request, coming at a time of post-Suez reappraisal of Britain's world-wide role, met with heated Parliamentary debate.[14] Nevertheless, British military aid was forthcoming. Air support was provided by RAF jets based in Sharjah. An army column was formed to retake the interior and included elements from the Cameronians and the TOS and a squadron of Ferret armoured cars, in addition to the Sultanate's Northern Frontier Regiment (NFR); it was commanded by General J. A. R. Robertson, a former Gurkha commander brought in from Cyprus.[15] The force left 'Ibrī in early August and captured Firq after several days of fighting. After Nizwā fell without a shot on 11 August, the other towns of the area readily capitulated. The Anglo–Omani force was joined at Nizwā by another column composed of the Sultanate's Muscat Regiment, which had marched inland from Muscat *via* the Wādī Samā'il without incident. Government casualties had been four wounded personnel; while the rebels suffered an estimated thirty deaths. The short campaign had been run at a cost of £270,000 to the British Exchequer.[16]

The insurrection was brief and its dénouement unspectacular. The rebels retreated to the vastness of the Jabal al-Akhḍar, while the British troops were withdrawn and Sa'īd appointed Aḥmad bin Ibrāhīm as civil administrator of the area with Ṭāriq bin Taymūr as his assistant. Internally, the situation had reached stalemate, with the rebels mining roads used by the Sultanate's military and PDO. Outside the country, the 'progressive' Arab bloc joined Saudi Arabia in denouncing Britain's support of the Sulṭān. Both the Sulṭān and the British realised that further action was necessary to resolve the situation and to prevent a future recurrence of revolt among the tribes of the former Imamate. With this in mind, the Under-Secretary of State for War, Julian Amery, visited Muscat in January 1958 and laid down the foundations for an exchange of letters between the Sulṭān and the British government, concluded during Sa'īd's visit to London in July. In exchange for an extension of RAF rights on al-Maṣīra Island, the Sultanate received material and personnel assistance for the creation of the Sultan's Armed Forces (SAF).[17]

The next step was to dislodge the rebels from the Jabal al-Akhḍar. In late 1958, several squadrons of the Special Air Service (SAS) were routed to Oman on their withdrawal from Malaya.[18] A combined SAS/SAF assault on the mountain plateau in January 1959 was completely successful.[19] The three rebel leaders, Sulaymān bin Ḥimyar and Ṭālib and Ghālib, however, managed to escape and lay the basis for a continued propaganda campaign. Training camps for the rebel movement's Oman Liberation Army were set up, first in Saudi Arabia and then in Iraq. The fitful guerrilla war carried on inside Oman was transformed into a terrorist campaign outside the country, with bombs planted in the Sultanate's mail, aboard British India ships and on various aircraft.[20] This activity only ceased after a British cruiser captured a dhow of rebel mine-layers off Ra's Suwādī on the Bāṭina in August 1961 and subsequent interrogation led to the capture of many of the rebel leaders in Oman and the Gulf.

Faced with continuing criticism in the world press and at the United Nations, the British attempted to negotiate with the rebels. These meetings grew out of contacts initiated between the PRPG and the leaders of the Imamate in September 1959 and June 1960. On 17 July 1960, the first meeting between the two sides took place in Beirut with a Residency official and Sulaymān bin Ḥimyar present. At this time, Sulaymān presented a list of conditions for further negotiations.[21] The British conditions were presented at a second meeting in Beirut in December.[22] A third meeting was arranged at the Beirut headquarters of the Omani delegation on 4 January 1961; but it and a subsequent meeting of 24 February both ended in failure when neither side appeared willing to drop its preconditions.[23] The only other contact between the Sultanate and the erstwhile Imamate was arranged by the Arab League in 1971 after the change of leadership in Muscat and came to an equally unsuccessful outcome.[24]

The failure of these attempts at reconciliation resulted in the continuation of the propaganda war between the opposing sides and their supporters. This aspect of the struggle had first emerged during the events of 1957, when Ṣāliḥ bin 'Īsā had appeared in Cairo as the spokesman of the 'Imamate of Oman' and 'Imamate' offices were subsequently established in Cairo, Damascus, al-Riyāḍ and Beirut. As soon as the rebels' military position in Oman had begun to collapse, their Arab supporters sought to bring the 'question of Oman' before the United Nations. An initial attempt to place the item on the agenda of the Security Council was narrowly defeated. However, the 'question of Oman' was included in the agenda of the General Assembly the following year. Gradually a pattern was established whereby the question was regularly introduced in General Assembly sessions and then assigned to various committees for further deliberation. These meetings were marked by Arab–British debates over the merits of the Sultanate's and Imamate's respective cases; and a number of witnesses appeared before the Special Political Committee, the Fourth Committee and the 'Special Committee on the Situation With Regard to the Implementation of the Declaration on the Granting of Independence to Colonial Countries and Peoples'.[25]

The only substantive results of UN consideration were reports submitted in 1963 and 1965. Herbert de Ribbing, the Swedish Ambassador to Spain appointed by the Secretary-General to examine the situation, visited Oman, Saudi Arabia and London in 1962 and submitted his report in the autumn of 1963. His conclusions were more or less in keeping with the Sulṭān's position. stating that the rebellion was long over, that the majority of the populace denied the existence of political repression, and that the British officers in SAF apparently had nothing to do with general policy-making. He also recommended that UN assistance be granted to help improve health and social conditions in Oman. Despite these conclusions, the Arab states continued to press for UN action favourable to their position. Consequently, in December 1963, the General Assembly created an '*Ad Hoc* Committee' to engage not only in a fact-finding mission on Oman but also to render a judgement on the relative merits of the conflicting views of the parties to the issue.[26] This committee conducted discussions in London, al-Dammām, al-Kuwayt and Cairo; Sa'īd bin Taymūr, however, refused permission for the committee's entry to Oman.[27] Partly as a result of this attitude, the committee reported in January 1965 that the 'question of Oman' was indeed an international issue, as it was the result of 'imperialistic policies and foreign intervention in Muscat and Oman'.[8] The General Assembly noted the report but took no action: the same pattern was continued in subsequent Assembly sessions until the admittance of the Sultanate to the UN in 1971 resulted in the long-delayed termination of discussion on the 'question of Oman'.

At the heart of the dispute was the legality of the 1957 rebellion and the subsequent steps taken by the Sulṭān and the British to suppress it. The major contention by sympathisers of the Imamate group was that a separate, independent state had existed in the interior of Oman since the conclusion of the 'Treaty' of al-Sīb in 1920.[29] Frequently, this argument was coupled with charges that the Sultanate was a 'British colony', which seems to contradict the alleged validity of the document signed at al-Sīb as an international instrument. The British responded to the allegation by pointing out that the Sīb agreement made no mention of the Imamate and simply granted a measure of autonomy to the tribes of the interior who were beyond the control of a weakened Sulṭān. They also cited Sultanate treaties with the United States, France and the Netherlands as proof of the Sultanate's independence. In short, most objections to the British role were based on wider political considerations rather than strictly on the merits of the situation in Oman. Similar arguments were used in the years to come by increasingly radical groups, particularly the National Liberation Front in Aden and the revolutionaries in Dhufar, to attack Britain's position in Arabia. The 1950s rebellion and the subsequent Dhufar insurrection were thus linked by their anti-British character as well as by their rebellion against the Sultanate. The ideological shift from a traditional and strictly religio-tribal opposition to a completely secular and Marxist–Leninist centre of rebellion was completed by the revolt in Dhufar.

Revolt in Dhufar: The Ideological Challenge

Dhufar, the isolated and long-neglected southern province of the Sultanate, found its traditional position reversed in the mid-1960s when it provided the Āl Bū Saʿīd state with a challenge more serious than that of the Imamate issue. The Dhufar problem was to vex the Sultanate for over a decade, bring about the downfall of the country's ruler and focus world attention on the hitherto forgotten Arabian principality. Prior to this position in the spotlight, Dhufar had been noted mainly as a source of frankincense from time immemorial. But with the development of full-scale revolt, its fate was to become the concern of the entire Arabian Peninsula and beyond.

In many ways, Dhufar resembles an island. It is bordered by the Arabian Sea to the south and east, and by the Jiddat al-Ḥarāsīs and Rubʿ al-Khālī deserts to the north. Although the nearby Mahrā and Ḥaḍramawt regions form a natural continuation to the west, the rough terrain of western Dhufar has prevented any substantial ties to those areas and afforded ideal guerrilla territory. The province is divided into three distinct zones: Ṣalāla Plain, facing the Arabian Sea and about thirty miles long and ten miles wide; a series of three mountain ranges, the Jabal Samhān in the east, the Jabal Qarā in the centre and the Jabal Qamar in the west, which form a crescent around the Plain; and the Najd, a stony plateau lying behind the mountains and separating them from the sands of the Rubʿ al-Khālī. The province is sparsely populated with the total number of inhabitants estimated at 60,000; by the mid-1970s, roughly half of these had gravitated to the capital at Ṣalāla.[30] The rest were either residents of a few coastal towns, principally Mirbāṭ, Ṭaqa, Raysūt and Rakhyūt, or herdsmen in the mountains and Najd. The majority of the inhabitants of Ṣalāla Plain and the Najd are Arabs of the widespread Kathīr tribe.[31] The population of the mountains and eastern plain, however, is largely derived from several intertwined ethnic groups, commonly referred to as *jibālīs* (mountain people) and thought to be descended from ancient South Arabian bloodstocks. These are the Qarā, the Mahrā and the Śḥerā.[32]

Traditionally, Dhufar has been separate from Oman with the first modern connection being its annexation by Saʿīd bin Sulṭān in

1829 following the death of Sayyid Muḥammad bin 'Āqil, a local ruler and freebooter.[33] However, the Sultanate's control was extremely loose and, during the period 1829–79, each village was generally independent in internal affairs.[34] In 1879, an Omani expedition successfully retook Ṣalāla and the province has, with a few brief exceptions, remained under Sultanate control ever since.

Fayṣal bin Turkī was the first Sulṭān to visit Dhufar in order to enjoy its mild climate and his son, Taymūr, spent more time in Ṣalāla than in Muscat. Nevertheless, it was Sa'īd bin Taymūr who was responsible for extending the Sultanate's authority throughout Ṣalāla Plain and into the mountains. As early as 1935, he had improved the palace at al-Ḥuṣn, between the old town of Ṣalāla and the beach, and built up agricultural estates at Arzāt and Jarzayz.[35] The Sulṭān spent much of the World War II period there and was a frequent visitor between 1945 and 1955. He finally made Ṣalāla his permanent residence in 1958 and never returned to Muscat. But his attitude in treating Dhufar as a private fiefdom was clearly unsuited to the twentieth century. Petty restrictions on the population aroused resentment and many Dhufaris left clandestinely for jobs in the Gulf. The Sulṭān's refusal to acknowledge Dhufari grievances and his angry reactions to the first expressions of discontent began the cycle of violence that ended in open revolt.[36]

Armed rebellion in Dhufar began with disaffected members of the Bayt Kathīr, who received some aid from Saudi Arabia and carried out a series of minor raids during 1963 and 1964. These tribesmen were soon joined by other Dhufaris and the rebellion assumed a more systematic form with the appearance and then the merger of such groups as the Dhufar Benevolent Society (DBS), the Dhufar Soldiers' Organisation (DSO) and the local branch of the Arab Nationalists' Movement (ANM).[37] As a result, the newly-formed Dhufar Liberation Front (DLF) held its first conference in central Dhufar in early June 1965.[38] A DLF attack launched against a government patrol at this time provided the organisation's official date for the beginning of the revolution—9 June 1965.[39] Nevertheless, the scope of the rebellion remained limited over the next several years, with the most notable exploit being the near-successful assassination attempt on Sa'īd bin Taymūr on 26 April 1966.[40]

Gradually, the moderate 'nationalist' tenor of the DLF became increasingly radicalised and at the movement's second congress at Ḥamrīn in central Dhufar in September 1968, the uneasy balance between the nationalist and radical camps was tipped in favour of the latter. At this point, the organisation's name was changed from DLF to the Popular Front for the Liberation of the Occupied Arabian Gulf (PFLOAG).[41] The movement began to rely increasingly on ideological and logistical support from the newly-independent Democratic Republic of Southern Yemen (later People's Democratic Republic of Yemen; PDRY), People's Republic of China, the Soviet Union, Iraq and various Palestinian guerrilla organisations. With new sources of support assured, the guerrilla campaign was stepped up. By late 1969, most of the province's three mountain ranges had fallen under rebel control, and Rakhyūt, one of the major coastal towns, had also been captured. The one road from Ṣalāla to the north—passing through the desert military base at Thamarīt—came under increasing attack and was eventually severed. Ṣalāla itself faced mortar attacks and as a defensive measure was surrounded by a barbed-wire perimeter and the jibālīs denied entrance. The success enjoyed by PFLOAG encouraged the emergence of similar groups in northern Oman, the most prominent of these being the National Democratic Front for the Liberation of Oman and the Arabian Gulf (NDFLOAG), born out of a coalition of various minor dissident groups and loosely connected to PFLOAG. NDFLOAG's mortar attacks launched on Nizwā and Izkī on 12 June 1970 were military failures, leading to the arrest of a number of NDFLOAG members. More importantly, however, they prompted quick action on the part of the various groups plotting the overthrow of Sulṭān Sa'īd bin Taymūr.

A few weeks later, a gun battle in Sa'īd's Ṣalāla palace resulted in his forced abdication and exile. His successor was his British-educated son Qābūs who promised a complete change from the archaic policies employed by his father. In Dhufar, his approach to the insurrection involved a 'carrot and stick' method of attempting to undo the damage caused by Sa'īd's petty restrictions on the population while simultaneously engaging in a heavy military build-up to reverse the tide of battle. The new Sulṭān's concern for Dhufar ran deep: his mother was a Qarawī from the Bayt Ma'ashānī of Ṭāqa and Qābūs was born and raised in Dhufar. His first action on assuming the throne included the issuance of a pardon for surrendering rebels—which attracted many of the 'tribal' or 'nationalist' rebels but was spurned by the 'ideologues'—and the provision of schools, health facilities and water distribution for the tribesmen of Dhufar, as well as access to Ṣalāla which had been closed to them since the beginning of the rebellion. At the same time, the Sultanate began to make use of its burgeoning financial reserves to reorganise and enlarge the Sultan's Armed Forces (SAF) and purchase sophisticated military matériel. Defence expenditures quickly rose to nearly 50 per cent of the national budget and remained at that level until after the end of the revolt.

By the beginning of 1971, the Sultanate's forces, hitherto continually on the defensive, finally began to carry the battle to the rebels. The government offensive briefly held the eastern mountains before withdrawing because of the annual monsoon. The forward thrust was resumed in the autumn and the Leopard Line, the first in a series of lines of containment, was constructed.[42]

As a result of intensified government efforts, the revolutionary movements in Oman were merged in 1971 to form the Popular Front for the Liberation of Oman and the Arabian Gulf (also known as PFLOAG). Shortly afterwards, PFLOAG undertook its last forward thrust, launching a rocket attack on Ṣalāla Air Base and organising twin assaults on the coastal villages of Mirbāṭ and Ṭāqa. The failure of these attempts marked a major turning-point in the war: from then on, the rebels were steadily pushed back. Operations in the eastern mountains were limited to hit-and-run attacks and rocket barrages of Ṣalāla Plain had ceased by October 1973. A further attempt to extend the rebellion to the northern part of Oman failed as plans for a co-ordinated series of uprisings to take place on New Year's Eve 1972 in various northern towns were discovered and some eighty conspirators were rounded up.

Government advances continued to appear. A notable achievement was SAF's success in establishing Mainbrace Line—a set of fortified mountaintop positions centred on the border post at Ṣarfayt and overlooking the strip of wooded hills between the sea-coast and the desert—as well as maintaining this advanced line during the 1972 monsoon season. The foothold in the west was complemented by the gradual clearing of rebel positions in the eastern and then the central mountain regions. With considerable assistance from Iranian combat troops, the road between Ṣalāla and Thamarīt was recaptured in late 1973 and from then on permanently held by the government. In early 1974, the Hornbeam Line was built parallel to the Thamarīt road and roughly twenty miles west of it. With its construction, supplies to rebel troops to its east were severely limited and eventually that sector was cleared of all but small guerrilla groups.

With both its military and political positions crumbling by mid-

1974, PFLOAG seemed ready to co-operate with an Arab League mediation committee. However, although the committee visited Muscat in May 1974, it was refused admission to PDRY and consequently the effort came to naught. Internal dissension within PFLOAG paralleled the reverses in the field. The organisation's May 1974 conference saw an open split between militant Dhufari members, determined to carry on with the guerrilla war, and more conciliatory members from the Gulf states, who sought to become legitimate political opposition within the various states. The controversial decision of the conference to concentrate military activity in Oman only was reflected in the truncation of the Front's name to the Popular Front for the Liberation of Oman (PFLO).

PFLO's problems continued unabated. SAF accelerated its pressure and in December 1974 a new series of positions—the Hammer Line—were built to the west of Hornbeam Line. In January 1975, a combined Omani–Iranian force captured the important coastal town of Rakhyūt, touted as the revolutionary capital of Dhufar, and subsequently the Damavand Line was built north from there to bisect the strip between the Hornbeam Line and the border. The government's final push began at the close of the 1975 monsoon season when Iranian troops moved into areas north of Rakhyūt. Other Iranian contingents moved south from Ṣarfayt towards the sea while the PFLO base at Ḥawf in PDRY was attacked by Sultanate of Oman Air Force (SOAF) fighters. The offensive became a rout by late November as Omani troops occupied the final villages in western Dhufar, unopposed by the rebels who had slipped back into PDRY. On 11 December 1975, before 50,000 enthusiastic citizens in Muscat, Sultan Qābūs declared that the Dhufar War was officially over. In the following months, a steady stream of rebel defectors severely truncated PFLO efforts to continue the movement's military viability.

The Sultanate's success in the war was due to a combination of factors, particularly the outside support it was able to marshal. Prominent among external sources of assistance was Great Britain, which suffered casualties in the fighting as early as 1966. By the end of the rebellion, the British presence in Dhufar had grown to 700, including seconded officers, those on private contract, various Special Air Service (SAS) contingents, a group of Royal Engineers and various RAF personnel stationed at Ṣalāla and al-Maṣīra Air Bases. In addition to personnel, the Sultanate relied heavily on British equipment and weapons. These included various fighter aircraft—including the top-of-the-line Jaguar—as well as transport aircraft, arms, patrol craft and the Rapier missile system. Furthermore, British interests were also present in commercial activities in Dhufar, such as port construction at Raysūt, roadbuilding, banking and communications.

Other significant assistance had been extended by Iran, whose presence in Arabia was almost universally condemned by Arab states. Nevertheless, Iranian aid appeared relatively soon after Sulṭān Qābūs's accession and Iranian paratroopers were being stationed in Oman by early 1973, although their central role in the clearing of the Thamarīt road was not officially acknowledged until February 1974. Subsequent Iranian troops were rotated in and out of Dhufar at three-month intervals in order to allow as many as possible to gain combat experience: this policy resulted in alarming losses among Iranian personnel.[43]

The Shah's reasons for involvement in Dhufar reflected his concern over Communist penetration on his southern flank, in addition to the north and east (i.e. the Soviet Union and its close relationship with Iraq), and the potential security threat posed if Oman and/or the Gulf states should fall to revolutionaries. An additional factor was Oman's strategic location on the southern shore of the Strait of Hormuz: a concern for its security led to joint naval operations by the Iranian and Omani navies there. Nevertheless, continued Sultanate reliance on Iranian military assistance proved to be a considerable obstacle in Oman's pursuit of good relations with its fellow Arab states.

Although Oman's traditional and wealthier neighbours in Arabia shared a common concern over the threat that revolutionary success in Dhufar posed to the traditional political structure of most of the Peninsula, these states were not prepared to provide much tangible assistance beyond moderate financial grants. The only Arab state which produced substantial support was Jordan, which loaned combat troops in mid-1975 to hold the Thamarīt road. Additional Jordanian army personnel were assigned to training duty and engineering units in Oman, and King Ḥusayn provided Oman with thirty-one Hawker Hunter jets in March 1975.

The moral support provided by the moderate or traditional Arab states was countered by that given by the radical states to PFLO and its predecessors. Chief among these was PDRY of course, which had stood firmly behind the rebels in matters of ideology and logistics since it received independence in 1967. Aden also served as an important link between the Dhufari revolutionaries and the Communist world. At various times, both the USSR and the PRC provided moral support and matériel to PFLO and rebel soldiers received training in both countries. Chinese support declined following the Sino–Iranian rapprochement of early 1973 and although Soviet aid was subsequently increased, the breach was never adequately filled. Lesser radical states also voiced support, primarily Iraq and Cuba. Iraqi involvement had been noticeable since the beginning of the rebellion and while never as strong as PDRY support, Baghdad continued to aid dissidents in Dhufar at least until diplomatic relations were established with Muscat in late 1975. In line with the extension of Cuban military aid to various Third World states, Cuban soldiers trained PDRY and Dhufari troops while Cuban pilots flew PDRY's MIG–21s.[44] Another largely marginal supporter of the revolutionaries was Libya, which reversed its 1972 offer of aid to the Sultanate and, by 1975, was passing on Soviet missiles to PFLO.

Much of the international concern over the war in Dhufar focused on the ideological schism of the struggle and the high stakes involved, i.e. the Gulf with all its petroleum wealth. Thus, it is not surprising that the 'domino theory' was frequently mentioned and the comparison with Vietnam made. The similarity resulted in a paradox in US policy. Fearful that a rebel victory would result in eventual Communist control over all the Gulf, the US sought to guarantee the Sultanate's victory. Yet, traumatised by the Vietnam experience, there could be no direct involvement. Consequently, the US encouraged Britain in the role of principal supporter, invoked the Nixon Doctrine to wage war by Iranian and Jordanian proxy and kept its own profile suitably low. Its closest connection came during Sulṭān Qābūs's first visit to Washington in January 1975 when the US requested landing rights at the then British RAF base on al-Maṣīra Island—beyond that, American involvement in Dhufar was limited to the sale of a few arms and helicopters.

Despite the predominant attention lavished on the international and ideological aspects of the revolt, true success in Dhufar will ultimately be measured by the attitudes and allegiance shown by the people of the province. By the time of the virtual cessation of military action in late 1975, the Sultanate's leadership had shown its willingness and even determination to attack the social and economic problems of Dhufar. The province's share of the state's development budget far outweighed its proportion of population, and Dhufaris were prominent in government positions, including three ministerial portfolios. Seemingly, not only military victory was within the Sultanate's grasp, but a good deal of progress had been made towards replacing a situation of mistrust and neglect with a spirit of unification and mutual co-operation throughout the Sultanate of Oman.

Notes

1. The election process has been discussed in Kelly, 'Sultanate and Imamate in Oman'; ibid., 'A Prevalence of Furies', pp. 127–8; Landen, *Oman Since 1856*, p. 418; and Wendell Phillips, *Oman: A History* (London: Longman, 1967), pp. 188–9. The following discussion is drawn largely from interviews held in Oman with members of most of the major tribes involved in the selection process, and with members of the ruling family.

2. Interview with a relative of Imām Muḥammad.

3. He was Ṣāliḥ's tutor and also resided in al-Bidīya in the Sharqīya.

4. The Sulṭān reportedly referred to assertions of his candidacy as 'nonsense'. UN General Assembly, 19th Session, 22 Jan. 1965, *Question of Oman; Report of the Ad Hoc Committee on Oman*, A/5846 (the 'Jiménez Report'), p. 112.

5. According to one source, however, Imām Muḥammad withdrew his endorsement of Ghālib on his deathbed after Aḥmad bin Muḥammad al-Ḥārithī warned him that the succession of Ghālib would result in dissension among the Omanis. Letter to the present writer from Muḥammad bin 'Abd Allāh al-Sālimī, 7 Ṣafar 1395/19 Feb. 1975.

6. Sulaymān had allegedly travelled to the Saudi capital at al-Riyāḍ in Nov. 1952 *via* the Saudi outpost at al-Buraymī. See Kelly, 'A Prevalence of Furies', p. 127. Ṭālib was also alleged to have visited Saudi Arabia in 1952. Phillips, *Oman: A History*, p. 189. For details on financial support and arms sent to the interior of Oman by the Saudis as revealed by documents captured at al-Buraymī in 1955, see J. B. Kelly, *Eastern Arabian Frontiers* (London: Faber and Faber, 1964), pp. 175–206.

7. There have been doubts raised as to whether this was a proper Ibāḍī election. Most sources seem to agree that it was but that Ghālib failed to receive support from all the shaykhs, particularly from the tamīma of his own tribe, 'Abd Allāh bin Zāhir al-Hinā'ī, and the faction of the Ḥirth led by Aḥmad bin Muḥammad, son of the late tamīma, Muḥammad bin 'Īsā.

8. Information on the events of the 1950s discussed here is partially based on numerous interviews held in Muscat with members of the Āl Bū Sa'īd and military officers involved in the activity. Among the principal published sources are the accounts of the fighting carried in *The Times* and the *New York Times*; Kelly, 'A Prevalence of Furies'; ibid., 'Sultanate and Imamate in Oman'; David deC. Smiley, *Arabian Assignment* (London: Leo Cooper, 1975); ibid., 'Muscat and Oman', *Journal of the Royal United Service Institution*, vol. 105, no. 617 (Feb. 1960), pp. 29–47; P. S. Allfree, *Warlords of Oman* (London: Robert Hale, 1967); Anthony Shepherd, *Arabian Adventure* (London: Collins, 1961). Also helpful was the document by Colin C. Maxwell, *Short History of the Sultan's Armed Forces* (mimeographed, Bayt al-Falaj, Nov. 1969). A chronology of events during this period is contained in the 'Jiménez Report', pp. 134–41. The present writer has also discussed the events of that decade in greater detail in 'Britain and the "Oman War": An Arabian Entanglement', *Asian Affairs*, vol. 63, pt. 3 (Oct. 1976), pp. 285–98.

9. The TOS action had come after the breakdown of the Buraymī arbitration talks in Geneva between Saudi Arabia and Great Britain, acting for Abu Dhabi and the Sultanate.

10. Ṣāliḥ had travelled overland to Ṣalāla in hopes of presenting his case to the Sulṭān personally. However, on his arrival, he discovered that the Sulṭān had already left for Oman and had left a message for Ṣāliḥ, suggesting that he keep going until he reached Russia. Personal interviews.

11. This journey was described by an accompanying journalist: James Morris, *Sultan in Oman* (London: Faber and Faber, 1957). Soon after Sa'īd's arrival in Nizwā, Sulaymān bin Ḥimyar came to make his peace. Afterwards, the Sulṭān visited al-Buraymī, where he met Shaykh Shakhbūt bin Sulṭān Āl Nuhayyān of Abu Dhabi, then returned to Muscat *via* Ṣuḥār.

12. When Aḥmad subsequently returned to the Sharqīya, his cousin, Khalīfa bin 'Alī, succeeded him as wālī until May 1957, when Aḥmad's uncle Ibrāhīm rose in revolt. Khalīfa was then replaced by Ḥamad bin Sa'ūd Āl Bū Sa'īd, who fled Nizwā before its occupation by the rebels in July 1957.

13. Their arrival was to have coincided with an uprising in the Sharqīya as well. However, when Ṭālib was delayed, Ibrāhīm bin 'Īsā al-Ḥārithī led some of the Ḥirth in a premature revolt in May. On the point of defeat by the Sulṭān's forces, Ibrāhīm accepted an invitation to meet with Sa'īd bin Taymūr at Bawshar—on his arrival, the Sulṭān had him put in prison at Fort Jalālī, where he languished until 1970. At the same time, Sulaymān bin Himyar had been 'invited' to Muscat. However, when Ṭālib bin 'Alī arrived a month later, Sulaymān slipped out of Muscat and led the Banī Riyām in revolt.

14. The Labour opposition expressed fears of a 'second Suez'. The Conservative Government replied that the situation in Oman was simply a tribal rebellion. Part of the British concern was over the rebels' use of American arms—although military spokesmen pointedly refused to identify them as such.

15. The role of the Cameronians in this campaign has been described in John Baynes, *The History of the Cameronians; vol. 4: The Close of Empire, 1948–1968* (London: Cassell, 1971), pp. 91–126.

16. *The Times*, 21 Nov. 1957.

17. A fuller account of SAF is included in Chapter 3. Col. David deC. Smiley was seconded from the British Army at that time to become the first Commander of SAF—the practice of using seconded commanders continued through the mid-1970s.

18. The SAS was reportedly chosen for the job because it would be less conspicuous than a drop by the Parachute Regiment, for example. Philip Warner, *The Special Air Service* (London: William Kimber, 1971), p. 19.

19. This assault has been described in *The Times*, 9 Apr. 1959; Smiley, *Arabian Assignment*, pp. 72–88; ibid., 'Muscat and Oman'; and Warner, *The Special Air Service*, pp. 209–21.

20. Two of the most consequential incidents were the attempted assassination of Aḥmad bin Ibrāhīm, the Minister of the Interior, aboard the British India steamer *Dwarka* in Dec. 1959, and the sinking of another steamer, the *Dara*, in April 1961 off Dubay, when 338 lives were lost. A personal account of the disaster, combined with a report on the subsequent London inquiry, has been published in P. J. Abraham, *Last Hours on Dara* (London: Peter Davies, 1963).

21. These conditions were: (1) a return to the *status quo ante* of 1954 and independence for the people of Oman; (2) withdrawal of British forces from Oman; (3) the release of political prisoners in Oman; and (4) reparations for property destroyed in the 1957 campaign. Mu'ayyad Ḥusayn al-Majīd, 'al-Qaḍiya al-'Umānīya al-'Arabīya', *al-Aqlām*, vol. 2, no. 2 (Oct. 1965), pp. 19–20. See also UN General Assembly, 18th Session, 8 Oct. 1963, *Report of the Special*

Representative of the Secretary-General on his Visit to Oman, A/5562 (the 'de Ribbing Report'), and the 'Jiménez Report'.

22. Their two conditions were: (1) implementation of a cease-fire in Oman and (2) the withdrawal of the Oman question from UN consideration. The Imām's reply to these requirements was that a cease-fire would be automatic when the British troops left and that withdrawal of UN consideration was impossible. al-Majīd, 'al-Qaḍīya al-'Umānīya al-'Arabīya', p. 20.

23. Ibid. See also *The Times*, 5 Jan. and 22, 24, and 25 Feb. 1961.

24. Albaharna, *The Arabian Gulf States*, p. lviii, note 3. Ṭālib subsequently wrote to a long-time expatriate in Muscat indicating that he wished to return. Interview with expatriate in question.

25. Discussion of UN activity regarding the 'question of Oman' is based on the annual *Yearbook of the United Nations* (1957–71), and the 'de Ribbing' and 'Jiménez Reports'.

26. The Committee consisted of Abdul Rahman Pazhwak (Afghanistan), Chairman; Fernando Volio Jiménez (Costa Rica), Rapporteur; Ram C. Malhotra (Nepal); Ali Monguno (Nigeria); and Ciss Abdou (Senegal).

27. The Sulṭān had been extremely reluctant to allow de Ribbing to visit Oman in 1962, claiming that the matter was entirely internal and therefore outside the UN's jurisdiction. His refusal to recognise the '*Ad Hoc* Committee' was a result of his conviction that the 'de Ribbing Report' had settled the matter once and for all.

28. 'Jiménez Report', p. 222.

29. Representative accounts of the pro-Imamate argument are Ezeldin Foda, 'Controversy over Oman', *Egyptian Economic and Political Review*, vol. 4, no. 4 (March 1958), pp. 12–14; *British Imperialism in Southern Arabia* (New York: Arab Information Centre, 1968); *The Question of Oman: An Analysis of the British Oman Dispute* (New York: Arab Information Centre, 1960; largely rewritten from the former paper); and the letters of H. St. John B. Philby to the *Middle East Journal*, vols. 13 and 14 (1959–1960; see 'Comment: Muscat and Oman', in the bibliography for a complete citation). The British position has been advanced by J. B. Kelly, 'Sultanate and Imamate in Oman', among others.

30. The present town of Ṣalāla is actually a conglomeration of smaller settlements, including the town of Ṣalāla proper and the villages of al-Ḥuṣn, al-Ḥāfa, Daḥarīz, al-Bālid/al-Bilād and al-Rubāṭ. The new government offices are concentrated in al-Ḥuṣn, which received its name from the Sulṭān's palace there.

31. The Bayt Kathīr predominate in the Najd while Ṣalāla Plain is inhabited largely by three sections of the Āl Kathīr: the Shanāfir, the Marhūn and the Rawwās. Some Kathīr live in the Jabal Qarā and several nomadic tribes, such as the Rawāshid and 'Awāmir range across the Rub' al-Khālī and Najd. Like most Dhufaris and unlike many Omanis, the Kathīr are Shāfi'ī Sunnīs in religion.

32. The Ṣ́herā are thought to have been the original inhabitants whose mountain habitat was over-run by the Qarā and Mahrā sometime before the rise of Islām, and who were followed at a later date by the Kathīr. The Qarā and Ṣ́herā live in close proximity in the Jabal Qarā, Jabal Qamar and eastern Ṣalāla Plain, with the Qarā speaking the Ṣ́herī language and exercising a protective status over the Ṣ́herā, similar to the *da'īf* (weak) status of certain groups of the coastal towns. The Mahrā of Dhufar are concentrated on the eastern fringes of the Jabal Samhān although the majority of Mahrā in Arabia are found in what is now the Sixth Governorate of the People's Democratic Republic of the Yemen. The Mahrī and Ṣ́herī languages, although Semitic, are not intelligible to Arabic speakers. In addition to these groups, there are a few members of the Yafa'ī tribe of southern Yemen, who were originally brought in as 'askarīs to Sulṭān Taymūr bin Fayṣal; some Sādāt, descendants of the Prophet Muḥammad, also

called Hāshimīyīn; and a large number of African blacks of slave descent. For more information, see Bertram S. Thomas, *Arabia Felix: Across the Empty Quarter* (London: Jonathan Cape, 1932); ibid., 'Among Some Unknown Tribes of South Arabia', *Journal of the Royal Anthropological Institute*, vol. 59, no. 1 (1929), pp. 97–111; ibid., 'Four Strange Tongues from South Arabia—the Hadara Group', *Proceedings of the British Academy*, vol. 23 (1937); ibid., 'Anthropological Observations in South Arabia', *Journal of the Royal Anthropological Institute*, vol. 62 (Jan.–June 1932), pp. 83–103; Fawwaz Trabulsi, 'The Liberation of Dhofar', *MERIP Reports*, no. 6 (Jan. 1972), pp. 3–11; Walter Dostal, 'Two South Arabian Tribes: al-Qarā and al-Ḥarāsīs', *Arabian Studies*, vol. 2 (1975), pp. 33–41. In addition, much information is contained in *Lorimer's Gazetteer*, vol. 2, pp. 442–53, 'Dhufar'; and 'The Arab Tribes of Dhufar', mimeographed study for Petroleum Development (Oman) Ltd.

33. Muḥammad's despotic reign ended when he was killed during a Qarawī uprising. For more information, see Hermann F. Eilts, 'Sayyid Muhammad bin 'Aqil of Dhufar; Malevolent or Maligned?', *Essex Institute Historical Collections*, vol. 109, no. 3 (July 1973). Almost the only substantial histories of Dhufar are contained in *Lorimer's Gazetteer*, vol. 1, pt. 1, pp. 589–601; IO, R/15/3/182; 'History of Dhufar', by R. E. L. Wingate (intended to serve as a continuation of *Lorimer's Gazetteer* from 1906 to 1923); and S. B. Miles, *The Countries and Tribes of the Persian Gulf*, 2nd edn (London: Frank Cass, 1966), pp. 498–514. An account of a visit by two nineteenth-century visitors is in J. Theodore and Mabel V. Bent, *Southern Arabia* (London: Smith, Elder, 1900).

34. An American who had been raised by Sayyid Muḥammad, 'Abd Allāh Lorleyd, exercised some authority after the Sayyid's death and the province was later ruled briefly by a Moplah, i.e. an Indian of Ḥadramī descent, Sayyid Faḍl bin 'Alawī, from 1876. However, a Qarawī uprising in 1879 forced him to flee to Constantinople where he sought Ottoman support in regaining Dhufar. One of his descendants, Hāshim bin 'Abd Allāh, was active in Beirut in the mid-1960s in drumming up support for Dhufari rebels. See J. B. Kelly, *Britain and the Persian Gulf, 1795–1880* (Oxford: Clarendon Press, 1968), pp. 772–5; and Joseph J. Malone, letter to the editor of *New Middle East*, no. 45 (June 1972), pp. 37–8.

35. The latter name is also spelled Qarzayz and pronounced Garzayz. IO, R/15/3/338; Annual Muscat Administration Report for 1935; R/15/3/242; PAM to PRPG, No. S.1126, 19 Aug. 1945. For more information on Sa'īd's activities in Dhufar, see Chapter 2.

36. After attacks were carried out on personnel of the John Mecom–Pure Oil Company in 1964, Ṣalāla was surrounded by barbed-wire fences and the jibālīs were refused entry. This action disrupted traditional trading patterns, caused economic hardship and provoked more discontent. Oil exploration in Dhufar had begun originally by PDO under a concession granted in 1937 (described in Chapter 3, note 54). However, they later relinquished the concession and Sulṭān Sa'īd bin Taymūr subsequently granted a new one to Wendell Phillips. His assignee, Dhufar-Cities Service, began exploration in 1952 but likewise was unable to discover commercially viable quantities of oil. The concession was surrendered to John Mecom–Pure Oil in 1962, which was also unsuccessful after several years of activity. Following a brief attempt by Continental Oil, the concession was once again taken up by PDO in 1969, which continued exploration through the mid-1970s.

37. For more information on early dissident activity in Dhufar and the Gulf, see Walid Kazziha, *Revolutionary Transformation in the Arab World* (London: Charles Knight, 1975). This work is the first extensive study of the ANM (in Arabic, Ḥarakat al-Qawmīyīn al-'Arab).

38. DLF in Arabic is Jabhat al-Taḥrīr al-Ẓufārīya. There have been a number of works written on the Dhufar rebellion, differing considerably in scope, accuracy and ideological viewpoint. Among the most comprehensive are D. L. Price. 'Oman: Insurgency and Development', *Conflict Studies*, no. 53 (Jan. 1975); and Fred Halliday, *Arabia Without Sultans* (Harmondsworth: Penguin, 1974), especially the chapter on 'Guerrilla War in Dhofar', pp. 304–60. Price visited Muscat and Dhufar and writes from a pro-British viewpoint while Halliday visited Dhufar at the invitation of the guerrillas and reports from the opposite end of the spectrum. Two other excellent articles written with opposing views are Ray Cleveland, 'Revolution in Dhofar; Sultanate of Oman', *Middle East Forum*, vol. 48, nos. 3–4 (1971), pp. 93–102; and Trabulsi, 'The Liberation of Dhofar'. In addition, the revolt has been treated by Kutschera, 'Révolution arabe'; R. M. Burrell, 'Rebellion in Dhofar: The Spectre of Vietnam', *New Middle East*, nos. 42–43 (March–April 1972), pp. 55–8; ibid., 'Politics and Participation Where Britannia Once Ruled', *New Middle East*, no. 51 (Dec. 1972), pp. 32–6; ibid. and Alvin Cottrell, *Iran, the Arabian Peninsula, and the Indian Ocean* (New York: National Strategy Information Centre, 1972), pp. 24–30; Andrew Wilson, 'Sultan Qabus Faces Dhofar Rebels', *Middle East International*, no. 3 (June 1971), pp. 32–3; Gérard Laliberté, 'La Guérilla du Dhofar', *Etudes Internationales*, vol. 4, nos. 1-2 (March–June 1973), pp. 159–81; R. P. Owen, 'The Rebellion in Dhofar—A Threat to Western Interests in the Gulf', *The World Today*, vol. 29, no. 6 (June 1973), pp. 266–72; Philippe Rondot, 'Le Sultanat d'Oman devant la Rébellion du Dhofar', *Maghreb-Machrek*, no. 70 (Oct.–Dec. 1975), pp. 38–46; J. B. Kelly, 'Hadramaut, Oman, Dhufar: The Experience of Revolution', *Middle Eastern Studies*, vol. 12, no. 2 (May 1976); John Townsend, *Oman: The Making of a Modern State* (London: Croom Helm, 1977), pp. 95–112; *et al.* The summary given here draws largely on the present writer's article, 'Guerrilla Warfare and Ideological Confrontation in the Arabian Peninsula: The Rebellion in Dhufar', *World Affairs*, vol. 139, no. 4 (1977), pp. 278–95.

39. The text of a declaration issued on 9 June is to be found in *Documents of the National Struggle in Oman and the Arabian Gulf* (London: The Gulf Committee, 1974), pp. 7–9. This is a good source of statements and communiques made by the Dhufari rebels during the first decade of the rebellion, and is a translation of *Wathā'iq al-Niḍāl al-Waṭanī, 1965–1974* (Beirut: Dār al-Ṭalī'a, 1974). The Gulf Committee has translated a number of publications put out by the rebel organisation.

40. Sa'īd had been inspecting the Dhofar Force headquarters at Arzāt, just outside Ṣalāla. As he was taking the salute from the honour guard, approximately a dozen members of the guard followed their leader's command to fire at the Sulṭān. Since they shot into the setting sun and the Sulṭān was standing at a lower level than the soldiers (and being short himself), the fusillade passed over his head. The Pakistani commander of Dhofar Force was then wounded by the leader of the guard who was in turn killed by one of the Sulṭān's slaves. Sa'īd later remarked that he finally realised what it was like to be in front of a firing squad. Interview with a member of SAF at the time of the attempt. Other versions are to be found in *The Times*, 29 Apr. 1966; *Arab Report and Record* (ARR), 16–30 Apr. 1966; and Halliday, *Arabia*, p. 319. The incident caused Sa'īd to retreat even deeper into his Ṣalāla palace and to introduce SAF (predominantly Baluchi in composition) into Dhufar to counterbalance the suspect Dhofar Force (which was mainly jibālī).

41. In Arabic, al-Jabha al-Sha'bīya li-Taḥrīr al-Khalīj al-'Arabī al-Muḥtall.

42. These lines consisted of a series of fortified positions linked by barbed-wire fences and frequent patrols. Their purpose was to divide the province into isolated sectors: when one area was cleared of rebel activity, the sector to its west could

then be isolated and cleared. Another line was attempted during Operation Simba in 1972 in order to seal off the border with PDRY; the effort proved premature, however.

43. Estimates of Iranian deaths range up to 1,000 men. *Financial Times*, 14 January 1977.

44. An important article on Cuban involvement in Africa and Asia was published in the *Christian Science Monitor*, 14 Jan. 1976. See also Wolfgang Berner, 'Cuban Intervention in Africa and Arabia', *Aussenpolitik*, English edn, vol. 27, no. 3/76 (1976), pp. 328–35.

CHAPTER 8

Coup d'Etat of 1970 and Volte-Face

The long century of Oman's isolation came to an abrupt end with a palace *coup d'état* in the summer of 1970. Although the *coup* was dramatic in its sudden reversal of the Sultanate's outward appearance, it was not unexpected. Indeed, the need for a substantial change in Oman had been perceived for a number of years, as the traditional character of most of the Sultanate's neighbours was inexorably modified. The economic and social transformation occurring in the Gulf, wrought by the advent of oil revenues, gradually worked its way south towards Oman. Meanwhile, southern Yemen gained its independence to the accompaniment of radical rhetoric. Even the Imamate of the Yemen, the Arabian Peninsula's other mountainous bastion of traditional rule, was plunged into civil war in the early 1960s and emerged years later considerably more affected by the outside world and its demands.

Pressures for Change

As the 1960s drew to a close, pressures for change in the Sultanate intensified as a result of the discovery of oil in 1964 and its subsequent exportation. The atmosphere was further charged by the spiralling violence of the revolt in Dhufar and intensified by the increasing belief, held inside and outside the country, that if Sa'īd bin Taymūr were to remain in power, the entire Sultanate would fall prey to subversion. Great Britain, long the protector of eastern Arabia, was particularly nervous over the fate of the Sultanate following its decision of 1968 to withdraw militarily from the Gulf by late 1971. London sought comfort in a possible analogy between Oman and Abu Dhabi, where a reactionary and obstinate ruler, Shakhbūt bin Sulṭān Āl Nuhayyān, had been removed by *coup d'état* in 1966 and replaced by his more adaptable and progressive brother, Zāyid. Consequently, Whitehall's position was to encourage a similar dénouement in Oman—under these benevolent circumstances, the actual transition was relatively painless for both Britain and Oman.

Opposition to Sa'īd bin Taymūr had become increasingly widespread in the last years of his reign. The leaders of the old Imamate revolt still maintained the 'Oman Liberation Army' in Saudi Arabia and Iraq, and had also established contact with the Dhufar Liberation Front, although co-operation was hampered by the rebellion's leftist orientation after 1968. Guerrilla activity in Dhufar provided the strongest opposition and the inability of the Sulṭān to control rebel actions there produced mounting concern over the country's fate and disenchantment with Sa'īd's ability to continue as Sulṭān. This disenchantment permeated the ruling family and various Āl Bū Sa'īd individuals left Muscat for other Arab countries and Europe. The strongest challenge from this quarter came from the Sulṭān's brother, Ṭāriq bin Taymūr. Frustrated by Sa'īd's diffident attitude towards him, Ṭāriq left the country in November 1962. Four years later, he called for Sa'īd's removal and disclosed that he had been in contact with other dissident groups and was establishing an armed force of his own.[1] He had also established a working relationship with the DLF in the mid-1960s but his association was rejected by the radical leaders of the post-1968 period because of his conservative background. His ties to the 'Imamate' camp consequently provided the working basis of his plans for an invasion of Oman in 1970, using several hundred members of the 'Oman Liberation Army' then based in Iraq.[2] At the same time, several minor organisations also professed intentions to overthrow the government. Of these, only the Arab Action Party, led by 'Abd Allāh bin Thānī al-Shiḥūḥī, was to pose any sort of threat and only a short-lived one at that.[3] The major threat of this kind was to come from the NDFLOAG with its abortive programme of attacks in June 1970.

The Coup d'Etat of 23 July

Underground opposition was centred around the Sulṭān's son Qābūs. Following his return to Oman—after education in England, a stint of military service with the Cameronians in Germany and then a world tour—the Heir Apparent had been almost completely isolated in Ṣalāla. There he had been given his own house and was put to work studying Islamic law. Since personal contact with his father was rare, Qābūs began to persuade his infrequent visitors to ask the Sulṭān to give him a responsible position. His father's refusal to do so eventually embittered Qābūs and by 1970 the Heir Apparent had reached the conclusion that Sa'īd should be overthrown. Feelers were put out to sympathisers both in Ṣalāla and Muscat. In Ṣalāla, these included Burayk bin Ḥamūd al-Ghāfirī, the son of the wālī of Dhufar; Ḥamad bin Ḥamūd Āl Bū Sa'īd, secretary to the Sulṭān; and one of the SAF intelligence officers in Dhufar and a former classmate of Qābūs at Sandhurst. Contact was made with allies in Muscat through a PDO official who made regular trips to Ṣalāla for discussions with Sulṭān Sa'īd and took advantage of the opportunity these afforded to converse with Qābūs. Although the British government was not directly concerned with the planning for the *coup*, Whitehall's sympathetic attitude was responsible for the co-operation of the Consul General in Muscat, David G. Crawford, and the PRPG, Geoffrey Arthur, as well as the seconded SAF Commander. The long-term expatriate community in the Sultanate was split between those loyal to Sa'īd and those who felt he had to go. One of the former, the Military Secretary, Brig. P. R. M. Waterfield, retired in January 1970 and was replaced by Col. Hugh Oldman, a former SAF Commander. Thus a major obstacle to the planning was removed and simultaneously an individual able to provide administrative continuity immediately following the *coup* had been acquired.[4] The Sultanate's director of intelligence secured Ṭāriq's co-operation and endorsement of Qābūs at a meeting in Dubay in May 1970, and the stage was set.[5] Despite the improvement in communication provided by Oldman's replacement of Waterfield, the date of the *coup* was continually postponed until the NDFLOAG's June raid on Izkī galvanised Qābūs and his supporters into action.[6]

After months of procrastination, the date was finally set for the night of 23 July 1970. Since the palace guards allegedly had been bribed to be absent on that night, Burayk bin Ḥamūd easily led a group of Ḥawāsina retainers through the palace doors and up to Sa'īd's apartments. There they were met by a fusillade fired by the Sulṭān and his personal slaves. Burayk was wounded and retreated to the courtyard where he was met by a senior SAF officer and some soldiers from the SAF Northern Frontier Regiment. The second charge into the palace was successful and Sa'īd was eventually persuaded to surrender. Reluctantly, he signed the abdication document and was bundled off to the RAF base and flown on to al-Baḥrayn where his wounds were tended.[7] From there, he was sent on to a private hospital in England where he spent several months. He subsequently took up residence in a suite at the Dorchester Hotel on London's Park Lane, where he died on 19 October 1972. Although plans had been made for a reconciliation between the old and new Sulṭāns, Sa'īd died before he was to meet his son.

News of the successful *coup* was suppressed until after the weekend. On 26 July, the new Sulṭān made a brief announcement to the country and the world:

> In the past I had marked with mounting concern and intense dissatisfaction the inability of my father to control affairs.
>
> Now my family and my armed forces have sworn their allegiance to me. The Old Sultan has left the country and I promise that the first thing I shall dedicate myself to will be the speedy establishment of a modern government.[8]

A few days later, Sulṭān Qābūs made his first visit ever to Muscat and was received by enthusiastic crowds. Almost simultaneously, Ṭāriq bin Taymūr arrived to take up the post of Prime Minister. The old administration existing in Muscat was quickly altered: most of the expatriate advisers were invited to leave and those Omani officials of long service, such as Aḥmad bin Ibrāhīm Āl Bū Sa'īd, Shihāb bin Fayṣal Āl Sa'īd and Ismā'īl bin Khalīl al-Raṣāṣī, found it expedient to retire. On 8 August, Ṭāriq announced the appointment of the new regime's first ministers: Sa'ūd bin 'Alī al-Khalīlī for education, Dr 'Āṣim al-Jamālī for health, Badr bin Sa'ūd Āl Bū Sa'īd for the interior and Muḥammad bin Aḥmad Āl Bū Sa'īd for justice.[9] Shortly afterwards, Ṭāriq departed to clear up his personal affairs in Germany and to recruit other Omani exiles to join the new government.

During his absence, the routine matters of government were handled by an 'Interim Council', a sort of kitchen cabinet serving as a bridge between the antiquated administration of Sa'īd bin Taymūr and the expanded bureaucracy that was to follow under Qābūs. Membership was composed of a mixture of individuals who had been involved in the *coup* and some newer elements of the 'old guard' who had only relatively recently been employed by the old Sulṭān, acting under pressure. Military Secretary Hugh Oldman served as chairman, and other members included: SAF Commander John Graham; David Ogram, the Director of Development; Robin Young and William Heber-Percy, who had been attached to the new Planning and Development Board; and Thuwaynī bin Shihāb Āl Sa'īd. Occasionally, others such as Francis Hughes, Peter Mason and Qays bin 'Abd al-Mun'im al-Zawāwī took part in deliberations.[10] The council's short-lived role was largely confined to such routine matters as review of contracts and determining which side of the road to drive on, as well as serving as caretaker for Ṭāriq. Upon the new Prime Minister's return at the end of August, the council was dissolved and active administration was transferred to Ṭāriq's cabinet of Omanis. The haphazard and largely eccentric method of governing that had been hitherto traditional in the Sultanate was radically altered in favour of a new and comprehensive administration.

Administrative and Socio-Economic Expansion

The substitution of a new Sulṭān for an old one was by no means the only consequence of the events of July–August 1970. The first violent change of leadership that the Āl Bū Sa'īd state had experienced in nearly a century also put an end to the isolationist policy of Sa'īd bin Taymūr by a government fully committed to development and international co-operation. The change of the country's name from the Sultanate of Muscat and Oman to the Sultanate of Oman symbolised this new policy of expansion.

Application was soon made for membership in the Arab League and a delegation spent much of early 1971 travelling to various Arab capitals seeking support for the new regime. The Sulṭān visited many of his fellow Arab heads of state in a campaign that also took him to al-Riyāḍ in December 1971 for a dramatic meeting with King Fayṣal and a welcome rapprochement between the two traditionally antagonistic states.[11] The Sulṭān's journeys also took him to the Iranian celebrations of 2,500 years of statehood at Persepolis in October 1971, the Algiers conference of non-aligned nations in September 1973, the Algiers Arab summit conference in November 1973, and the Islamic summit conference in Lahore in February 1974. His itinerary also included state visits to London, Paris, Tehran and Washington. Following the Sultanate's admission into the Arab League in 1971, the country joined the United Nations on 7 October 1971, and subsequently the IMF, IBRD, WHO, UNESCO and other organisations.[12] As a result, Oman established correct relations with all Arab states except PDRY and Iraq—although Libya later turned against the Sultanate, and Iraq agreed to establish diplomatic relations in 1976.[13] Twenty-one states were represented in Muscat by late 1975 in a significant contrast to Sa'īd's time when only Great Britain and India maintained representatives there.

One of the new Sulṭān's first campaigns was to abolish the myriad of restrictions imposed by the old regime. These ranged from such vagaries as the daily closing of Muscat's three gates three hours after sundown, and the rigid enforcement of a law requiring nocturnal pedestrians in the capital to carry a hurricane lantern, to serious strictures on trade—such as the customs post at nearby Ruwī for taxing products moving from the interior to Muscat/Maṭraḥ—and personal freedom.[14] Such strictures, although perhaps useful when first instituted, had clearly become anachronistic by the 1960s.

It should be noted that contrary to sweeping condemnations of Sa'īd bin Taymūr in the years following the *coup*, a certain measure of development and freedom of movement had existed under the old Sulṭān. By way of example, over a thousand vehicles had been imported into Muscat prior to 1970—although most were for military or oil company use and private import had to be approved personally by the Sulṭān. Omanis who left the country to find work elsewhere were not automatically prohibited from returning: many returned to visit their families periodically and others came back permanently with enough savings to buy some land or purchase a taxi. Nevertheless, many stayed away if for no other reason than there was little money to be made in stagnant Muscat. In addition, various capital projects had been either planned, under construction or completed by July 1970. These included a water supply scheme for the capital, a new electrical plant, hospital, girls' school, port, government office building, paved road to Ṣuḥār and a master plan for Greater Maṭraḥ.[15] Nevertheless, the creeping, almost grudging, pace of pre-1970 development was quickly overturned by a plethora of crash projects for schools, hospitals, health clinics, housing, roads, government buildings, an international airport, and water, agricultural and fishing resources surveys.[16] The dramatic increase in both government and private sector services is illustrated in Table 1.[17]

In view of the immediate spur to the *coup*, i.e. the rebel attack on Izkī in June, it is not surprising that another of Sulṭān Qābūs's

Table 1: Government and Private Sector Services

	1969	1970	1971	1972	1973
Government revenues (million riyāls)	—	—	50.1	53.0	68.5
Government expenditures (million riyāls)	4.8	—	46.0	71.6	92.9
Government development expenditures (million riyāls)	.2	—	20.0	29.9	29.9
Total imports (million riyāls)	11.2	12.0	40.2	61.6	85.8
Dutiable imports (million riyāls)	5.6	7.6	13.8	18.7	33.7
Schools	3	3	16	41	68
Students	—	900	6,941	15,332	24,481
Hospitals	3	5	8	13	15
Health clinics	10	13	17	20	29
Post offices	—	2	10	12	17
Telephone lines	416	557	989	1,208	2,226
Government employees	—	1,750	3,112	5,318	9,073
Kilometres of paved roads	10	10	26	210	300
Kilometres of graded roads	—	1,817	2,168	3,060	3,620
Vehicles registered	1,029[18]	840	5,540	4,191	4,803

primary concerns was to undercut dissident inroads and sympathy by a show of military strength and a 'hearts and minds' campaign in Dhufar.[19] Despite the increased emphasis on the southern province, Dhufar retained its quasi-autonomous status in the Sultanate with local government agencies falling under the jurisdiction of the Wālī, whose role and responsibilities far surpassed those of his counterparts in the north. A pertinent example of this autonomy was the Dhofar Development Department (DDD), established in 1971 and administered separately from the ministries in Muscat. The new Sulṭān's stress on Dhufar's development was shown by the wide scope of projects instituted there, including a port at Raysūt, schools, housing, a hospital and a government administration building in Ṣalāla, paved roads from Ṣalāla to Raysūt and Ṭaqa, as well as a projected paving of the entire route from

Ṣalāla to Muscat, two experimental farms outside Ṣalāla and radio and colour television stations. In the mountains, the Sultanate sought to gain the loyalty of the jibālīs through its Civil Action Teams (CAT), which dug wells and set up shops, health clinics and schools.[20]

In order to initiate the 'new era', however, the country found itself in dire need of manpower, which was partially met only by recourse to large numbers of expatriates, including Europeans, Americans, Indians, Pakistanis, Egyptians, Palestinians, Jordanians and Lebanese. Conscious efforts were also made to draw upon the reservoir of Omanis abroad. By the late 1960s, there were over 50,000 Omanis living in various Gulf states, with more than 12,000 in al-Baḥrayn and 14,000 in al-Kuwayt alone—many of these returned following the *coup d'état.*[21] In addition, the Sultanate welcomed surrendering Dhufari rebels and several gained the rank of Under-Secretary in Omani ministries. Another rich source was that of the 'Zanzibari' Omanis, who had been shunned by Sulṭān Sa'īd but were welcomed after 1970, especially because of their education and training, although many faced the problem of not speaking Arabic.[22]

The process of building a new government, begun immediately following the *coup*, continued throughout the early years of Sulṭān Qābūs's reign. In addition to the four ministries announced by Ṭāriq bin Taymūr in August 1970, administrative machinery was soon set up for foreign affairs, economy, communication and public services, information, social affairs and labour, land affairs, awqāf and Islamic affairs, and the Sulṭān's *dīwān.*[23] On National Day 1974 (18 November), the Sulṭān announced a major realignment of ministries. The new line-up consisted of: Defence; Foreign Affairs; Information; Interior; Education; Justice; Land Affairs; Communications; Public Works; Commerce and Industry; Agriculture, Fisheries, Petroleum and Minerals; Health; Labour and Social Affairs; Awqāf and Islamic Affairs; and Dīwān Affairs. In addition, two Ministers without Portfolio were appointed.[24] Furthermore, agencies were created outside the ministerial framework, including the Dhufar Administration, the Royal Oman Police and the Oman Currency Board.[25] With the multiplication of offices came the requirement for qualified personnel to staff them.

Despite the liberal and 'modern' nature of the new regime, the emergence of Omani officials at the top positions of government on non-ascriptive terms was a recent and still rare phenomenon.

Although bases for recruitment remained as varied as under Sulṭān Sa'īd, there was a decidedly more Omani tilt, and, given that, a more specifically Arab tendency. In the first few years after 1970, at least six major groups of high-level government personnel emerged, excluding Europeans who were officially termed 'advisers' everywhere except in the military. These groups included: (1) close members of the ruling family who received the most important portfolios as a matter of rank regardless of their qualifications; (2) the traditional Āl Bū Sa'īd 'civil servants' whose long service as wālīs and private secretaries gave them the experience for such traditional posts as the ministries of interior, justice, land affairs and the dīwān; (3) members of the tribal 'establishment', i.e. representatives of the interior region who were brought into the government to integrate the traditional power system of that area into the new regime; (4) those individuals who had links to the old Sulṭān, either on their own account or through their fathers' service, and who subsequently declared their allegiance to Qābūs bin Sa'īd; (5) Omani Arab merchants—a category quite closely linked to the previous one, as these individuals' positions in the 1970s were due to more than their ability as businessmen; and (6) Omanis on non-ascriptive terms, which remained the most difficult route to attainment of high position.

This last category was limited mainly by the lack of qualified (i.e. educated) candidates as well as by the conservative nature of the regime. The pool of qualified candidates was limited still further by the omission of several otherwise eligible groups. Of these, the 'Zanzibaris' were the most prominent. Their disqualification rested on the inability of many of them to speak Arabic in addition to their native Swahili and English. There was also some apprehension over their alleged radical orientation, since some were educated in Tanzania. Although Arabic-speaking 'Zanzibaris' acquired several important positions, none had gained ministerial rank by the mid-1970s.

Another ethnic group that was largely denied responsible positions was the Baluchi. This was probably due to a combination of their traditional status as 'second-class citizens' and the scarcity of qualified candidates because of the historical lack of educational opportunities. A more serious omission in terms of expertise lost to the government and country has been that of the Omanis of Indian origin. The Khojas and Hindus of Muscat and Maṭraḥ have for centuries provided the commercial backbone of the country.

Since the abolition of British extra-territorial privileges in the 1950s, many of the Hindus became Omani citizens while most of the Khojas inadvertently lost British citizenship nearly a century previously. Their relative prosperity and mobility have long allowed them to educate their children abroad but their placement in high government positions was prevented on ethnic and religious grounds. The Baḥārina, who are Shī'ī like the Khojas, have also been excluded from top government posts, with one exception.

Despite the new regime's more liberal emphasis when compared to its predecessors, Sulṭān Qābūs soon made it clear that he would retain many of the traditional prerogatives of Arabian monarchs. The tug-of-war between the Sulṭān and his uncle and Prime Minister, Ṭāriq bin Taymūr, which reached a climax in 1971, was at least partially provoked by a difference of opinion over the continuation of highly personalised rule by the Sulṭān, as favoured by Sulṭān Qābūs, and the gradual implementation of a constitutional monarchy, as it was espoused by Ṭāriq. The latter acquired the services of an Australian consultant, John Townsend, of the Whitehead Consulting Group based in London, who had previously been engaged by Sulṭān Sa'īd and then by Shaykh Zāyid bin Sulṭān Āl Nuhayyān of Abu Dhabi, to produce a study of the political system of Oman which Ṭāriq hoped would support his viewpoint. In the end, however, Townsend's report backed the Sulṭān.

Compounding the philosophical differences was Ṭāriq's enthusiastic approach to his duties as Prime Minister, arousing the enmity of several individuals in the British 'establishment' in Muscat who had helped plan the *coup* and subsequently dominated the Interim Council. These parties voiced their complaints to the Sulṭān: eventually, 'Qābūs thought Ṭāriq was out for his job; Ṭāriq thought Qābūs was out for his head.'[26] After *Le Monde* reporter Eric Rouleau brought the situation to public attention in the course of a series of articles on the emergence of Oman, the misunderstanding deteriorated into a potentially damaging power struggle.[27] The crisis reached the point of no return in November 1971 when Oman's Ambassador to the UN received opposing instructions for an upcoming vote and so abstained; Ṭāriq thereupon submitted his resignation from Germany in December. After a short period during which 'Āṣim al-Jamālī acted as Prime Minister, the Sulṭān assumed the title himself in addition to the portfolios of foreign affairs and defence.

The loss of Ṭāriq's experience and political talents was a serious handicap for the government. Various reports strongly suggested that the Sulṭān was left vulnerable to outside pressures and controversial relationships.[28] A certain amount of criticism of the Sulṭān was also raised in some quarters over his tendency to remain secluded in his palaces in Ṣalāla and elsewhere.[29] But the criticism was far outweighed by the spectacular transformation exhibited by the Sultanate, particularly in the capital area, and by the emergence of a responsive and relatively efficient structure of government which was slowly developing.

Ṭāriq returned to Muscat not long after his resignation and assumed a low profile as adviser to the Sulṭān and his representative at various international conferences.[30] A budgetary crisis in early 1975 was accompanied by the creation of a Supreme Development Council with the Sulṭān as Chairman and members drawn from those ministers directly concerned with the development process—a distinct improvement over the previous helter-skelter approach. Even as the first flushes of enthusiasm wore off in the years following the change in government, the high expectations of the Omanis were kept comparatively satisfied by the expansion of physical improvements in the infrastructure and services from the capital to the interior.

Traditional Themes in a New Era: A Reassessment

Given the enormous impact of rapid change, it is inevitable that the four major themes in Omani politics outlined in previous chapters—the Sulṭāns and the ruling family, administration, the tribes and external influences—should be greatly affected and transformed. Perhaps the role of the Āl Sa'īd and the Āl Bū Sa'īd has changed the least, as the ruling family has remained firmly entrenched in the mainstream of the nation's political life. The historical basis of the dynasty assured the Sultanate of an ideological affinity with its neighbours in the Gulf, Saudi Arabia and Iran—close relationships made vital by the threat posed by the Dhufar rebellion.[31]

In the November 1974 cabinet, the Āl Sa'īd held the portfolios of defence, foreign affairs, information, interior and education. In addition, Āl Bū Sa'īds were ministers of justice, land affairs and dīwān affairs. The family continued to be a highly visible élite in Muscat, in tandem with the established merchant families and expatriate advisers—an Āl Bū Sa'īd member of any commercial partnership, such as real estate, seemed to assure success. But the family's position remained even more important in the interior, which felt the post-1970 changes less than the capital. There the traditional presence of an Āl Bū Sa'īd wālī, a neutral figure amidst tribal rivalries, continued. In short, the family seemed destined to dominate the country's politics for some time to come, with the dynastic Āl Sa'īd undoubtedly retaining importance after the wider role of the Āl Bū Sa'īd elements has been forgotten.

The Sultanate's administration, almost by definition, changed the most as it expanded beyond recognition. It began to dominate life completely in the capital region,[32] and extended basic services to the interior for the first time. The proliferation of ministries, departments and agencies may have seemed to have been created out of thin air, but, nevertheless, there were solid roots in the past. For example, the Ministries of Interior and Justice and the Customs Department continued to function in basically the same channels that had existed for a half century or more, while the Ministries of Education, Health and Public Works, as well as the Department of Agriculture, grew out of offices belonging to the old Development Department of 1950s vintage. The difference between the old and new variations lay in the latter's ability to respond adequately to the needs of the country rather than to the whims of an eccentric Sulṭān. Only the military establishment, as a result of the exacting requirements for national security, possessed a solid framework; yet it too expanded considerably after 1970.

In contrast to the ruling family, the role of the tribes was severely curtailed by the new face of Oman. The demise of their importance on the national stage, stretching back in origin to the failure of the 1950s revolt, was concisely symbolised in the fate of Aḥmad bin Muḥammad al-Ḥārithī. Once the most powerful tribal figure of the interior, Aḥmad's uncompromising attitude toward the new Sulṭān resulted in his house arrest in Muscat from 1971 and loss of his political position. The few tamīmas remaining after 1970 managed to retain their status only by acknowledging the supreme role of the state and confining their political ambitions to activities within their own tribes. Resentment at being excluded from wider Omani power politics undoubtedly contributed to the co-operation of tribal elements with NDFLOAG and PFLOAG schemes for subversion in Oman, but their inability to carry out those plans pointed up the futility of resisting the new order by traditional means.

Even though the national arena was closed to tribal intrigue, the shaykhs still exercised predominant influence in the countryside. They held local authority for many settlements and administered the law in tribal dīras: it was still the shaykh who journeyed to the Ministry of the Interior in Muscat to seek settlement of a grievance for a member of his tribe.[33] But the countryside was changing as well. Traditional authority patterns were eroded in the larger towns by the establishment of municipalities responsible to Muscat and municipal councils initially appointed from the capital. The traditional responsibility of the shaykh to serve as intermediary between the government and his people in procuring basic services was largely superseded by the establishment of government clinics, agricultural extension units and schools, all of which encouraged direct contact between the government's representatives and the individual.

In keeping with the new regime's rejection of isolation, external contacts were deepened and multiplied. Ties with Britain remained close but London lost relative influence due to the openness of post-1970 Muscat. The transition in the title of London's representative in Oman from Political Agent to Consul General to Ambassador coincided with Britain's loss of position in Aden to the south and in the Gulf to the north. Furthermore, the severity of the challenge in Dhufar caused the Sultanate to turn to other sources of aid, primarily the United States through its allies in the area such as Iran, Jordan and Saudi Arabia. Paradoxically, Oman's increased liberalisation and entry into the international arena meant a closer identification with the Arab world's traditional bloc and facilitated the potential for internal disruption.

In conclusion, the post-1970 era should not be viewed entirely as the abrupt departure from the past that slogans such as 'new dawn' would have it. Sulṭān Qābūs bin Sa'īd remains very much an Āl Bū Sa'īd Sulṭān and his actions in the first five years of power seemed to indicate that he was not radically different in personality from his predecessors, even though he was clearly much more responsive to the needs of his people. Clothed in the aura of a 'modern' or 'developing' country, Omani politics have become more pluralistic than at any time in its history—a trend which will undoubtedly increase at a steady and measured pace. But Ṭāriq bin Taymūr's conception of a constitutional monarchy and parliament is not likely to be a reality for some time, until the increased emphasis on education has obtained results and the narrowly-based political system, with all its predominant elements of Āl Bū Sa'īds, tribal notables and powerful merchant families, has broadened significantly. In terms of political development and participation, the Sultanate remained several decades behind al-Kuwayt and al-Baḥrayn.

In the 1970s, Oman entered a position of balance between the traditional past and a heavily Westernised future. Its dilemma was captured in the typical picture of an Omani individual, who still carried a *khanjar* but adorned it with a wristwatch, who carried a camelstick but travelled by Land Rover or Datsun, who dressed in white *dishdāsha* and skullcap yet concluded business deals by telephone in English and spent his holidays in London. The path that the country has chosen will almost certainly alter that which is quintessentially 'Omani' but, as the preceding pages have attempted to show, that is not the first challenge of great magnitude that Oman has faced and conquered.

Notes

1. See David Holden's interview with Ṭāriq in *The Sunday Times*, 20 Nov. 1966, held in Dubay. For a biographical sketch of Tāriq, see Chapter 2.

2. Interviews with Sayyid Ṭāriq bin Taymūr, 28 Dec. 1974, and a senior intelligence official in Muscat.

3. This group had been organised in al-Kuwayt with the help of ANM and NDFLOAG and subsequently established a base in Dubay from where attacks were to be launched on the Ru'ūs al-Jibāl region. However, SAF, TOS and British SAS contingents managed to round up the potential rebels before their campaign began. *ARR*, 16–31 Dec. 1970; interview with above official. Two other embryonic groups were 'Abd Allāh al-Rasbī's POLO organisation which was captured intact in the Wādī al-Jizzī in early 1970, and the Arab Labour Front, sponsored by NDFLOAG and concentrated in Ja'lān and Ṣūr but never really operative. Ibid.

4. Various prominent expatriates had not been informed of the plotting for fear that their loyalty to Sulṭān Sa'īd would give the game away. These included the Sulṭān's Personal Adviser, F. C. L. Chauncy, the Deputy Commander of SAF, Brig. C. C. Maxwell, and the Manager of the British Bank of the Middle East (BBME). Indeed, when Qābūs apparently mentioned his activities to the BBME Manager during a Ṣalāla visit by the latter, the banker incredulously repeated the conversation on his return to Muscat and the word was passed to Qābūs to be more selective in his confidants. Interviews with individuals involved in the planning.

5. Ibid.

6. In the immediate confusion following the rocket attack, there was some fear that Ṭāriq had reneged on his agreement and had begun his invasion. However, the quick capture of the rebels responsible for the attack proved conclusively that NDFLOAG was to blame. Ibid.

7. During the course of the attack, Sa'īd shot himself in the foot while

cocking one of two pistols he used to defend himself. He also suffered a second wound in his side, claiming afterwards that the SAF officer had shot him. After he had been taken to the airfield, it was discovered that he had not signed the Arabic copy of the abdication and so was brought back to the palace for his signature and then back to the waiting plane. Although the RAF provided transport, they did so reluctantly and only because the Sulṭān was wounded. This account of the event is based primarily on various interviews conducted in Muscat in late 1974 and early 1975. Published accounts appeared in *The Times*, the *Guardian*, the *Daily Telegraph*, *et al.*, in the days following the coup. Another account is given in Riyāḍ Najīb al-Rayyis, *Ṣirā' al-Wāḥāt wa-al-Nafṭ: Humūm al-Khalīj al-'Arabī Bayna 1968–1971* (Beirut: al-Nahār—al-Khidmāt al-Ṣiḥāfīya, 1973), pp. 228–9.

8. Sultanate of Oman, Ministry of Information, Labour and Social Welfare, *The New Oman* (Muscat, 1971), p. 7.

9. Ibid.

10. Interviews with several members of the council in late 1974/early 1975.

11. It was only at this time that Saudi Arabia dropped its recognition of the 'Oman Revolutionary Movement' and withdrew its vestigial support of 'Imām' Ghālib bin 'Alī, partly because of Ghālib's arrogance towards the Sulṭān at a conciliation meeting.

12. See Chapter 7 for a summary of the deliberation in the UN over the 'question of Oman'.

13. The reason for the Libyan and Iraqi shifts are discussed in the previous chapter.

14. The closing of the gates was an anachronistic custom dating from the period when rebellious tribes of the interior posed a threat to Muscat's security. The regulation for carrying lanterns was oriented in logic of a sort: it made identification easy for police following the murder of a sailor in the sūq in the 1940s. The customs post at Ruwī also dated from the period when the Sultanate's control over the interior was less secure and export fees on interior products were the Sulṭān's only means of gathering taxes from his nominal subjects. A lively description of these practices is contained in Ian Skeet, *Muscat and Oman: The End of an Era* (London: Faber and Faber, 1974).

15. For a closer look at pre-1970 development, see Barbara Wace, 'Master Plan for Muscat and Oman', *Geographical Magazine*, vol. 41, no. 12 (Sept. 1969), pp. 892–905.

16. Comprehensive examinations of economic development in the Sultanate have been published in: Sultanate of Oman, Ministry of Development, National Statistical Department, *Development in Oman, 1970–1974* (Muscat, 1975); *Middle East Economic Digest*, *Oman, A MEED Special Report* (20 July 1973) which contains a convenient checklist of development projects initiated up to that time; ibid. (June 1976); *Africa* (London), no. 27 (Nov. 1973), pp. 97–106; Ragaei El Mallakh, 'Economic Requirements for Development, Oman', *Middle East Journal*, vol. 26, no. 4 (1972), pp. 415–27; Robert A. Mertz, *Education and Manpower in the Arabian Gulf* (Washington: American Friends of the Middle East, 1972), pp. 38–109; Sa'ūd al-'Awnsī, *Aḍwa' 'alā al-Tanmīya fī 'Umān* (Beirut: Maktab al-Rāzī, 1974; a thesis for Beirut Arab University); and various National Day supplements put out by the Sultanate's London Embassy and UN Mission, as well as *The Times* and the *Gulf Mirror*. The *IMF Survey* publishes periodical reports on the state's financial position, as in vol. 1, no. 9 (11 Dec. 1972), vol. 2, no. 19 (9 Sept. 1974), and vol. 5, no. 3 (2 Feb. 1976). An essential source is the Whitehead Consulting Group's *Economic Survey of Oman 1972* (London: Harold Whitehead and Partners, 1972). A more general view of

change in Oman after two and a half years under Qābūs is that of Robert Azzi, 'Oman, Land of Frankincense and Oil', *National Geographical Magazine*, vol. 143, no. 2 (Feb. 1973), pp. 205–29.

17. Sources used include: *Development in Oman, 1970–1974;* Sultanate of Oman, General Development Organisation, National Statistical Department, *Statistical Yearbook 1972* (Muscat, 1973); Whitehead, *Economic Survey of Oman 1972; IMF Survey*, vol. 5, no. 3 (2 Feb. 1976); and Sultanate of Muscat and Oman, 1969 Budget (unpublished).

18. Total up to July 1970.

19. See the previous chapter.

20. There were twelve CAT centres by early 1976. The province's special place in Omani development was adversely affected by the austerity measures of 1974 and 1975 and many of the hitherto independent agencies, including the DDD, were integrated into the Muscat bureaucracy at that time. Nevertheless, an additional development scheme was announced in Nov. 1975 as the Dhufar rebellion came to an end.

21. Al-Baḥrayn's census of 1965 listed 12,628 Omanis while the 1971 census showed only 10,785. State of al-Baḥrayn, Central Statistical Office, *Statistical Abstract 1972* (al-Manāma, 1973), p. 10. The 1970 Kuwayti census showed 14,670 Omanis. State of al-Kuwayt, Central Statistical Office, *Statistical Yearbook of Kuwayt 1974* (al-Kuwayt, 1974), p. 23. Al-Kuwayt issued 1,108 residence permits to Omanis in 1965. By 1970, the figure had swelled to 6,042 but by 1974 it had dropped to 762. Ibid., p. 59.

22. The Āl Bū Sa'īd dynasty in Zanzibar had been overthrown by a violent black nationalist revolution in January 1964. As a consequence, many Zanzibaris of Omani descent were killed or persecuted. The Sulṭān, Jamshīd bin 'Abd Allāh, managed to escape to England with many of his followers but the leading Arab politician, 'Alī Muḥsin, head of the Zanzibar Nationalist Party (ZNP) and Minister of Internal Affairs, was imprisoned and only released in late 1973. The *Observer*, 23 Dec. 1973. For in-depth studies of the revolution and politics in Zanzibar, see Michael F. Lofchie, *Zanzibar: Background to Revolution* (Princeton: Princeton University Press, 1965); and Richard M. Preece, 'Constitutional Development and Political Change in the Zanzibar Protectorate, 1890–1962' (unpublished Ph.D. dissertation, Johns Hopkins University, 1975). One prominent example of a Zanzibari Omani is Nāṣir bin Sayf Āl Bū 'Alī (Elbualy), who escaped the revolution on a ship full of refugees. When the ship reached Muscat, the Zanzibaris were refused permission to disembark and were finally accepted by Shaykh Rāshid of Dubay, filtering from there throughout the Gulf. After working in Abu Dhabi, Nāṣir bin Sayf entered Oman as Director of Information in Sept. 1970 and subsequently was named Ambassador to the United Kingdom. Interview with Ambassador Elbualy, London, 2 Oct. 1974.

23. Basic information on the early development of these departments is contained in *The New Oman*. In addition, most of the ministries have published or distributed reports on their activities, such as the Ministry of Foreign Affairs' *Wizārat al-Khārijīya fī al-'Ahd al-Jadīd* (Muscat, 1974).

24. The respective ministers named to head these ministries were: the Sulṭān himself; Qays bin 'Abd al-Mun'im al-Zawāwī (technically, Minister of State for Foreign Affairs); Fahd bin Maḥmūd Āl Sa'īd; Fahr bin Taymūr Āl Sa'īd; Fayṣal bin 'Alī Āl Sa'īd; Hilāl bin Ḥamad al-Sammār; Muḥammad bin Aḥmad Āl Bū Sa'īd; 'Abd al-Ḥāfiz Sālim Rajab; Karīm Aḥmad al-Ḥaramī; Muḥammad bin Zubayr; Sa'īd bin Aḥmad al-Shanfarī; Dr Mubārak al-Khaḍḍūrī; Khalfān bin Nāṣir al-Wuhaybī; al-Walīd bin Zāhir al-Hinā'ī; and Ḥamad bin Ḥamūd Āl Bū Sa'īd. The two Ministers without Portfolio were Burayk bin Ḥamūd al-

Ghāfirī, the Wālī of Dhufār, and Dr 'Āṣim al-Jamālī. Further adjustments were announced on 10 April 1976.

25. The Currency Board actually dates from 1968 and had issued the Sa'īdī riyāl, later Omani riyāl, in May 1970. Prior to this time, the Sultanate used three different currencies for various parts of the country: the Gulf or External Rupee served Muscat and the coast, along with locally minted baiza coins of various denominations; the interior used Maria Theresa dollars almost exclusively while Sulṭān Sa'īd sought to introduce Dhufari riyāls in the south in addition to the Maria Theresa dollars used there. For more information on these units of currency, see John Duke Anthony, with J. E. Peterson and Donald S. Abelson, *The Sultanate of Oman and the Amirates of Eastern Arabia: A Cultural and Historical Dictionary* (Metuchen, N. J.: The Scarecrow Press, 1976); and Michael E. Edo, 'Arabian Currency Arrangements Seen Evolving in Context of Rapid Change', *IMF Survey*, vol. 2, no. 25 (9 Dec. 1974). In early 1975, the Oman Currency Board was absorbed into the new Central Bank of Oman.

26. The background for this episode is drawn from a number of interviews in Muscat with advisers to the Sulṭān, as well as a discussion with Sayyid Ṭāriq bin Taymūr on 28 Dec. 1974. Sayyid Ṭāriq briefly mentioned the interference of the 'old guard' in an interview with Eric Rouleau, *Le Monde*, 30–31 May 1971. According to a recently published account by a Lebanese journalist, another source of conflict lay in the political debts (*fawātīr sīyāsīya*) which Ṭāriq had acquired during his years in exile. Thus he was supposedly induced to appoint certain ministers lacking in qualifications (*kafāyāt mutawāḍi'a*) and to invite a particular West German firm to build the Muscat–Ṣuḥār road. According to this account, when the Sulṭān blocked the discharge of these debts, Ṭāriq began systematically to thwart all the Sulṭān's programmes, thus precipitating the crisis. See al-Rayyis, *Ṣirā' al-Wāḥāt wa-al-Nafṭ*, pp. 257–9.

27. Rouleau reported, *inter alia*, that he had received conflicting replies to queries as to when a constitutional monarchy might be instituted in Oman. *Le Monde*, 26–31 May 1971.

28. One person to gain access to the Sulṭān was the former US Secretary of the Treasury, Robert Anderson. According to one report, Anderson's connection with the Sulṭān was established in London at the same time that the CIA allegedly arranged for the December 1971 meeting between Sulṭān Qābūs and King Fayṣal of Saudi Arabia. *Foreign Report*, 3 Feb. 1972. Anderson made only one brief visit to Oman, in late 1971. At about the same time, two other businessmen, Yaḥyā 'Umar and Ghassān Shākir, also established interests in the Sultanate. For a discussion of their background and influence, see the series of articles by Jim Hoagland on 'The Arab Money Men' in the *Washington Post*, 14–19 Sept. 1975. These two individuals were apparently involved in Libyan politics as well. See Patrick Seale and Maureen McConville, *The Hilton Assignment* (London: Temple Smith, 1973). One apparent victim of the manoeuvring was the maverick oil man, Wendell Phillips. The holder of two previous concessions from Sulṭān Sa'īd bin Taymūr, Phillips was granted another concession after his visit to Muscat in Feb. 1971. However, following his apparent difficulty in raising the $1 million bonus required to seal the agreement, Phillips was refused entry to Oman in September of that year. In a bizarre turn of events, the Sultanate charged that Phillips had no intention of fulfilling the terms of the agreement while Phillips called a London press conference and claimed that he had been refused an entry visa to Oman, thus preventing him from presenting his cheque to the Sulṭān. Subsequently, the offshore concession was granted to Anderson, who turned it over to Oman Sun Oil Company. See the *Legal Decision for the Sultan of Oman Regarding Wendell Phillips Concession*, by Spear and Hill,

19 Feb. 1972. In addition, an early fishing survey operated by an American firm, Mardella, was alleged to be 'an undercover spy operation'. Fred Halliday, 'The Americanization of the Persian Gulf', *Ramparts*, vol. 11, no. 4 (Oct. 1972), pp. 18–20.

29. By 1975, the Sulṭān enjoyed the use of two palaces in Ṣalāla and one at al-Sīb, as well as the former residence of Sulṭān Sa'īd's Personal Adviser in Muscat and the new Muscat palace, which in its unfinished state towered above the old city. The *New York Times* reported on 22 Jan. 1976 that the Sulṭān retained approximately 10 per cent of the country's oil revenues for his own use.

30. The reconciliation between Qābūs and his uncle was sealed by the marriage of the Sulṭān to Ṭāriq's daughter on 22 March 1976.

31. The rulers and tribes of the former Trucial Coast, now the United Arab Amirates, traditionally looked towards Muscat as a source of authority and frequently sought Āl Bū Sa'īd assistance in settling local disputes, a role that the Sultanate played up to the mid-twentieth century.

32. Before 1970, 'capital' meant Muscat. The governorate was subsequently expanded another thirty miles to the west to include al-Sīb.

33. In this connection, it will be recalled that the Durū' shaykhs have adapted to new circumstances by acting as labour brokers for the oil company. See Chapter 4.

Glossary

āl — family; used as part of name of distinguished family, dynasty or tribe; not to be confused with the article, 'al-'.

'askarī (plural, 'askar) — traditional armed retainer of Sulṭān or wālī.

awqāf (singular, waqf) — property which has been deeded to a purpose of the Islamic faith and administered by religious officials, generally through a government department.

badū (singular, badawī) — nomads, often used in contrast to hadar (settled).

banī (singular, bin) — sons; frequently used as a preface to a tribal name.

bayt al-māl — public treasury in traditional Islamic state; also used for crown property.

dhow — the Western generic term for the native wooden boats of Arabia and the Indian Ocean.

jabal (plural, jibāl) — mountain.

jibālī — an individual from the mountains; frequently used in Dhufar to indicate the peoples inhabiting the three mountain ranges of that province.

khanjar — traditional curved dagger with its ornamental sheath.

lakh — Indian term for one hundred thousand; numerically written as 1,00,000.

muṭawwi' (plural, muṭāwi'a) — religious leader of the Ibāḍī sect; the equivalent of the 'ulamā' of Sunnī Islām.

qāḍī (plural, quḍā) — Islamic religious judge; frequently serving as an assistant to a wālī.

sharī'a — traditional code of Islamic law.

shaykh (plural, shuyūkh) — title ordinarily given to chief of a tribe; also used as title for rulers of the amirates of the Arabian Gulf.
sūq (plural, aswāq) — market or bazaar.
tamīma (plural, tamā'im) — paramount shaykh; a tribal leader having control over all sections of his tribe.
'urf — traditional code of pre-Islamic or tribal law.
wādī (plural, awdiya or widyān) — valley or watercourse.
wālī (plural, wulā) — governor of town for either the Sulṭān or Imām.
wilāya (plural, wilāyāt) — area under the jurisdiction of a wālī.
zakāt — Islamic alms tax; collected on property by the state and used for the benefit of the poor and needy.

APPENDIX B

Abridged Genealogy of the Āl Sa'īd

Descendants of Sulṭān Turkī bin Sa'īd

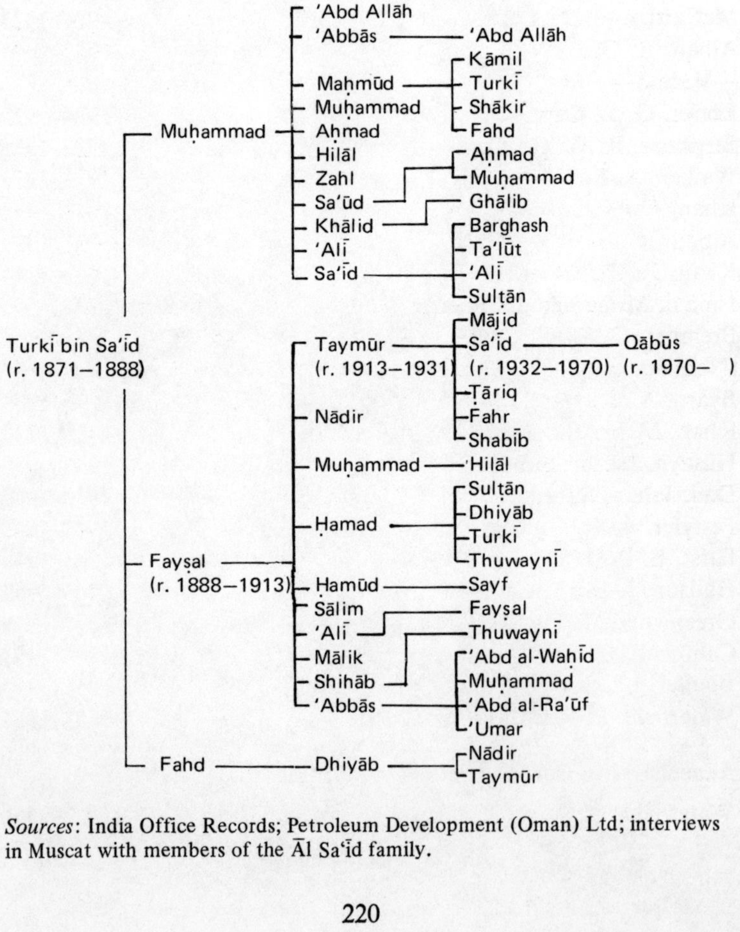

Sources: India Office Records; Petroleum Development (Oman) Ltd; interviews in Muscat with members of the Āl Sa'īd family.

Military Commanders in the Sultanate

Commandant, Muscat Levy Corps (MLC)[1]

McCarthy, E. D., Capt.		1921–1923
Alban, R. G. E. W., Lt.		1923–1924
—Vacant—	(Mar.-July)	1924
Eccles, G. J., Capt.		1924–1926
Stephens, R. W. G., Capt.		1926–1928
Walker, A. R., Capt.		1928–1931
Khan, Fateh, Subedar		1931–1932
Alban, R. G. E. W., Capt.		1932–1933
Khan, Fateh, Subedar		1933–1934
Isma'il, Muhammad, Subedar	(Feb.-Oct.)	1934
Bremner, C. E. U., Capt.	(Oct.-Dec.)	1934
(Nominal control by Sulṭān)	(Jan.-Dec.)	1935
Byard, A. C., Capt.		1935–1938
Khan, Mehr, Subedar		1938–1939
Husayn, Hazur, Subedar	(Jan.-Mar.)	1939
Dad, Jahan, Subedar		1939–1940
Pettyfer, A. O. C., Maj.		1940–1942
Hirst, L. B., Maj.		1942–1946
Hudson, J. E. H., Capt.		1946–1947
Greenwood, T. P., Maj.		1947–1949
Campbell, G. C., Maj.		1949–1951
Boulter, Lt. Col.		1951–1953
Waterfield, P. R. M., Lt. Col.		1953–1955

Administrative Commandant/Chief of Staff

Waterfield, P. R. M., Col.	1955–1958

Military Secretary/Defence Secretary[2]

Waterfield, P. R. M., Brig.	1958–1970
Oldman, H. R. D., Col.	1970–1973

Commander, Sultan's Armed Forces (SAF)[3]

Smiley, David deC., Col.	1958–1961
Oldman, Hugh R. D., Col.	1961–1964
Lewis, Anthony O., Col.	1964–1967
Purdom, Corin W., Brig.	1967–1970
Graham, John D. C., Brig.	1970–1972
Creasey, Timothy M., Brig.	1972–1975

Notes

1. From 1921 until late 1940s, all British Commandants also held the title of Military Adviser.
2. The post of Defence Secretary was replaced by Minister of Defence in 1973. At that time, Sulṭān Qābūs became Minister and Fahd bin Taymūr became Deputy Minister.
3. All SAF Commanders have been on secondment from the British army; the Deputy Commander since 1958 has been Col./Brig. Colin C. Maxwell.

Sources: India Office Records and interviews with members of SAF.

Genealogies of the Tamimas of Five Principal Tribes

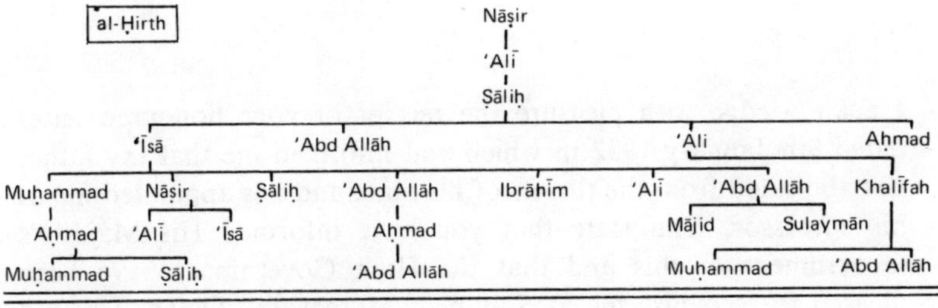

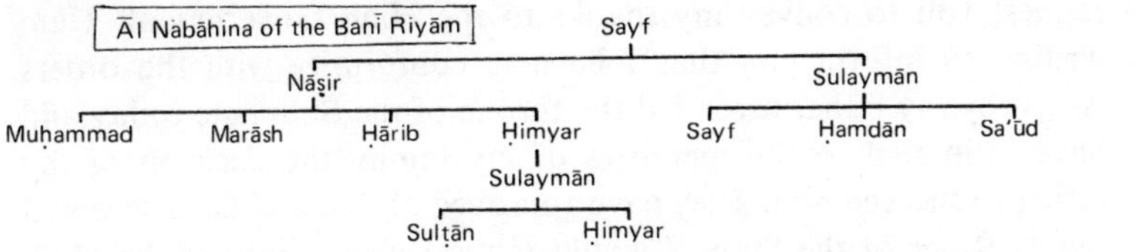

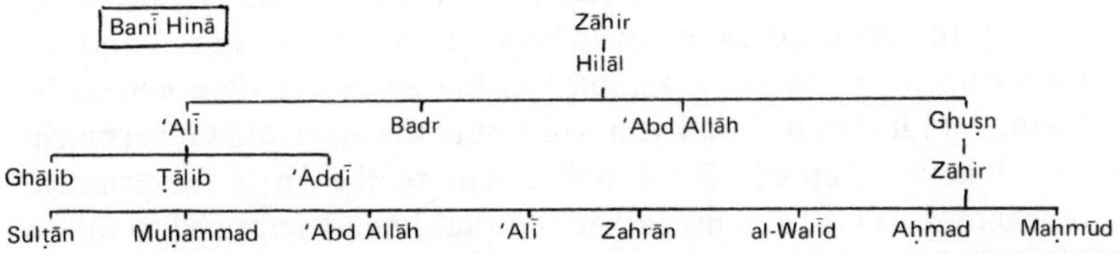

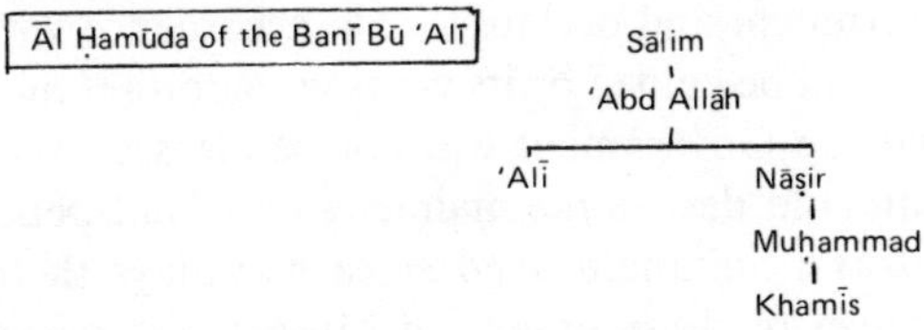

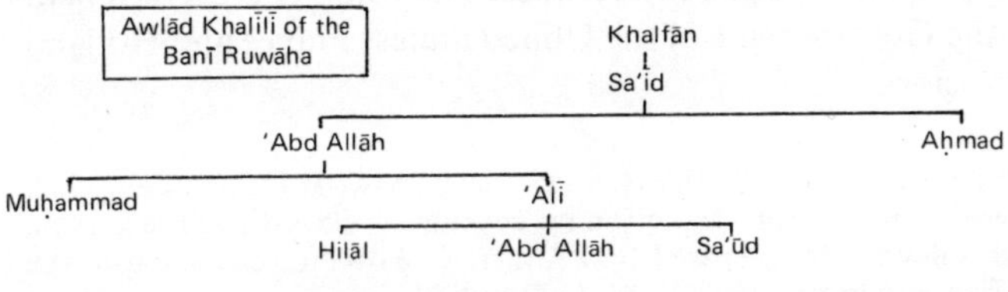

Sources: Muḥammad bin 'Abd Allāh al-Sālimī, *Nahḍat al-A'yān bi-Ḥurrīyat 'Umān* (Cairo: Dār al-Kitāb al-'Arabī, 1380/1961); interviews in Oman with members of the shaykhly families of the respective tribes.

Letter of Accession of Sa'īd Bin Taymūr (1932)

I acknowledge with pleasure the receipt of your honoured letter dated 9th January 1932 in which you informed me that my father has abdicated from the throne of his State and has appointed me as his successor. You state that you have informed His Majesty's Government of this and that the High Government have been pleased to recognise me as Sultan of Muscat and Oman. I would request you to convey my thanks to the High Government. I am writing to inform you that I have in conformity with the orders issued by my father ascended the throne of the Sultanate today and have intimated to the members of my family the decision of my father to succeed him. They have approved of that and have accepted me as Ruler of the State. I would request you to inform the High Government that it is not hidden from me that I shall endure in my rule by the continuance of their help and assistance to me and my Government in the same manner as my ancestors were helped by them. And it is hoped that you will assure the aforesaid Government that I have accepted all the obligations to the High Government descending to me from my father and that I am determined to follow his policy in all my relations with Government and that I rely on the help of the Government and declare that in accordance with the wishes of my father I will be guided by its views in important matters, as I am assured that the Government will not be pleased except in what profits my State and desires the maintenance of independence of our Government and Sultanate. And since nowadays there are no other representatives of those powers in Muscat with whom we are in treaty relations we would request His Majesty's Government to inform the Governments of the United States, France and Holland of our accession.

Source: Sa'īd bin Taymūr to PRPG H. V. Biscoe, 2 Shawwāl 1350/10 Feb. 1932. This letter was amended from that given by Taymūr bin Fayṣal on his accession in 1913 and follows draft prepared by PAM T. C. Fowle as contained in IO, R/15/3/54; Fowle to Biscoe, No. C–284, 15 Dec. 1931.

APPENDIX F

British Official Representation at Muscat

Political Residents

Bogle, A. H., Assistant Surgeon (died in the appointment)	1800	
Seton, D., Capt. (on sick leave, 1802–3; died in the appointment)	1801 to	Aug. 1809
Watts, Lt. (A)[1] (died in the appointment)	1808	
Bunce, (A) (died in the appointment, Dec. 1809)	1809	
Hamerton, A., Capt.	1840	

Political Agents and Consuls

Pengelley, W. M., Lt.	May 1861 to	Jan. 1862
Green, M., Maj.	Feb. 1862 to	Oct. 1862
Disbrowe, H., Lt. Col.	Jan. 1863 to	Feb. 1867
Atkinson, G. A., Capt.	Mar. 1867 to	Feb. 1869
Way, A. C., Maj. (died in the appointment)	8 Jan. 1870 to	1 May 1871
Ross, E. C., Maj.	8 May 1871 to	14 Dec. 1872
Miles, S. B., Capt.	30 Dec. 1872 to	6 June 1877
Robertson, P. J. C.	7 June 1877 to	3 Jan. 1878
Miles, S. B., Lt. Col.	4 Jan. 1878 to	14 June 1879
Smith, C. B. E., Maj.	16 July 1879 to	2 Jan. 1880
Grant, C., Maj.	16 Aug. 1881 to	22 Mar. 1883
Mockler, E., Maj.	20 Apr. 1883 to	17 Sept. 1883
Miles, S. B., Lt. Col.	20 Sept. 1883 to	1 Apr. 1886

Mockler, E., Lt. Col.	2 Apr. 1886 to 25 Oct. 1886
Miles, S. B., Lt. Col.	1 Nov. 1886 to 15 Apr. 1887
Mockler, E., Lt. Col.	16 Apr. 1887 to 1 Mar. 1889
Jayakar, A. S., Agency Surgeon (A)	2 Mar. 1889 to 30 Mar. 1889
Stratton, W., Lt.	31 Mar. 1889 to 15 Dec. 1889
Yate, C. E., Maj.	16 Dec. 1889 to 28 Mar. 1890
Jayakar, A. S., Agency Surgeon (A)	29 Mar. 1890 to 30 Nov. 1890
Mockler, E., Lt. Col.	1 Dec. 1890 to 13 Oct. 1891
Jayakar, A. S., Agency Surgeon (A)	14 Oct. 1891 to 26 Nov. 1892
Hayes Sadler, J., Maj.	27 Nov. 1892 to 18 Apr. 1895
Jayakar, A. S., Agency Surgeon (A)	19 Apr. 1895 to 22 May 1895
Whyte, J. F., Capt.	23 May 1895 to 23 Nov. 1895
Hayes Sadler, J., Maj.	24 Nov. 1895 to 16 Apr. 1896
Beville, F. A., Capt.	17 Apr. 1896 to 11 June 1897
Jayakar, A. S., Agency Surgeon (A)	12 June 1897 to 15 Sept. 1897
Fagan, C. G. F., Maj.	16 Sept. 1897 to 30 Sept. 1899
Cox, P. Z., Maj.	1 Oct. 1899 to 2 Jan. 1904
Grey, W. G., Maj.	11 Jan. 1904 to July 1906
Shakespear, W. H. I., Capt. (O)	July 1906 to Nov. 1906
Grey, W. G., Maj.	Nov. 1906 to Apr. 1908
Scott, N., Capt. (O)	Apr. 1908 to July 1908
McConaghy, F., Capt.	July 1908 to Nov. 1908
Holland, R. E.	Nov. 1908 to Apr. 1910
Trevor, A. P., Maj.	Apr. 1910 to Apr. 1911
Knox, S. G., Maj.	Apr. 1911 to Mar. 1914
Benn, R. A. E., Lt. Col.	Mar. 1914 to Oct. 1915
Stewart, H., Maj.	Oct. 1915 to 15 Jan. 1916
Ducat, C. T., Lt. Col.	16 Jan. 1916 to 16 Feb. 1916
Stewart, H., Maj.	17 Feb. 1916 to 8 Mar. 1916
Ducat, C. T., Lt. Col.	9 Mar. 1916 to 14 June 1916
Burton, A. R., Maj. (O)	15 June 1916 to 22 June 1916
Howell, E. B., Maj.	23 June 1916 to 9 Oct. 1916
King-Mason, A., Maj. (O)	10 Oct. 1916 to 7 Nov. 1916
Haworth, L. B. H., Maj.	8 Nov. 1916 to 11 Oct. 1917
Brickman, J. M., Capt. (i/c)	12 Oct. 1917 to 30 Nov. 1917
Haworth, L. B. H., Maj.	1 Dec. 1917 to 16 Oct. 1919
Wingate, R. E. L.	17 Oct. 1919 to 2 Mar. 1920
Gazdar, M. J., Head Clerk (i/c)	3 Mar. 1920 to 10 Apr. 1920
Wingate, R. E. L.	11 Apr. 1920 to Oct. 1921
Rae, M. E., Maj.	Oct. 1921 to Feb. 1923
Wingate, R. E. L.	Feb. 1923 to Sept. 1923

Gazdar, M. J., Head Clerk (i/c)	Sept. 1923	to	Sept. 1923
Hinde, R. G., Maj.	Sept. 1923	to	30 Oct. 1924
Crosthwaite, C. G., Lt. Col.	31 Oct. 1924	to	23 May 1925
Alban, R. G. E. W., Capt. (A)	24 May 1925	to	7 Oct. 1925
Crosthwaite, C. G., Lt. Col.	8 Oct. 1925	to	11 Feb. 1926
Barrett, C. C. J., Maj.	12 Feb. 1926	to	9 Sept. 1926
Richardson, G. A. (i/c)	10 Sept. 1926	to	22 Sept. 1926
Murphy, G. P., Maj.	23 Sept. 1926	to	14 June 1930
Fowle, T. C., Maj.	15 June 1930	to	29 May 1931
Alban, R. G. E. W., Capt. (O)	30 May 1931	to	31 Oct. 1931
Fowle, T. C., Maj.	1 Nov. 1931	to	24 July 1932
Alban, R. G. E. W., Capt. (O)	25 July 1932	to	13 Nov. 1932
Bremner, C. E. U., Maj.	14 Nov. 1932	to	22 Mar. 1933
Alban, R. G. E. W., Capt. (O)	23 Mar. 1933	to	16 June 1933
Bremner, C. E. U., Maj.	17 June 1933	to	5 June 1935
Watts, R. P., Maj.	6 June 1935	to	18 May 1938
—Vacant—	19 May 1938	to	12 July 1938
Watts, R. P., Maj.	13 July 1938	to	25 Apr. 1939
Hickinbotham, T., Capt./Maj.	26 Apr. 1939	to	2 Apr. 1940
Howes, J. B., Capt. (A)	3 Apr. 1940	to	26 July 1940
Hickinbotham, T., Maj.	27 July 1940	to	13 Aug. 1941
Howes, J. B., Capt.	14 Aug. 1941	to	21 Jan. 1942
Alban, R. G. E. W., Maj.	22 Jan. 1942	to	22 May 1942
Pelly, C. J.	23 May 1942	to	20 Sept. 1943
Bird, R. E. R., Capt.	21 Sept. 1943	to	31 Oct. 1943
Metcalfe, R. D., Capt.	1 Nov. 1943	to	31 Oct. 1944
Galloway, A. C., Lt. Col.	1 Nov. 1944	to	21 Apr. 1945
Hallows, R. I.	22 Apr. 1945	to	29 Nov. 1945 (forenoon)
Hudson, J. E. H., Maj.	29 Nov. 1945 (afternoon)	to	30 Nov. 1946
Stewart, A. C., Maj.	1 Dec. 1946	to	13 June 1947
Hudson, J. E. H., Maj.	13 June 1947	to	Aug. 1947
Stewart, A. C., Maj.	Aug. 1947	to	Aug. 1948
Ellison, R. E.	Aug. 1948	to	Sept. 1949

Consul Generals[2]

Chauncy, F. C. L., Maj.	Sept. 1949	to	Oct. 1958
Monteith, W. N.	Oct. 1958	to	May 1960
Phillips, J. F. S.	May 1960	to	May 1963

Duncan, J. S. R.	May 1963 to	Oct. 1965
Carden, D. C.	Oct. 1965 to	Sept. 1969
Crawford, D. G.	Sept. 1969 to	May 1971

Ambassadors[3]

Hawley, D. F.	May 1971 to	Feb. 1975
Treadwell, C. J.	Mar. 1975 to	

Notes

1. Abbreviations: (A) Acting; (O) Officiating; (i/c) in charge.
2. Maj. Chauncy held the personal rank of Consul General from his appointment; Muscat was not upgraded from Consulate to Consulate General until 1 Sept. 1957.
3. The Muscat Consulate General became an Embassy in July 1971.

Sources: Lorimer's Gazetteer, vol. 1, pt. 1, pp. 2675–7; B. C. Busch, *Britain and the Persian Gulf, 1894–1914* (Berkeley: University of California Press, 1967), Appendix H; 10, Annual Muscat Administration Reports, and Annual Reports on the Working of the Muscat Orders-in-Council; *Persian Gulf Gazette*; and Ruth Hawley, *The British Embassy in Muscat, A Short History* (Maṭraḥ: privately printed, 1974), pp. 20–3.

APPENDIX G

Summaries of Sultanate Budgets, 1921-47

RECEIPTS

In Rupees	(Acts: Actuals; Ests: Estimates)					
Item	1921[2] Acts	1922[3] Ests	1922[4] Acts	1923 Ests	1923 Acts	1924[5] Ests
1. Subsidies[1]	1,86,400	1,86,400	1,86,400	1,86,400		93,200
2. Customs	8,33,700	8,62,000	6,87,500	7,00,000		4,00,500
3. Landing charges	8,500	8,000	35,700	40,000		19,000
4. Zakāt	–	–	14,600	15,000		20,000
5. Quarantine fees	5,086	6,000	2,000	6,000		3,000
6. Passport fees	–	–	–	–		–
7. Court fees & stamps	–	–	–	–		–
8. Boat registration	–	–	–	–		–
9. Brokerage tax	–	–	–	–		–
10. Bayt al-Māl	–	–	–	–		–
11. Liquor licences	–	–	–	–		–
12. Municipalities	–	–	–	–		–
13. Wilāya of Ṣuḥār	–	–	–	1,05,000		36,250
14. Profit on exchange	–	–	–	7,000		1,000
15. Mineral concession	–	–	–	–		–
16. Advances recoverable	–	–	–	–		–
17. Sales of dates & tobacco	–	–	–	–		–
18. Miscellaneous	35,920	35,000	21,200	15,000		25,000
(a) Sale of forms & publications						
(b) Sale of weights & measures						
(c) Interest and commissions						
(d) Rent of Gwadur & Shināṣ aerodromes						
TOTALS	10,69,606	10,97,400	9,47,400	10,74,400		5,97,950

Notes:
1. Both Zanzibar & Arms Traffic Subsidies (86,400 plus 1,00,000)
2. Budget runs from 1 Oct. 1920 to 30 Sept. 1921
3. Budget runs from 1 Oct. 1921 to 30 Sept. 1922
4. Budget adjusted for calendar year: 1 Jan. 1922 to 31 Dec. 1922
5. Estimates for period of July–December 1924 only.

In Rupees

Item no.	1924[6] Acts	1925 Ests	1925[7] Acts	1926 Ests	1926[9] Acts	1927 Ests	1927[10] Acts	1928 Ests
1.	1,86,400	1,86,400	93,200	1,86,400	93,200	1,86,400	93,200	1,86,400
2.	8,14,064	7,37,000	3,67,892	7,62,000	2,82,332	7,30,000	2,82,847	7,00,000
3.	38,493	37,000	16,139	37,000	10,479	27,000	13,058	35,000
4.	16,137	76,000	2,112	76,000	870	61,500	26,142	61,500
5.	5,210	5,000	1,581	5,000	1,943	4,000	2,272	5,000
6.	–	4,500	1,710	4,500	2,045	4,500	4,233	5,500
7.	–	1,500	618	1,200	730	1,000	485	1,000
8.	–	–	–	–	–	8,500	2,304	5,500
9.	–	–	–	–	–	–	–	–
10.	–	6,200	1,758	8,000	2,144	6,000	2,448	6,000
11.	–	–	–	–	–	–	–	–
12.	–	–	–	–	461	1,000	330	1,000
13.	56,515	–	2,800	–	50	–	–	–
14.	5,597	[8]	[8]	[8]	[8]	[8]	[8]	[8]
15.	–	12,400	10,000	2,400	2,100	12,100	–	12,100
16.	–	5,000	1,860	5,000	158	13,000	3,000	3,500
17.	–	–	–	–	–	–	–	–
18.	13,144	5,000	9,289	5,000	26,165	5,000	95,785	5,000
(a)								
(b)								
(c)								
(d)								
TOTALS	11,35,560	10,76,000	5,08,959	10,92,500	4,22,677	10,60,000	5,26,104	10,27,500

Notes:

6. Including Rs. 50 for 'Refund of Advance'.
7. Includes Jan.–June 1925 only.
8. Included under item no. 18.
9. Includes Jan.–June 1926 only.
10. Includes Jan.–June 1927 only.

In Rupees

Item no.	1928[11] Acts	1929 Ests	1929[11] Acts	1930 Ests	1930[11] Acts	1931[13] Ests	1931 Acts
1.		1,86,400		1,86,400		1,86,400	1,86,400
2.		6,95,000		6,84,000		4,93,000	4,95,711/10
3.		25,000		22,000		20,000	—
4.		61,500		65,000		7,000	7,688/12
5.		3,500		4,000		6,000	6,681/4
6.		3,000		4,500		4,000	1,492/8
7.		1,200		2,300		4,000	2,148/1
8.		5,500		4,000		—	2,817/15
9.		—		—		—	5,200/6
10.		4,000		4,000		—	1,459/14
11.		—[12]		—[12]		—	1,250/—
12.						—	444/4
13.		—[8]		—[8]		—	—
14.						—	—
15.		2,000		500		—	—
16.		1,700		—		—	—
17.		—		—		—	—
18.		1,000		1,000		11,000	41/6
(a)							
(b)							
(c)							
(d)							
TOTALS		9,89,800		9,77,700		7,74,400	7,11,336/—

Notes:
11. Actual totals for year indicated, not available.
12. Included with item no. 18.
13. Revised in early 1931; breakdown is incomplete, not having accounted for Rs. 43,000.

In Rupees

Item no.	1932 Ests	1932[11] Acts	1933 Ests	1933 Acts	1934 Ests	1934 Acts	1935 Ests
1.	1,86,400		1,86,400	1,86,400/–	1,86,400	1,86,400/–	97,710[16]
2.	4,50,000		3,92,000	4,21,385/2	4,00,000	4,85,228/10	4,30,000
3.	[14]		8,000	16,783/6	16,000	11,719/3	10,000
4.	7,000		7,000	29,784/–	15,000	17,392/15	15,000
5.	7,000		7,000	6,027/12	6,000	6,050/15	6,000
6.	1,500		1,700	1,765/8	1,500	1,649/7	1,500
7.	2,000		2,000	2,315/15	2,000	2,396/13	2,000
8.	3,000		3,000	5,130/13	5,000	4,730/8	5,000
9.	5,000		5,500	12,312/2	8,000	13,114/13	10,000
10.	1,500		2,000	2,640/14	2,000	4,671/–	4,000
11.	1,200		1,200	1,250/–	1,200	1,200/–	1,200
12.	500		500	540/15	500	682/9	510
13.	37,000		25,000	47,496/15	35,000	36,247/13	35,000
14.	–		–	819/4	–	–	–
15.	–		–	–	–	–	–
16.	–		–	–	–	–	–
17.	–		–	–	–	–	–
18.	–		200	[15]			
(a)				889/–	400	2,381/9	2,000
(b)				559/5	400	78/6	200
(c)				–	1,800	1,853/2	1,200
(d)				–	–	–	–
TOTALS	7,02,100		6,41,500	7,36,495/13	6,81,200	7,75,797/11	6,21,320

Notes:

14. Included with item no. 2.

15. Includes Rs. 394/14 not included with (a) to (d).

16. Arms Traffic Subsidy expected to be extended for only one month, 10 days.

In Rupees

Item no.	1935 Acts	1936 Ests	1936 Acts	1937 Ests	1937 Acts	1938 Ests	1938 Acts
1.	1,86,399/15	86,400	86,400/–	86,400	86,400/–	86,400	86,400/–
2.	4,65,954/11	4,30,000	5,10,445/6	4,50,000	5,18,945/3	4,55,000	5,50,832/2
3.	13,519/14	10,000	14	10,000	11,146/1	2,000	2,907/11
4.	15,672/2	15,000	17,952/6	15,000	22,045/2	15,000	16,170/8
5.	4,635/1	5,000	5,032/6	5,000	5,092/8	5,000	5,742/13
6.	1,601/6	1,000	1,643/–	1,500	1,799/8	1,500	3,573/–
7.	2,780/14	2,000	2,982/2	2,500	4,532/7	3,500	5,166/6
8.	4,213/12	4,000	4,934/14	4,500	4,655/8	4,500	5,236/10
9.	17,214/7	10,000	17,880/11	15,000	20,305/3	16,000	15,077/15
10.	3,525/15	4,000	4,216/12	4,000	3,741/2	4,000	126/7
11.	1,200/–	1,200	1,375/–	1,200	1,800/–	1,500	1,800/–
12.	996/11	650	797/8	700	832/10	–	–
13.	22,746/12	30,000	27,884/3	30,000	30,992/14	30,000	24,956/7
14.	–	–	–	–	–	–	–
15.	–	–	–	–	–	–	–
16.	–	–	–	–	–	–	–
17.	–	–	–	–	–	–	–
18.							
(a)	2,803/–	2,000	2,655/10	2,550	3,099/3	2,550	3,203/6
(b)	136/–	100	339/12	100	343/12	100	84/–
(c)	5,735/4	4,000	6,505/9	5,000	9,564/10	6,300	5,730/6
(d)	42,172/12	6,650	–	6,650	13,218/9	6,650	–
TOTALS	7,91,308/8	6,12,000	6,91,045/3	6,40,100	7,38,514/4	6,40,000	7,27,007/11

In Rupees

Item no.	1939 Ests	1939 Acts	1940 Ests	1940 Acts	1941 Ests	1941 Acts
1.	86,400	86,400/–	86,400	86,400/–	86,400	86,400/–
2.	4,70,000	5,12,473/4	4,75,000	5,83,187/1	5,80,000	6,22,085/12
3.	2,500	3,880/7	2,500	2,660/3	2,500	2,404/5
4.	15,000	13,051/13	15,000	13,177/6	15,000	29,701/12
5.	5,000	6,259/14	5,000	3,336/13	4,000	3,277/10
6.	2,000	3,271/–	2,000	1,698/–	1,500	2,587/–
7.	4,500	5,106/3	4,500	5,543/4	4,500	5,137/3
8.	5,000	4,489/15	4,600	4,519/14	5,000	5,141/14
9.	16,000	15,762/7	15,000	14,081/11	15,000	12,605/11
10.	4,000	4,969/15	4,000	2,075/6	4,000	
11.	2,000	1,650/–	1,500	1,050/–	–	
12.	–	–	–	–	–	
13.	30,000	25,956/7	30,000	4,967/8	28,000	
14.	–	–	–	–	–	
15.	–	–	–	–	–	
16.	–	–	–	–	–	
17.	–	–	–	–	–	
18.			9,600			6,717/5
(a)	3,000	2,855/6		2,839/–	2,000	
(b)	200	224/2		71/–	17	
(c)	6,400	6,505/10		2,743/15	4,000	4,905/14
(d)	–	–	–	–	–	
TOTALS	6,52,000	6,92,856/7	6,55,100	7,28,351/1	7,52,900	7,80,964/6

Notes:
17. Included with item (c).

In Rupees

Item no.	1942 Ests	1942 Acts	1943 Ests	1943 Acts	1944 Ests	1944 Acts
1.	86,400	86,400/–	86,400	86,400/–	86,400	86,400/–
2.	5,40,000	6,49,851/15	5,64,000	12,09,056/15	6,00,000	23,57,264/8
3.	1,500	5,138/15	4,000	1,308/2	3,000	1,877/2
4.	37,000	67,198/10	39,000	1,29,651/5	50,000	74,668/1
5.	2,000	3,475/7	2,000	1,309/–	2,000	6,927/9
6.	1,000	1,092/12	1,000	1,175/–	1,000	5,893/–
7.	4,000	7,418/14	6,000	5,708/4	6,000	6,200/13
8.	5,000	7,037/3	5,400	9,998/11	5,000	8,893/–
9.	15,000	16,378/9	15,000	24,579/4	15,000	18,501/15
10.	3,000	—	—	—	—	—
13.	[18]	[18]	[18]	[18]	[18]	[18]
18. (a)	4,500	7,015/13	7,200	15,312/1	8,000	14,145/11
(b)	100	123/–	[19]	[19]	[19]	[19]
(c)	1,000	11,661/15	6,000	4,60,497/8	15,600	68,180/3
19. Weighing Charges		16,563/10		15,147/–	8,000	19,834/15
TOTALS	7,00,500	8,79,356/11	7,36,000	19,60,143/2	8,00,000	26,68,786/13

Notes:
18. Included under no. 4.
19. Included under (a).

In Rupees

Item no.	1945 Ests	1945 Acts	1946 Ests	1946 Acts	1947 Ests	1947 Acts
1.	86,400	86,400/–	86,400	86,400/–	86,400	86,400/–
2.	10,00,000	27,63,547/9	15,00,000		15,00,000	20,02,566/1
3.	3,000	5,596/2	5,000		5,000	6,028/1
4.	50,000	66,217/6	60,000		70,000	56,538/7
5.	2,500	9,032/12	4,000		8,000	12,379/8
6.	1,500	5,913/10	4,800		5,000	8,005/–
7.	7,500	7,812/7	6,000		6,000	6,200/3
8.	6,000	11,592/–	8,000		10,000	13,891/11
9.	15,000	44,169/12	20,000		30,000	58,558/8
10.	10,000	12,102/–	7,500		10,000	18,921/8
18. (a)	10,000	17,044/–	10,000		10,000	5,610/3
(b)	[19]	[19]	[19]		[19]	[19]
(c)	8,100	1,09,360/5	5,300		–	–
19.	10,000	25,086/3	13,000		13,000	19,790/7
TOTALS	12,10,000	31,63,874/2	18,60,000[20]		17,53,400	25,49,515/3[21]

Notes:
20. Includes 1,30,000 from Gwadur Customs.
21. Includes 2,54,626/10 from Gwadur Customs.

EXPENDITURES

In Rupees (Acts: Actuals; Ests: Estimates)

Name of Item	1921[1] Acts	1922[1] Ests	1922[5] Acts	1923 Ests	1923[9] Acts	1924[10] Ests
1. Civil list	3,32,307[2]	3,34,000[2]	2,12,200[2]	2,13,000[2]		1,70,000[2]
2. Dīwān al-Sulṭān (central administration)	1,93,492	1,64,000	3,21,300	2,94,400		82,500
3. Judicial dept.	–	–	–	–		–
4. Jalālī Fort (prison)	–	–	–	–		–
5. Mīrānī Fort	–	–	–	–		
(a) Police						3,250
(b) 'Askarīs						–
6. Defence (Muscat Infantry)	1,18,146	2,04,200	2,35,500	1,89,000		84,800[11]
7. Marine	76,272	25,000	[6]	[6]		[6]
8. Customs & revenues	1,25,246	1,03,000	95,500	99,000		69,550
9. Wālīs & staff	[3]	[3]	[3]	[3]		–
10. Wilāya of Ṣuḥār	–	–	–	85,000		24,000
11. Pensioners	8,636	18,000	8,500	13,000		4,250
12. Public works dept. & municipalities	[4]	[4]	–	–		–
13. Quarantine	5,448	5,000	4,000	7,000[8]		1,750
14. Education (school)	–	–	–	–		–
15. Repayment of loan	93,480	93,480	93,500	93,500		46,750
16. Subsidies to shaykhs	–	–	–	–		1,500
17. Improvement schemes	–	–	–	–		–
18. Miscellaneous	1,07,232	53,520	1,02,700[7]	70,000		25,000
TOTALS	10,60,259	10,00,200	10,73,200	10,63,900		5,13,350

Notes
1. Covers period: 1 Oct. to 30 Sept.
2. Includes Sultan's Privy Purse.
3. Included under item 2.
4. Included under item 15.
5. Adjusted so that 1922 and years after are budgeted for 1 Jan. to 31 Dec.
6. Included with item 6.
7. Includes loss on exchange, amount of Rs. 6,200.
8. Includes 3,000 for Maṭraḥ Hospital.
9. Figures not available.
10. Estimates for period of July–December only.
11. Includes Maṭraḥ Hospital (and Marine)

In Rupees

Item no.	1924 Acts	1925 Ests	1925[16] Acts	1926[10] Ests	1926[16] Acts	1927 Ests	1927[16] Acts	1928 Ests
1.	2,21,428[2]	1,20,000	60,000	1,64,000	1,65,292	3,25,000	1,60,795	3,25,000
2.	1,63,295	74,000	26,591	35,000	33,993	70,000	30,600	77,500
3.	—	18,500	9,289	9,500	9,534	21,000	9,810	20,000
4.	—	13	13	13	13	13	13	13
5.		—	—	—	—	13	13	13
(a)	3,009							
(b)	—							
6.	1,69,738[11]	1,70,000	95,395	80,000	86,964	82,901	1,65,600	1,70,000
7.	6	6,000	3,808	44,000	559	42,000	15,167	35,000
8.	1,40,007	1,27,900	45,348	50,000	49,374	1,15,650	58,813	1,29,000
9.	—	1,46,550	48,383	75,000	49,285	1,45,000	70,944	1,48,800
10.	—	—	—	—	—	—	—	—
11.	8,058	—	—	5,750	4,708	10,800	4,389	9,600
12.	—	15,000	16,994	2,000	3,126	13,000	6,109	14,000
13.	3,467	4,600[14]	4,525[17]	4,100[19]	1,964[20]	7,250[21]	3,580[21]	7,250[21]
14.	—	—	—	—	—	—	—	18,400
15.	93,480	1,01,500[15]	53,240[18]	46,760	46,740	93,500	46,740	46,750
16.	2,610	3,050	1,306	1,500	1,302	4,000	1,086	—
17.	—	—	—	—	—	—	—	—
18.	52,790	34,300	43,762	15,500	56,682	33,021	1,06,002	27,000
TOTALS	8,63,182[12]	8,21,400	4,08,641	5,33,110	5,09,523	9,63,122	6,79,635	10,28,300

Notes

12. Includes 5,300 in advances.
13. Included in item 3.
14. Includes 3,600 for Maṭraḥ Hospital.
15. Includes Ṣuḥār Customs loan of 8,000.
16. Figures for January to June only.
17. Includes 2,314 for Maṭraḥ Hospital.
18. Includes 7,500 for Ṣuḥār Customs loan.
19. Includes 1,800 for Maṭraḥ Hospital.
20. Includes 1,886 for Maṭraḥ Hospital.
21. Includes Maṭraḥ Hospital.

In Rupees

Item no.	1928[9] Acts	1929 Ests	1929[9] Acts	1930 Ests	1930[9] Acts	1931[22] Ests	1931 Acts	1932 Ests
1.		3,13,500		3,20,000		2,90,000	2,22,947/4	2,60,500
2.		73,500		66,000		1,12,200	1,52,151/4	[24]
3.		20,000		24,500		—	—	18,400
4.		[13]		[13]		—	—	5,100
5.		[13]		[13]		—	—	
(a)								10,200
(b)								24,180
6.		1,65,480		1,61,000		1,69,000	89,239/6	98,000
7.		47,000		28,000		30,000	20,711/8	21,000
8.		1,20,750		1,14,900		1,07,000	98,978/8	87,500
9.		1,43,650		1,47,000		—	—	52,700
10.		—		—		—	—	20,400
11.		9,200		9,300		9,000	8,609/10	10,000
12.		11,500		13,500		12,000	8,282/1	29,100
13.		4,000		4,000		2,300	2,551/13	7,000
14.		12,500		12,000		16,000	13,937/3	14,600
15.		43,520		43,500		43,000	30,000/–	2,00,060[25]
16.		—		—		—	—	—
17.		—		—		—	—	—
18.		26,000		34,000		35,000	31,304/10	14,000
TOTALS		9,90,600		9,77,700		8,68,100[23]	6,78,713/12	9,00,300

Notes
22. Revised in early 1931.
23, Includes 42,600 for Shamālīya Administration.
24. Includes 10,000 for Ministry of Finance, and 17,560 for Council of Ministers.
25. Includes debts.

In Rupees

Item no.	1932[9] Acts	1933 Ests	1933 Acts	1934 Ests	1934 Acts	1935 Ests	1935 Acts
1.		2,64,700 [26]	2,46,073/3 [28]	2,31,180 [29]	2,78,460/9	2,23,272	2,37,890/9
2.					17,552/8	15,828	20,323/–
3.		18,780	19,104/12	18,240	17,895/10	17,616	17,543/13
4.		4,630	5,095/6	4,700	5,692/14	4,700	5,710/15
5.		8,870	8,092/12	8,800	8,142/8	8,960	9,034/5
(a)							
(b)		[27]	[27]	[27]	[27]		
6.		87,050	80,197/5	89,480	68,393/3	85,810	68,047/2
7.		6,000	7,625/3	–	--	13,000	–
8.		73,240	81,158/1	[30]	85,482/8	93,308	96,275/14
9.		71,510	75,254/10	75,980	75,804/3	77,892	77,204/15
10.		19,790	20,417/1	21,227	23,798/5	26,670	24,071/5
11.		8,300	9,505/10	10,572	10,076/11	10,200	10,146/14
12.		14,400	24,509/7	19,472	34,785/6	16,000	32,523/11
13.		7,000	5,725/14	6,000	2,575/13	6,000	2,770/4
14.		–	–	–	–	2,400	1,512/–
15.		–	–	–	–	–	–
16.		–	–	–	–	–	–
17.		–	–	–	–	–	1,606/1
18.		12,100	11,434/–	11,528	37,164/10	19,664	67,131/5
TOTALS		6,17,750	6,17,984/14	6,04,845	6,65,824/12	6,21,320	6,71,792/1

Notes
26. Includes 10,000 for Interior and 11,380 for Finance.
27. Included with item 8.
28. Includes 11,704/5 for Interior and 12,087/5 for Finance.
29. Includes 11,000 for Interior and 96,666 for Finance.
30. Included with Finance Dept.

In Rupees

Item no.	1936 Ests	1936 Acts	1937 Ests	1937 Acts	1938 Ests	1938 Acts	1939 Ests
1.	2,22,072	2,50,698/12	2,46,312	2,26,675/14	2,38,992	2,45,146/2	2,37,078
2.	22,128	22,623/–	23,238	22,448/–	23,676	24,983/–	34,247
3.	17,676	16,953/11	17,374	16,096/–	18,408	17,519/11	8,937
4.	5,400	5,788/5	5,800	6,036/12	5,300	5,899/13	5,619
5.	9,200		9,160				
(a)		3,966/8	(5,260)	4,661/2	7,048	5,328/3	–
(b)		3,900/–	(3,900)	3,890/8	3,900	3,580/–	11,082
6.	84,610	85,291/12	83,610	84,447/9	84,810	91,774/9	69,478
7.	–	–	–	–	–	–	–
8.	93,346	92,826/–	93,310	89,006/10	82,916	78,716/1	66,771
9.	72,000	71,487/14	71,000	70,705/15	74,000	70,636/13	83,596
10.	26,000	27,373/10	26,000	24,418/15	27,000	23,087/8	27,000
11.	9,504	8,211/–	8,544	11,925/–	12,780	12,339/6	12,689
12.	15,508	25,763/2	17,000	41,111/11	20,000	45,163/12	20,240
13.	5,000	2,709/6	5,000	2,469/14	5,000	2,848/3	4,805
14.	2,400	2,016/–	4,800	4,979/7	6,000	7,131/4	10,101
15.	–	–	–	–	–	–	–
16.	–	–	–	–	–	–	–
17.	–	–	–	–	–	–	–
18.	20,900	27,235/2	25,900	1,04,501/4	30,170	43,351/4	29,296
TOTALS	6,05,744	6,46,844/2	6,37,048	7,13,374/9	6,40,000	6,77,505/9	6,36,835[31]

Note
31. Includes 1,600 for Electric Subsidy, and 14,296 for Defence old Bills.

In Rupees

Item no.	1939 Acts	1940 Ests	1940 Acts	1941 Ests	1941 Acts	1942 Ests	1942 Acts
1.	2,36,446/2	2,46,984	2,44,098/6	2,48,004	2,42,726/2	2,47,900	2,53,081/8
2.	34,232/–	41,436	38,617/4	38,808	38,161/8	8,900	8,596/–
3.	9,442/7	8,364	8,258/–	8,800	8,800	[37]	[37]
4.	5,763/9	6,080	6,997/14	6,200	13,497/12	26,100	25,279/13
5.	9,802/8	16,500	16,646/7	18,000	14,204/2	29,900	30,987/8
(a)							
(b)							
6.	61,192/14	70,000	67,845/13	70,000	70,000/–	70,000	70,000/–
7.	–	–	–	–	–	–	–
8.	67,500/14	65,500	65,345/10	75,500	74,039/8	1,06,600	97,509/7
9.	80,609/6	79,516	78,763/3	83,472	1,10,514/11	1,02,900	95,540/5
10.	26,033/13	26,800	23,912/4	30,000	30,000	[38]	[38]
11.	12,521/14	12,360	13,455/–	13,680	64,264/13[36]	32,000	29,145/14
12.	47,892/6	12,500	33,944/2	8,500	14,356/13	10,200	11,578/3
13.	4,469/–	5,000	2,935/2	4,000	26,364/4	21,300	21,051/4
14.	10,615/4	13,500	14,363/9	17,500	17,500	[39]	[39]
15.	–	–	–	–			
16.	–	–	–	–			
17.	–	–	–	–			
18.	47,167/4	33,000	33,750/5	39,542	–	44,200[40]	2,36,586/13[41]
TOTALS	6,67,985/4[32]	6,48,000[33]	6,65,475/ [34]	6,67,500[35]	7,24,429/9	7,00,000	8,79,356/11

Notes

32. Includes Defence old Bills of 14,295/15.
33. Includes 5,494 for Defence old Bills, and 4,966 for Unforeseen Expenditure.
34. Includes 5,493/6 for Defence old Bills, 9,597/13 for Unforeseen Expenditure, and 1,450/14 for Zakāt Expenditure.
35. Includes 5,494 for Defence old Bills.
36 Includes Ceremonials.
37. Included with no. 4.
38. Included with no. 9.
39. Included with no. 13.
40. Reserve.
41. Net saving for 1942.

In Rupees

Item no.	1943 Ests	1943 Acts	1944 Ests	1944 Acts	1945 Ests
1.	2,55,000	2,68,318/4	2,85,000	2,84,971/15	2,98,060
2.	8,640	9,600/–	10,000	9,930/–	15,775
3.	[37]	[37]	8,200	6,797/–	10,030
4.	23,520	21,371/10	10,000	10,435/–	4,795
5.	27,600	29,463/–	36,700	35,011/15	27,535
6.	70,000	70,000/–	70,000	70,000/–	70,000
7.	–	–	–	–	–
8.	83,000	83,149/3	1,14,100	1,13,646/7	1,55,070
9.	99,100	95,342/6	1,15,100	1,15,120/–	1,47,305
10.	[38]	[38]	–	–	–
11.	31,200	66,043/7	36,000	44,626/7	18,410
12.	10,900	8,025/14	12,000	28,447/11	36,175
13.	15,900	16,500/5	19,800	20,774/2	3,600
14.	[39]	[39]	[39]	[39]	31,610
18.	70,540[42]	[43]	38,100[44]	[45]	5,485[46]
19. External Affairs					9,595
20. Treasury					8,025
21. Internal Affairs					13,960
22. Ceremonial, gifts and presents					62,320
23. General contingencies					7,500
24. Stationery					6,500
25. Transport, travel and mission					44,250
26. Posts and telegrams					600
27. Gwadur					23,000
TOTALS	6,95,400	7,26,490/–	7,55,000	7,81,359/9	9,99,600

Notes

42. Reserve; and includes 3,000 for leave pay, etc.; 28,200 for general contingencies; 5,400 for travelling allowance; and 12,000 for dearness allowance.
43. No total, but includes: 2,718/8 for leave pay, etc.; 41,359/– for general contingencies; 2,598/7 for travelling allowance; and 12,000/– for dearness allowance.
44. Reserve; and includes: 3,000 for leave pay, etc.; 36,600 for general contingencies; and 5,400 for travelling allowance.
45. No total, but includes: 1,834/11 for leave pay, etc.; 31,663/6 for general contingencies; and 8,100/15 for travelling allowance.
46. Unforeseen expenditures.

In Rupees

Item no.	1945 Acts	1946 Ests	1946 Acts	1947 Ests	1947 Acts
1.	3,04,827/4	3,48,000		3,46,000	3,36,602/2
2.	15,884/8	31,400		32,000	30,875/–
3.	9,315/–	11,400		14,200	13,257/14
4.	5,285/12	7,500		8,900	7,362/2
5.	27,140/8	31,300		33,100	31,084/6
6.	70,000/–	2,40,000		2,48,200	2,72,995/4
7.	–	–		37,000	37,102/11
8.	1,84,895/8	1,49,600		1,43,000	1,43,175/1
9.	1,60,543/11	1,80,000		1,73,000	1,80,697/–
10.	–	–		–	–
11.	19,487/5	30,100		35,100	33,638/6
12.	65,991/10	80,000		43,000	28,448/13
13.	3,614/1	5,700		5,000	4,503/7
14.	28,694/7	41,000		34,000	29,237/–
18.	30,817/14[46]	18,400[46]		16,000[46]	3,327/–[46]
19.	10,020/4	29,500		1,200	1,140/–
20.	7,928/8	7,900		8,300	7,381/6
21.	14,943/15	16,800		24,200	24,577/13
22.	87,056/–	90,000		20,000	27,011/5
23.	4,209/15	4,800		4,800	370/4
24.	1,752/11	10,000		10,000	14,211/5
25.	23,770/10	30,000		12,000	13,231/8
26.	162/12	600		1,000	1,080/15
27.	23,000/2	36,000		[47]	46,861/12
TOTALS	10,99,342/5	14,00,000		12,50,000	12,88,176/6

Notes
47. Gwadur not included in budget.

Source: India Office Records, especially files R/15/3/196 and R/15/1/448 - R/15/1/451.

Selected Bibliography

Primary Sources

Unpublished Documentary Sources

India Office Records, London (IO)

Foreign Department, Political and Secret Proceedings, Correspondence to and from the Persian Gulf (L/P&S/10).
Persian Gulf Residency Records (R/15/1).
Muscat Political Agency Records (R/15/3).

Public Records Office, London

Foreign Office Records, Series 54 (Muscat). (FO)

Petroleum Development (Oman) Ltd Records, Mīnā' al-Faḥl, Oman (PDO)

Various correspondence relating to tribal matters.
Various mimeographed monographs prepared as studies on particular tribes or as quick reference to the tribes of Oman.

Miscellaneous

Kalīmat al-Sulṭān Sa'īd bin Taymūr, Sulṭān Masqaṭ wa-'Umān, 'an Tārīkh al-Wāḍ' al-Mālī fī al-Salṭana fī al-Māḍī wa-Mā Yu'milu an Yukūn 'alayhi al-Ḥāl fī al-Mustaqbal Ba'da Taṣdīr al-Nafṭ. 'The Word of Sulṭān Sa'īd bin Taymūr, Sulṭān of Muscat and Oman, About the History of the Financial Position of the

Sultanate in the Past and What It Is Hoped It Will Be in the Future, After the Export of Oil.' In Arabic and English edns. N.p., Shawwāl 1387/January 1968.
Maxwell, Colin C. 'Short History of the Sultan's Armed Forces', mimeographed paper. Bayt al-Falaj, Oman. Nov. 1969.
Wingate, Sir Ronald E. L. 'Mesopotamia and South Eastern Arabia During and Just After the First World War', paper delivered at the Middle East Centre, St Antony's College, Oxford, 2 March 1965.

Interviews and Correspondence

In the course of research, interviews were conducted during 1974, 1975 and 1976 with approximately one hundred individuals in the United States, Great Britain, Beirut, al-Kuwayt, al-Baḥrayn, Qaṭar, the United Arab Amirates and the Sultanate of Oman. These individuals included: former officials of the Government of India, principally Political Residents in the Persian Gulf and Political Agents in Muscat; current and former officials of the British Foreign Office; civilian and military expatriates either currently or formerly in the employment of or on secondment to the Sultanate of Oman; several cabinet ministers and most of the ministry under-secretaries of the Sultanate of Oman; various members of the Omani ruling family; and other Omani nationals and non-Omanis knowledgeable on one or more facets of Omani politics, history, economics and/or society.

In addition, communications were received from individuals in all of the above categories. These letters either supplanted interviews held previously or were received from individuals with whom it was not possible to meet personally.

Published Documentary Sources and Government Publications

Aitchison, C. U., comp. *A Collection of Treaties, Engagements and Sanads Relating to India and Neighbouring Countries.* 14 vols. 5th edn Delhi: Manager of Publications, Government of India, 1933. Reprinted Neudeln, Liechtenstein: Kraus Reprint, 1973.
British Trade Mission to Kuwait, the Gulf States, Muscat, and Oman. [sic] *Report.* London: Council for Middle East Trade, Nov. 1964.
Great Britain. *Arbitration Concerning Buraimi and the Common Frontier Between Abu Dhabi and Sa'udi Arabia, Memorial.* London: HMSO, 1955.

——. Admiralty. Admiralty War Staff. Intelligence Division. *A Handbook of Arabia.* London: Prepared on behalf of the Admiralty and the War Office, vol 1: 1916, vol. 2: 1917.

——. Department of Overseas Trade. *Report on Economic and Commercial Conditions in the Persian Gulf.* London: HMSO, Dec. 1936.

——. Foreign Office. Foreign Office Confidential Reprint. *The Affairs of Arabia, 1905–1906.* Robin L. Bidwell, ed. London: Frank Cass, 1971.

——. Foreign Office. Historical Section. *Persian Gulf.* Handbook No. 81. London: HMSO, June 1919.

——. India Office. *The India List and the India Office List.* London: HMSO, annually to 1947.

——. Political Residency in the Persian Gulf. *The Persian Gulf Gazette.* vol. 1, no. 1 (1 October 1953) through vol. 20, no. 1 (May 1972), plus Supplements 1 (1 October 1953) through 58 (August 1968). London: HMSO.

Hurewitz, Jacob C., comp., tr., and ed. *The Middle East and North Africa in World Politics: A Documentary Record.* vol. 1: *European Expansion, 1535–1914.* 2nd edn New Haven: Yale University Press, 1975.

India, Government of. General Staff. *Military Report and Route Book: The Arabian States of the Persian Gulf, 1939.* New Delhi: Government Printing, 1940.

——. Political Agent, Muscat. *Muscat Trade Report for 1942/43.* Simla: Government of India Press, 1943.

——. Political Agent, Muscat. *Muscat Trade Report for 1943/44.* Simla: Government of India Press, 1944.

League of Nations. Treaty Series. *Publication of Treaties and International Engagements Registered with the Secretariat of the League.* vols. 1–205 (Sept. 1920 to July 1946).

Lorimer, J. G., comp. *Gazetteer of the Persian Gulf, 'Omān, and Central Arabia.* Calcutta: Superintendent, Government Printing, vol. 1: 1915; vol. 2: 1908. Reprinted Farnborough, Hants.: Gregg International Publishers, 1970; Shannon: Irish Universities Press, 1970; in six volumes.

Muscat and Oman, Sultanate of. *The Sultanate of Muscat and Oman.* Muscat: Sultanate Printing Press, 1969.

Oman, Sultanate of. Department of Information. *Oman.* Muscat: 1972. Published in both English and Arabic editions.

——. General Development Organisation. National Statistical Department. *Oman at a Glance*. Muscat: 1972.

——. General Development Organisation. National Statistical Department. *Statistical Yearbook, 1972*. Muscat: 1973.

——. General Directorate for Information and Tourism. *'Umān al-Yawm, Ma'a Khuṭab li-Jalālat al-Sulṭān Qābūs bin Sa'īd al-Mu'aẓẓam* ('Oman Today, With Speeches by His Majesty, Sulṭān Qābūs bin Sa'īd'). Muscat: Shawwāl 1392/November 1972.

——. Ministry of Development. National Statistical Department. *Development in Oman, 1970–1974*. Muscat: 1975.

——. Ministry of Development. National Statistical Department. *Statistical Yearbook, 1973*. Muscat: 1974.

——. Ministry of Foreign Affairs. *Wizārat al-Khārijīya fī al-'Ahd al-Jadīd*. Muscat: Wizārat al-Khārijīya, Idārat al-Ṣaḥāfa wa-al-Tarjima, Shawwāl 1394/November 1974.

——. Ministry of Information and Tourism. *Sultanate of Oman: Economic Development*. Muscat: 1975.

——. Ministry of Information and Tourism. *Sultanate of Oman: History and Archaeology*. Muscat: 1975.

——. Ministry of Information and Tourism. *Sultanate of Oman: Southern Region—Dhofar*. Muscat: 1975.

——. Ministry of Information, Labour and Social Welfare. *The New Oman*. Muscat: 1971.

Petroleum Development (Oman) Ltd. *Annual Report to His Majesty the Sultan of Oman*. Mīnā' al-Faḥl, Oman: 1968–1974.

Popular Front for the Liberation of Oman. *Wathā'iq al-Niḍāl al-Waṭanī, 1965–1974*. Beirut: Dār al-Ṭalī'a, 1974. Translated and published as *Documents of the National Struggle in Oman and the Arabian Gulf*. 9th June Studies. London: Gulf Committee, 1974.

Popular Front for the Liberation of the Occupied Arabian Gulf. 'Gulf Liberation Manifesto', in *NLF: National Liberation Fronts, 1960/1970*, ed. by Donald C. Hodges and Robert Elias Abu Shanab (New York: Wm. Morrow, 1972), pp. 143–5.

Qāsim, Jamāl Zakarīyā, ed. *Mukhtārāt min Wathā'iq al-Khalīj al-'Arabī* ('Selections from Documents on the Arabian Gulf'). al-Kuwayt: Jāmi'at al-Kuwayt, 1972.

Saudi Arabia. *Arbitration for the Settlement of the Territorial Dispute between Muscat and Abu Dhabi on one side and Saudi Arabia on the Other, Memorial*. Cairo: Government of Saudi Arabia, 11 Dhu al-Ḥijja 1374/31 July 1955. Published in English and Arabic editions.

United Nations. *Yearbook of the United Nations*. 1957–1971.

——. Economic and Social Office, Beirut. *Interdisciplinary Reconnaissance Mission to Oman, Report*. ESOB/D/72/73, July 1972.

——. General Assembly, 18th Session, 8 October 1963. *Report of the Special Representative of the Secretary-General on his Visit to Oman*, A/5562. ('The de Ribbing Report'.) Included in General Assembly, Official Records, 18th Session, Annexes, Agenda Item No. 78, pp. 2–24.

——. General Assembly, 19th Session, 22 January 1965. *Question of Oman; Report of the Ad Hoc Committee on Oman*, A/5846. ('The Jiménez Report'.)

——. Treaty Series. *Treaties and International Agreements Registered or Filed and Recorded with the Secretariat of the United Nations*. vols. 1–700 (1946/1947–1969).

Whitehead Consulting Group. *Economic Survey of Oman 1972*. London: Harold Whitehead and Partners, 1972.

Autobiographical Accounts

Abraham, Parappillil John. *Last Hours of Dara*. London: Peter Davies, 1963.

Allfree, P. S. *Warlords of Oman*. London: Robert Hale, 1967; South Brunswick, N. J.: A. S. Barnes, 1967.

Bent, J. Theodore, and Mabel V. A. Bent. *Southern Arabia*. London: Smith, Elder, 1900.

Boustead, Sir Hugh R. D. *The Wind of Morning*. London: Chatto and Windus, 1972.

Craufurd, C. E. V. *Treasure of Ophir*. London: Skeffington & Son, 1929.

Fiennes, Sir Ranulph. *A Talent for Trouble*. London: Hodder and Stoughton, 1970.

——. *Where Soldiers Fear to Tread*. London: Hodder and Stoughton, 1975.

Harrison, David L. *Footsteps in the Sand*. London: Ernest Benn, 1959.

Harrison, Paul W. *Doctor in Arabia*. New York: John Day, 1940; London: Robert Hale, 1943.

Morris, James H. *Sultan in Oman*. London: Faber and Faber, 1957; New York: Pantheon, 1957.

Murphy, Lt. Col. C. C. R. *Soldiers of the Prophet*. London: John Hogg, 1921.
Ponajidine, Emma Cochran. *My Life in the Moslem East*. Indianapolis: Bobbs-Merrill, 1932.
Shepherd, Anthony. *Arabian Adventure*. London: Collins, 1961.
Smiley, David deC., with Peter Kemp. *Arabian Assignment*. London: Leo Cooper, 1975.
Thesiger, Wilfred P. *Arabian Sands*. London: Longman, 1959; New York: E. P. Dutton, 1959. Reprinted Harmondsworth: Penguin, 1964.
Thomas, Bertram S. *Alarms and Excursions in Arabia*. London: George Allen and Unwin, 1931; Indianapolis: Bobbs-Merrill, 1931.
——. *Arabia Felix: Across the Empty Quarter of Arabia*. London: Jonathan Cape, 1932.
Wingate, Sir Ronald E. L. *Not in the Limelight*. London: Hutchinson, 1959.

Secondary Sources

Books, Dissertations and Unpublished Manuscripts

Albaharna, Husain M. *The Legal Status of the Arabian Gulf States*. Oxford: Manchester University Press, 1968; Dobbs Ferry, N. Y.: Oceana Publications, 1968. 2nd rev. edn published as *The Arabian Gulf States: Their Legal and Political Status and Their International Problems*. Beirut: Librairie du Liban, 1975.
al-ʻAnsī, Saʻūd. *Aḍwāʼ ʻalā al-Tanmīya fī ʻUmān* (ʻLight on Development in Omanʼ). Beirut: Maktab al-Rāzī li-al-Khidmāt al-Jāmiʻīya, 1974.
Anthony, John Duke, with J. E. Peterson and Donald S. Abelson. *Historical and Cultural Dictionary of the Sultanate of Oman and the Amirates of Eastern Arabia*. Metuchen, N. J.: The Scarecrow Press, 1976.
al-ʻAzzād, Ṣalāḥ. *al-Tayyarāt al-Sīyasīya fī al-Khalīj al-ʻArabī* (ʻPolitical Currents in the Arabian Gulfʼ). Cairo: Maktabat al-Anjilū al-Miṣrīya, 1974.
Arabian American Oil Company. Relations Department. Research Division. *Oman and the Southern Shore of the Persian Gulf*. Cairo: Arabian American Oil Company, 1952. Published in English and Arabic editions.

Badger, G. P., ed. and tr. *The History of the Imams and Seyyids of 'Umân, by Salîl-ibn-Razîk, from 661–1856*. London: Hakluyt Society, 1871.

Bannerman, M. Graeme. 'Unity and Disunity in Oman: 1895–1920.' Unpublished Ph.D. dissertation, University of Wisconsin, 1976.

Baynes, John. *The History of the Cameronians*. vol. 4: *The Close of Empire, 1948–1968*. London: Cassell, 1971.

Bertram, G. C. L. *The Fisheries of Muscat and Oman*. N.p., *c.* 1949. For the Government of the Sultanate of Muscat and Oman.

Busch, Briton Cooper. *Britain and the Persian Gulf, 1894–1914*. Berkeley: University of California Press, 1967.

——. *Britain, India and the Arabs, 1914–1921*. Berkeley: University of California Press, 1971.

Carter, John. 'Some Tribes of the Omani Interior.' Unpublished Manuscript, London, 1975.

Chirol, Sir Valentine. *Fifty Years in a Changing World*. London: Jonathan Cape, 1972.

Clark, Dean O., and Robert Anton Mertz. *The Coastal Countries of the Arabian Peninsula: A Guide to the Academic Placement of Students from Kuwait, Bahrain, Qatar, United Arab Emirates, Sultanate of Oman, People's Democratic Republic of Yemen and Yemen Arab Republic in Educational Institutions in the USA*. Washington: American Association of Collegiate Registrars and Admissions Officers, 1974. World Education Series.

Cole, Donald Powell. *Nomads of the Nomads: The Āl Murrah Bedouin of the Empty Quarter*. Chicago: Aldine, 1975.

Darby, Phillip G. C. *British Defence Policy East of Suez, 1947–1968*. London: Oxford University Press for the Royal Institute of International Affairs, 1973.

Darlow, Michael, and Richard Fawkes. *The Last Corner of Arabia*. London: Namara Publications/Quartet Books, 1976.

al-Dā'ūd, Maḥmūd 'Alī. *al-Khalīj al-'Arabī wa-al-'Alāqāt al-Duwalīya* ('The Arabian Gulf and International Relations'). vol. 1: *1890–1914*. Cairo: Jāmi'at al-Duwal al-'Arabīya, Ma'had al-Dirāsāt al-'Arabī al-'Ālīya, 1961?

——. *Muḥāḍarāt 'an al-Taṭawwur al-Siyāsī al-Ḥadīth li-Qaḍīyat 'Umān* ('Lectures on Recent Political Developments Concerning the Question of Oman'). Cairo: Jāmi'at al-Duwal al-'Arabīya, Ma'had al-Dirāsāt al-'Arabīya al-'Ālīya, 1964.

Dickson, Harold Richard Patrick. *The Arab of the Desert*. London: George Allen and Unwin, 1949. 2nd edn.: 1951.

Dostal, Walter. *Die Beduinen in Südarabien: Eine ethnologische Studie zur Entwicklung der Kamelhirtenkultur in Arabien*. vol. 16. Vienna: Wiener Beiträge zur Kulturgeschichte und Linguistik, 1967.

Fawdah, Farīd. *Ṣafaḥāt Majīda min Kifāḥ 'Umān* ('Glorious Pages in the Struggle of Oman'). Cairo: Dār al-Fikr al-'Arabī, 1962.

Fox, Cyril S. *The Geology and Mineral Resources of Dhufar Province, Muscat and Oman*. Calcutta: Baptist Mission Press for the Government of the Sultanate of Muscat and Oman, 1947.

al-Ghazzālī, 'Abd al-Mun'im. *al-'Adwān al-Brīṭānī 'alā 'Umān wa-al-Yaman* ('British Aggression Against Oman and Yemen'). Cairo: Dār al-Fikr, 1957.

Gorman, Major J. T. *Historical Record of the 2nd Battalion, 4th Bombay Grenadiers (King Edward's Own), formerly 102nd King Edward's Own Grenadiers*, 1776–1933. New edn. Weston-super-Mare, Somerset: Lawrence Brothers, 1933.

Graves, Philip. *The Life of Sir Percy Cox*. London: Hutchinson, 1941.

Gray, Audrey Ward, comp. *Oman: A Selected and Annotated Bibliography*. Beirut: Ford Foundation, 1973.

Ḥāfiẓ, Ḥamdī, and Maḥmūd al-Sharqāwī. *Qaḍīyat 'Umān* ('The Question of Oman'). Cairo: Dār al-Qawmīya li-al-Ṭibā'a wa-al-Nashr, 1962?

Halliday, Fred. *Arabia Without Sultans*. Harmondsworth: Penguin, 1974; New York: Vintage, 1975.

Harrison, Ann M. *A Tool in His Hand*. New York: Friendship Press, 1958.

Harrison, Paul W. *The Arab at Home*. New York: Thomas Y. Crowell, 1924.

Higham, Robin D. S. *Britain's Imperial Air Routes, 1918 to 1939*. London: G. T. Foulis, 1960.

Hill, Ann and Daryl. *Sultanate of Oman, a Heritage*. London: Longman, 1976.

Holden, David. *Farewell to Arabia*. London: Faber and Faber, 1966; New York: Walker, 1966.

Hoskins, Halford Lancaster. *British Routes to India*. New York: Longmans, Green, 1928.

Iraq Petroleum Company Ltd. *Handbook of the Territories which*

Form the Theatre of Operations of the Iraq Petroleum Company Limited and its Associated Companies. London: Compiled in the Companies' Head Office, 1948.

al-Jināḥī, Sa'īd Aḥmad. *Kunt fī Ẓufār, Mushāhadāt fī Arḍ al-Thawrah* ('I Was in Dhufar, Sights in the Land of Revolution'). Beirut: Dār Ibn Khaldūn, 1974.

Johnstone, T. M. *A Harsusi Lexicon.* Oxford: Oxford University Press, 1976.

Kajare, Prince Firouz. *Le Sultanat d'Omân: La Question de Muscate.* Etude d'histoire diplomatique et de droit international. Paris: A. Pedone, 1914.

Kazziha, Walid W. *Revolutionary Transformation in the Arab World: Habash and his Comrades from Nationalism to Marxism.* London: Charles Knight, 1975; New York: St Martin's Press, 1975.

Kelly, J. B. *Britain and the Persian Gulf, 1795–1880.* Oxford: Clarendon Press, 1968.

——. *Eastern Arabian Frontiers.* London: Faber and Faber, 1964; New York: Praeger, 1964.

King, Russell, and J. H. Stevens, comps. *A Bibliography of Oman, 1900–1970.* Durham: University of Durham, Centre for Middle Eastern and Islamic Studies, 1973. Occasional Papers Series, No. 2.

Kumar, Ravinder. *India and the Persian Gulf Region, 1858–1907: A Study in British Imperial Policy.* Bombay: Asia Publishing House, 1965.

Landen, Robert G. *Oman Since 1856: Disruptive Modernization in a Traditional Arab Society.* Princeton: Princeton University Press, 1967.

Marlowe, John. *The Persian Gulf in the Twentieth Century.* London: The Cresset Press, 1962.

Mason, Alfred DeWitt, and Frederick J. Barny. *History of the Arabian Mission.* New York: The Board of Foreign Missions, Reformed Church in America, 1926.

Mertz, Robert Anton. *Education and Manpower in the Arabian Gulf.* Washington, D.C.: American Friends of the Middle East, 1972.

Miles, Samuel Barrett. *The Countries and Tribes of the Persian Gulf.* London: Harrison and Sons, 1919. 2nd edn: London: Frank Cass, 1966.

Morris, James H. *The Market of Seleukia.* London: Faber and Faber, 1957. Also published under title, *Islam Inflamed, A Middle*

East Picture. New York: Pantheon, 1957.

Muṣṭafā, 'Awnī. *Salṭanat al-Ẓalām fī Masqat wa-'Umān* ('Sultanate of Darkness in Muscat and Oman'). Beirut: Dār al-Ādāb, 1964.

Nawful, Sayyid. *al-Awḍā' al-Sīyāsīya li-Imārāt al-Khalīj al-'Arabī wa-Junūb al-Jazīra* ('Political Conditions in the Amirates of the Arabian Gulf and South Arabia'). Cairo: Dār al-Ma'ārif, 1961. 2nd edn: Cairo: Jāmi'at al-Duwal al-'Arabīya, Ma'had al-Buḥūth wa-al-Dirāsāt al-'Arabīya, 1962. 3rd edn: 1966–67.

Page, Stephen. *The USSR and Arabia: The Development of Soviet Policies and Attitudes Towards the Countries of the Arabian Peninsula 1955–1970*. London: Central Asian Research Centre in association with the Canadian Institute of International Affairs, 1971.

Philby, H. St. John B. *The Empty Quarter, Being a Description of the Great South Desert of Arabia Known as Rub' al-Khali*. London: Constable, 1933; New York: Henry Holt, 1933.

Phillips, Wendell. *Oman: A History*. London: Longman, 1967. Reprinted Beirut: Librairie du Liban, 1971.

——. *Unknown Oman*. London: Longman, 1966; New York: David McKay, 1966.

Preece, Richard Matheson. 'Anglo–Omani Relations, 1913–1957.' Unpublished M.A. dissertation, Georgetown University, 1960.

Qal'ajī, Qadrī. *al-Khalīj al-'Arabī* ('The Arabian Gulf'). Beirut: Dār al-Kātib al-'Arabī, 1965.

Qāsim, Jamāl Zakarīyā. *Dawlat Bū Sa'īd fī 'Umān wa-Sharq Ifrīqīyā, 1741–1861*. ('The Bū Sa'īd State in Oman and East Africa, 1741–1861'). Cairo: Maktabat al-Qāhira al-Ḥadītha, 1968.

——. *Dirāsa li-Tārīkh al-Imārāt al-'Arabīya* (*1840–1914*) ('A Study in the History of the Arabian Amirates, 1840–1914'). Cairo: Maṭba'at Jāmi'at 'Ayn Shams, 1966; 2nd edn, al-Kuwayt: Dār al-Buḥūth al-'Ilmīya, 1974.

——. *al-Khalīj al-'Arabī: Dirāsa li-Tārīkh al-Imārāt al-'Arabīya, 1914–1945* ('The Arabian Gulf: A Study in the History of the Arabian Amirates, 1914–1945'). Cairo: Dār al-Fikr al-'Arabī, 1973.

——. *al-Khalīj al-'Arabī: Dirāsa li-Tārīkhihi al-Mu'āṣir, 1945–1971* ('The Arabian Gulf: A Study in its Modern History, 1945–1971'). Cairo: Jāmi'at al-Duwal al-'Arabīya, Ma'had al-Buḥūth wa-al-Dirāsāt al-'Arabīya, 1974.

al-Rayyis, Riyāḍ Najīb. *Ṣirā' al-Wāḥāt wa-al-Nafṭ: Humūm al-*

Khalīj al-'Arabī Bayna 1968–1971 ('The Struggle of Oases and Oil: Troubles of the Arabian Gulf, 1968–1971'). Beirut: al-Nahār, al-Khidmāt al-Ṣiḥāfīya, 1973.

Riḍā, 'Ādil. *'Umān wa-al-Khalīj: Qaḍāyā wa-Munāqashāt* ('Oman and the Gulf: Problems and Disputes'). Cairo: Dār al-Kātib al-'Arabī, 1969.

al-Rumayḥi, Muḥammad Ghānim. *al-Bitrūl wa-al-Taghayyur al-Ijtimā'ī fī al-Khalīj al-'Arabī* ('Petroleum and Social Change in the Arabian Gulf'). Cairo: Jāmi'at al-Duwal al-'Arabīya, Ma'had al-Buḥūth wa-al-Dirāsāt al-'Arabīya, 1975.

Said-Ruete, Rudolph. *Said bin Sultan (1791–1856), Ruler of Oman and Zanzibar: His Place in the History of Arabia and East Africa.* London: Alexander-Ouseley, 1929.

Salem, Elie A. *Political Theory and Institutions of the Khawarij.* Johns Hopkins University Studies in Historical and Political Science, vol. 74, no. 2. Baltimore: Johns Hopkins University Press, 1956.

al-Sālimī, 'Abd Allāh bin Ḥumayd. *Tuḥfat al-A'yān bi-Sīrat Ahl 'Umān* ('Gems of the Notables in the History of the People of Oman'). 5th edn al-Kuwayt: Dār al-Ṭalī'a, 1394/1974.

al-Sālimī, Muḥammad bin 'Abd Allāh. *Nahḍat al-A'yān bi-Ḥurrīyat 'Umān* ('Renaissance of the Notables in the Freedom of Oman'). Cairo: Dār al-Kitāb al-'Arabī, 1380/1961.

——, and Nājī 'Assāf. *'Umān . . . Tārīkh Yatakallim* ('Oman . . . History Speaks'). Damascus: al-Maṭba'a al-Umūmīya, 1383/1963.

al-Sammān, Zakī, and Muḥammad Khayr Ḥuṣrīya. *'Umān: Arḍ al-Buṭulāt wa-Maqburat al-Ghazā* ('Oman: Land of Bravery and Grave of Aggression'). 2nd edn Damascus: Maktab Silsilat al-Buḥūth al-'Arabīya li-al-Ṣaḥāfa wa-al-Nashr wa-al-I'lān, 1964.

Sanger, Richard H. *The Arabian Peninsula.* Ithaca, New York: Cornell University Press, 1954.

Searle, Pauline. *Dawn Over Oman.* Beirut: Khayats, 1975.

Shāmis, Sālimī bin Ḥamūd bin. *al-'Anwān 'an Tārīkh 'Umān* ('Aggression in the History of Oman'). N.p., n.d.

al-Shītī, 'Abd Allāh. *'Umān fī Ma'rakat al-Ḥurrīyah* ('Oman in the Struggle for Freedom'). Damascus: n.p., 1962.

al-Sīyābī, Sālim bin Ḥamūd. *Is'āf al-A'yān fī Insāb Ahl 'Umān* ('The Assistance of the Notables in the Origins of the People of Oman'). Damascus: al-Maktab al-Islāmī, n.d.

Stanford Research Institute, for American University, Foreign Area

Studies. *Area Handbook for the Peripheral States of the Arabian Peninsula*. Washington, D.C.: USGPO, 1971.

Stanton Hope, W. E. *Arabian Adventurer: The Story of Haji Williamson*. London: Robert Hale, 1951.

Storm, W. Harold. *Whither Arabia? A Survey of Missionary Opportunity*. London: World Dominion Press, 1938.

Townsend, John. *Oman: The Making of a Modern State*. London: Croom Helm, 1977.

Warner, Philip. *The Special Air Service*. London: William Kimber, 1971.

Wilson, Sir Arnold T. *The Persian Gulf: An Historical Sketch from the Earliest Times to the Beginning of the Twentieth Century*. London: George Allen and Unwin, 1928.

Winder, R. Bayly. *Saudi Arabia in the Nineteenth Century*. London: Macmillan, 1965; New York: St Martin's Press, 1965.

Young, T. Cuyler, ed. *Middle East Focus: The Persian Gulf*. Proceedings of the Twentieth Annual Near East Conference. Princeton: Princeton University Conference, 1969.

al-Zarqā, Muḥammad 'Alī. *'Umān: Qadīman . . . wa-Ḥadīthan* ('Oman: Past . . . and Present'). Cairo: Dār al-Qāhira lil-Ṭibā'a, 1959.

Zwemer, Samuel M. *Arabia: The Cradle of Islam*. New York: Fleming H. Revell, 1900.

Articles, Chapters, Monographs and Pamphlets

Abdullah, M. Morsy. 'The First Sa'udi Dynasty and Oman, 1795–1818.' *Proceedings of the Fourth Seminar for Arabian Studies* (1970), pp. 34–40.

Anthony, John Duke. 'Insurrection and Intervention: The War in Dhofar', in Abbas Amirie, ed., *The Persian Gulf and Indian Ocean in International Politics* (Teheran: Institute for International Politics and Economic Studies, 1975), pp. 287–303.

——. 'Political Dynamics in the Sultanate of Oman.' Unpublished paper written for the External Research Program of the US Department of State (October 1974).

Arab Information Centre. *British Imperialism in Southern Arabia*. Information Paper, No. 6. New York: Arab Information Centre, 1958.

——. *The Question of Oman: An Analysis of the British Oman*

Dispute. Information Paper, No. 13. New York: Arab Information Centre, 1960.

Austria. Bundeskammer der Gewerblichen Wirtschaft. *Trucial States, Muscat und Oman*. Vienna: Wirtschaftring-Verlagsgesellschaft für die Gewerbliche Wirtschaft, 1960.

Azzi, Robert. 'Oman, Land of Frankincense and Oil.' *National Geographic Magazine*, vol. 143, no. 2 (Feb. 1973), pp. 205–29.

'Bahrain Dinar, a Gulf Currency.' *Orient* (Hamburg), vol. 11, no. 1 (1970), pp. 3–5.

Bardt, W. 'German Economic Mission to Bahrain, Qatar, Abu Dhabi, Oman and Dubai.' *Orient* (Hamburg), vol. 12, no. 4 (1971), pp. 119–23.

Bates, Michael L. 'Unpublished Wajīhid and Būyid Coins from 'Umān in the American Numismatic Society.' *Arabian Studies*, vol. 1 (1974), pp. 171–5.

Bathurst, R. D. 'Maritime Trade and Imamate Government: Two Principal Themes in the History of Oman to 1728', in Derek Hopwood, ed., *The Arabian Peninsula: Society and Politics* (London: George Allen and Unwin, 1972; Totowa, N.J.: Rowman and Littlefield, 1972), pp. 86–106.

Beckingham, C. F. 'Bū Sa'īd.' *Encyclopedia of Islam*. 2nd edn, vol. 1, pp. 1281–3.

——. 'The Reign of Ahmad ibn-Sa'īd, Imam of Oman.' *Journal of the Royal Asiatic Society*, vol. 28, pt. 3 (1941), pp. 257–60.

Bell, Gertrude. 'The Rebellion Against the Sultan of Muscat, May 1913 to July 1916', in *The Arab War: Confidential Information for General Headquarters from Gertrude Bell; being Despatches reprinted from the Secret 'Arab Bulletin'* (London: Golden Cockerel Press, 1940), pp. 20–8.

Bennett, Thomas Jewel. 'The Past and Present Connection of England with the Persian Gulf.' *Journal of the Royal Society of Arts*, vol. 50 (13 June 1902), pp. 634–52.

Bent, J. Theodore. 'Muscat.' *The Contemporary Review* (London), vol. 68, no. 360 (Dec. 1895), pp. 871–82.

Bentley, G. W. 'The Development of the Air Route in the Persian Gulf.' *Journal of the Royal Central Asian Society*, vol. 20, pt. 2 (1933), pp. 173–89.

Berner, Wolfgang. 'Cuban Intervention in Africa and Arabia.' *Aussenpolitik* (English edition), vol. 27, no. 3/76 (1976), pp. 328–35.

Bondarevskiy, G. L. 'The Continuing Western Interest in Oman—as Seen from Moscow.' *New Middle East*, no. 35 (Aug. 1971), pp. 11–15.

Brinton, Jasper Y. 'The Arabian Peninsula: The Protectorates and Sheikdoms.' *Revue Egyptienne de Droit International*, vol. 3 (1947), pp. 25–38.

Brizuela, P. de. 'Apuntes históricas sobre el reino de Omán.' *Boletin de la Real Academia de la Historia*, vol. 57 (1910), pp. 337–64.

Buchan, Alistair. 'Britain in the Indian Ocean.' *International Affairs* (London), vol. 42, no. 2 (1966), pp. 184–93.

Burrell, R. M. 'Politics and Participation Where Britannia Once Ruled.' *New Middle East*, no. 51 (Dec. 1972), pp. 32–6.

——. 'Rebellion in Dhofar: The Spectre of Vietnam.' *New Middle East*, nos. 42/43 (Mar./Apr. 1972), pp. 55–8.

——, and Alvin J. Cottrell. 'Revolutionary War in Dhofar', in *Iran, the Arabian Peninsula, and the Indian Ocean* (New York: National Strategy Information Centre, Sept. 1972), pp. 24–30.

Carret, Jacques. 'Le particularisme ibadite au Mzab.' *L'Afrique et l'Asie*, vol. 49, no. 1 (1960), pp. 38–46.

Carter, John. 'Changes in the Bedouin Way of Life.' *Arab World*, pp. 4–7.

——. 'Graves of Three Descendants of Badr Bū Ṭuwayriq in Ẓafār of Oman.' *Arabian Studies*, vol. 2 (1975), pp. 211–12.

Caskel, Werner. 'The Bedouinization of Arabia.' *American Anthropologist*, vol. 56, no. 2, pt. 2, Memoir No. 76 (Apr. 1954), pp. 36–46.

Churba, Joseph. *Conflict and Tension Among the States of the Persian Gulf, Oman and South Arabia*. Foreign Affairs Research Paper, No. 15346-P. Documentary Research Study AU-204-71-IPD. Montgomery, Alabama: The Institute for Professional Development, Air University, Maxwell Air Force Base, 1971.

Clements, Frank. 'The Islands of Kuria Muria: A Civil Aid Project in the Sultanate of Oman Administered from Salalah, Regional Capital of Dhofar.' *British Society of Middle Eastern Studies Bulletin*, vol. 4, no. 1 (1977), pp. 37–9.

Cleveland, Ray. 'Muscat: Capital City of Oman.' *Middle East Forum*, vol. 35, no. 9 (Nov. 1959), pp. 27–9.

——. 'Oman: Tradition and Transition.' *Viewpoints*, vol. 3, no. 2 (1963), pp. 14–16.

——. 'Revolution in Dhofar; Sultanate of Oman.' *Middle East*

Forum, vol. 47, nos. 3/4 (1971), pp. 93–102.
——. 'Zur Landes- und Völkerkunde von Dhofar.' *Bustan*, vol. 7, ht. 2/3 (1966), pp. 41–4.
Codrai, Ronald A. "Oman, Including the Trucial Coast.' *Canadian Geographical Journal*, vol. 40, no. 4 (Apr. 1950), pp. 184–92.
'Comment: Muscat and Oman.' *Middle East Journal*, vol. 11, no. 3 (1957), pp. 282–4. Also letters to the editor in the following issues: vol. 13, no. 1 (1959), pp. 126–7; vol. 13, no. 3 (1959), p. 355; vol. 13, no. 4 (1959), p. 487; vol. 14, no. 2 (1960), p. 246; vol. 14, no. 3 (1960), p. 365.
Cornelius, P. F. S., N. L. Falcon, D. South and C. Vita-Finzi. 'The Musandam Expedition, 1971–72: Scientific Results, Part I.' *The Geographical Journal*, vol. 139, pt. 3 (Oct. 1973), pp. 400–25.
Cox, Sir Percy Z. 'Overland Journey from the Persian Gulf to Maskat.' *The Geographical Journal*, vol. 20, no. 4 (Oct. 1902), p. 452.
——. 'Some Excursions in Oman.' *The Geographical Journal*, vol. 66, no. 3 (Sept. 1925), pp. 193–227.
Craufurd, C. 'The Dhofar District.' *The Geographical Journal*, vol. 53, no. 2 (Feb. 1919), pp. 97–105.
Croizat, Victor J. 'Oman and the Dhofar Rebellion.' *Marine Corps Gazette*, vol. 59, no. 2 (February 1975), pp. 18–22.
Dalyell of the Binns, Gordon. 'The Persian Gulf.' *Journal of the Royal Central Asian Society*, vol. 25, pt. 3 (1938), pp. 349–64.
Deffarge, Claude, and Gordian Troeller. 'Secret War Number Eleven: Slavery and oil are the stakes on the Arabian Peninsula.' *Atlas*, vol. 18, no. 5 (Nov. 1969), pp. 32–7. Trans. from *Der Stern* (Hamburg).
'Dhofar: No More a Desolate Land.' *Arab Economist*, vol. 7, no. 72 (Jan. 1975), pp. 18–20.
Dostal, Walter. 'The Shiḥūḥ of Northern Oman: A Contribution to Cultural Ecology.' *The Geographical Journal*, vol. 138, pt. 1 (Mar. 1972), pp. 1–7.
——. 'Two South Arabian Tribes: al-Qarā and al-Ḥarasīs.' *Arabian Studies*, vol. 2 (1975), pp. 33–41.
Dowson, V. H. W. 'A Short Tour of Southern Arabia, British Somaliland, and the Northern Sudan.' *Journal of the Royal Central Asian Society*, vol. 35, pt. 2 (Apr. 1948), pp. 105–15.
Eccles, G. J. 'The Sultanate of Muscat and Oman, With a Description of a Journey into the Interior Undertaken in 1925.' *Journal of the Royal Central Asian Society*, vol. 14, pt. 1 (1927), pp. 19–38.

Edo, Michael E. 'Arabian Currency Arrangements Seen Evolving in Context of Rapid Change.' *IMF Survey*, vol. 3, no. 23 (9 Dec. 1974), pp. 374–5.

——. 'Character of Currencies of Arabian Peninsula Shaped by Recent Origin, Area's Resources.' *IMF Survey*, vol. 4, no. 1 (6 Jan. 1975), pp. 10–12.

Eilts, Hermann F. 'Ahmad bin Na'man's Mission to the United States in 1840: The Voyage of Al-Sultanah to New York City.' *Essex Institute Historical Collections*, vol. 98, no. 4 (Oct. 1962), pp. 219–77. Reprinted by Petroleum Development (Oman) Ltd.

——. 'Sayyid Muhammed bin 'Aqil [sic] of Dhufar; Malevolent or Maligned?' *Essex Institute Historical Collections*, vol. 109, no. 3 (July 1973), pp. 179–230. Reprinted by Petroleum Development (Oman) Ltd.

Elboushi, Ismail Mudathir. 'National Report About the Geologic and Mineral Activities in the Sultanate of Oman.' Muscat: Ministry of Development, Directorate General of Petroleum and Minerals, March 1974. Paper presented to the Second Pan-Arab Conference on Mineral Resources, Nov. 1974.

Ençer, Ahmet G. 'A Desert Palace of the Seventeenth Century.' *Crossroads, The World of Islam*, no. 2 (July/August 1977), pp. 19–26.

Fairchild, David G. 'Persian Gulf Dates and Their Introduction into America.' US Department of Agriculture, Bureau of Plant Industry, *Bulletin*, no. 54 (19 Dec. 1903).

Falcon, N. L. 'The Musandam (Northern Oman) Expedition, 1971/72.' *The Geographical Journal*, vol. 139, pt. 1 (Feb. 1973), pp. 1–19.

Faris, Nabih Amin. 'Derivation and Orthography of Rub' al-Khāli.' *Journal of the Royal Central Asian Society*, vol. 44, pt. 1 (Jan. 1957), pp. 28–30.

Fawzī, Fārūq 'Umar. 'Biblīyūjrāfīyā fī Tārīkh 'Umān' ('Bibliography on the History of Oman'). *al-Khalīj al-'Arabī*, vol. 2, no. 2 (1975), pp. 174–91.

Fayein, Claudie. 'Révolution arabe: il n'y a pas que la Palestine.' *Jeune Afrique*, no. 530 (2 Mar. 1971), pp. 15–17.

Fisher, W. B., and H. Bowen-Jones. 'Development Surveys in the Middle East.' *The Geographical Journal*, vol. 140, pt. 3 (Oct. 1974), pp. 454–66.

Foda, Ezeldin. 'Controversy over Oman.' *Egyptian Economic and Political Review*, vol. 4, no. 4 (Mar. 1958), pp. 12–14.

de Gaury, Gerald. 'A Note on Masirah Island.' *The Geographical Journal*, vol. 123, pt. 4 (Dec. 1957), pp. 499–502.

Glubb, Faris. 'Britain's Feudal Friends in Oman.' *Venture*, vol. 18, no. 9 (Oct. 1966), pp. 14–16.

Grey, W. G. 'Trade and Races of Oman.' *The Quarterly Journal of the Mythic Society*, vol. 2, no. 2 (Jan. 1911), pp. 60–1.

Grohmann, Adolf. 'Khūryān Mūryān.' *Encyclopedia of Islam*. 1st edn, vol. 2, pp. 975–6.

——. 'Masḳaṭ. '*Encyclopedia of Islam*. 1st edn, vol. 3, pp. 391–3.

——. 'Maṭraḥ.' *Encyclopedia of Islam*. 1st edn, vol. 3, p. 414.

——. "Omān.' *Encyclopedia of Islam*. 1st edn, vol. 3, pp. 975–7.

Haines, S. B. 'Memoir of the South and East Coasts of Arabia, Part II.' *The Journal of the Royal Geographic Society*, vol. 15 (1845), pp. 104–60.

Halliday, Fred. 'The Americanization of the Persian Gulf.' *Ramparts*, vol. 11, no. 4 (Oct. 1972), pp. 18–20.

——. 'Class Struggle in the Arab Gulf.' *New Left Review*, no. 58 (Nov./Dec. 1969), pp. 31–7.

——. 'Counter Insurgency Old and New: The Case of Oman.' *Gulf Studies*, no. 1 (April 1976), pp. 13–35.

——. 'Interview with Talal Saad and Said Seif on the Political Situation in Oman and Dhofar.' *New Left Review*, no. 66 (Mar./Apr. 1971), pp. 53–8.

——. 'Oil and Revolution in the Persian Gulf.' *Ramparts*, vol. 9, no. 9 (Apr. 1971), pp. 52–4.

Harris, Christina Phelps. 'The Persian Gulf Submarine Telegraph of 1864.' *The Geographical Journal*, vol. 135, pt. 2 (June 1969), pp. 169–90.

Harrison, David L. 'A Plan to Save the Arabian Tahr.' *Asian Affairs*, vol. 63 (N.S. 7), pt. 1 (Feb. 1976), pp. 33–4.

Harrison, Paul, and W. Harold Storm. 'The Arabs of Oman.' *The Moslem World*, vol. 24, no. 3 (July 1934), pp. 262–70.

Hawley, Ruth. *The British Embassy in Muscat: A Short History*. Muscat: Privately printed, May 1974.

Hay, Rupert. 'Great Britain's Relations with Yemen and Oman.' *Middle Eastern Affairs*, vol. 11, no. 5 (May 1960), pp. 142–9.

Headley, R. L. "Awāmir.' *Encyclopedia of Islam*. 2nd edn, vol. 1, p. 759.

——. 'al-Bāṭina.' *Encyclopedia of Islam*. 2nd edn, vol. 1, p. 1098.

Heard-Bey, Frauke. 'Development Anomalies in the Beduin Oases of al-Liwa.' *Asian Affairs*, vol. 61 (N.S. 5), pt. 3 (Oct. 1974), pp. 272–86.

——. 'The Gulf States and Oman in Transition.' *Asian Affairs*, vol. 59 (N.S. 3), pt. 1 (Feb. 1972), pp. 14–22.

——. 'Social Changes in the Gulf States and Oman.' *Asian Affairs*, vol. 59 (N.S. 3), pt. 3 (Oct. 1972), pp. 309–16.

Heath, M. L. 'Arabian Extremities.' *Journal of the Royal Central Asian Society*, vol. 47, pts. 3/4 (July/Oct. 1960), pp. 260–9.

——. 'Stability in the Arabian Peninsula.' *Journal of the Royal United Service Institution*, vol. 105, no. 618 (May 1960), pp. 174–85.

Holden, David. 'A Season in Oman.' *Horizon*, vol. 18, no. 3 (1976), pp. 22–31.

Howard, Bushrod, Jr. 'Buraimi, A Study in Diplomacy by Default.' *The Reporter*, 23 Jan. 1958, pp. 13–16.

Hurewitz, J. C. *The Persian Gulf: Prospects for Stability*. Headline Series, No. 220. New York: Foreign Policy Association, 1974.

'Increasing Role for Women in Oman.' *The Middle East*, no. 8 (May 1975), pp. 24–5.

Johns, Richard. 'Muscat: The Way Ahead.' *Middle East International*, no. 6 (Sept. 1971), pp. 7–12.

Johnson, Maxwell O. 'The Arab–Persian Gulf: A Strategic Analysis.' *Marine Corps Gazette*, vol. 59, no. 2 (February 1975), pp. 23–8.

Johnstone, T. M. 'Folklore and Folk Literature in Oman and Socotra.' *Arabian Studies*, vol. 1 (1974), pp. 7–23.

——. 'Knots and Curses.' *Arabian Studies*, vol. 3 (1976), pp. 79–83.

——. 'The Language of Poetry in Dhofar.' *Bulletin of the School of Oriental and African Studies*, vol. 35, pt. 1 (1972), pp. 1–17.

——. 'The Modern South Arabian Languages.' *Afroasiatic Linguistics*, vol. 1, no. 5 (Feb. 1975), pp. 93–121.

——. 'Oath-taking and Vows in Oman.' *Arabian Studies*, vol. 2 (1975), pp. 7–18.

Karabuda, Barbro. 'Red Guerrillas of the Arabian Gulf.' *Eastern Horizon*, vol. 9, no. 5 (1970), pp. 48–54.

Karam, Fu'ād. *Thawrat Ẓufār: Ṣirā' Bayna al-Shuyū'īa wa-al-Islām* ('The Dhufar Revolt: A Struggle Between Communism and Islam'). Beirut: Ḥaqā'iq 'an al-Marksīya, no. 9, n.d.

Kelly, J. B. 'The British Position in the Persian Gulf.' *The World Today*, vol. 20, no. 6 (June 1964), pp. 238–49.

——. 'The Buraimi Oasis Dispute.' *International Affairs* (London), vol. 32, no. 3 (July 1956), pp. 318–26.

——. 'The Future in Arabia.' *International Affairs* (London), vol. 42, no. 4 (Oct. 1966), pp. 619–40.

——. 'Hadramaut, Oman, Dhufar: the experience of revolution.' *Middle Eastern Studies*, vol. 12, no. 2 (May 1976), pp. 213–30.

——. 'The Legal and Historical Basis of the British Position in the Persian Gulf', in *St Antony's Papers*, no. 4; Middle Eastern Affairs, no. 1 (London: Chatto and Windus, 1958; New York: Praeger, 1959), pp. 119–40.

——. 'A Prevalence of Furies: Tribes, Politics, and Religion in Oman and Trucial Oman', in Derek Hopwood, ed., *The Arabian Peninsula: Society and Politics* (London: George Allen and Unwin, 1972; Totowa, N. J.: Rowman and Littlefield, 1972), pp. 107–41.

——. 'Sovereignty and Jurisdiction in Eastern Arabia.' *International Affairs* (London), vol. 34, no. 1 (1958), pp. 16–24.

——. 'Sultanate and Imamate in Oman.' *Chatham House Memoranda*. London: Royal Institute for International Affairs, 1959.

Khamis, A. 'Oman: Balance of Payments (1972–1973).' *Arab Economist*, vol. 7, no. 72 (Jan. 1975), pp. 22–3.

King, Noel Q., and Seyyid Saeed Akhtar Risvi. 'The Khoja Shia Ithna-Asheriya Community in East Africa (1840–1967).' *Muslim World*, vol. 64, no. 3 (July 1974), pp. 194–204.

Knabenshue, Denis. 'A Mission to Muscat.' *The American Foreign Service Journal*, vol. 11, no. 8 (Aug. 1934), pp. 412–15 and 432–5.

Kruse, Hans. 'Disturbances in Oman.' *International Studies*, vol. 7, no. 4 (Apr. 1966), pp. 589–94.

Kumar, Ravinder. 'British Attitudes towards the Ibadiyya Revivalist Movement in East Arabia.' *International Studies*, vol. 3, no. 4 (Apr. 1962), pp. 443–50.

——. 'The Dismemberment of Oman and British Policy Towards the Persian Gulf.' *Islamic Culture*, vol. 36, no. 1 (Jan. 1962), pp. 8–19.

Kutschera, Chris. 'Révolution arabe: il n'y a pas que la Palestine.' *Jeune Afrique*, no. 529 (23 Feb. 1971), pp. 19–25.

Lake, Michael. 'New Direction in Oman.' *Venture*, vol. 22, no. 9 (Oct. 1970), pp. 20–4.

Laliberté, Gérard. 'La Guérilla du Dhofar.' *Etudes Internationales*, vol. 4, nos. 1/2 (Mar./June 1973), pp. 159–81.

Lee, Marc, and Geoffrey Matthews. 'The United Nations and the Politics of the Arabian Peninsula.' *Contemporary Review*, vol. 211, no. 1222 (Nov. 1967), pp. 230–4.

Lees, G. M. 'The Physical Geography of South-East Arabia.' *The Geographical Journal*, vol. 71, no. 5 (May 1928), pp. 441–70.

Lewicki, Tadeusz. 'al-Ibāḍīyya.' *Encyclopedia of Islam*. 2nd edn, vol. 3, pp. 648–60.

——. 'Les subdivisions de l'Ibāḍiyya.' *Studia Islamica*, vol. 9 (1958), pp. 71–82.

Liebesny, Herbert. 'Administration and Legal Development in Arabia: The Persian Gulf Principalities.' *Middle East Journal*, vol. 10, no. 1 (1956), pp. 33–42.

——. 'International Relations of Arabia: The Dependent Areas.' *Middle East Journal*, vol. 1, no. 2 (Apr. 1947), pp. 148–68.

Lindt, A. R. 'Politics in the Persian Gulf.' *Journal of the Royal Central Asian Society*, vol. 36, pt. 4 (Oct. 1939), pp. 619–33.

Lockhart, Laurence. 'The Menace of Muscat and its Consequences in the late Seventeenth and early Eighteenth Centuries.' *Asiatic Review*, N.S. vol. 42, no. 112 (Oct. 1946), pp. 363–9.

——. 'Nādir Shāh's Campaign in 'Umān in 1737–1744.' *Bulletin of the School of Oriental and African Studies*, vol. 8, pt. 1 (1935–1937), pp. 157–71.

Luce, Sir William. 'Britain's Withdrawal from the Middle East and Persian Gulf.' *Journal of the Royal United Service Institution*, vol. 114, no. 653 (Mar. 1969), pp. 4–10.

McDermott, Anthony. 'Oman: Winning the Peace.' *Middle East International*, no. 66 (December 1976), pp. 9–11.

MacLauren, E. C. B. 'Oman and the Trucial Coast.' *Australian Quarterly*, vol. 30, no. 1 (Mar. 1958), pp. 65–76.

Mahan, Alfred Thayer. 'The Persian Gulf and International Relations.' *National and English Review*, vol. 40 (Sept. 1902), pp. 27–45.

al-Majīd, Mu'ayyad Ḥusayn. 'al-Qaḍīya al-'Umānīya al-'Arabīya' ('The Arab Question of Oman'). *al-Aqlām*, vol. 2, no. 2 (Oct. 1965), pp. 10–29.

El Mallakh, Ragaei. 'Economic Requirements for Development, Oman.' *Middle East Journal*, vol. 26, no. 4 (1972), pp. 415–27.

Malone, Joseph J. 'Echoes of Dhofar's early history' (letter to the editor). *New Middle East*, no. 45 (June 1972), pp. 37–8.

——. 'The Sultanate of Oman', in *The Arab Lands of Western Asia*

(Englewood Cliffs, N.J.: Prentice-Hall, 1973), pp. 211–25.
Mandaville, Jon. 'Banū Hinā.' *Encyclopedia of Islam*. 2nd edn, vol. 3, p. 403.
——. 'al-Ḥubūs.' *Encyclopedia of Islam*. 2nd edn, vol. 3, p. 537.
Mansfield, Peter. 'Oman Emerges.' *Middle East International*, no. 19 (Jan. 1973), pp. 12–14.
al-Marayati, Abid. 'The Problem of Oman.' *Foreign Affairs Reports*, vol. 15, no. 8 (Aug. 1966), pp. 99–109.
Matthews, Charles D. 'al-Baṭāḥira.' *Encyclopedia of Islam*. 2nd edn, vol. 1, p. 1091.
——. 'al-Durū'.' *Encyclopedia of Islam*. 2nd edn, vol. 2, pp. 630–1.
——. 'al-Ḥarāsīs.' *Encyclopedia of Islam*. 2nd edn, vol. 3, pp. 176–7.
——. Letter to the editor on South Arabian languages. *Middle East Journal*, vol. 13, no. 2 (1959), pp. 232–4.
May, H. P., and G. P. G. Robinson. 'The Musandam Expedition: Scientific Results, Part II.' *The Geographical Journal*, vol. 140, pt. 1 (Feb. 1974), pp. 94–104.
Meade, M. J. 'The Sultanate of Muscat and Oman.' *Asiatic Review*, N.S. vol. 24, no. 80 (Oct. 1928), pp. 571–5.
Melamid, Alexander. 'Boundaries and Petroleum Developments in Southern Arabia.' *Geographical Review*, vol. 47, no. 4 (Oct. 1957), pp 589–91.
——. 'The Buraimi Oasis Dispute.' *Middle Eastern Affairs*, vol. 7, no. 2 (Feb. 1956), pp. 56–63.
——. 'Economic Changes in Yemen, Aden and Dhofar.' *Middle Eastern Affairs*, vol. 5, no. 3 (Mar. 1954), pp. 88–91.
——. 'Oil and the Evolution of Boundaries in Eastern Arabia.' *Geographical Review*, vol. 44, no. 2 (Apr. 1954), pp. 295–6.
——. 'Political Boundaries and Nomadic Grazing.' *Geographical Review*, vol. 55, no. 2 (1965), pp. 287–90.
Mertz, Robert A. 'Portrait of Oman: Change Amidst Tradition.' *AFME Report*, July 1973, pp. 1, 3–4.
Messaoud, Said. 'Our Struggle Continues: The People's Front for the Liberation of Oman.' *Gulf Studies*, no. 1 (April 1976), pp. 11–12.
Miles, Samuel Barrett. 'Across the Green Mountains of Oman.' *The Geographical Journal*, vol. 18, no. 5 (Nov. 1901), pp. 465–98.
——. 'Journal of an Excursion in Oman, in South-east Arabia.' *The Geographical Journal*, vol. 7, no. 5 (May 1896), pp. 522–37.
——. 'On the Border of the Great Desert: a Journey in Oman.' *The Geographical Journal*, vol. 36, no. 2 (Aug. 1910), pp. 159–78;

and no. 4 (Oct. 1910), pp. 405–25.

——. 'On the Route between Sohár and el-Bereymí in 'Omán, with a note on the Zatt, or Gypsies in Arabia.' *Journal of the Asiatic Society of Bengal*, vol. 46, pt. 1, no. 1 (1877), pp. 41–60.

Miske, A. B. 'Dhofar: la révolution dans les grottes.' *Africasia*, vol. 52 (1–14 Nov. 1971), pp. 31–4.

Nocentini, Diletto. 'L'Oman, ai margini della civilta.' *Le Vie del Mondo*, vol. 22, no. 3 (1960), pp. 285–300.

Nouri, Moufid M. 'The Growth of the Revolutionary Movements in the Arab Gulf: Oman.' *al-Khalīj al-'Arabī*, vol. 2, no. 2 (1975), pp. 385–418.

Nunè, Enrico. 'L'Inghilterra nella Penisola Arabica.' *Oriente Moderno*, vol. 21, no. 5 (May 1941), pp. 209–32.

'Oil and a Troubled Oasis.' *The World Today*, vol. 7, no. 11 (Nov. 1952), pp. 448–9.

'Oil Price Rises Help Oman's Economy Catch Up with Pace of Its Development.' *IMF Survey*, vol. 2, no. 19 (2 Sept. 1974), pp. 283–5.

'Oman', in *The Middle East and North Africa* (London: Europa Publications, annually).

'Oman—A New Start.' *Africa* (London), no. 27 (Nov. 1973), pp. 97–106.

'Oman: A MEED Special Report.' *Middle East Economic Digest*, vol. 17, no. 29 (20 July 1973), pp. 818–44.

'——.' *Middle East Economic Digest* (June 1976).

'Oman Seeks Modernization of Economy, Emphasizes Income-Generating Projects.' *IMF Survey*, vol. 5, no. 3 (2 Feb. 1976), pp. 46–8.

'Oman Supplement.' *Arab Economist*, vol. 7, no. 74 (Mar. 1975), Suppl. pp. 1–46.

Owen, R. P. 'Developments in the Sultanate of Muscat and Oman.' *The World Today*, vol. 26, no. 9 (Sept. 1970), pp. 379–83.

——. 'Oman: A New Chapter.' *Middle East International*, no. 33 (Mar. 1974), pp. 6–8.

——. 'The Rebellion in Dhofar—A Threat to Western Interests in the Gulf.' *The World Today*, vol. 29, no. 6 (June 1973), pp. 266–72.

Page, Stephen. 'Moscow and the Persian Gulf Countries, 1967–1970.' *Mizan*, vol. 13, no. 2 (Oct. 1971), pp. 72–88.

Pelly, Lewis. 'Remarks on the Tribes, Trade and Resources around the Shore Line of the Persian Gulf.' *Transactions of the Bombay Geographical Society*, vol. 17 (1863), pp. 32–112.

Peterson, J. E. 'Britain and "the Oman War": An Arabian Entanglement.' *Asian Affairs*, vol. 63 (N.S. 7), pt. 3 (Oct. 1976), pp. 285–98.

——. 'Guerrilla Warfare and Ideological Confrontation: The Rebellion in Dhufar.' *World Affairs*, vol. 139, no. 4 (1977), pp. 278–95.

——. 'The Revival of the Ibāḍī Imāmate in Oman and the Threat to Muscat, 1913–1920.' *Arabian Studies*, vol. 3 (1976), pp. 165–88.

——. 'Tribes and Politics in Eastern Arabia.' *Middle East Journal*, vol. 31, no. 3 (1977), pp. 297–312.

Philby, H. St. John B. 'Rub' Al Khali.' *Journal of the Royal Central Asian Society*, vol. 19, pt. 4 (1932), pp. 569–84. Also correspondence with Bertram S. Thomas in vol. 20, pt. 3 (1933), pp. 488–95.

Popular Front for the Liberation of Oman and the Arabian Gulf. *Oman: A Class Analysis*. 9th June Studies. London: Gulf Committee, 1974. Trans. from 1973 Arabic edition published in Beirut.

——. *The Oman War: 1957–1959, A Critical History*. 9th June Studies. London: Gulf Committee, 1974. Trans. from 1973 Arabic edition published in Beirut.

Preece, Richard Matheson. 'The Traditional State of 'Uman—a Sketch.' *SAIS Review*, vol. 10 (1965), pp. 26–32.

Price, D. L. *Oman: Insurgency and Development*. Conflict Studies, no. 53. London: Institute for the Study of Conflict, Jan. 1975.

Purini, G. 'Il nuovi stati del Golfo Arabico.' *Levante*, vol. 20, nos. 3/4 (Dec. 1973), pp. 5–25.

Rentz, George. 'al-Buraymī.' *Encyclopedia of Islam*. 2nd edn., vol. 1, pp. 1313–4.

——. 'al-Djanaba.' *Encyclopedia of Islam*. 2nd edn, vol. 2, p. 40.

——. "Ibrī.' *Encyclopedia of Islam*. 2nd edn, vol. 2, pp. 1004–5.

——. 'al-'Ifār.' *Encyclopedia of Islam*. 2nd edn, vol. 3, pp. 1037–8.

Richter, Siegfried. 'Some Remarks on the First Stage of Military Infiltration of the Arab Gulf Region (Masirah) by US Imperialism.' *al-Khalīj al-'Arabī*, vol. 4 (1975), pp. 9–14.

Rondot, Philippe. 'Le Sultanat d'Oman devant la rébellion du Dhofar.' *Maghreb-Machrek*, no. 70 (Oct./Dec. 1975), pp. 38–46.

Ross, E. C., tr. 'Annals of 'Omán, from early times to the year 1728 A.D.' *Journal of the Asiatic Society of Bengal*, vol. 43 (1874).

——. 'Memorandum on the Tribal Divisions in the Principality of 'Omán.' *Transactions of the Bombay Geographical Society*, vol. 19, pt. 3 (1873), pp. 187–98.

Rubinacci, Roberto. 'The Ibāḍīs', in *Religion in the Middle East:*

Three Religions in Concord and Conflict, A. J. Arberry, gen. ed.; C. F. Beckingham, ed. for Islām; vol. 2 (Cambridge: Cambridge University Press, 1969), pp. 302–17.

Said-Ruete, Rudolph. 'The Al-bu-Said Dynasty in Arabia and East Africa.' *Journal of the Royal Central Asian Society*, vol. 16, pt. 4 (1929), pp. 417–32.

——. 'Dates and References of the History of the Al Bu Said Dynasty (1741–1856).' *Journal of the Royal Central Asian Society*, vol. 18, pt. 3 (Apr. 1931), pp. 233–55.

Salisbury, Matthew. 'End of a Rebellion?' *Middle East International*, no. 57 (Mar. 1976), pp. 18–20.

Salṭanat 'Umān: 'Adad Khāṣ ('Sultanate of Oman: Special Report'). Beirut: al-Nahār, July 1973.

'Sappers and Sultan's Men Cement the Peace.' *Soldier*, vol. 33, no. 5 (May 1977), pp. 12–15.

al-Sha'fī, Muḥammad Sa'īd. 'al-'Alāqāt al-Sa'ūdīya—al-'Umānīya, 1800–1818' ('Omani–Saudi Relations, 1800–1818'). *Majallat Kullīyat al-Ādāb li-Jāmi'at al-Riyaḍ*, vol. 1 (1970), pp. 206–29.

Simpson, M. G. 'The Indo-European Telegraph Department.' *Journal of the Royal Society of Arts*, vol. 76 (2 Mar. 1928), pp. 382–400.

Smiley, David deC. 'Muscat and Oman.' *Journal of the Royal United Service Institution*, vol. 105, no. 617 (Feb. 1960), pp. 29–47.

Stevens, J. H. 'The Role of Major Agricultural Projects in the Economic Development of Arabian Peninsula Countries.' *Proceedings of the Seventh Seminar for Arabian Studies* (1973), pp. 140–4.

——, and E. Cresswell. 'The Future of Date Cultivation in the Arabian Peninsula.' *Asian Affairs*, vol. 59 (N.S. 3), pt. 2 (June 1972), pp. 191–7.

Stiffe, Arthur W. 'Ancient Trading Centers of the Persian Gulf: Muscat.' *The Geographical Journal*, vol. 10, no. 6 (Dec. 1897), pp. 608–18.

'Sultanate of Muscat and Oman.' *Near East and India*, vol. 30, no. 807 (4 Nov. 1926), pp. 516–17.

'——.' *Asiatic Review*, vol. 24, no. 80 (Oct. 1928), pp. 571–5.

Thawrat Ẓufār ('The Revolution of Dhufar'). Milaff al-Sab'īnāt, Qaḍāyā Duwalīya, no. 5. Beirut: al-Nahār, May 1973.

Thesiger, Wilfred P. 'Across the Empty Quarter.' *The Geographical Journal*, vol. 111, nos. 1–3 (Jan.-Mar. 1948), pp. 1–21.

——. 'The Badu of Southern Arabia.' *Journal of the Royal Central*

Asian Society, vol. 37, pt. 1 (Jan. 1950), pp. 53–61.
——. 'Desert Borderlands of Oman.' *The Geographical Journal*, vol. 116, nos. 4–6 (Oct.-Dec. 1950), pp. 137–71.
——. 'A Further Journey Across the Empty Quarter.' *The Geographical Journal*, vol. 113, nos. 1–5 (Jan.-June 1949), pp. 21–46.
——. 'A New Journey in Southern Arabia.' *The Geographical Journal*, vol. 108, nos. 4–6 (Oct.-Dec. 1946), pp. 129–45.
Thomas, Bertram S. 'Among Some Unknown Tribes of South Arabia.' *Journal of the Royal Anthropological Institute*, vol. 59, pts. 1/2 (1929), pp. 97–111.
——. 'Anthropological Observations in South Arabia.' *Journal of the Royal Anthropological Institute*, vol. 62 (Jan.-June 1932), pp. 83–103.
——. 'Arab Rule under the Al Bu Sa'id Dynasty of Oman.' *Proceedings of the British Academy*, vol. 24 (1938), pp. 27–53. Reprinted London: Humphrey Milford, 1938.
——. 'Four Strange Tongues from South Arabia—the Hadara Group.' *Proceedings of the British Academy*, vol. 23 (1937), pp. 239–331. Reprinted London: Humphrey Milford, 1937.
——. 'The Kumzari Dialect of the Shihuh Tribe, Arabia, and a Vocabulary.' *Journal of the Royal Asiatic Society*, pt. 4 (Oct. 1930), pp. 785–854. Reprinted as an Asiatic Society Monograph, no. 21. London: Royal Asiatic Society, 1930.
——. 'The Musandam Peninsula and Its People the Shihuh.' *Journal of the Royal Central Asian Society*, vol. 16, pt. 1 (Jan. 1929), pp. 71–86.
——. 'The South-Eastern Borderlands of Rub' al-Khali.' *The Geographical Journal*, vol. 73, no. 3 (Mar. 1929), pp. 193–215.
——. 'Ūbār—The Atlantis of the Sands of Rub' al-Khali.' *Journal of the Royal Central Asian Society*, vol. 20, pt. 2 (June 1933), pp. 259–65. Also correspondence with H. St John B. Philby in vol. 20, pt. 3 (Oct. 1933), pp. 488–95.
Tkatsch, J. 'Ẓafār.' *Encyclopedia of Islam*. 1st edn., vol. 4, pp. 1185–90.
Trabulsi, Fawwaz. 'The Liberation of Dhofar.' *MERIP Reports*, vol. 1, no. 6 (Jan. 1972), pp. 3–11.
'Transportation Development Likely to Aid Modestly Rising National Income of Oman.' *IMF Survey*, vol. 1, no. 9 (11 Dec. 1972), p. 142.

Tremayne, Penelope. 'From Resistance to Revolution.' *Army Quarterly and Defense Journal*, vol. 105, no. 1 (January 1975), pp. 46–50.

——. 'Guevara through the Looking Glass: A View of the Dhofar War.' *Journal of the Royal United Institute for Defence Studies*, vol. 119, no. 3 (Sept. 1974), pp. 39–43.

Vadala, R. 'Mascate.' *L'Asie Française*, vol. 23 (May 1923), pp. 135–7.

Vainney, J. J. 'The Social and Economic Evolution of Bahrein, Qatar, Muscat and Oman.' *Levante*, vol. 15, nos. 1/2 (1968), pp. 37–42.

Van Peursem, Gerrit D. 'The Arabian Mission and Saudi Arabia.' *Muslim World*, vol. 38, no. 1 (Jan. 1948), pp. 6–10.

Veccia Vaglieri, Laura. 'al-Bārūnī, Sulaymān.' *Encyclopedia of Islam*. 2nd edn, vol. 1, pp. 1070–1.

——. 'L'Imāmato Ibāḍita dell''Oman: La Ricostituzione dell' Imāmato Ibāḍita nell'interno dell''Omān.' *Annali dell'Istituto Universitario Orientale di Napoli*, N.S. vol. 3 (1949), pp. 245–82.

——. 'Il tripolitano ibadita Suleiman el-Baruni e sue notizie sull' 'Oman.' *Oriente Moderno*, vol. 14, no. 8 (Aug. 1934), pp. 392–6.

Vesey-Fitzgerald, Desmond. 'From Hasa to Oman by Car.' *Geographical Review*, vol. 41, no. 4 (Oct. 1951), pp. 544–60.

Wace, Barbara. 'Master Plan for Muscat and Oman.' *Geographical Magazine*, vol. 41, no. 12 (Sept. 1969), pp. 892–905.

Wakebridge, Charles. 'Dhofar: The Achilles Heel.' *Middle East International*, no. 33 (Mar. 1974), pp. 8–10.

Wall, Michael. 'A Jump of Centuries: A Survey of the Arabian Peninsula.' *The Economist*, 6 July 1970.

Watt, W. Montgomery. 'Traditional Arab Communities in the Modern World.' *International Affairs* (London), vol. 44, no. 3 (July 1968), pp. 494–500.

Wellsted, J. R. 'Narrative of a Journey into the Interior of Oman.' *Journal of the Royal Geographical Society*, vol. 7 (1837), pp. 102–13.

Whitelock, F. 'Descriptive Sketch of the Islands and Coast Situated at the Entrance of the Persian Gulf.' *Journal of the Royal Geographical Society*, vol. 8 (1838), pp. 170–84.

Wilkinson, John C. 'Arab–Persian Land Relationships in Late Sasānid Oman.' *Proceedings of the Sixth Seminar for Arabian*

Studies (1972), pp. 40–51.
——. 'Bayāsirah and Bayādīr.' *Arabian Studies*, vol. 1 (1974), pp. 75–85.
——. 'Bio-bibliographical Background to the Crisis Period in the Ibāḍī Imāmate of Oman (End of 9th to end of 14th century).' *Arabian Studies*, vol. 3 (1976), pp. 137–64.
——. 'The Ibāḍī Imāma.' *Bulletin of the School of Oriental and African Studies*, vol. 39, pt. 3 (1976), pp. 535–51.
——. 'The Julanda of Oman.' *The Journal of Oman Studies*, vol. 1 (1975), pp. 97–108.
——. 'Ḳalhāt.' *Encyclopedia of Islam*. 2nd edn, vol. 4, pp. 500–1.
——. 'The Oman Question: The Background to the Political Geography of South-East Arabia.' *The Geographical Journal*, vol. 137, pt. 3 (Sept. 1971), pp. 361–71.
——. 'The Origins of the Omani State', in Derek Hopwood, ed., *The Arabian Peninsula: Society and Politics* (London: George Allen and Unwin, 1972; Totowa, N. J.: Rowman and Littlefield, 1972), pp. 67–88.
——. *The Organisation of the Falaj Irrigation System in Oman*. Research Paper, No. 10. Oxford: School of Geography, University of Oxford, July 1974.
Wilson, Andrew. 'Sultan Qabus Faces Dhofar Rebels.' *Middle East International*, no. 3 (June 1971), pp. 32–3.
Young, Richard. 'Recent American Policy Concerning the Capitulations in the States of the Middle East.' *American Journal of International Law*, vol. 42, no. 2 (Apr. 1948), pp. 418–23.
——. 'United Kingdom–Muscat Treaty of 1951.' *American Journal of International Law*, vol. 46, no. 4 (Oct. 1952), pp. 704–8.
Yusuf Ali, A. 'Khodja.' *Encyclopedia of Islam*. 1st edn, vol. 2, pp. 960–2.
Zabbāl, S. "Umān' ('Oman'). *al-'Arabī*, no. 151 (June 1971), pp. 100–23.
Zabih, Sepehr. 'Iran's Policy Towards the Persian Gulf.' *International Journal of Middle East Studies*, vol. 7, no. 3 (July 1976), pp. 345–58.
Zwemer, Samuel M. 'Notes on Oman.' *National Geographic Magazine*, vol. 22, no. 1 (Jan. 1911), pp. 89–98.
——. 'Three Journeys in Northern Oman.' *The Geographical Journal*, vol. 19, no. 1 (Jan. 1902), pp. 54–64.

Serials

Arab Report and Record (ARR), 1966–76.
Christian Science Monitor, 1970–6.
The Economist, 1953–76.
Foreign Broadcast and Information Service—Middle East and North Africa (FBIS), 1975–6.
Foreign Report, 1970–6.
Gulf Bulletin (London), 1972–5.
Gulf Weekly Mirror (al-Manāma), 1972–5.
Middle East Economic Digest (MEED), 1970–6.
Middle East Economic Survey, 1974–6.
Le Monde, 1971–6.
The New York Times, 1945–76.
The Observer (London), 1973–6.
Oman (Embassy of Oman, London), 1973–5.
Oman News (Embassy of Oman, Washington), 1973–6.
Oman News (Permanent Mission of Oman to the UN, New York), 1975–6.
The Times (London), 1934–76.
Voice of the Arab World (London), 1973–6.
Washington Post, 1970–6.

Index

Qarūt 122, 128
al-Qawāsim 152
Quetta 64, 145
Qurayshi, Muhammad Sayyid 83
Qurīyāt 17
Qurum Hills 17

al-Raḥbīyīn 16
Rakhyūt 187, 189
Rapier missiles 192
Ra's al-Ḥadd 17, 93, 128, 139
Ra's al-Khayma 27
Ra's Suwādī 184
al-Raṣāṣī, Ismā'īl bin Khalīl 57, 81, 83, 97, 98, 105 n26, 106 n33, 106 n39, 203; as head of justice 82; responsibility for wālīs 100, 101
al-Rasbī, 'Abd Allāh 213 n3
al-Rawāshid 196 n31
al-Rawwās 196 n31
Raysūt 187, 192, 206
Reformed Church of America 22, 23
al-Riyāḍ 129, 185, 204
riyāl, Sa'īdī 85
Riyām (town) 85, 106
Robertson, General J. A. R. 183
Roosevelt, President Franklin D. 53
Rouleau, Eric 209
Royal Air Force (British) 31–2, 127, 142, 183, 184, 191; installations in Oman 139; possible use of in Omani interior 54
Royal Engineers (British) 191
Royal Oman Police 207
Rub 'al-Khālī 14, 18, 19, 77, 129, 153, 157 n36, 187
al-Rubāt 196 n30
al-Ruqayshī, Muḥammad bin Sālim 124–5
Russia, challenge to British in Gulf 29; relations with Oman 152
al-Rustāq 16, 26, 27, 97, 99, 111, 113, 124, 126, 165, 172, 174, 181, 182, 183; Āl Bū Sa'īd control over 60
Ru'ūs al-Jibāl 80, 100, 114, 119, 157 n36, 213 n3
al-Ruwāḥī, 'Abd al-'Aziz 73
Ruwī 167, 168, 214 n14; attack on (1915) 171–2
Ruwī Hospital 85

al-Sādāt (Hāshimīyīn) 196 n32
Saḥam 17, 60
Ṣalāla 19, 32, 63, 80, 85, 93, 97, 101, 117, 118, 138, 154, 183, 101–2, 210; and Dhufar rebellion 187; British representation in 145; description of 187; development in 206–7; Sa'īd bin Taymūr's residence in 55–6
Ṣalāla Air Base 139, 190, 191, 202
Ṣalāla Plain 187, 190
al-Sālimī, 'Abd Allāh bin Ḥumayd 74, 120, 122, 123, 169, 170
al-Sālimī, Muḥammad bin 'Abd Allāh, candidature for Imām 181
Saljūqs 20
Samad 18
Samā'il 16, 46, 84, 97, 128, 129; and rebellion of 1913–20 170–2; tribes in 114
al-Sammār family 69 n64
Sandhurst 63, 202
Saudi Arabia 18, 32, 115, 129; and al-Buraymī crisis 93, 94; relations with Banī Bū 'Alī 127; relations with Oman 55, 150, 151, 152–4; relations with Sulaymān bin Ḥimyar al-Nabhānī 124; role in al-Jabal al-Akhḍar rebellion 182–6 *passim*; sharī'a of Mecca 150
Saudis in Oman 116
'Ṣawt al-'Arab' 165
Sayq 100, 122, 124
Sayyid, use of title 40 n55
Seistan Levy Corps 92
Shāfi'ī school of Islām 196 n31
Shākir, Ghassān 216 n28
al-Shanāfir 196 n31
al-Shanfarī, Sa'īd bin Aḥmad 215 n24
Sharayja 122
sharī'a courts 81, 82
Sharjah 89, 144
al-Sharqīya 54, 99, 100, 114, 119, 121, 152; description of 17–18
shāwīya 37 n36
shaykh, declining importance of 116–18; function of 101; participation in Sultanate government 208; role of, after 1970 211–12
Shebbeare, John D. 81, 86, 97, 117
Sḥerā 21, 187
al-Shiḥūḥ 21, 119, 171; as Sultanate retainers 91
al-Shiḥūḥī, 'Abd Allāh bin Thānī 201
Shī'ī Muslims 21–2, 82, 209
Shināṣ 17, 60, 139, 152
al-Sīb 17, 95, 217 n29; Agreement of